*The Frightful Stage*

# The Frightful Stage

## Political Censorship of the Theater in Nineteenth-Century Europe

Edited by
Robert Justin Goldstein

*Berghahn Books*
New York • Oxford

First published in 2009 by
*Berghahn Books*

www.berghahnbooks.com

©2009, 2011 Robert Justin Goldstein
First paperback edition published in 2011

All rights reserved. Except for the quotation of short passages for the purposes of criticism and review, no part of this book may be reproduced in any form or by any means, electronic or mechanical, including photocopying, recording, or any information storage and retrieval system now known or to be invented, without written permission of the publisher.

**Library of Congress Cataloging-in-Publication Data**

The frightful stage : political censorship of the theater in nineteenth-century Europe / edited by Robert Justin Goldstein.
   p. cm.
   Includes bibliographical references and index.
   ISBN 978-1-84545-459-3 (hbk) -- ISBN 978-0-85745-171-2 (pbk)
   1. Theater—Censorship—Europe—History—19th century. 2. Theater and state—Europe—History—19th century. 3. Theater—Political aspects—Europe—History—19th century. 4. Censorship—Europe—History—19th century. I. Goldstein, Robert Justin.

PN2044.E85 F75 2009
792.094'09034—dc22

2008052534

**British Library Cataloguing in Publication Data**

A catalogue record for this book is available from the British Library

Printed in the United States on acid-free paper.

ISBN 978-1-84545-459-3 (hardback)
ISBN 978-0-85745-171-2 (paperback)
ISBN 978-0-85745-419-5 (ebook)

# Contents

**Preface**
*vii*

**INTRODUCTION**
Robert Justin Goldstein
*1*

**GERMANY**
Gary D. Stark
*22*

**FRANCE**
Robert Justin Goldstein
*70*

**RUSSIA**
Anthony Swift
*130*

**SPAIN**
David T. Gies
*162*

## Italy
John A. Davis
*190*

## The Habsburg Monarchy
Norbert Bachleitner
*228*

## Summary
Robert Justin Goldstein
*265*

## List of Contributors
*300*

## Index
*302*

# Preface

This volume is the second in what has been conceived as a trilogy of edited collections about political censorship in nineteenth-century Europe. Its origins date to my 1983 book *Political Repression in Nineteenth-Century Europe,* which was, in retrospect, a rather foolishly ambitious attempt to survey all aspects of political repression for all of Europe between 1815 and 1914. As the general subject continued to interest me, I decided to focus thereafter especially upon one key aspect of the overall topic: political censorship. This led to two further books published in 1989, *Censorship of Political Caricature in Nineteenth-Century France* (Kent State) and *Political Censorship of the Arts and the Press in Nineteenth-Century Europe* (MacMillan). They were based on both archival research and extensive readings in secondary sources in English and French, the two European languages accessible to me.

The further and deeper I explored the general subject of nineteenth-century European political censorship, the more it became clear that this was an issue of enormous significance both to the ruling elites and to opposition movements, each of whom invested extraordinary amounts of time and energy in attempting to, respectively, implement and resist it. It also became increasingly clear that my language limitations were a serious impediment to further research, since most relevant publications, not to mention archival materials, have not been translated into English or French. Therefore, I decided to recruit a group of multilingual scholars who could penetrate materials for all of the major countries of nineteenth-century continental Europe—namely France (which I could handle), Germany, the Habsburg Monarchy, Italy, Russia, and Spain—to create a book that focused especially on print censorship in nineteenth-century Europe, which resulted in the 2000 publication of *The War for the Public Mind:*

*Political Censorship in Nineteenth-Century Europe* (Praeger). Although focusing on censorship of newspapers, books, and journals, this volume touched briefly on censorship of other media, including theater, opera, caricature, and cinema—just enough to make clear that, although in the twentieth and twenty-first centuries we tend to think of print censorship as especially important, in nineteenth-century Europe, when large segments of the population were illiterate, censorship of the stage and the visual arts was perhaps even more significant. Thus, as detailed in this volume, most European regimes continued prior censorship of such media long after ceasing print censorship. Therefore, a second book, focused on censorship of the stage (including both spoken and musical theater, such as opera)—the one that is now in your hands—seemed called for. A third and final volume, focused on censorship of the visual arts (such as caricature, posters, sculpture, painting, and early photography and cinema) is now in the planning stages.

As with *The War for the Public Mind,* the primary purpose of this volume is to provide reliable and comprehensive summaries, for an English-language audience, of the latest research available from the most important countries of nineteenth-century Europe. In most cases a large (and sometimes overwhelming) literature (in non-English languages) is available on this topic, and the contributors to this book were therefore not asked or required to do archival research (although they were certainly not discouraged from such). To hold the number of endnotes down to a reasonable level, they have generally been grouped together, in the appropriate order, at the end of paragraphs; in addition, each chapter includes an extensive bibliographical essay, including whatever sources are available in English, designed to highlight the most important sources.

*The War for the Public Mind* received overwhelmingly positive reviews in a wide diversity of academic journals, with the primary criticism that it lacked a chapter on England. The reason for this, and why there is no England chapter in this book either, is simply that material on English censorship—of the theater in particular—is both abundant and easily accessible to English-language readers, and this book seeks to make available to them material that is not. However, I have included many references to England, as well as to other countries that do not have individual chapters devoted to them, in the introductory and summary essays, which attempt to point out similarities and differences in nineteenth-century theater censorship across the European continent. The introductory chapter seeks primarily to provide some brief general background context for readers more knowledgeable about (or interested in) theater than European history in general, and to briefly summarize both the reasons why European political authorities feared especially the theater and the history of pre–nineteenth-century European political theater censorship. The heart of the book consists of individual country chapters on Germany, France, Russia, Spain, Italy, and the Habsburg Monarchy. A summary seeks to recapitulate major themes about the substance of nineteenth-century European drama censorship. Although the introduction and summary are massively informed by the country chapters, they also draw heavily on my own research. Inevitably there is some duplication of both general content and specific incidents/quotations between the introduction and (especially) the summary and the country chapters. I have tried to keep this to a minimum, but have deliberately erred on the side of repetition in certain cases, both because I view the information as particularly apt and/or eloquent and because, realistically, some readers will examine some, but not all, of the country chapters, and would otherwise miss some critical material. The introductory and summary chapters lack bibliographic essays because there is virtually no significant comparative or summary literature dealing with nineteenth-century *European* political theater censorship, as opposed to material on individual countries; what little is available is included in endnotes 19 in the introduction and 2 in the summary. In writing the introduction, in particular, I have liberally borrowed from my earlier publications, which are mentioned in the latter endnote.

I am deeply indebted to the chapter contributors, who have of course made this book a reality, and have exhibited seemingly limitless patience as the delays that inevitably impact all multi-authored collections came into play. I also want to thank Janice Best, professor of languages and literature at Acadia University (Canada), and Robin Lenman, formerly history professor at the University of Warwick (UK), for reading a draft manuscript and providing many helpful suggestions. I am also much indebted to Berghahn Books and to my editor, Marion Berghahn, for her confidence in this work from its early days and, more generally, for keeping the faith at a time when marketplace pressures are probably a greater and more ruthless censorship threat to academic freedom and publication than anything wielded (or dreamed of) by the authorities.

# Introduction

Robert Justin Goldstein

## The Social and Political Context of Nineteenth-Century European Theater Censorship

In studying political theater censorship in nineteenth-century Europe, what is especially striking is how similar were the concerns and practices of authorities across the continent, as well as the responses of those who suffered from the censorship. Throughout Europe the theater was viewed by ruling elites as a form of communication that had enormous importance, and therefore drama censorship occupied a great deal of their time and energy, with a particular focus on proposed scripts that were viewed as potentially threatening to the existing political, legal, and social order. Moreover, given the especial fear of the poor and illiterate throughout Europe following the French revolution, and the far greater access of this element of the population to the stage as compared with print media, the authorities tended to pay particular attention to productions presented in venues that were especially popular among the lower classes. An examination of precisely which material the authorities sought to ban or circumscribe provides an unusually detailed glimpse into their mentalities, and especially their fears. In response to similar attempts by ruling elites across Europe to control the theater, dramatists and theater audiences throughout the continent developed common techniques of evasion and resistance.

Political controls over the theater were part of a much broader network of attempts to maintain the social and political status quo in nineteenth-century Europe, a fact that makes it very difficult to isolate its specific impact. For example, among the major countries or regions of Europe (Italy before 1860 and Germany before 1870 were each divided into numerous small states), the printed press (with the exception of England) was generally subject to prior censorship before about 1850. National elections and legislatures did not exist in Russia before 1905 and in the Habsburg Monarchy before 1860, while in those countries that had elected parliaments, the right to vote was generally restricted to, at most, the wealthiest 5 percent of the population before 1850, with universal adult (male only) suffrage generally dating at best from 1890 or later. Even then broader suffrage was often made meaningless by massive vote rigging (as in Spain, Portugal, and Hungary) or complicated electoral schemes that heavily weighted the votes of the rich (as in Austria, Belgium, Rumania, Russia, and the dominant German state of Prussia). Most European countries also outlawed or strictly limited freedom of assembly and association until mid century or thereafter, and harsh restrictions on the right to form trade unions and/or to strike were generally enforced until late in the nineteenth century or beyond.[1]

Another form of extremely important, if indirect, control maintained by European rulers over the ability of their citizens to effectively voice their views or otherwise participate in public affairs was that most countries did not provide even free elementary education until 1830 or after, and virtually none provided free education beyond that level. The result was that in 1850 over half of European adults were literate only in France, Germany, Switzerland, England, the Netherlands, and the Scandinavian countries, while adult literacy rates were 20 percent or less in Iberia, Italy, the Balkans, and Russia. As late as 1914 fewer than 3 percent of children between the ages of fourteen and eighteen across Europe were enrolled in secondary schools, and less than 1 percent of the university-age population in any country attended institutions of higher education. Moreover, when and where free education was made available (or required), it was generally designed to keep the poor in their "place" by depriving them of any knowledge beyond the basics required to provide a minimally adequate work force or that might upset the existing social structure. Thus, even in "advanced" France, leading politician Adolph Thiers (president, 1871–73) defined the purpose of education as teaching that "suffering is necessary in all estates" and that "when the poor have a fever, it is not the rich who have sent it to them." Russian minister of education Ivan Delianov decreed in 1887 that state-supported secondary schools should bar children of "coachmen, menials, cooks, washerwomen, small shopkeepers and the like" since it was "completely unwarranted for the children of such people to leave their position in life."[2]

Despite such restrictions, the seemingly unstoppable tide of modernization in nineteenth-century Europe, especially marked by rapid growth of literacy, urbanization and industrialization, and breakthroughs in communication and transportation (particularly the invention of the telegraph, the railroad, and technical breakthroughs in printing, which greatly reduced costs) led to the emergence—for the first time in world history—of a large mass of ordinary people with at least the potential for the desire and capacity to participate in public life. Thus, as the result of the greatest and fastest transformation until then in world history, in Europe as a whole between 1815 and 1914, adult literacy increased from under 30 percent to over 70 percent, the population living in towns of twenty thousand or more jumped from about 5 percent to about 20 percent, and the industrial labor force increased from about 15 percent to about 30 percent of the total labor force (as suggested above with regard to literacy rates, these overall figures hide massive variations among countries, with central, southern, and eastern Europe generally lagging substantially behind). This development deeply frightened traditional and emerging elites, especially due to the extraordinary number of political rebellions during the 1789–1850 period (the French Revolution of 1789, revolts in Spain, Portugal, and Naples in 1820–21, uprisings in France, Poland, Belgium, and parts of Switzerland, Italy, and Germany in 1830–32, and revolutions almost everywhere in Europe in 1848), generally led by elements of the emerging middle class, but typically supported by significant segments of the poor. In a statement that has become famous among modern historians because it so well captured both the political emergence of ordinary citizens and the horror such provoked among ruling elites, French legislative deputy Saint-Marc Girardin warned his colleagues in the early 1830s that "the barbarians which threaten society are [the working classes] in the outlying districts of our manufacturing towns, not in the Tartary of Russia [a reference suggestive of Mongol hordes]."[3]

Most Europeans, as earlier, lived in or on the margins of poverty during the nineteenth century. As the two best overall measures of social wealth and health, the infant mortality rate (about 5 per 1,000 in the wealthiest countries in 2007) was approximately 200 per 1,000 for all of Europe in 1815 (although it dropped substantially to about 150 by 1914), and life expectancy (today about 80 in wealthy countries) was under 40 years in 1815 (although jumping to almost 50 by 1914). Of course, such indicators were far higher than average for the relatively small European elite. Despite the generally impoverished state of the European masses, the rapid growth of literacy, industrialization and urbanization, and improvements in transportation and communication, as well as improved living conditions by 1900 (especially in western and northern Europe), for the first time gave large segments of the poor both an increasing awareness of their condition and a sense that change was possible. This contrasted sharply with the many centuries during which Europeans typically lived their entire lives encased in narrow geographical, vocational, and ideological frameworks that made it almost impossible to envision, much less demand, better lives from their rulers, who had not only far better material conditions of life, but alone enjoyed any significant freedom and power. Thus, on the eve of the 1905 Russian revolution, jurist A. F. Koni wrote to a friend: "The current situation in Russia is strange, and … frightening. Society is bursting out of its swaddling clothes, in which it was forcibly kept [by poverty and repression] and which dulled the mind and atrophied any feelings of self-dignity. But it already wants to run, although it doesn't yet know how to walk, and indeed to stand on its own feet." Similarly, John Stuart Mills observed in 1848 in England, where the social and economic transformation of Europe was especially advanced, that the working classes would no longer accept a "patriarchal or paternal system of government" and had irrevocably "taken their interests into their own hands" once they had been "taught to read," brought "together in numbers to work socially under the same roof," and enabled by railways to "shift from place to place." Or, in the astonishingly eloquent words of Hungarian peasant Albert Szilagi, testifying before a government commission investigating outbursts of rural unrest in his country in the 1890s, "The rightful demands of the laborers increased because the people of the land study more, know more, see more. How can you blame us? We have learnt how to read and write. We would now like to wear better clothes, eat like human beings and send our children to schools."[4]

## The Authorities' Fear of the Theater

In an age before the development of radio, television, cinema, and the internet, when large segments of adult populations were illiterate, and when political assembly and association were strictly regulated or completely banned, the theater provided the most important form of mass entertainment, and the only arena, aside from the church, in which regular mass gatherings were permissible in nineteenth-century Europe. Thus, as historian Eda Sagarra notes for Austria, the theater was the "center of public life" before 1850, "a substitute it was aptly said for [the lack of a] parliament"; similarly, in Russia, which lacked an elected national legislature before 1905, as Anthony Swift notes in his chapter below, one drama critic remarked in 1899, "for us plays and theaters are the same things as, for example, parliamentary events and political speeches are for a Western European." According to early nineteenth-century Bavarian reformer Wilhelm Riehl, "public life stormed and raged in the theater and concert hall because there was nowhere else it was allowed to storm and rage"; German theater historian Monika Steinhauser endorses this view, writing that "the proverbial theater mania of the pre-1848 period is explained by the fact that public opinion could not express itself except via the theatre because there was no [national] legislature, no free press and no right of assembly." With regard to France, F. W. J. Hemmings writes that the theater engaged the "attention of every class of people throughout the length and breadth of the land," serving as the "one and only purveyor of excitement, amusement and pathos that the mass of the population knew," as well as the "one and only escape from their usually laborious and lackluster existence." The mid-century Parisian theater industry alone employed over 10,000 people, with over 32,000 seats available nightly. According to contemporary observer Pierre Giffard, "the population of Paris lives at the theater, of the theater and by the theater." Similarly, according to historians of nineteenth-century Italian opera, "to all intents and purposes there was no other amusement whatever available," so everyone's attention "focused on the theater, which served as a kind of club where all sections of the population met to discuss both business and private affairs," and a new opera's success was "a capital event that stirred to its depths the city lucky enough to have witnessed it, and word of it ran all over Italy."[5]

While the authorities' fears of the printed press were unquestionably substantial and intense, they were even more alarmed by media such as the theater (as well as caricature, and, subsequently, cinema), which communicated with a far wider public than that reached by the press, including even the dreaded "dark masses," who, if often illiterate, were rarely blind or deaf, and were able to afford at least cheap theater tickets far more easily than they could buy newspapers or books. This was especially true before 1850, when press circulations rarely exceeded several thousand, due both to the general practice of selling newspapers only via long-term and expensive subscriptions and to the high illiteracy rates. That the stage was perceived as posing a far greater threat than the printed word by European authorities is clearly demonstrated by the fact that prior (or preventive) censorship of theater generally continued long after the press was freed from prior restraint (although usually remaining subject to potentially severe post-publication penalties). The most extreme example was England, where the press was freed from prior restraint in 1695, yet preventive drama censorship continued until 1968, or for almost another 275 years (!). In other countries the gap between the end of press and theater censorship was far shorter, but the differential treatment always favored the press: in France prior censorship was never enforced for the printed word after 1822, but preventive theater censorship continued until 1906; the Russian press was largely freed from prior press censorship in 1865 (although not entirely until 1905), yet theater censorship continued until the very end of the tsarist regime (only to be quickly reimposed by the Bolsheviks); Austrian press censorship ended in 1867, yet drama censorship continued until 1926; prior Swedish and Dutch press censorship were abolished by 1815, yet preventive theater censorship ended, respectively, only in 1872 and 1977; and prior German and Danish press censorship were abolished by 1850, yet drama censorship continued, respectively, until 1918 (before being restored by the Nazis) and 1953.[6]

The theater was viewed as so important and so potentially subversive that it was not unusual for rulers to personally intervene in establishing censorship regulations or even in making determinations concerning individual plays. The stage was deemed more threatening than the press not only because of its ability to reach even the illiterate, but also because it was generally perceived as more powerful and direct in impact, and because, unlike with the printed word, the audience was a collective one that, it was feared, might be stirred to immediate mob action. Print was perceived as "consumed" primarily by relatively educated people, often in private, who would not be immediately affected even by subversive matter; therefore, if a publication proved dangerous, unsold copies could be confiscated before their ill effects were evident. The impact of subversive theater, however, could apparently be virtually instantaneous: according to a French prison director, "When they put on a bad drama, a number of young new criminals soon arrive at my prison." The fact that the theater addressed a collective audience was also stressed: according to a French stage-censorship advocate speaking in 1830, the press "only addresses each reader in isolation, separately; dramatic works present themselves to ardent spectators, gathered together in great numbers, upon whom the actors' craft produces impassioned spontaneous sensations which could be translated immediately into outbreaks of disorder, violence, public unrest." Similarly, the governor-general of Moscow, explaining in 1805 why he was forbidding a play based on a tolerated book, declared that the "average person reads to himself alone, while a theatrical performance is attended by the masses," who might be swayed by occasional "daring expressions and thought against the government." A supporter of stage censorship made essentially the same argument before a 1909 British parliamentary inquiry, testifying that "the intellectual pitch of the crowd is lowered and its emotional pitch is raised," thus making theater audiences typically "irrational, excitable, lacking in self-control." Throughout the nineteenth century, drama-censorship supporters cited the widespread (if probably highly exaggerated) belief that presentation of the opera *La Muette de Portici* triggered the successful 1830 Belgian revolution against Dutch rule (the opera originally had been banned in Brussels and German towns near France). Similarly, French theater censor Victor Hallays-Dabot wrote in 1862 that plays that had provoked opposition demonstrations in the 1840s provided "a sort of dress rehearsal" for the 1848 revolution and, as Anthony Swift points out in his chapter below, a Russian minister declared in 1858 that "in all revolutions privately-owned theaters served as a means for arousing passions."[7]

Such arguments and fears were common throughout Europe. As Gary Stark notes in his chapter below, French social scientist Gustave Le Bon's tremendously influential 1895 book, *The Psychology of the Crowd*, argued that theatrical performances "have an enormous influence on the crowd" and "nothing arouses the fantasies of people as strongly" as when the audience "simultaneously feels the same emotions," which were sometimes strong enough to "translate themselves into action," especially as theater spectators had a "remarkable inclination" not to distinguish between the "real" and "unreal." When French minister of justice Jean-Charles Persil successfully urged legislators to reimpose prior censorship for the theater (and caricature, but not for the written word) in 1835 (all such censorship had ceased after the 1830 Revolution), he characterized the stage as posing a special danger, because, rather than addressing the "mind," it spoke to the "eyes," thus amounting to "a deed, an action, a behavior," rather than "the expression of an opinion." He declared, "Let an author be content with printing his plays, he will be subjected to no preventive measures," but "when opinions are converted into acts by the presentation of a play" they must be subject to the "high direction of the established power." A high-ranking Austrian official explained in a 1795 memorandum that drama censorship should be "much stricter" than for print due to the "different" and "infinitely more powerful" impression "which can be made on the minds and emotions of the audiences by a work enacted with the illusions of real life, by comparison with that which can be made by a play which is merely read at a desk"; he added that this was especially so because printed material could be restricted "only to a certain kind of reader [i.e., the middle and upper classes], whereas the playhouse by contrast is open to the entire public, which consists of people of every class, every walk of life and every age." Such views were reflected in drama censorship rules in Austrian-ruled Lombardy in the early nineteenth century, which warned that "theatrical performances can exercise the strongest impressions on those who watch them" and "are frequented by every sort of person," and an 1822 decree in the Austrian-dominated (if technically independent) Italian duchy of Tuscany, which ordered that restrictions applying to printed matter that disseminated "subversive" ideas threatening to "weaken or destroy veneration for Religion or for the Throne" be "applied more strictly to theatrical performances." An 1890s German court upheld the police power to ban plays for political reasons, not only because audiences might be incited to "disturbances of order" through "rowdyism and other excesses," but also because they might be "inwardly misled to views that endanger public well-being and order," such as "the disturbance caused by the thought that the existing political order does not grant the individual citizen his rights" (thus inadvertently literally demonstrating the accuracy of such perceptions!).[8]

In mid nineteenth-century Spain even book publishers, who bitterly protested against the censorship of novels, viewed the theater as entirely different: they declared that although it was "undeniable" that the "abuse of cleverness" in novels could be "very harmful and warrants the vigilance of a wise and prudent government, there is no way that it can have as much influence in subverting good ideas and even less that it can cause as immediate damage as an ardent dramatic presentation." The president of the French Society of Dramatic Authors, Baron Isidore Taylor, supported theater censorship based on similar arguments before an 1849 state inquiry, declaring that the stage "produces, among all those watching, a sort of electric communication, even more seductive for the masses than a speech, and one thousand times more dangerous than the most vehement article in the daily press." Similarly, the Viennese actor Friedrich Ziegler argued in 1820 that drama that attacked "religion, law, and monarchy" had done more damage than "all the political pamphlets" together, as the "inspiration of the spoken word, heard by many thousands, strikes more deeply than any cold political writings read only by a few." In Russia an interior ministry official warned in 1905 that theaters were among "the most powerful instruments of influence on the public" and were "penetrating the widest possible circles and becoming available at a price everyone can afford"; he echoed the 1868 words of a minister of the imperial Russian court, who lamented that popular theaters would become the "most powerful and simplest means to cultivate in the people ideas hostile to the existing order," especially since the "press influences only the educated class, which is capable of discerning the truth and is not easily carried away," but the stage could "distort the comprehension of the simple folk and install in them the germs of disorder." The London *Times*, too, in a 1907 editorial backing a ban on a play about abortion, was particularly concerned about theatrical influence on the unwashed masses. It declared that although the play provided "probably the most authentic presentation we have yet had on the English stage of great social and political questions," its subject, and the "sincere realism with which it is treated, makes it in our judgment wholly unfit for performance, under ordinary conditions, before a miscellaneous public of various ages, moods and standards of intelligence."[9]

Such concerns over the perceived power of the stage led most European governments to not only censor the theater before presentations, but also to require theater owners to undergo police scrutiny, to obtain licenses, and to post sometimes extremely heavy bonds to be forfeited in the case of legal violations. For example, the director of the Vaudeville theater in Paris had to deposit a bond of 300,000 francs in 1846, a staggering amount equivalent to approximately $60,000 in 2000. Theater licensing requirements were in effect, for example, in Britain until 1843, in France until 1864, in Germany until 1870, and in Russia until 1882. The number of theaters generally increased dramatically after licensing requirements were lifted in each of these countries, suggesting that, when enforced, they substantially limited the number of stage venues. Thus, in Germany the abolition of theater licensing led to the estimated immediate founding of almost ninety new theaters.[10]

Fear of the theater's potential subversive power was especially marked before the advent of free, compulsory primary education (around mid century outside of southern and eastern Europe), because the stage was so widely considered to be the most important forum for education of the lower classes. Thus, during the 1830–48 reign of French king Louis-Philippe, theater inspectors were directed to report in great detail about what they observed in theaters "in which the coarsest classes of people gather," since such venues had "become the only school in which the lower class of society goes to learn its lessons." An 1819 decree in Wallachia, the

Turkish-controlled province that later formed part of Romania, declared that theater censorship was required because while theaters could be a school for "good morals," able to "combat wickedness and make virtue, showing us how to distinguish between vice and virtue," when "the selection of plays is poorly made, they abuse the law, become a school for laxity and bad habits and defile civic custom." Similarly, as David Gies notes in his chapter below, the Madrid theater censor defined his job in the 1830s as ensuring that a "school of customs not become a house of prostitution." In 1888 Russian interior minister Dmitrii Tolstoi told Tsar Alexander III that "since the theater unquestionably has an important educational significance, it would seem necessary to ensure that the people receive from it sober and beneficial impressions and nothing that would promote their moral corruption." Earlier, eighteenth-century Russian tsarina Catherine the Great had termed the theater a "school for the people," with potential for fostering children's "moral education," while adding that it was "absolutely essential that it be under my supervision," as "I am the teacher in charge of this school and mine is the prime responsibility to God for the nation's morals."[11]

## Hopes for the Theater

As some of these quotations suggest, while the potentially subversive power of the theater was deeply feared by European elites, the stage was also perceived as potentially enlightening the masses (especially—although not only—by private, rather than government, elites), or at least diverting them from even more dangerous activities. Thus, among leading eighteenth-century European Enlightenment figures, France's Voltaire (who spent much of his life in exile for his political views) termed the theater a "powerful instrument of civilization, a great school for the people," while Germany's Friedrich Schiller, in a famous 1784 lecture on theater as a "moral institution," declared that the stage could open up "infinite horizons to the spirit thirsting" for an alternative to the "bestial condition" and "monotonous, often oppressive affairs of daily life," providing "nourishment to the soul's every power" and "uniting the acculturation of mind and heart with the noblest sort of entertainment." In a 1789 book, *Discourse on Freedom of the Theater,* French author Marie-Joseph Chénier labeled the theater "the most active and quickest means of invincibly arming the forces of human reason and shining a great deal of light simultaneously upon the people." The oft-censored Russian playwright Nikolai Gogol termed the stage a "kind of pulpit from which much good can be spoken to the world," while a Russian magazine that supported inexpensive theaters wrote in 1886 that such venues would provide "ennobling artistic impressions to the masses" and become a "higher school" from which Russia's greatest talents could "teach us goodness and truth, until now only a luxury accessible to the prosperous classes." Similarly, even a late nineteenth-century Russian provincial governor wrote that "no moral book, no moralistic lecture can have the kind of powerful corrective influence on a person as a play," while the great Russian director Konstantin Stanislavsky told his Moscow Art Theater company in 1898 to "never forget that we are striving to brighten the dark existence of the poor classes, to give them minutes of happiness and aesthetic uplift to relieve the muck which envelops them." In Germany in 1890 the founders of the socialist-oriented Freie Volksbühne similarly viewed the theater's benefits for the lower classes, declaring that the stage "should be a source of high artistic gratification, moral uplift and a powerful stimulus to thinking about the great topics of the day," potentially serving as a source of "emancipation and social regeneration" unlike the existing stage, which, "subjugated to capitalism," corrupted mass tastes by presenting plays on the level of "society small talk … the circus and comic papers." A proponent of the "social theater" in Belgium called for dramas that celebrated working-class virtues by describing "all the devotion, all the self-abnegation, all the sacrifices and all the heroism of the proletariat," while a similar advocate in France, Louis Lumet, who founded a "popular" Parisian stage in 1897, declared his purpose to "elevate man, to give him joy, not from gayety but to support in him ideas of justice and independence," and to provide "immortal light" that would provide the means to "become a free people."[12]

Other proponents of the educational role of the theater argued that drama could instruct and invigorate the middle classes or prove the salvation of entire societies. Thus, the German liberal newspaper *Grenzboten*, hailing the foundation of the Leipzig Stadttheater in 1868, declared that the stage produced "an immeasurable effect on the thought and sensitivity of the people" and termed the theater the "conscience of the nation, the integration-point of middle-class desires and hopes, the seat of self-identity of middle class society." The great French republican historian Jules Michelet, who was twice dismissed from university professorships for his political views, declared that the "theater, the true theater, will revive the world," and that "an immensely popular theater" would in the future "unquestionably be the most powerful means of education" and "the best hope perhaps of a national renovation." Victor Hugo, perhaps his country's leading opponent of theater censorship, termed the theater "a crucible of civilization" that "forms the public soul" and that, if subsidized and uncensored by the state, could reconcile class differences in France by "developing moral sentiment and education in the lower classes" and thus "make calm reign in that part of the population." He added, "The rich and poor, the happy and unhappy, the Parisian and the provincial, the French and the foreigners will meet each other every night, mix their souls fraternally and share in the contemplation of great works of the human spirit. From that will result popular and universal improvement."[13]

If an unregulated and politicized theater was seen by European rulers as threatening subversion, a controlled and frothy stage was perceived as potentially shoring up the establishment by diverting the minds of the potentially discontented middle and lower classes to non-political matters. Thus, in 1775 a French official declared that

> spectacles [i.e., the theater and other entertainments] in large cities are necessary in order to divert the man of affairs, in order to amuse upstanding people and well-to-do persons and finally to occupy the people who, when not attached to any spectacle, can be induced to factionalism. You know that the populace is stirred up, thrown into confusion, flighty; it is necessary then to stabilize it; well, one cannot do it except by spectacles. ... For that reason, legislators have established different ones in every age, and I dare to suggest that it is sound politics ... even to increase them. ... The days of the Virgin and the solemn fetes that the church dedicates to the grandeur of religion, in which our theaters are closed out of respect ... there is committed in the capital more evil on these days of every kind, whether debaucheries, drunkenness, libertinage, thefts and even assassination.

In Austria in 1806, during the Napoleonic wars, when price increases were about to be announced and economic problems led the authorities to consider closing the theaters, the police sent the emperor a similar report urging that the theaters should remain open, because "in times like the present, when such manifold sufferings depress the character of the people, the police must co-operate more than ever before in distracting the citizens in every moral way. The most dangerous hours of the day are the evening hours. They cannot be filled less harmfully than in the theater. ... Prudence demands ... since entertainment and distraction of the people have always been a state maxim ... that an entertainment familiar for years should not be closed down just at such a moment."[14]

Austrian police continued to stress the same points during the 1820s, declaring that "lacking moral entertainment" the poor "could easily be misled," while providing "respectable cheap entertainment" such as the theater led people, "especially the lower classes," away from the "more expensive, often unsalubrious pubs, coffeehouses and gambling houses to better amusements, with some influence on education and morals," while also keeping them "under public observation and order for the duration of the performance." Government support of the theater, the police stressed, tended to "restrain those activities endangering morality and public order," while bringing "variety to daily conversation and supplying for the latter material that is as abundant as it is harmless." The chief minister of Austrian-ruled Lombardy Venetia during the 1815–48 period similarly urged that Milan's famous La Scala opera house be kept busy as it "attracts to a place open to observation during the hours of darkness a large part of the educated population," and, as John A. Davis notes in his chapter below, in 1820 a leading Neapolitan minister termed theaters a "political and moral necessity that keeps the multitude from engaging in more pernicious gatherings." A Papal advisory committee reported in 1837 (a period of general unrest in Europe and especially in Italy, where the Papal States occupied the central portion of that then-divided country) that "particularly at this time the distraction and entertainment of the people is the healthiest cure for the wounds that have been inflicted in almost every part of the world," and that a "suitably distracting theater, decently entertaining and soberly diverting" had been "confirmed by the experience of centuries" to be the "means most fitting and conducive" to help create a people "more calm and content with the government to which it finds itself subjected." French authorities in 1852 expressed a comparable hope in urging that censorship ensure that the stage "completely avoid" all scenes "imprinted with a revolutionary spirit" as well as "all forms of factionalism, based on the principle that the theater must be a place of repose and of distraction and not an overt arena of political passions." Similarly, Russian czar Nicholas I (ruled 1825–55) overrode the opposition of his secret police in allowing the production of sensational "blood and thunder" dramas because he saw them as "a sort of emotional lightning conductor which grounded the energy of social protest." Decades later Russian authorities in 1897 declared popular theaters a useful means of "drawing the folk away from drinking establishments" and "spreading the idea of the dangers of alcohol abuse," thus serving "not only as entertainment but as a means of exercising moral influence on the masses."[15]

## Class and Theater Censorship

Not only were communications media such as the theater (and caricature) perceived as particularly accessible to lower-class audiences strictly controlled, but, even *within* each media category, material that the authorities viewed as particularly targeted at the "dark masses" was typically subjected to particularly strict controls. As John House notes in a study of the censorship of images in France in the 1860s, while the authorities were in general "particularly wary of the potency of visual experience, in the form of a print or a stage representation or a performance of popular café-concert songs," the "question of class—of determining what types of material should be permitted for which social groups—seems to have been the most fundamental concern." Thus, in 1852 the French police minister termed drawings "one of the most dangerous" of the "means employed to shake and destroy the sentiments of reserve and morality which are so essential to conserve in the bosom of a well-ordered society," because "the worst page of a bad book requires some time to read and a certain degree of intelligence to understand," while the drawing "offers a sort of personification of the thought, it puts it in relief, it communicates it with movement and life, so as to thus present spontaneously, in a translation which *everyone* can understand, the most dangerous of all seductions, that of example" (emphasis added). Many European countries took special steps to keep even books and newspapers out of the hands of the poor, for example imposing licensing requirements and so-called "caution bonds" on newspaper publishers and special taxes on the press to insure that only the "respectable classes" could own or purchase newspapers. In some cases, as in Germany between 1819 and 1848, lengthy books that presumably would be too complex and expensive to appeal to the lower classes were exempted from prior censorship requirements (the German cutoff was 320 pages), or, as in Austria, the same book might be approved for some elements of the population, but not for others. As one historian has summarized the Austrian system, which had five separate categories of books, "the lower the social and educational status, the more information was to be withheld." Thus, the Austrian category of "*erga schedam*" included books containing "more evil than good" but which could nonetheless be allowed under special procedures for individual readers known to be "wise, talented, of good reputation, or holding high office." The Russian book-censorship system regularly directed censors to pay the "strictest attention to censoring the publications destined for the general public." The Russian censors approved Karl Marx's *Das Kapital* because they concluded it was a "difficult, inaccessible strictly scientific work" that few would read, and "even fewer [would] understand" its socialist message, buried in a "colossal mass of abstruse, somewhat obscure politico-economic argumentation."[16]

It is not surprising, therefore, that the severity of the European theater censorship often depended upon the perceived class nature of the audience. As French theater censorship historian Odile Krakovitch summarizes, "The more modest and popular the theater, the harsher the censors' judgments and the more numerous the required modifications." Thus, French plays that might be approved for so-called "legitimate" theaters typically patronized by the middle and upper classes were often barred from the popular stage: the censors' reports repeatedly contain phrases such as "this appears to us to contain passages which could be troublesome given the [working-class] theater for which this work is destined" and "there is reason to fear that, in [a theater] currently frequented by the working class, such a spectacle would only arouse [class] animosities." Before the 1864 termination of French theater licensing requirements, theoretically only a handful of stages could legally present "legitimate" drama, while the so-called "popular" theaters could officially only present material such as pantomimes, vaudevilles, melodramas, and short skits and songs that were unlikely to encompass serious political critiques (although in practice such restrictions were enforced with increasing laxity after about 1830). Censorship of French café-concerts tended to be especially harsh, as their audience was highly working-class based: during the 1850–1900 period, about 10 percent of all songs proposed for performance at such venues were forbidden, a percentage far exceeding that for theatrical plays.[17]

Similar class-based distinctions were common in nineteenth-century Europe. Thus, in Germany, the expensive court theaters had a near monopoly on the performance of opera and serious drama during the first half of the century, while the censors clearly differentiated on the basis of proposed venues thereafter. For example, Gerhart Hauptmann's famous drama, *The Weavers,* based on an 1844 uprising by Silesian weavers, was repeatedly banned from public performances until the Berlin Supreme Administrative Court agreed in 1894 to allow a production at Berlin's Deutsches Theater, since the high admission prices there would exclude the "common masses" who would be "most susceptible" to any possible pernicious influences and this venue was "visited primarily by members of those circles of society who do not tend towards acts of violence and other disturbances of public order." The great German director Max Reinhardt played on such official orientations in appealing for 1906 censorship approval of Frank Wedekind's sexually oriented *Spring Awaken-*

*ing;* Reinhardt assured the censors that the play would not be performed "for the general public" but "in the Kammerspiele, a theater which seats only some 300 and which, owing to the high prices, will draw its public from the most exclusive social circles." As John A. Davis points out in his chapter below, the 1852 Piedmont theater regulations directed that special attention be paid to "popular theaters," from which "anything" should be removed "that might incite sympathy for crime and hatred for the punitive activities of the state." Russia went beyond this in 1888 by establishing a separate censorship administration to censor inexpensive "popular" theaters; thereafter hundreds of plays previously approved for the more-expensive venues were banned from popular theaters. Minister of the Interior Dmitrii Tolstoy proposed this policy to Tsar Alexander III by explaining that while "in examining plays the censor has in view the more or less educated public," the "common man," due to his "level of mental development, his outlook and conceptions," will "often interpret in an utterly wrong sense something that would present no temptation for a somewhat educated person, and thus a play containing nothing blameworthy from a general point of view may be unsuitable and even harmful for him." Thus, Alexander Ostrovsky's 1891 play *A Happy Day,* featuring a corrupt provincial official plotting to marry off his daughters, was cleared as a "harmless farce" for the regular stage, but, according to the censors, could not be tolerated in the popular theaters, because to "depict before the ignorant crowd the lowest-ranking representatives of the government in a ridiculous light, to have them commit crimes with impunity—this is extremely inappropriate."[18]

## Early Theatrical Censorship

Stage censorship originated in the long-held view, dating back to Roman times, that the theater was a den of sexual immorality, religious heresy, and political sedition. Although in Greece actors were so venerated and drama so influential that Plato referred to his country as a "theatrocracy," by Roman times the theater had become increasingly bawdy and disorderly. During the Roman Empire the stage was in such low repute that actors were forbidden to vote or hold public office and were viewed as so contaminated that neither they nor their children were allowed to engage in any other profession. Early Christian theologians such as Tertullian, Caesarius, and Augustine responded to the licentious and sacrilegious character of much of the later Roman stage by referring to theaters as the "shrine of Venus," "celebrations of the devil," and "dens of iniquity." During the Middle Ages, the Church forbade actors to practice their craft on pain of excommunication, and, in AD 568 and 692 respectively, authorities in the Western and Eastern Roman Empires, acting under Church pressure, banned all theatrical spectacles. Although theater slowly revived during the late Middle Ages, often in the form of liturgical dramas, passion plays, or other religiously inspired spectacles, distrust and suspicion of the secular stage continued. Thus, in 1662 Cardinal Carlo Borromeo of Milan described the theater as "the source and base of nearly all evils and all crimes," while in a 1666 article French writer Pierre Nicole termed playwrights "public poisoners." During the Puritan Revolution in England stages were shut down completely between 1642 and 1660 under a law that deemed all actors "Rogues" and denounced theaters as "Spectacles of pleasure, too commonly expressing lascivious Mirth and Levitie." The sixteenth-century ban on the theater in Geneva, imposed by Calvin to guard against the "dissipation and libertinism which the actor troops disseminate among the youth," remained effective for two hundred years. All theatrical performances were banned during the American Revolution (1776–83), while, in a famous eighteenth-century controversy over theatrical freedom, leading Enlightenment spokesman Jean Jacques Rousseau expressed views later summed up by a theater critic as concluding: "Man is depraved, the first time by society, and the second time by the theater."[19]

More typical than complete suppression of the stage were attempts to regulate the theater, usually through administrative decrees that were enforced in a rather haphazard manner. Thus, in 1559 English Queen Elizabeth I barred the presentation of all unapproved plays and forbade all works on political and religious subjects, while attempts to regulate French theater date to 1398, with the first of a series of sporadic attempts to impose prior censorship on all dramatic presentations. In 1641 French Louis XIII banned representations of "all dishonest actions, all lascivious words and double entendres which could affect the honest public." Systematic theater censorship in France began only under Louis XIV, who in 1701 directed that all plays be submitted in advance to the Paris police to ensure that all characters conformed to standards of "the highest purity," or, as theater historian Glynne Wickham has put it, to make sure that "any public utterance thought to be critical of the monarchy or suspect to the Church" would be stifled. In Spain modern theater censorship dates from the seventeenth century, while in Austria, where similar restrictions originate in the mid eighteenth century, Emperor Joseph II in 1770 gave clear instructions to actors that no deviation from approved scripts would be tolerated: "No one is allowed deliberately to add or alter anything in his part or to employ unseemly gestures; everyone, on the contrary, should keep exclusively to the terms prescribed by the author and authorized by the imperial and royal theater censorship; in case of infraction, the offender is fined one-eighth of his monthly salary." In a number of countries theater censorship was drastically tightened in response to the ideological threat posed by the French Revolution. Thus, in the German state of Bavaria, "all plays bearing on our country's history" were banned in the 1790s. Those who violated theater licensing and censorship rules typically were threatened with serious reprisals, and in a number of instances actors and playwrights were fined, jailed, or deported for their infractions. Thus, the illustrious seventeenth-century English playwright Ben Jonson was twice briefly jailed for dramatic indiscretions, although eventually Jonson aspired to be a censor himself.

## Notes

1. For documentation and elaboration on these points, see Robert Justin Goldstein, *Political Repression in Nineteenth-Century Europe* (London, 1983).
2. Roger Price, *The French Second Republic* (Ithaca, NY, 1972), 254; P. Alston, *Education and the State in Tsarist Russia* (Stanford, CA, 1969), 129.
3. These general trends are discussed in all good general histories of nineteenth-century Europe, such as M. S. Anderson, *The Ascendancy of Europe, 1815–1914*, 3rd ed. (London, 2003), Leo Loubère, *Nineteenth-Century Europe: The Revolution of Life* (Englewood Cliffs, NJ, 1994), and Theodore Hamerow, *The Birth of a New Europe: State and Society in the Nineteenth Century* (Chapel Hill, NC, 1983), which includes an excellent collection of statistics. Clive Church, *Europe in 1830: Revolution and Social Change* (London, 1983), and Jonathan Sperber, *The European Revolutions, 1848–1851*, 2nd ed. (Cambridge, 2005), provide good coverage on the revolutionary outbursts of those years. The Girardin quote is in John Merriman, "Contested Freedoms in the French Revolutions, 1830–1871," in Isser Woloch, ed., *Revolution and the Meanings of Freedom in the Nineteenth-Century* (Stanford, CA, 1996), 187.
4. Gary Thurston, *The Popular Theater Movement in Russia, 1862–1919* (Evanston, IL, 1998); Hamerow, 135; Andrew Janos, *The Politics of Backwardsness in Hungary, 1824–1945* (Princeton, NJ, 1983), 162–63.
5. Eda Sagarra, *Tradition and Revolution: German Literature and Society, 1830–1890* (New York, 1971), 79; Robert Nemes, *The Once and Future Budapest* (Dekalb, IL, 2005), 32; Monika Steinhauser, "Théâtre et théâtralité urbaine au XIXe siècle en Allemagne," in Christophe Charle, ed., *Capitales culturelelles, Capitales symboliques: Paris et les experiences européennes XVIIIe-Xxe siècles* (Paris, 2002), 204;

F. W. J. Hemmings, *Theater and State in France, 1760–1905* (Cambridge, 1994), 1; Harold Hobson, *French Theater Since 1800* (London, 1978), 4–5; Francis Toye, *Rossini* (London, 1954), 24; John Rosselli, *The Opera Industry in Italy from Cimarosa to Verdi* (Cambridge, 1984), 169. Christophe Charle, "L'attraction théâtrale des capitales aux XIXe siècle: problèmes de comparison," in Charle, ed., *Capitales Européenes et Rayonnement Culturel, XVIIIe-Xxe siècle* (Paris, 2004), 155, has useful statistical information about the number of theaters and seats available in a variety of European cities.

6. For surveys of nineteenth-century European political repression and, especially, press censorship, see Goldstein, *Political Repression;* Robert Justin Goldstein, *Political Censorship of the Arts and the Press in Nineteenth-Century Europe* (London, 1989), 26–71; Goldstein, ed., *The War for the Public Mind: Political Censorship in Nineteenth-Century Europe* (Westport, CT, 2000); Anthony Smith, *The Newspaper: An International History* (London, 1979), 105–43; and John Hohenberg, *Free Press/Free People: The Best Cause* (New York, 1971), 46–161. French press censorship is compared with that elsewhere in Goldstein, "Nineteenth-century French Political Censorship in Comparative European Perspective," *Proceedings of the Western Society for French History* 29 (2003): 117–32.

7. Albert Delpit, "La Liberté des Théâtres," *Revue des deux mondes* (1878): 623; Louis Allard, "Un Épisode de la Censure Dramatique: La Comédie et la Censure sous Louis-Philippe," *Romanic Review* 34 (1943): 332; Jack Weiner, *Mantillas in Moscovy: The Spanish Golden Age Theater in Tsarist Russia, 1672–1917* (Lawrence, KS, 1970), 25; John Palmer, *The Censor and the Theater* (New York, 1913), 189; Vincent Adoumie, "Du chant à la sedition: *La Muette de Portici* et la revolution belge de 1830," in *Le chant, acteur de l'histoire* (Rennes, France, 1999), 243–54; Sonia Slatin, "Opera and Revolution: *Muette de Portici* and the Belgian Revolution of 1830 Revisited," *Journal of Musicological Research* 3 (1979): 45–62; Janet Fulcher, *The Nation's Image: French Grand Opera as Politics and Politicized Art* (Cambridge, 1987), 11–46; Victor Hallays-Dabot, *Histoire de censure théâtrale en France* (1862), 116.

8. [French] *Archives Parlementaire de 1787 à 1860* (1989), 257–58; Donald Kimbell, *Verdi in the Age of Italian Romanticism* (Cambridge, 1981), 25; W. E. Yates, *Theater in Vienna: A Critical History, 1776–1995* (Cambridge, 1996), 25–26; Roy Pascal, *From Naturalism to Expressionism: German Literature and Society, 1880–1918* (New York, 1973), 266.

9. Adrian Shubert, "Spain," in Goldstein, ed., *War,* 189–90; Odile Krakovitch, *Les Pièces de théâtre soumises a La Censure (1800–1830)* (Paris, 1982), 14; Johann Hüttner, "Theater Censorship in Metternich's Vienna," *Theater Quarterly* 37 (1980): 64; Gary Thurston, "The Impact of Russian Popular Theater, 1886–1895," *Journal of Modern History* 55 (1983): 262; E. Anthony Swift, "Fighting the Germs of Disorder: The Censorship of Russian Popular Theater, 1888–1917," *Russian History* 18 (Spring 1991): 11; Richard Findlater, *Banned! A Review of Theater Censorship in Britain* (London, 1967), 99.

10. For France, F. W. J. Hemmings, *Theater and State in France, 1760–1905* (Cambridge, 1994), 160–75; for Russia, Murray Frame, *Schools for Citizens: Theater*

and *Society in Imperial Russia* (New Haven, CT, 2006), 74–106, and Frame, "'Freedom of the Theatres': The Abolition of the Russian Imperial Theatre Monopoly," *Slavic and East European Studies* 83 (2005): 254–89.
11. Odile Krakovitch, *Hugo Censuré: La Liberté au Théâtre au XIXe Siècle* (Paris, 1985), 83; "Prince Alexandru Sutu's decree founding an Office of theater to exercise censorship, 8 November, 1819," in Laurence Senelick, ed., *National Theater in Northern and Eastern Europe, 1746–1900* (Cambridge, 1991), 303; Frame, *Schools*, 22–23.
12. Sally Charnow, *Theater, Politics and Markets in Fin-de-Siècle Paris* (New York, 2005), 55; translation of Schiller lecture on website <www.schillerinstitute.org/tranls/schil_theatermoral.html> (accessed 3 July 2007); Edward Braun, *The Director and the Stage* (London, 1982), 60; Frame, *Schools*, 137; Gary Thurston, *The Popular Theatre Movement in Russia, 1862-1919* (Evanston, IL 1998), 58; Cecil Davies, *Theatre for the People: The Story of the Volksbühne* (Austin, TX, 1977), 2; Raphael Samuel, et al., *Theatres of the Left: Workers' Theatre Movements in Britain and America* (London, 1985), 17; Cecilia Beach, *Staging Politics and Gender: French Women's Drama, 1880–1923* (New York, 2005), 12, 15.
13. Anne Marie Koller, *The Theatre Duke: Georg II of Saxe-Meiningen and the German Stage* (Stanford, CA, 1984), 12; Stephen Kippur, *Jules Michelet* (Albany, NY, 1981), 120, 130; Krakovitch, *Hugo*, 217.
14. Robert Isherwood, *Popular Farce and Fantasy: Popular Entertainment in Eighteenth-Century Paris* (New York, 1986), 255; Hüttner, 61–62.
15. Alice Hanson, *Musical Life in Biedermeier Vienna* (Cambridge, 1985), 75; John Rosselli, *The Opera Industry in Italy from Cimarosa to Verdi* (Cambridge, 1984), 82; David Kimbell, *Verdi in the Age of Italian Romanticism* (Cambridge, 1981), 40; Odile Krakovitch, *Censure des Répertoires des Grands Théâtres Parisians (1835–1906)* (Paris, 2003), 15; Thurston, *Popular,* 148; Herbert Marshall, *The Pictorial History of the Russian Theater* (New York, 1976), 247.
16. John House, "Manet's Maximilian: Censorship and the Salon," in Elizabeth Childs, ed., *Suspended License: Censorship and the Visual Arts* (Seattle, WA, 1997), 187; Archives Nationales (hereafter AN), Paris, F18 2342; David Laven, *Venice and Venetia under the Habsburgs, 1815–1835* (Cambridge, 2002), 178; Jeffrey Brooks, *When Russia Learned to Read: Literacy and Popular Literature* (Princeton, NJ, 1985), 299–306; Albert Resis, "*Das Kapital* comes to Russia," *Slavic Review* 19 (1970): 221. On French caricature–censorship generally, see Robert Justin Goldstein, *Censorship of Political Caricature in Nineteenth-Century France* (Kent, OH, 1989). On class-based newspaper and book censorship generally, see Goldstein, "Introduction," and Lothar Hobelt, "The Austrian Empire," in Goldstein, ed., *War,* 17–18, 218.
17. Odile Krakovitch, "Robert Macaire ou la Grande Peur des Censeurs," *Europe: Revue litteraire mensuelle* (1987): 55–56; Jean-Marie Thomasseau, "Le Melodrama et La Censure sous le Premier Empire et la Restauration," *Revue des sciences humaines* 162 (1976): 179; Krakovitch, *Hugo*, 114, 131, 140; Nicholas Harrison, "Colluding with the Censor: Theater Censorship in France After the Revolution," *Romance Studies* 25 (1995): 12; Odile Krakovitch, "La Censure

des Spectacles sous le Second Empire," in Pascal Orly, ed., *La Censure en France a l'ère démocratique* (Paris, 1997), 71–72, 77; Concetta Condemi, *Les Café-Concerts* (Paris, 1992), 39. On especial fear of café-concerts, see also Eva Kimminich, "Chansons étouffée: Recherche sur le café-concert au XIXe siècle," *Politix* 14 (1991): 19–26.

18. Dawn Sova, *Banned Plays: Censorship Histories of 125 Stage Dramas* (New York, 2004), 313; Peter Jelavich, *Munich and Theatrical Modernism: Politics, Playwriting and Performance, 1890–1914* (Cambridge, MA, 1985), 118; Horst Claus, *The Theater Director Otto Brahm* (Ann Arbor, MI, 1981), 11; Swift, "Germs," 31; E. Anthony Swift, *Popular Theater and Society in Tsarist Russia* (Berkeley, CA, 2002), 106.

19. For a longer and documented account of early theatrical controls discussed in this and the following paragraph, see Goldstein, *Political Censorship*, 123–26. I have relied most heavily on Jonas Barish, *The Anti-Theatrical Prejudice* (Berkeley, CA, 1981); Mendel Kohansky, *The Disreputable Profession: The Actor in Society* (Westport, CT, 1984); Glynne Wickham, *A History of the Theater* (London, 1992); and Kenneth MacGowan et al., *Golden Ages of the Theater* (Englewood Cliffs, NJ, 1979). For the Rousseau characterization, see Charnow, *Theater, Politics and Markets in Fin-de-Siècle Paris* (New York, 2005), 56.

# Germany

### Gary D. Stark

## Theater and German Culture

Theater stood at the center of nineteenth-century German cultural life: according to one scholar, it was the "focal point of public culture, princely representation, and civic communication."[1] In the baroque courts of the kings, dukes, princes, and counts who governed the many petty principalities that made up the eighteenth-century Holy Roman Empire, princely authority and ostentatious theatrics went hand in hand. Several of these sovereigns established royal or court theaters (*Hoftheaters*) for the amusement of their aristocratic courtiers, but also to display their wealth and status and to impress their subjects and rivals with the pomp and grandeur of their rule. From the eighteenth century until the end of monarchy in Germany in 1918, these court theaters under royal patronage functioned as dynastic showcases and prominent centers of social life, especially in the smaller princely residences such as Kassel, Karlsruhe, Mannheim, Darmstadt, and Meiningen.

When middle-class German intellectuals in the late eighteenth and early nineteenth century sought to create and nurture a national literary culture—a truly "German" literature that would transcend and unify the various local territorial cultures and dialects—many regarded theater as the primary means toward this end. During the "classical" period of German literature, Lessing, Goethe, Schiller, and others made drama a key medium of literary expression and general vehicle for culture. Contemporaries spoke of a widespread "cult of the theater" that ascribed to this medium a unique moral, spiritual, educational, and even political mission. In his famous 1784 essay, "The Stage Considered as a Moral Institution," Friedrich Schiller venerated the theater as a source of moral enlightenment and civic education for the broad populace, an agent of social progress, and a source of national self-consciousness and unity. The unique power and appeal of the stage was comparable to that of religion, Schiller believed, and he foresaw a time when it would replace religion as a moral force in public life.[2] There were repeated calls from the 1780s to the late 1840s for the creation of a permanent "national" repertory theater (*Nationaltheater*), modeled on France's Comedie-Française. Its appeal would reach beyond the narrow ruling class that frequented the court theaters, but because it would be supported by royal and private patrons, it would not become commercially dependent on the crude tastes of the broad, semi-educated populace that sought cheap entertainment. Such a theater, performing German dramas written in a standard national language for the educated national community, would be a force for cultural integration and unity, an expression of Germany's emerging cultural nationalism, and a source, not of amusement and diversion, but of enlightenment that would raise the moral and cultural level of German society.[3] Efforts were made in Hamburg, Dresden, and Mannheim to create a national theater, but none succeeded for very long.

In the early nineteenth century, theater in Germany served a quasi-political as well as a cultural function. Worried about the surge of popular political consciousness and patriotic sentiment that swept the German states during the Napoleonic era and War of Liberation (1813–15), the ruling classes after 1815 were determined to restore order, resist demands for national unification, and push their subjects back into the non-political private sphere. Establishment authorities in the Restoration era (1815–48) discouraged the public discussion of social and political issues and hoped the theater, by focusing on light entertainment, could serve as a safety valve or diversion for rising discontent. They did not grasp, as Schiller had in his famous theater treatise, that the stage might also play a positive role in building public support for the government. "Sovereigns and guardians of the state," Schiller wrote, "if they knew how to do it, could use the stage to correct and enlighten popular opinion about government and the governing class. Legislative power might speak to its subjects in unfamiliar symbols, might defend its actions before they had time to utter a complaint, might silence their doubts without appearing to do so."[4]

For many in the frustrated middle classes, however, the theater became instead a surrogate for public life. At a time when public and political life was still tightly controlled by the aristocracy, political assemblies and associations forbidden or tightly regulated, and the press heavily censored, theaters provided one of the few arenas outside church where regular mass gatherings were allowed. For educated middle class audiences, theaters were not merely vehicles of entertainment, but sometimes served also as places where ideas and news could be exchanged and social and political ideas could be aired.[5] Some liberals considered the theater as a vehicle for national reform and as a substitute parliament. In any case, in the decades before 1848 a real theater craze swept many levels of society: interest in the theater grew, audiences expanded, and attendance rose. While local theaters may not have become sites of public worship (as the dramatist Franz Grillparzer once predicted), in many places they did become centers of public life. As one observer noted in 1841, "Not only has the German theater come to occupy an honorable place among all the arts in the course of the last fifty years, it has actually become a social necessity. In all the princely capitals you find richly equipped theaters; all important towns vie with each other in building magnificent temples to the art of drama and establishing it within their walls. The greatest minds have devoted their interest and their activity to the theater."[6]

Popular enthusiasm for theater remained high after the German states were unified under Prussian leadership in 1871. The English writer Henry Vizetelly, a frequent visitor to Berlin in the 1870s, observed: "The Berlinese of today are steady playgoers, and pass much of their time at the theaters, which, on Sunday evenings especially, are filled to overflowing."[7] Schiller's idealized cult of the theater as an institution of personal cultivation and national consciousness was so pervasive in the imperial era (1871–1918) that nearly every social stratum expressed reverence for its uplifting spiritual power and national mission. Emperor Wilhelm II (ruled 1888–1918) ardently endorsed the "noble, idealistic viewpoint" of Schiller's famous essay. The Hohenzollern monarchy, the emperor affirmed, had always regarded the theater as "a weapon of enormous power" in the "struggle against materialism and un-Germanness"; like the school and the university, he believed the function of the stage was to cultivate idealism and character in the younger generation, to ennoble their moral views, and to "prepare them for their task of preserving the highest spiritual values of our wonderful German fatherland."[8] The educated, cultivated bourgeoisie that formed the backbone of imperial culture shared similar views, while various cultural "outsiders," including radical avant-garde modernists and committed Social Democrats, also acknowledged the theater's unique power and believed it was capable of sparking a national cultural, social, and political transformation.[9]

This cult of the theater and perception of its power was regularly invoked to justify extensive state controls over stage productions. Because nineteenth-century Germans believed so strongly in the remarkable cultural and political power of the stage, state authorities were determined to control and censor it. Even at the dawn of the twentieth century, various Prussian ministers of interior expressed their duty to protect the stage as "a place of cultivation and spiritual uplift for wide segments of the population" and to prevent "any performance that the uneducated 'common man' might misconstrue"; similarly, Munich's police director considered police censorship of theaters "a positive, state-sustaining, national, and monarchical institution."[10]

Germans' love of the stage in the nineteenth century stimulated a steady proliferation of new theater venues. Although aristocratic court theaters remained important up until World War I (after 1810 the number of princely states with royal theaters rose to about twenty), in the first half of the century two new types of theater emerged to serve the middle classes. Beginning in the 1790s, and especially after 1815, cities such as Augsburg, Bremen, Breslau, Braunschweig, Düsseldorf, Frankfurt am Main, Hamburg, Hanover, Leipzig, Magdeburg, and Nuremberg established their own city or municipal theaters (*Stadttheaters*). Typically the city council or a committee of prominent citizens appointed by the municipal government formed a joint stock company, erected a theater building in the city, and then leased it to a tenant director to operate. These leaseholders were usually chosen on the basis of purely commercial, not artistic considerations. The municipal government did not subsidize the theater, but rather earned income from the rent and the theater license it granted; the tenant director, in turn, generally regarded the theater as a purely commercial enterprise. His degree of autonomy varied, depending on circumstances and local personalities. In some cities, including Hamburg, the joint stock company allowed the director extensive freedom regarding artistic questions, while in others, such as Leipzig, the city government's theater committee and mayor insisted on being involved or at least consulted on daily operations.[11] By 1848 there were about thirty municipally owned theaters in Germany; by the end of the century there were four times as many.

Privately owned commercial theaters, tied neither to a royal court nor a municipal government, began to thrive during the theater craze of the

Restoration era. To establish a standing commercial theater (in contrast to itinerant bands of actors, or *Wanderbühne*) required the permission of the government authorities. Although the Prussian Commercial Code of 1810 abolished medieval corporative restrictions and established freedom of enterprise in most occupations, those who wished to found and operate a privately owned theater were required to apply to the local police or provincial governor for a license. Most other German states adopted similar requirements. As the law read in the 1840s, "Theater directors need the special permission of the governor of the province in which they will hold performances. Such permission will be granted only after the applicant provides evidence of the necessary reliability and education, although on the judgment of the governor, permission can be denied even if these requirements are met."[12] Theater licenses, which were valid for a specific time and location, frequently had limiting conditions attached: to protect the repertoire and audience of the royal or municipal theaters, private commercial theaters were often forbidden from performing certain genres (e.g., the classics or opera, which were considered monopolies of the court and municipal theaters), were limited to certain performance times or admission prices, and had to abide by censorship restrictions (to be discussed below). When a more liberal commercial code was adopted by the new German Empire in 1871, theater licensing was extended to the entire nation. Subsequent amendments tightened restrictions on the granting of theater licenses, requiring authorities to examine an applicant's "moral, artistic, and financial qualifications." Licensees were obligated to observe all local laws and ordinances; police in Munich went further still, admonishing all new theater operators that they were required to respect "religion and decency." Licenses could be revoked if a theater failed to comply with the terms and restrictions of its license or if the operator no longer met the necessary financial, artistic, or moral qualifications. While the most common ground for revocation was financial, this weapon was also used against theaters whose repertoire the authorities found objectionable. Despite these restrictions, and the difficulty privately owned commercial theaters incurred during the first half of the nineteenth century in competing with court and municipal theaters, the number of such theaters rose steadily: by 1830 there were approximately twenty in Germany, and by 1842 over sixty had emerged.

After unification in 1871 and the heady economic boom that followed, new theaters sprang up everywhere, especially in Berlin and other large cities. In the 1870s, Berlin, for example, granted over 140 licenses for new theaters, although in the 1880s, due to tighter licensing requirements, only 27 new licenses were approved, while 50 were denied. On the eve of World War I, the nation's theater association listed a total of 463 stages in the German Empire. Along with 116 privately owned commercial theaters (the majority of which were founded after 1871), 132 were operated by city or town governments, serving as a source of civic pride. At the beginning of the twentieth century, Berlin, with a population of 1.9 million and the "theater capital" of the nation, hosted three royal theaters and over 25 conventional commercial theaters (not counting scores of less reputable vaudeville and variety halls). Munich (population nearly 600,000), its primary rival, claimed 2 royal and 14 commercial theaters.[13]

## Legal Controls

As theaters spread in Germany, so too did official efforts to control them. Until the creation of a central federal government in 1871, theaters fell under the idiosyncratic oversight of a multitude of independent local authorities. The Holy Roman Empire of the German Nation that collapsed in 1806 consisted of more than eighteen hundred sovereign territories, ranging from large- or medium-sized kingdoms like Austria, Prussia, Bavaria, and Saxony, to small "free cities" and tiny estates, some less than a square mile in size. Despite an upsurge of nationalistic sentiment during the War of Liberation that toppled Napoleon, the 1815 Congress of Vienna, hoping to restore the "legitimate" authority of church, monarchy, and aristocracy that had been threatened by the French Revolution, established a German Confederation of thirty-five loosely associated sovereign states and principalities and four free cities. Dominated by Austria and its arch-conservative chancellor, Klemens von Metternich, this confederation squelched any movement toward liberalism or a stronger central government, both of which would infringe on local rule by the traditional elites.

German playwrights, like other writers, had to contend with repressive censorship laws for much of the century. Although the Congress of Vienna promised freedom of the press for subjects of the German Confederation, Prussia, Austria, Saxony, Hesse, and most other German states retained or enacted strict pre-publication censorship laws. Following the 1819 Karlsbad decrees (which remained in force until 1848), the ruling authorities entirely suppressed several opposition newspapers and journals and required all publications of less than 320 pages to submit to rigorous prior censorship. When authorities feared the "Young Germany" literary movement of the 1830s was challenging the established political, social, or religious order, works by Heinrich Heine, Karl Gutzkow, Heinrich Laube, and other authors were confiscated; anyone who published, printed, or distributed their works risked prosecution; and Gutzkow and Laube were briefly imprisoned. Since none of these authors wrote drama, however (their preferred literary genres were novels and lyric poetry), the ban on Young German literature had little immediate impact on the German stage; by the time some of them turned to drama later in the decade, their work had lost its political edge and authorities no longer found it a threat. The strict controls over printed material in this period probably deterred some dramatists from writing or publishing works that dealt with politically sensitive topics, and it meant that some dramas (see *Dantons Tod*, below) could not be published without modifications. But since few German authors in this period were interested in serious drama, and those who were, like Christian Grabbe, usually chose distant, safe historical subjects, press censorship was not a significant problem for German theaters.

The Revolution of March 1848 briefly introduced freedom of the press in Germany, but after the collapse of the revolution in late 1848 and the resurgence of the traditional ruling elites, most German states passed new press laws reimposing many restrictions on the press and printed works (although not prior censorship). While one could now publish what one wished, a copy of every printed work had to be submitted to local authorities and the author, editor, publisher, printer, and distributor could all be held liable for prosecution if the work violated the criminal code.

The founding of the German Empire in 1871 created a federal system of four kingdoms, six grand duchies, seven principalities, three free cities, and one imperial province. While Germany now had its first central, national government, its powers were limited and much of life still remained under the control of authorities in the individual states. Freedom of the press and book trade was finally guaranteed by the Imperial Press Law of May 1874, which lifted most legal controls over printed materials. A publication could be confiscated and its author prosecuted after publication if it violated specific provisions of the criminal code, such as inciting others to criminal acts, inciting the social classes to violence against each other, or libeling officials, clergymen, or members of the armed forces. Playwrights and other creative writers were most affected by the criminal statutes prohibiting *lèse majesté*, blasphemy, and obscenity, and several writers were prosecuted for these offenses, especially obscenity, after 1874. No drama in the imperial period led its playwright to be prosecuted for a political offense, however.

It was not printed dramas that nineteenth-century German authorities most feared and most closely controlled, but rather dramatic performances. Live theatrical performances were viewed as posing a very different and more immediate threat to public order and security than the print media, because they were perceived as potentially stirring or inciting an audience to direct action. In his famous essay on the theater, Schiller had discussed how the stage presented living, visual representations upon the senses in ways that dead texts could not, and for this reason exercised a more profound and lasting influence on theatergoers, greater even than morality and law. This powerful effect, Schiller maintained, derived from the greater, more immediate impact of the spoken as compared to the printed word, and from the fact that spoken dialog was coupled on stage with physical action; the influence could be especially strong when actors addressed an audience directly. Dramatic art, and especially tragedy, Schiller argued, also had a cathartic element: for centuries dramatists had sought to create an illusion of reality that aroused the audience's empathetic identification with the characters on stage and stimulated and vicariously satisfied spectators' emotions. Viewing a theatrical production was intended to be an intense emotional experience, and a skillfully staged piece could thus provoke a strong emotional audience reaction.

In the pre-1848 Restoration era when publications were strictly censored, local authorities generally assumed that any work the censor allowed to be printed was also safe for live performance. But as theaters proliferated and after controversial theater performances in 1830 were widely blamed for sparking pitched verbal and physical battles in Paris and for touching off revolution in Belgium, guardians of order in Germany became increasingly conscious of the unique power the stage could exercise over its audience and fearful that theatergoers could be incited to disorderly or even violent behavior by what they witnessed. Since theaters are collective enterprises in a public space and a social setting, dramatic performances were viewed as posing potential dangers far greater than reading dramatic literature. Unlike reading, a private, solitary activity that the reader ultimately controls (if a reader is enraged or disturbed by what s/he reads, the experience can be immediately terminated), those attending the theater are not isolated individuals but members of an assembled public group participating in a collective experience over which they have little control. Above all, as members of an assembled group—as part of a crowd—theatergoers were perceived as susceptible to the powerful influences of crowd psychology. As Gustave Le Bon asserted in his enormously influential 1895 study *La psychologie des foules* (The Psychology of the Crowd), the theater was a particularly dangerous breeding ground for unpredictable, irrational crowd behavior. He was convinced that crowds think only in images, which are able to horrify, inspire, or incite a crowd to action.

> Theatrical performances, which present the image in its clearest form, always have an enormous influence on the crowd. ... Nothing arouses the fantasies of people as strongly as a theater piece. The assembled spectators simultaneously feel the same emotions ... [and] sometimes the feelings that are suggested by these images are strong enough to ... translate themselves into action. ... The unreal is in their eyes nearly as important as the real. They have a remarkable inclination not to distinguish between the two.[14]

Because the nature, function, and effect of the theatrical medium differed so radically from that of the press, by the late nineteenth century high government officials, local police, many legal scholars, and even some German dramatists generally agreed that it had to be subjected to more stringent legal controls. Close state supervision over the stage was considered necessary to not only safeguard the theater's special moral and national-political mission, but also to protect established society against theatergoers who might, after viewing particularly stirring performances, be transformed into a disorderly mob.[15]

In the royal court theaters that still dominated theatrical life in the first half of the century (and that enjoyed a monopoly over operatic productions), the monarch himself or a high-court official decided what would or would not be performed onstage. In Bavaria, for example, King Ludwig I (ruled 1825–48) carefully scrutinized the weekly repertoire of his court theater, sometimes ordering that one piece replace another, or deciding which actors would play specific roles; at other times he edited the scripts of works he found objectionable. Germany's various territorial rulers had different concerns and obsessions. Ludwig, for example, was less concerned about political issues than about moral and religious ones; he followed closely the lead of Vienna's royal theaters and would permit certain performances in Bavaria that were not welcome in the Prussian royal theaters. Prussian kings Friedrich Wilhelm III (ruled 1797–1840) and Friedrich Wilhelm IV (ruled 1840–61), on the other hand, were particularly sensitive about dramas portraying their Hohenzollern ancestors (see below); moreover, in the late 1840s the latter told his intendant to avoid all works that would elicit any kind of political demonstration. The intendants who oversaw the daily operations of the royal theaters for the monarch were invariably barons, or other members of the high nobility with impeccable pedigrees: most had military or bureaucratic, but no theatrical, experience. Carefully avoiding controversial works, they generally filled the repertoire with safe classics or lavish opera productions, favored French and Italian authors over Germans, and exercised careful censorship over all scripts. Botho von Hülsen, for example, while serving as intendant of the Royal Theater in Berlin (1869–86), spent hours at night scrutinizing scripts word by word, eliminating anything that might be remotely offensive or carry any double meaning. (It was no wonder the acerbic critic Maximilian Harden, surveying Berlin theatrical life in the 1880s, considered the Royal Theater "boring" and its "shameful repertoire" to be "simple artistic bankruptcy and the complete renunciation of any leading position in German theater life."[16]) There were exceptions to the stuffy conservatism of German court theaters, however. In small Saxe-Meiningen the "Theater Duke" Georg II (ruled 1866–1914) developed one of Europe's most innovative and influential theaters and laid important groundwork for the modern, realistic theater; in 1886 his Meiningen Players held Germany's first public performances of Ibsen's controversial *Ghosts*. Munich's royal theater performed Ibsen's *Pillars of Society* in 1878 and *A Doll's House* in 1880, while the court theater of Stuttgart premiered his *When We Dead Awaken* in 1900.

For added security, military guards were stationed at public entrances and the public seating areas of most German court theaters. As one 1840s account explains:

> These guards are responsible for the maintenance of public order, and if there is any danger of this being disturbed, their numbers are to be doubled. ... Above all, on the opening of the box office ... guards have to keep back pushy and obstreperous persons in a firm but calm and humane manner; on the other hand they have to arrest trouble-makers, quarrelers and drunks. In court theaters, guards will take instant action against any open expression on the part of spectators which contravenes the orders and directions given by the prince. ... [They] are permitted to fall out only after the house has been entirely vacated by the public.[17]

Control over the repertoire and audiences in municipal theaters was only slightly more relaxed. Since these were licensed by the city government and the director usually had to answer to the mayor, a city commission, or a board of directors and submit the entire repertoire for review and approval, they too generally steered well clear of any work that was potentially controversial or offensive. Police, rather than military guards, were also stationed in such theaters, with orders to act if there was any reason to fear public disorder and lawlessness.

It was not performances in the closely supervised royal or municipal theaters that the state worried about, but rather those in the independent private theaters. Prior censorship of dramatic performances—that is, the need to obtain the authorities' approval before a work could be performed publicly—had been instituted in Vienna in the late eighteenth century when private theaters began to appear there. As private theaters emerged in the other German states after 1815, prior censorship was introduced there as well. Thus, after an 1820 performance in Coblenz created a minor scandal, Prussian state chancellor Prince Karl von Hardenberg decided that, even if the book censors approved a work for publication, its public performance could nonetheless be forbidden or halted by police for reasons of public order or security. The chancellor empowered the Royal Police Presidium of Berlin to ensure that "in the future, no published or unpublished tragedy, drama, comedy, or operetta can be performed in any public theater (with the exception of those operated from the royal budget) without the prior approval of the royal District Administrative Presidents or those they assign to this task."[18]

Because there were relatively few private theaters even in Berlin before 1848, the new requirement for prior official approval at first had limited impact. When press censorship was abolished in the early days of the Revolution of 1848, there was some confusion as to whether this applied also to theater censorship, until the Prussian interior minister ruled in September that the 1820 censorship order lacked any legal basis and was incompatible with the new rights of freedom of expression and of the press. The need for prior approval was abolished and the state's control of public dramatic performances was limited to cases where a presentation violated some aspect of the criminal code, in which case authorities had to follow the usual legal process of prosecuting the offender (i.e., after the performance). For several months private theaters in Prussia enjoyed unrestricted freedom to perform virtually any drama they wished—and did so. But when the revolution collapsed and reactionary winds resumed, Berlin police placed new restrictions on theater performances. In February 1850 Police President Carl von Hinckeldey—who, like Schiller, regarded the theater as a "moral institution, a school ... [which] the state can use as a lever for furthering general morality and all its other objectives"—ordered police officials to regularly visit the performances of new plays and submit a written report "when the content of the work contains something especially striking [*Auffälliges*]."[19] Authorities became increasingly concerned that the public stage was being used to attack the government and that they lacked effective legal means to stop this and to punish offenders; at the same time, the presence of police observers in the theaters and their often capricious behavior created tensions with the theater directors.

In July 1851, responding to complaints from exasperated theater operators about arbitrary and unpredictable police meddling, von Hinckeldey ordered that henceforth "no public theatrical performance may take place within the greater Berlin police district without the express [advance] approval of the Police Presidium."[20] Because the Prussian Constitution guaranteed freedom of assembly and expression, the government denied this was a reintroduction of censorship; rather, it argued, the ordinance was grounded in the police's legal authority and responsibility to uphold public peace, security, and order by regulating various public activities, especially public entertainments. Though challenged repeatedly in Prussian courts as unconstitutional, judges consistently upheld the 1851 censorship ordinance. All commercial theaters in the city were now required to submit to the police fourteen days in advance the text of any new theatrical work they wished to perform; permission was granted only if police had no objections to it "from a commercial or moral standpoint or for reasons of [public] security or order." An unauthorized performance could be immediately halted by the police; the theater operator could have his license revoked and be fined or imprisoned for "insubordination." Police officers could attend any performance in order to "prevent disturbances of public peace and order during the performance, to uphold the audiences' and the actors' respect for the law, and to prevent any deviation for the conditions under which police permission was granted."[21] Compared to the relatively limited state oversight of private theaters before 1848, the controls instituted after 1851 were stringent indeed.

Berlin's handling of theater censorship soon became a model for other Prussian cities. During the next decades, the Prussian minister of interior continually urged local police throughout Prussia to adopt Berlin's theater censorship ordinance in their areas, and some cities like Breslau and Cologne did so.[22] Although police in other Prussian cities such as Frankfurt, Düsseldorf, Hanover, and Aachen never formally promulgated theater censorship ordinances, they nevertheless exercised a de facto system of prior censorship under which theaters "voluntarily" submitted their works for approval; police censors then decided what excisions or alterations had to be made in the text or whether the work had to be dropped from the repertoire altogether.[23] Following national unification under Prussian leadership, Berlin's system of prior censorship was adopted in the other large states of Saxony and Bavaria: after 1871, police in Dresden, Leipzig, and Munich issued ordinances nearly identical to Berlin's and these, in turn, were soon imitated by authorities in many smaller Saxon and Bavarian municipalities. Police in Munich seemed especially worried about extemporaneous improvisations on stage and included an additional clause stating, "It is the obligation of theater managers to ensure that their actors do not improvise during performances; [this is to be done] by inserting in the contract of every permanent member of the ensemble and of every guest performer special disciplinary clauses that forbid improvisation. To guarantee that these conditions are being observed, such contracts must be made available to the Police Direction on demand."[24] Several medium-sized states in the German Empire (e.g., Württemberg, Baden, and Hesse), free cities like Hamburg and Bremen, and most of the remaining tiny states did not subject privately owned theaters to prior censorship, though in some places theaters had to notify police in advance of works they intended to perform, and authorities anywhere could halt any performance that violated the criminal code or that threatened the public peace.

Royal theaters were exempt from this police censorship, as were municipal theaters operated by a local government: their self-censorship sufficed. In Münster, for example, the director of the municipally owned theater had to receive permission from the city council for every work to be performed, while in Mannheim, the city-controlled National Theater established a standing subcommittee of board members to "ensure that no uncensored works are performed, and no offense against religion, good morals, and also no politically inflammatory material takes place."[25] So-called "private" theaters, on the other hand, which were also exempt, posed constant headaches for the authorities. The licensing requirements of the commercial code and the various local ordinances requiring prior censorship of dramatic works applied only to commercial theaters operated for a profit (i.e., those charging admission) and to "public" performances. Clubs or associations whose members staged informal performances for their own enjoyment only or for educational purposes were not required to obtain an operating license, provided they did not charge admission to their performances and used only amateur performers who received no pay for their work. Likewise, any "private" theatrical performance that was closed to the general public did not require prior censorship approval. Thus, church and educational organizations, amateur theatrical clubs, literary societies, and various other "closed" (i.e., private) associations could freely stage theatrical productions for their own members or for a small circle of invited guests so long as the general public was excluded.

Where theater censorship existed in the latter half of the century, if police refused to permit a drama or authorized its performance with certain conditions (e.g., that portions of the script be excised or altered), the decision could usually be appealed, either to a higher level within the administration or sometimes through the state courts. While the police decisions were usually upheld (especially in Bavaria), the courts in Prussia, Saxony, and Baden at times overturned police censorship bans. Around the turn of the century, after a series of embarrassing incidents in which police banned highly respected works only to have their action reversed by the courts, Prussian authorities began to consult literary experts about the artistic merit of certain works before reaching their decisions. The Bavarian city of Munich went further, creating in 1908 a Censorship Advisory Board of distinguished civilian literary experts (including, briefly, noted author Thomas Mann) who, "by the high level of their general education and/or their recognized expertise, can be relied on to give an objective, authoritative opinion" whenever the authorities had reservations about approving dramas.[26] The board was regularly consulted over the next decade about "borderline" cases that raised strong moral concerns, but not about politically sensitive dramas.

## Censorship Controversies

State censorship of the theaters and of literature in general naturally incensed many German writers as well as broad sectors of the liberal public. Heinrich Heine, whose works were frequently heavily censored or outlawed in the repressive Restoration era, published a famous satire that read simply:

Chapter XII

The German censors----------------------------------------------------------
-----------------------------------idiots-----------------------------------
----------------------------------------------------------------------.

His contemporary Karl Gutzkow remarked:

Censorship might still be bearable if from the outset it did not, as a branch of administrative bureaucracy, bear the stamp of literary incompetence. An official who has perhaps studied all the commentaries on the laws of the land but who has never studied a work of a different scholarly discipline, not to mention art, an official whose ideas are all directed towards small spaces in the administrative buildings, who has only one God, namely his superior, and only one heaven, namely promotion—such a man should pass judgment on your writing?[27]

In one of his satirical plays the Austrian playwright Johann Nestroy characterized a censor as "a human pencil or a pencilized human, a living blue line scratched across the products of human genius, a crocodile lying in wait along the bank of the river of ideas and biting off the heads of the writers swimming there."[28] Gutzkow, Heine, and other Young German writers of the Restoration era blamed censorship for thwarting the creation of a German national theater because a whole range of subjects, such as the clergy, religious saints, the upper aristocracy, and marriages between aristocrats and commoners, could be discussed in prose but not portrayed on stage.[29]

In the latter half of the century, after theater censorship had become systematized and bureaucratized throughout much of the German Empire, critics frequently complained about the narrow, legalistic perspective police officials applied when reviewing the dramas submitted to them. One fin de siècle author protested that works were being judged simply from the "mentality of the bureaucrats ... who in most cases evaluate the intellectual creations entrusted to them the same way that a blind man evaluates colors"; another German parliamentarian, himself a judge, declared that juristically trained civil servants knew as much about art and literature as an elephant about playing the flute.[30] The playwright Frank Wedekind, whose sexually explicit works were frequently forbidden by the Munich Censorship Advisory Board in the years before World War I, compared their deliberations to the Inquisition, and denounced Germany's "fanatical muzzling of dramatic literature";[31] his colleague Thomas Mann condemned all preventive theater censorship as a "despicable tutelage of the public in matters of taste." For Mann, "censorship is a force that inhibits culture, for it substitutes suppression, a crude ban, for the education that the public really needs. Only art itself, in combination with free and serious criticism, is qualified to educate the public, not the state." (Four years later, however, Mann joined the Munich Censorship Advisory Board in the naïve hope that he could mediate between art and the state; after failing to sway the police and being roundly criticized by Wedekind and other writers, he resigned in frustration after a year.)[32]

After 1890, as conservatives campaigned (unsuccessfully) to tighten theater censorship and increase the punishment for writing or performing "immoral" works, the political left agitated (equally unsuccessfully) to loosen and even abolish altogether police licensing and censorship of theaters. In 1900 a coalition of liberals, progressives, and social democrats in parliament joined with writers, artists, publishers, journalists, academics, theater owners, and others in the intellectual and artistic community to form a network of local "Goethe Leagues for the Protection of Free Art and Learning" in order "to protect freedom of art and learning in the German Empire against attacks of every kind." A national conference of these groups approved a resolution condemning the censorship of theatrical performances by local authorities as antiquated and "an unworthy tutelage [for] the German nation" and demanded its abolition throughout Germany.[33] The Progressive Party introduced a bill in the Reichstag to abolish all local theater censorship. To the paragraphs of the commercial code that required the licensing of all theater and music hall operators, the Progressives proposed adding a clause declaring that "no prior approval is necessary" for staging an individual dramatic work in a legitimate theater.[34] Prior theater censorship, the bill argued, was an unnecessary form of police oversight, as the existing criminal code was adequate to deal with any theater excesses; if a performance violated the law, police retained the authority to halt it and prosecute those responsible. Dramatic art, the Progressives maintained, should enjoy the same freedom enjoyed by writers who published their work and who were subject only to the criminal code controls: "We want every author, every theater director, every actor to assume his own direct responsibility before the common criminal code; we want the actor and the theater director to bear responsibility for his work, just as authors [now] do for the contents of their books. And if the state authorities take energetic measures under the provisions of the existing criminal statutes, then surely we have no more need for any [prior] censorship."[35]

The bill was defeated, and prior stage censorship continued until the German Empire was overthrown and all forms of censorship were abolished on 12 November 1918.

## Political Censorship

German state authorities used their oversight of court, municipal, and commercial theaters to jealously guard their political power against the forces of liberalism, democracy, socialism, and revolution. Recognizing the importance of theater to national life and the great influence it might exert over audiences—and thus over public opinion—they did not hesitate to intervene against or censor the stage when it introduced politically sensitive topics. This political censorship was most apparent when theaters touched on the topics of political and social insurrection, the image and reputation of the monarchy and the military, or the integrity of the nation state at home and its alliances abroad.

## Insurrection and Socialism

Anxious defenders of the German social and political order were enormously apprehensive about dramatic performances that might favorably depict, glorify, or condone violent revolution or social rebellion, so they were especially wary of all dramas set during real or imagined instances of violent social insurrection, however distant in time and whatever the author's political orientation or social philosophy. In the reactionary period following the 1819 Karlsbad degrees, for example, royal theaters sometimes found certain German *Sturm und Drang* classics too politically threatening. Schiller's immensely popular *Die Räuber* (The Robbers), which bore the motto "*in tyrannos*" (against the tyrants) and dealt with youthful rebellion against the corruption, despotism, and injustices of the social elites, quickly disappeared from nearly all royal stages after 1819, as did his *Wilhelm Tell*, which depicted the assassination of an emperor and a mass democratic uprising of the Swiss against tyrannical Austrian rule. (The intendant of the Prussian royal theaters claimed the latter had not been censored, but rather that staging any new performances would simply be too costly.) Goethe's *Egmont*, about the sixteenth-century Dutch struggle for religious tolerance, free speech, and national independence against the tyrannical Spanish, met the same fate. Furthermore, because a newspaper review of one of its last performances in October 1819 spotlighted the play's political dimensions, the Berlin police president decreed that if theater critics continued to mix "unsuitable political allusions" with their reviews, the political press would be forbidden from carrying any theater reviews.[36] *Wilhelm Tell* and *Egmont* remained banished from the Prussian royal theaters until the 1840s. Rossini's 1829 opera about Tell, based on Schiller's play, was permitted in the Berlin and Darmstadt court theaters, but only with a completely modified text "because of its revolutionary spirit."[37] Royal aversion to *Die Räuber* lasted much longer; when the Berlin royal theater intendant allowed an 1829 production, Friedrich Wilhelm III was furious and banned further performances. It was not allowed again on the royal stage until after the 1848 revolution (July 1849), then was banished again the next month when the last revolutionary vestiges collapsed. Schiller's classic did not return to the Berlin royal stage until 1855.

Like Rossini's *William Tell*, other operas of this era dealing with themes of insurrection and national liberation met staunch resistance. In the 1820s Beethoven reportedly was planning an opera set in ancient Greece that would draw parallels to the contemporary Greek struggle for independence from the Ottoman Empire, but had to abandon the project because censors found the parallel too obvious. Albert Lortzing's 1832 opera *Andreas Hofer*, dealing with the Tyrolean patriot's uprising against Napoleon, was banned for many years because Austria, which controlled the area after 1814, objected to the allusion to Tyrolean nationalism. Wagner's opera *Rienzi* (1840), about a medieval Italian revolutionary whose call for Italian unification might spark contemporary nationalists to call for German unification, was altered by the Saxon censors. Rienzi's cry "Not only Rome shall be free! All Italy shall be free. Hail to united Italy!" was changed to "Not only Rome is great! All Italy shall be great. Hail to the ancient greatness of Italy!" After Wagner had to flee Saxony as a "traitor" for his participation in the 1848–49 revolutionary outbreaks, his opera was banned for the next decade.[38]

Memories of the 1848 revolution were still fresh when in March 1852 the Munich royal theater premiered Friedrich Hebbel's drama *Agnes Bernauer*, based on an incident from fifteenth-century Bavarian history in which Albrecht, son of Duke Ernst, instigated a rebellion against the sovereign and the nobility after the reigning duke, to protect his dynasty, murders Albrecht's commoner wife Agnes and strips Albrecht of his right to the throne. In the third act, when Albrecht calls upon the peasants and urban burghers to support him against the duke and the nobility, wild applause broke out from the upper balconies (where the middle classes sat) and loud hissing from the box seats (where the nobility sat). The tumult was so unsettling to Maximilian II (ruled 1848–64) that he ordered the play removed from the repertoire after only one performance.[39]

For much of the century, plays set during the French Revolution were viewed as a potential threat because they would likely contain inflammatory revolutionary rhetoric and action that might inspire an audience, especially one containing workers, to rebellion or social insurrection. Christian Grabbe's epic *Napoleon, oder Die hundert Tage* (Napoleon, or the Hundred Days), which surveyed the French Revolution and Restoration, was a veiled commentary on the reactionary regimes and petty tyrants that followed Napoleon; while published in 1831, it was not performed until 1895. An overtly political drama like *Dantons Tod* (Danton's Death), by the radical revolutionary exile Georg Büchner, could be published in 1835 only because Büchner's friend Karl Gutzkow removed any provocative language before the press censor saw it. As Gutzkkow later explained,

> To deny the censor the pleasure of expunging things himself, I took up that role myself and pruned the prolific democracy of the writing with the shears of pre-censorship. ... Long, suggestive dialogues from the scenes of the masses that bubbled with wit and imagination had to be discarded. The pointed wordplay had to be blunted or bent crooked with supplemental dumb expressions added here and there. The real Danton Büchner created doesn't come through; what emerged instead is a scant remainder, the ruins of a devastation.[40]

The uncensored version was only published in 1879 and not performed publicly until 1913.

In late 1879, when painful memories of the 1871 Paris Commune were still prevalent and shortly after the enactment of the reactionary 1878 Anti-Socialist Law, Berlin police banned Paolo Giacometti's *Maria Antonietta,* a historical drama set during the Revolution. Members of the city's lower classes, it was feared, might be "incited" by some of the stirring revolutionary scenes and speeches and might regard the revolutionary events on stage as something to be imitated in real life—despite the fact the work was to be performed in Italian! Similarly, in 1898 Berlin police refused to allow a public performance of Arthur Schnitzler's *Der grüne Kakadu* (The Green Cockatoo), an examination of the moral degeneracy of French society set on the eve of the storming of the Bastille, until several lines of revolutionary rhetoric were omitted. In Munich, Schnitzler's drama was banned altogether,[41] as was another work set during the French reign of terror, Ferdinand Bonn's *Eine deutsche Kaisertöchter* (A German Emperor's Daughter).[42]

Concerns about historical dramas with revolutionary settings were deeply rooted in German authorities' profound anxiety about the "social question" and the threat it posed to established society. The social question, which arose in the 1840s with the beginnings of industrialization in Germany, referred to the plight of the working classes, their miserable working and living conditions, their growing alienation from the traditional rural order and from the emerging urban, bourgeois world, the polarization of modern society into two antagonistic classes, and the possibility of a revolutionary overthrow of the social order by embittered workers. The rise of organized labor and socialist trade unions in the 1860s produced a strong, united, Social Democratic political party in the 1870s that embraced Marxism and demanded the political and economic emancipation of the working class. Bismarck regarded Social Democracy as "an enemy against whom the state and society are bound to defend themselves"[43] and after 1871 waged an energetic political and legal war against it. The notorious 1878 "Anti-Socialist Law" allowed the government to conduct a ruthless campaign against Social Democratic activity of every kind. Although the law expired in 1890, the anti-Socialist crusade continued: Bismarck's successor, Chancellor Caprivi, declared in 1891 that "the struggle against Social Democracy is the most serious question of our time. ... I consider it currently the greatest danger to the Reich, and so I believe the means of fighting against it must be fully utilized with each new opportunity."[44]

Amateur workers' dramatic societies and dramatic works by and about German workers played an important role in the organized German labor movement, both as recreation and as a means of disseminating reform ideas. In the 1890s these workers' theaters were supplemented by a number of Freie Volksbühne Vereine (Free People's Stage Associations) that provided working-class subscribers with inexpensive tickets to special, members-only (private) performances commissioned from professional theaters. Under the Anti-Socialist Law, German police outlawed numerous workers' dramatic societies as "cover[s] for socialist agitation."[45] They also confiscated and banned dramatic literature written by Social Democrats like August Otto-Walster and dramas alleged to have a "socialist content"; the plays of radical writers like John Makay and Karl Henckell, published anonymously in Switzerland, were also seized and proscribed.

After 1890, police in Saxony used local laws regarding associations and assemblies to prevent Social Democratic gatherings from performing notoriously tendentious socialist dramas like *Friede auf Erden! Oder Der Ausweisung am Weihnachtsabend* (Peace on Earth! Or the Expulsion on Christmas Eve) because "the sole intent and likely result [of this work] is to use ... the dramatic arts to serve hateful political passions; to degrade religious behavior in a most gripping manner; to cast aspersions on royal personages; to arouse class hatred, envy, dissatisfaction, and enmity within members of the audience; and to thereby encourage them to immoral and illegal behavior."[46] Similarly, Berlin police forbade Social Democratic associations from performing various dramatic sketches and pro-socialist dramas because they were "animated by a revolutionary spirit," "blatantly express hatred against the existing state," "openly preach revolution from beginning to end," and because their revolutionary slogans and action would exert a strong influence on a working-class audience.[47]

Authorities waged a two-decade long campaign against the Berlin Freie Volksbühne, a popular theatrical association organized for the socialist working class. Because it held private performances open to members only, it neither had to obtain a commercial operating license nor was it subject to the 1851 censorship ordinance that required prior police approval of any public performance. Spurred on by Wilhelm II (who, upon learning of the founding of the Freie Volksbühne, declared "this business must by all means be stopped"[48]), police in 1892 used the laws regulating associations to require the organization to submit its membership list and information about its activities to the police and to allow police observers at all meetings and performances. The court upheld this police action because it recognized that theatrical texts and performances could be a highly effective vehicle for promoting Social Democratic ideas:

> Because such works directly evoke fantasy and passion, the reading, discussion, or mere theatrical performance of literary works that poetically portray workers' unjust treatment, exploitation, or oppression at the hands of the bourgeoisie or civil service must, without a doubt, be considered far more capable of disseminating and strengthening the Social-Democratic outlook among the working population—and, consequently, of gaining adherents for the [Social Democratic] party—than theoretical or sober factual treatments of the ... political and social position of the fourth estate ever could.

Whatever the original or stated artistic aims of the Freie Volksbühne, the court declared, in practice it "performs, reads, or discusses exclusively (or nearly exclusively) those literary works that are especially well suited for spreading the ideas of the Social Democratic Party." Each work chosen for its repertoire was

> calculated to expose the "hollowness and untenability" of the social relations and state institutions it portrays, to arouse the passions of the workers who see them, to increase as much as possible the workers' dissatisfaction with existing conditions, and to most effectively awaken and fortify in the workers a desire to change [these conditions] and to join with the goals of the Social Democratic Party. ... [The Freie Volksbühne] consciously and actively utilizes dramatic art to arouse the emotions, prejudices, and passions of wide segments of the population in the interests of party agitation and for the purpose of bringing about a change in the existing social order.[49]

After the Freie Volksbühne held a well-publicized private premier of *Die Weber* in 1893 (see below) and after membership grew to nearly ten thousand (because it was a source of inexpensive theater tickets), authorities were convinced the general public was easily obtaining access to the group's "private" performances; since it was allegedly becoming a commercial theater in disguise, police decided it should be subject to the same censorship ordinance as public, commercial theaters. (The Berlin police president confided his real motive for this action was to "prevent or partially prevent the social democratic plague from spreading its propaganda to the broad masses through the performance of socialist theatrical works."[50]) To avoid having to submit its performances to police censorship the Freie Volksbühne reorganized in 1897, tightening membership requirements enough to again qualify as a private theater society. By 1910, however, its membership had grown so large and its activities had come so closely to resemble a public commercial theater that police again demanded its performances be subject to prior censorship. After losing a court appeal, the Freie Volksbühne had to submit to the 1851 censorship ordinance. Other German cities took stronger action against their local Freie Volksbühnes: in Kiel and Hanover they were dissolved by police order, while in Munich police harassment forced cancellation or change of several scheduled performances, and in 1899 finally forced the organization to disband.

Besides intervening to prevent working class audiences in socialist organizations from seeing or performing socialist dramas, German authorities frequently also tried to keep plays about socialism, labor strife, or worker discontent away from the more general, middle-class audiences of the commercial theaters. For example, Ludwig Fulda's social drama *Verlorene Paradies* (Lost Paradise), which examined a bitter wage dispute between striking factory workers and a ruthless employer who wanted to forcibly suppress them, although approved for public performance in Berlin in November 1890, was banned in several smaller Prussian cities as threatening the social order and inciting illegal behavior. These provincial bans remained in force throughout the 1890s, but following the easing of class tensions after 1900 they were overturned by the courts in 1903.[51]

State authorities were especially worried about dramas dealing with actual recent nearby social insurrections, such as the 1844 Silesian workers revolt. Gerhart Hauptmann's 1892 work *Die Weber* (The Weavers), now regarded as a classic of the German naturalist literary movement, depicted the weavers' spontaneous, bloody uprising and the underlying social and economic misery that caused it. Because officials in the Silesian capital of Breslau and in Berlin regarded the drama as inflammatory socialist propaganda that threatened public order by provoking class hatred, inciting demonstrations, and strengthening the lower class's tendency toward violent rebellion, police in both cities banned public performances. They felt vindicated when the Freie Bühne, where performances were not subject to prior police approval, held a private premiere in February 1893 that caused the left-wing press to praise the play's "revolutionary spirit," "powerful inflammatory effect," and great contemporary relevance. Although the ban of *Die Weber* was appealed, a lower court upheld it because the work "clearly suggests violent rebellion is a solution to life's distress, … there is a legitimate concern that if [it] were performed in a public theater, it would arouse the passions of the dissatisfied elements in the audience in a way that would endanger public order."[52] However, in October 1893 a Prussian appeals court freed the play for public performance in Berlin and Breslau—provided ticket prices were kept high enough to guarantee that audiences would be drawn mostly from upper-class groups. Police in Hanover, Hamburg, Leipzig, and other German cities forbade public performances for a few years more, until the last police ban was overturned by court order in 1901.

In 1894 Franz Held's *Ein Fest auf der Bastille* (A Festival at the Bastille), depicting a young hero caught up in the storming of the Bastille and the following revolutionary events, was performed in Berlin commercial theaters until a Social Democratic reading club asked to hold a special performance for its members. The police president refused and also banned further public theater performances on the grounds that it was written by a long-time social-revolutionary agitator, distorted history, amounted to a provocative apology for and inflammatory glorification of violent insurrection, and would "suggest to dissatisfied and revolutionary dispositions the possibility of a repetition [of the revolutionary events it depicts]."[53] A court overturned the ban, arguing that the work's many public performances demonstrated it was unlikely any future audience would draw parallels between the French Revolution and present conditions, or that the drama would "agitate the audience against our state and its institutions, or will occasion similar [revolutionary] behavior here in the present." The court did, however, support the police's decision to prohibit the special performance before a socialist audience.[54]

In 1897 and again in 1901 Berlin censors banned the public performance of *Ausgewiesen* (Expelled), a drama by the Social Democrat Carl Böttcher about how the repressive Anti-Socialist Law frequently ruined the careers, families, and lives of many innocent people. Police objected to the "socialist content" of the drama and its portrayal of the authorities as coldhearted, ruthless tormenters of the workers; because memories of the law were still fresh and the passions it had aroused still intense, they feared the play might provoke violent outbursts from the "uncritical and highly excitable working-class audiences" that attended the two theaters where it was to be performed. A public performance at a third theater was permitted in 1907 because that playhouse was frequented by a more educated and respectable clientele.⁵⁵ In liberal Hamburg, which had no formal system of theater censorship, the political police "urgently advised" that Böttcher's drama *Streik!* be kept off the public stage there in late 1896. The piece had been publicly performed in Berlin, but in the midst of Hamburg's bitter 1896–97 dock strike a theater director there decided it would be wise to voluntarily submit it for police approval first. Although Böttcher claimed his piece was a "conciliatory work" more "inclined to unite than to divide agitated parties," the Hamburg police feared a public performance would "make crass propaganda for the striking masses and exaggerate the misery they are suffering." The theater waited until the strike collapsed in February 1897 to perform it (advertising it as having "the permission of the highest authorities"), but quickly dropped it from the repertoire when it proved a box office flop.⁵⁶

At the turn of the century Berlin police banned a public performance of Bjørnstjerne Bjørnson's *Über unsere Kraft II* (Beyond our Power II), which portrayed a desperate confrontation between oppressed factory workers and their brutal employer, ending with an anarchists' attempt to kill the industrialist and spark a workers' revolution by dynamiting a workers' meeting.⁵⁷ Likewise, Franz Adamas' *Familie Wawroch*, which strongly resembled Zola's *Germinal* (banned in France) and Hauptmann's *Die Weber*, focusing on a bloody confrontation between oppressed miners and their heartless employer, was banned in Berlin in 1900 because police feared the play's socialistic speeches and revolutionary slogans might provoke a lower-class audience to disruptive disturbances. After an expurgated version was publicly premiered in Vienna, the Berlin theater in question asked permission to perform that same revised version, but police refused again, citing reports that tumult and demonstrations had followed the Vienna performance.⁵⁸ A third, still further expurgated version of *Familie Wawroch*, stripped of its most militant political utterances, was finally approved by the Berlin police in October 1900, but after it opened at last in September 1901 the police threatened to revoke their decision if any repetition occurred of audience outbursts that were provoked by a scene in which the miners riot. The scene was promptly dropped and other revisions made for all future performances (all mention of Social Democracy, May Day demonstrations, and anti-state and anti-employer striker shouts were removed), resulting in a work so eviscerated and tame that the theater lost all interest in it and, after a few more performances, dropped it from the repertoire.[59]

In the years immediately following the Russian Revolution of 1905, Leopold Kampf's sympathetic account *Am Vorabend* (On the Eve) was suppressed in several German cities (including Essen, Frankfurt, Dresden, Düsseldorf, and Berlin-Charlottenberg). Police banned public and/or private performances—and in some cases even public readings—of the work because in their eyes it glorified revolutionaries and assassins. In Hamburg, where theater censorship did not legally exist, no reason was given when the scheduled public performances were suddenly canceled; the liberal press quickly suspected the police were behind it, however, and condemned the fact that art in Hamburg was being measured by "Prussian police batons."[60]

German officials remained worried about the Freie Volksbühne and its pro-socialist repertoire right up until World War I. Shortly after having obtained censorship authority over the theatrical society in 1910, police prohibited it from performing Emil Rosenow's *Die in Schatten Leben* (Those Who Live in the Shadows). Rosenow, a Social Democratic journalist and Reichstag delegate and the most successful of all socialist dramatists, modeled his drama on Zola's *Germinal;* it depicted the ruthless exploitation of an impoverished family of miners by a corrupt and powerful family of mine owners who were supported by the church. The Berlin censor, noting Rosenow's Social Democratic activism, found the work "provocative" and "tendentiously one-sided" because it deliberately and grossly misrepresented the actual legal rights and status of miners while stereotyping mine owners and managers as ruthless, exploitative tyrants. The courts upheld the ban because the play was held likely to agitate, inflame, and provoke the overwhelmingly working-class audiences of the Freie Volksbühne, "filling them with a deep embitterment and hatred [not only] against the entrepreneurial class, [but also against the church], state, and society that allows such [exploitive] conditions to exist."[61] Although police in Hanover also banned this work, between 1912 and 1914 it was publicly performed in Stuttgart, Frankfurt, and Mannheim, without (as one liberal paper dryly noted) revolution breaking out in any of those cities.[62]

## The Monarch

While nineteenth-century German authorities guarded against images of social disorder and political revolt on the public stage, they were equally cautious about theatrical depictions of the very symbol of political authority and social order—the monarch. Although its legal basis was dubious, in Germany as in other monarchies, reigning crowned heads, by long-standing tradition, could not be depicted on stage without their express consent. As the Berlin theater censor once explained, in order to protect "the unique position a reigning sovereign occupies in the life of a state, it cannot be permitted for just anyone to bring the personality of the monarch onto the stage. ... It is totally impermissible that the actions of a reigning ruler who appears in a dramatic presentation should be subjected to the critical evaluation either of a playwright or of an audience, much less to an audience's applause or hisses [*Bei- oder Mißfall*]."[63] Actors or entertainers were not permitted publicly to portray the monarch either in serious dramas or in light-hearted vaudeville skits.

While reigning sovereigns were never depicted in the theater, earlier members of a royal family sometimes were. Heinrich Kleist's 1810 drama *Prinz Friedrich von Homburg*, for example, dealt with the historic battle of Fehrbellin (1675) at which the title character led Prussian forces to victory but, having disobeyed orders, was sentenced to death by the king. Because in one scene Prince Friedrich is portrayed as a coward who is terrified about his impending execution, the director of the Berlin royal theater refused to have the drama performed there, justifying his decision on three grounds: first, "In a military state like Prussia, it is really utterly impossible to put an officer on stage who has so little *point d'honeur* in his body that he begs for his own meager life; that would ridicule our entire [military] caste, and that will not do"; second, the work allegedly was historically inaccurate since the real Prince Friedrich was brave and did not beg for his life; and third, no ancestor of the ruling dynasty should be portrayed on stage, least of all when the playwright depicted him so disparagingly. After some changes in the script (the prince now recoiled not from the thought of his execution, but rather at the dishonorable method that would be used), it was eventually performed in July 1828, but only three times and while Friedrich Wilhelm III was absent from the city; it was not performed in the royal theaters of Prussia again until the reign of Wilhelm I (king of Prussia 1861–88; German emperor 1871–88).[64] Since other German royal houses in the 1820s cared little about Hohenzollern pride, the royal theaters in Saxony, Bavaria, Hanover, Württemberg, and the municipal theater of Hamburg performed the work freely.

Friedrich Wilhelm III's successor established a strict policy regarding the depiction of any Hohenzollern forebears on stage that remained in force for the remainder of the century. In 1843 Karl Gutzkow (the Young German author briefly imprisoned in 1835) asked Friedrich Wilhelm IV to allow the Berlin royal stage to perform his new historical comedy *Zopf und Schwert* (Pigtail and Sword), which dealt with the cruel, narrow-minded martinet Friedrich Wilhelm I (ruled 1713–40). The royal cabinet, however, was opposed, not only because it "misrepresented" recent historical events, but also because it treated the former king as petty, base, lacking in royal dignity, and farcical; such a work would make the entire royal court "a laughing-stock." The king's cabinet forbade the intendant from presenting it, even though it was being performed in other Prussian and German theaters, including the Dresden court theater. To end this, at least in Prussia, in April 1844 Friedrich Wilhelm IV decreed that henceforth "dramas in which deceased members of my royal house appear on stage may be performed only if my express approval is granted."[65] (Gutzkow's drama immediately disappeared from Prussian theaters for two decades and was not performed on the Berlin royal stage again until 1893, although it was often permitted in non-Prussian court theaters.) In the 1880s this cabinet order regarding Hohenzollern ancestors was amended. No permission would be granted unless at least one hundred years had passed since the figure's death; once a piece had been performed in a royal theater or had been approved for a public theater, it could also be performed elsewhere without additional permission; and (after 1900) dramas submitted for royal approval were to be accompanied by a summary of the contents and the written opinions of two or three literary experts testifying to their literary value.[66] The purpose of such careful screening was quite simple: as the Berlin police president once explained, it was important nothing be permitted that might undermine loyalty to the ruling dynasty by arousing false impressions about the personalities, deeds, and character of its members, especially among society's lower and semi-educated strata.[67]

These restrictions on the portrayal of royal ancestors encompassed a great many figures and events crucial to European history. Since historical drama was a popular nineteenth-century genre with both playwrights and audiences, the desire of Friedrich Wilhelm IV and his successors to control their family's theatrical image inhibited an important aspect of the German theater. Between 1878 and 1918, for example, the royal Civil Cabinet (which had to approve any work performed in Prussia containing royal ancestors) rejected about 80 percent of the more than fifty works submitted for approval; less than 10 percent were approved outright, while another 10 percent were approved only after revisions were made. Emperor Wilhelm II often took a detailed interest in the works submitted for his approval, frequently wanting to know, for example, which actor was going to play the role of the Hohenzollern in question.[68] Although some of the works submitted were rejected as frivolous and undignified farces with which the dynasty wanted no association, most were light comedies, operettas, serious dramas, or historical tragedies by noted authors that were not critical or disparaging of the Hohenzollerns. Indeed, a good many were highly patriotic and historically accurate and contained idealized, even fawning portrayals of some of the dynasty's most popular and beloved figures, such as Friedrich the Great or Queen Luise, beloved consort of Friedrich Wilhelm III.

Dramas about Friedrich the Great presented the dynasty with a particularly difficult problem. On the one hand, he was the most famous, historically significant, and most widely loved Hohenzollern king and thus a favorite of playwrights, audiences, and theater managers. On the other hand, those aspects of his life that were often the most compelling and dramatically rich, such as his painful, humiliating treatment by his brutal father Friedrich Wilhelm I, reflected badly on the royal house. In the 1870s, for example, Heinrich Laube's *Prinz Friedrich* was banned because characterizing Friedrich Wilhelm I as an inhuman, tyrannical father might also imply he was an inhuman, tyrannical monarch.[69] Since Wilhelm II disapproved of how several dramas treated this bitter father-son conflict, after 1901 the emperor began approving such works only if literary experts would attest to their high artistic value. Then, peeved by Ferdinand Bonn's *Der junge Fritz* (Young Fritz) and *Friedrich der Große* (Friedrich the Great), in December 1909 Wilhelm II issued a cabinet order stating he no longer wanted this tragic episode from the history of his ancestors portrayed on the stage in any form, and that any dramas containing such material would be automatically rejected.[70]

In the end, the Hohenzollerns' hyper-sensitivity to their historic image and the heavy-handed controls they used to keep so many of their forebears off the public stages of Germany was sadly shortsighted. By prohibiting the performance of numerous highly patriotic plays dealing with some of the dynasty's most popular ancestors, the monarchy lost numerous opportunities to establish closer emotional ties with the populace and heighten nationalist feeling. Only the collapse of the monarchy in 1918 ended the stifling censorship of Hohenzollern characters on stage, resulting in the final irony that it was much easier to stage a drama about the Hohenzollerns in the Weimar Republic, after the dynasty was deposed, than in the imperial era, when it reigned.

Like the Hohenzollerns, other German royal dynasties also used theater censorship to protect their public image. In 1907, for example, the Bavarian government persuaded several other German states, including liberal

Hamburg, to ban the drama *Ludwig II von Bayern* because it "display[ed] a great lack of piety for the unfortunate King," would perpetuate the "idiotic myth" that Ludwig II (ruled 1864–86) was poisoned by one of his advisors, and "harm[ed] the good name of [the reigning] Prince Regent [Luitpold]."[71]

## The Military

Next to the monarchy, the military was the central institution in Prussia, and after 1871 in the German empire. A "state within the state" immune from civilian control, its function was as much to defend the monarchy and ruling elite against internal revolution as to defend the nation from external threats. As a reliable praetorian guard of the monarchy and a formidable opponent of any political change, the military was defended tenaciously by German rulers. So sacrosanct was the Prussian army that throughout the century, no Prussian military uniforms or standards were allowed to appear on stage. In the latter part of the century, especially after the Franco-Prussian war (1870–71), civilian esteem for the military was extraordinarily high, a development nowhere more apparent than in the theater: between 1870 and 1914 dramas about the military and military life flooded the German stage and proved enormously popular (one study has counted well over eight hundred theatrical works written and/ or performed in the imperial era simply about the *contemporary* German military).[72] This profusion of plays did much to increase the army's popularity and make it "an object of patriotic adoration."[73] Although Germany's press freedom allowed satirical journals like *Simplicissimus* to mount increasingly harsh attacks on a growing number of military scandals and abuses, especially the army's treatment of civilians, German theater audiences were carefully insulated from all negative portrayals of the military.

By stressing the more harmless, even comic aspects of military life and avoiding its sinister features, pro-military dramas propagated and reinforced a popular image that military service was an elevating and uplifting experience for young recruits. Maintaining public confidence in the ennobling quality of military service and in the officer corps that trained new soldiers was especially important because of universal compulsory military service: since every German male had to serve at least a year in the military, every family was likely to worry about what kind of men would be commanding their sons and what impact military service would have upon them. For this reason, German authorities were quick to react to plays that depicted officers and military service brutalizing and morally corrupting young recruits. Before 1900, mistreatment and harassment of conscripts by ruthless, sadistic officers and a harsh system of military justice that left victims with little legal redress and stripped defendants of most of the rights civilians enjoyed was a serious problem in Germany. Elsa von Schabelski's 1893 drama *Notwehr* (Self-Defense) dealt with a young recruit who is so mercilessly persecuted by a brutal officer that in a moment of desperation he is forced to kill the officer. The Berlin police forbade any public performances of this play because in their view it misrepresented actual conditions in the military and might encourage uninformed members of the public to believe that common soldiers were entirely defenseless against their superiors' cruelest whims. The courts upheld the ban on the grounds that such a sensationalistic distortion of reality was "likely to cause among common soldiers dissatisfaction with their condition and insubordination toward their superiors" and could "undermine [soldiers'] confidence in the wisdom of military institutions and respect for their superiors, thereby attacking the moral foundations essential for discipline and order in the army." The court concluded:

> There can be no doubt that the public performance of such a work would passionately arouse the majority of viewers, and that this would be expressed not only as sympathy for the victim and loathing for his tormentor, but also would direct itself against the state itself [for allowing or encouraging such abuses to take place]. ... The passionate bitterness that would be aroused against the state and its institutions and the resulting antipathy toward military service, based on universal conscription, presents a danger to the common good against which the police must justifiably intervene.[74]

Twenty years later Leo Jungman's *Die letzten sechs Wochen* (The Last Six Weeks) depicted how a young soldier, six weeks before his discharge, is pitilessly persecuted by his commanding officer, who holds a personal grudge against him; provoked into striking the officer, the soldier is, through false testimony, court-martialed and sentenced to three years imprisonment. Although this play was already being performed in Bremen (where the garrison commander ordered his soldiers not to attend), Saarbrücken, and a few other small cities, the Berlin police president banned it in March 1910 and wrote to these other cities strongly urging they do the same. Convinced that many of the events depicted in the drama simply could not occur under Germany's (recently revised) military penal code, he considered Jungman's play "an unjustified and embittered attack against state order. ... The piece *unjustly* attacks military law and judicial procedures, *unjustly* accuses these of harshness, and thereby *unjustly* arouses rage and bitterness toward the essential institution of the military and against military service itself." After an unsuccessful appeal to overturn the ban, the author repeatedly tried to rewrite the play to satisfy the Berlin censor's objections, but each revision was rejected.[75]

Censors objected also to any theatrical depiction of officers' brutality to civilians. After the minister of war refused to investigate or condemn an 1896 incident in which an army lieutenant drew a sword in a restaurant and killed a civilian, Hermann Sudermann's *Morituri* (We, Who Are About to Die, Salute You) mildly satirized the cruelty and arrogance often displayed by the military. Although approved for performance in Berlin in February 1897, some provincial governments, such as Baden, banned it.[76] Less fatal, more amusing confrontations between German officers and civilians were likewise taboo, such as the famous "Captain of Köpenick" incident of October 1906, in which an unemployed shoemaker and ex-convict, dressed in a secondhand captain's uniform, played upon civilian deference to military authority to arrest the obedient mayor of Köpenick and confiscate the city's treasury. The incident triggered a wave of theatrical satires in 1906–7; while some were allowed in liberal Hamburg or in smaller Bavarian cities such as Amberg, Passau, and Ulm, none were permitted in Berlin until 1911.

Besides jealously guarding the military against charges of petty brutality, German censors also vigilantly protected it from accusations of moral corruption. For example, the Cologne police required that some sexually suggestive lines spoken by a general be removed from a 1905 comedy there, and when a popular Berlin theater asked permission in 1909 to perform *Herzeleid* (Sorrow), a play about an officer's romantic involvements, the censor refused on the grounds that the lieutenant was presented in too negative a light and the uncritical petty-bourgeois audiences and social democratic workers who frequented that theater were likely to view him as typical of the entire officer corps.[77]

## The Polish Minority

As Germans struggled to create a nation state before 1871 and to preserve it thereafter, issues of national identity and national unity and the problem of resentful non-German ethnic minorities always vexed Prussia, and later the German Empire. The Congress of Vienna had restored Prussia's control over areas that had been forcibly annexed during the various partitions of Poland, thereby frustrating Polish desire for an independent nation. Dissident Poles in eastern Prussia and a rising Polish nationalist movement remained a constant worry, and authorities consistently suppressed works they feared might promote separatism or nationalist consciousness there. For example, Karl von Holtei's 1829 operetta *Der alte Feldherr* (The Old General) dealt with Tadeusz Kościuszko, the Polish hero of the War of Liberation, but the figure of Napoleon was also to appear briefly onstage. Fearing that the royal censor and intendant would not allow any reference to the former French emperor, through an intermediary von Holtei asked Friedrich Wilhelm III if he had any objection to a "worthy" portrayal of Napoleon. When the answer was no, von Holtei told the intendant the king had approved the performance and asked to have it scheduled for a time he knew the monarch could not attend. When the actor portraying Napoleon appeared on stage, the audience applauded so enthusiastically that the Berlin police president (who was also alarmed at the play's glorification of Kościuszko) wanted to forbid any further performances but backed down when told the king had given his prior approval. News of the controversy quickly spread and attendance at the operetta rose. When Friedrich Wilhelm III finally attended a performance, he noted how the audience seemed to pay close attention to the play's political undertones and applaud them vigorously (perhaps because of the king's presence). The following day he told von Holtei that while the Napoleon character was no problem, it was "unacceptable" to glorify a Polish nationalist; he ordered the play dropped from the repertoire after three final performances—which played to a packed house because by then it had become a real sensation.

During German unification, Prussia's eastern Polish provinces had opposed being included in a German national state. After 1871, parliamentary representatives from these regions championed the rights of Polish citizens there and resisted the government's increasing efforts to Germanize this area. Prussian authorities, pressured by radical German nationalist groups in the area, pursued a long and often bitter struggle to make German the required language in schools, all government business and public meetings. Local censors paid particularly close attention to Polish-language theatrical performances, sending observers to every performance, even after works had received police approval. When local police in 1894 began requiring that private as well as public theatrical performances receive prior approval and that Polish-language scripts submitted for censorship be accompanied by an officially notarized German translation, Polish spokesmen condemned the new policy as designed to prevent all Polish-language performances by making the approval process too costly and cumbersome.[78]

After 1900, when a blossoming of Polish societies, associations, and cultural institutions fostered Polish nationalist consciousness and agitation, German authorities tightened their control of Polish-language material. Numerous publications, including novels, songbooks, dramas, histories, pictures, and even certain prayer books and hymnals were confiscated and banned, often on the grounds they might threaten public order by arousing the Polish minority to violence against the German majority.[79] Police in eastern Prussia, but also in western German cities like Bochum, where there were large numbers of Polish speakers, allowed some dramas to be performed publicly in Polish, but they were very carefully screened and a number were banned or had to be revised because of their anti-German or overly Polish-nationalist tendencies. For example, after an initial performance in Posen, the historical drama *Eva Miaskowska,* set during the Poles' heroic seventeenth-century defeat of the Turks, was banned by police in Gembitz in 1909 because it was "likely to awaken and reinforce Polish nationalist consciousness to a dangerous degree." Courts upheld the ban because

> the continual emphasis on the Polish fatherland throughout the piece and its flaunting of Polish nationalist feeling strengthens Polish nationalist consciousness and, given the psychological situation that agitation for a Greater Poland has created among a great many Poles, would lead to a revival of hopes for a future Polish-national commonwealth. Perceptions would thereby be awakened that would lead to behavior that endangers the state order, namely, the existence and the constitution of the Prussian state. Under these circumstances, a performance would lead not to a state-preserving sense of Prussian and German patriotism, but rather to a yearning for a future Polish fatherland.[80]

The drama *Stary-Mundur,* which treated the 1863 Polish insurrection against Russia, was similarly banned by Stettin police in 1916 because it "glorified revolutionary ideas" and Polish national liberation.[81] Besides prohibiting public performances, authorities banned and confiscated printed versions of many Polish dramas, songs, poems, and novels.

## German Allies

Like their counterparts in France, England, and elsewhere, German authorities also intervened in theatrical life in the interests of foreign policy, banning plays and operettas that might prove diplomatically embarrassing or harmful.[82] Nowhere was concern over the domestic and foreign ramifications of drama greater than in the Prussian (and later, German) capital, Berlin. Police there, as in many other cities, considered it their duty "to prevent disruptions in the peaceful relations with other nations, insofar as such disruptions might result from the activities of private persons." Yet Berlin's situation and the responsibilities of its police were also unique. In their view, because of "the tendency of the populace here to commit disturbances of all kinds, the citizenry's lively interest in current political affairs, both domestic and foreign (as evidenced by the large number of newspapers here), the large number of foreigners who reside in Berlin and who frequent [the theaters]," and because of the presence of a large diplomatic community, performances in Berlin about controversial foreign events, personalities, or issues, besides offending foreign governments, might also profoundly agitate segments of the local populace and spark disturbances of public order.[83] Diplomatically sensitive theatrical performances that might be harmless in other cities were thus perceived as having a very different effect in the capital. For these reasons, performances in Berlin with any conceivable international ramifications came under close scrutiny. When dealing with such material, authorities had few established guidelines to follow. Police in most German cities, as a matter of course, banned all stage references to the reigning sovereigns of other nations. While negative or suggestive comments about a neighboring monarch could offend him/her, even neutral comments about a ruler might call forth embarrassing catcalls or hoots from a German audience; so it was considered best to simply ban them all.

At least in the years preceding World War I, there was a general attempt in Prussia to keep off the public stage "all distorting or insulting portrayals of the historical or contemporary life of other nations."[84] But in most cases authorities made their decisions and interventions on a case-by-case basis. A few examples, mostly involving relations with Russia and Austria-Hungary, will illustrate how theater censorship was used in Germany's national interest. In the Restoration era, when monarchs dominated political life and international relations, when court theaters dominated theatrical life and their repertoires was determined by the monarch's tastes and wishes, performances that other monarchs found offensive could easily be construed as a deliberate insult, with serious international repercussions. Thus, because the Russian ambassador to Prussia objected to any member of the Romanov dynasty being portrayed in an "unseemly light," the Berlin royal theater would not perform Karl Immermann's 1832 trilogy about the Russian czar Alexis. On the other hand, because of the pro-Russian policies of Prussia and Hesse-Darmstadt in the early 1840s, their royal theaters performed Karl Gutzkow's 1842 drama *Patkul* despite protests by Saxony (the play dealt with the late seventeenth-century Livonian national hero Patkul, who worked with Russia and Poland to liberate the Livonian gentry from Swedish rule, but was betrayed to the Swedes by Elector August II, ruler of Saxony and Poland).[85] When Schiller's *Wilhelm Tell* was performed in various court theaters of the (Austrian-dominated) German Confederation in the 1830s and 1840s, all references to tyrannical "Austrians" were dropped or changed to "foreigners." Deference to the other states of the German Confederation also led provincial Prussian authorities to ban performances of Heinrich Laube's comedy *Gottsched und Gellert* in 1845 because it promoted the idea of "German unity under Prussia's scepter."[86]

After unification, Bismarck regarded Austria-Hungary and Russia as Germany's two most reliable allies, and maintaining good relations with each became the cornerstone of his foreign policy. When performances in commercial theaters, especially in Berlin, threatened to offend either power, Bismarck, the Foreign Office, or local authorities were quick to act. In June 1875, for example, shortly after the signing of the Three Emperors' League between Germany, Austria-Hungary, and Russia, the Russian ambassador complained to Bismarck that the drama *Kaiser Paul*, which dealt with the cruel, unpopular czar who was assassinated in 1801, was an offense to the Russian royal family. Upon Bismarck's request, the Prussian interior minister instructed all provincial governors to ban the play from public performance in their provinces lest it damage Prussian-Russian relations.[87] When *Graf Hadubrand*, which contained several passages criticizing the corruption, brutality, and anti-Semitism of the Russian government, was planned for Berlin in late 1879—a year of tense relations with Russia following the Berlin Congress—police banned the work because of "the present political situation."[88] In January 1885 the operetta *Der Feldprediger* (The Army Chaplain) was being performed in Berlin; set during the Napoleonic wars, it contained a humorous scene in which rustic Russian Cossack troops, encountering German tallow candles for the first time, promptly ate them. Bismarck feared this scene would subject the military forces of an allied state to ridicule, so he had the Berlin theater censor eliminate it from all future performances.[89] In September 1907, long after Russia and the German Empire had drifted far apart and the czar had allied himself with Germany's rivals France and England, a Berlin theater asked permission to perform *Das Ungeheuer* (The Monster), which depicted the Russian bureaucracy as corrupt and the czar and his ministers as dupes and pawns. The Berlin police president banned the work as a derisive, slanderous attack on Russia that would provoke a protest from the Russian ambassador and damage attempts to reestablish better diplomatic relations. The ministry of interior later approved a revised script from which the most anti-Russian passages had been cut, but when it was performed the Russian ambassador protested even this expurgated version. Chancellor von Bülow and the Foreign Office reprimanded the interior minister for passing the work before consulting them.[90]

The architects of German foreign policy were even more sensitive about works that might offend their closest, most reliable ally, Austria-Hungary. One of the most famous examples involved Ernst von Wildenbruch's historical drama *Der Generalfeldoberst* (The Supreme Field Commander), set during the opening years of the Thirty Years War, which had as its protagonist a close relative of the Hohenzollern monarch who is executed (on stage) for participating in a rebellion against the tyrannical Habsburg Kaiser Ferdinand II, and which contained some disparaging dialogue about the house of Habsburg. When a Berlin theater asked permission to perform the play in 1889, it required Wilhelm II's personal approval because it contained a Hohenzollern ancestor, but he and members of his entourage wanted it banned because of its anti-Habsburg tone. Bismarck agreed it should be prohibited in Berlin—not only because of its anti-Habsburg content, but also because it might incite Czech nationalism and thus cause difficulties within the Austro-Hungarian Empire. Because von Wildenbruch held a minor Foreign Office post, Bismarck also feared the public might conclude the play somehow reflected official policy or was instigated as part of some complex diplomatic intrigue. The emperor therefore banned the work from public performance in all Prussian theaters and all private theaters in Berlin on the grounds that it was unfriendly toward Austria.[91] When another Berlin theater expressed interest in performing the play in 1901, the Foreign Office indicated it would approve provided the most pointed anti-Habsburg passages were cut, but the theater thereupon apparently lost interest and abandoned plans for a public performance.[92]

Because the play *Ludwig II von Bayern* (see above) also posed a threat to German-Austrian relations in March 1907, the Foreign Ministry again intervened. Since the work contained some unfavorable allusions about the beloved, assassinated Empress Elizabeth of Austria, Germany's diplomats feared a public performance would anger Emperor Franz Joseph and cause distress to Austria. For this reason the Foreign Office contacted the interior minister to make sure the work would not be allowed in Berlin.[93] Three years later *Der Feldherrnhügel* (The Commander's Hill) created another sensation. Set during the Austro-Prussian war of 1866, it was banned by censors in Berlin and several other German cities because it "was perceived in Vienna as an insult to the Austrian army, its equipment, and its commanders and for this reason caused offense and annoyance."[94] The Munich censors, however, decided the work might be acceptable with extensive changes, so they approved a script in which the names, uniforms, and geographic references were changed so that nothing would indicate it was set in Austria. Before permitting a performance, however, the Munich police made sure to explain their decision to the Austrian government and secure its consent.[95]

At various times after the turn of the century, the state also intervened against dramas that might exacerbate growing tensions with France, or threaten the nation's new alliance with Turkey. As German authorities seem to have realized, censoring dramas in order to avoid offending other nations is a sticky proposition: once a government has assumed the role of censor, no matter how liberal its policies or how infrequently it uses that power, it necessarily assumes responsibility for—and can legitimately be held responsible for—what it does and does not allow in public. Authorities can no longer take a position of neutrality or indifference: if they choose not to prohibit a potentially offensive work, it will be perceived as actually condoning or endorsing the work and the decision *not* to intervene to prevent a possible insult could and probably would be interpreted as an intentional insult by the foreign power in question. Thus, the German Empire felt it had little alternative but to respond to virtually every foreign complaint and intervene even where there was but the slightest chance of offending a foreign power.

## Conclusion

Like many other nineteenth-century European states, Germany required privately owned commercial theaters to be licensed and after mid century required most of these to obtain prior state approval for any dramas they performed. Unlike many of its neighbors, however, in much of Germany the decisions of the police theater censors could be—and frequently were—appealed to an administrative law court, which sometimes overturned the censor. The political fragmentation of Germany before 1871 and the decentralized, federal structure of the German Empire thereafter meant that laws, censorship policies, the criteria for granting theater licenses, and even the political will to control the theater differed from state to state and frequently from city to city; authorities in different places often made quite divergent decisions about the same drama. Nevertheless political censorship of the stage proved relatively effective in Germany. Authorities successfully intervened against many dramatic performances perceived as threatening basic political institutions (such as the monarch, the Hohenzollern dynasty, and the military) or the territorial unity of Prussia and the German Empire (especially expressions of Polish nationalism) or Germany's external diplomatic interests. They were also able to successfully thwart or limit the use of drama in socialist gatherings, to prevent or restrict the access of socialist audiences to tendentious or propagandistic socialist literature, and to prevent the performance of dramas that depicted social insurrection. Few of Germany's sovereigns or other state officials learned how to use the theater to build public support for the government or to correct and enlighten public opinion about the ruling class, as Schiller once had hoped. Many of them were able, however, to prevent the stage from being used to influence public opinion in ways that threatened the government and the interests of the ruling class.

## Bibliographical Essay

The best brief overviews of nineteenth-century Germany in English are David Blackbourn, *History of Germany, 1780–1918: The Long Nineteenth Century*, 2nd ed. (Malden, MA, 2003); John Breuilly, ed., *Nineteenth-Century Germany: Politics, Culture and Society, 1780–1918* (London, 2001); and Eda Sagarra, *An Introduction to Nineteenth-Century Germany* (Harrow, 1980). James Sheehan's *German History, 1770–1866* (Oxford, 1989) and Gordon Craig's *Germany, 1866–1945* (Oxford, 1978) provide more detailed analyses. For general outlines of nineteenth-century German literature in a social context, see Eda Sagarra, *Tradition and Revolution: German Literature and Society, 1830–1890* (New York, 1971), and Roy Pascal, *From Naturalism to Expressionism: German Literature and Society, 1880–1918* (London, 1973); while Hans Knudsen, *Deutsche Theatergeschichte*, 2nd ed. (Stuttgart, 1970); Max Martensteig, *Das deutsche Theater im neunzehnten Jahrhundert: Eine kulturgeschichtliche Darstellung*, 2nd ed. (Leipzig, 1924); and Marvin Carlson, *The German Stage in the Nineteenth Century* (Metuchen, NJ, 1972) provide useful surveys of the German theater. Robert Justin Goldstein's *Political Censorship of the Arts and the Press in Nineteenth-Century Europe* (New York, 1989) and his edited book, *The War for the Public Mind: Political Censorship in Nineteenth-Century Eu-*

*rope* (Westport, CT, 2000), are the best general introductions to political censorship in nineteenth-century Europe. There are currently no book-length English-language studies of nineteenth-century German theater censorship, but for press and caricature censorship, see Frederik Ohles, *Germany's Rude Awakening: Censorship in the Land of the Brothers Grimm* (Kent, OH, 1992); Alex Hall, *Scandal, Sensation and Social Democracy: The SPD Press and Wilhelmine Germany, 1890–1914* (Cambridge, 1977); Mary Lee Townsend, *Forbidden Laughter: Popular Humor and the Limits of Repression in Nineteenth-Century Prussia* (Ann Arbor, MI, 1992); and Ann Allen, *Satire and Society in Wilhelmine Germany: Kladderadatsch and Simplicissimus* (Lexington, KY, 1984). Theater censorship is discussed at some length in Gary Stark, *Banned in Berlin: Literacy Censorship in Imperial Germany, 1871–1918* (New York, 2009).

Focused studies of the interaction between German theater, society, and politics in the first half of the century can be found in Maria Porrmann and Florian Vaßen, eds., *Theaterverhältnisse im Vormärz* (Bielefeld, 2002); Horst Denkler, *Restauration und Revolution: Politische Tendenzen im Deutschen Drama zwischen Wiener Kongress and Märzrevolution* (Munich, 1973); and Suzanne Ghirardini-Kurzweill, "Das Theater in den Politischen Strömungen der Revolution von 1848," inaugural dissertation, Ludwig-Maximilians-Universität zu München (Munich, 1960). For the later nineteenth century, see Helmut Schanze, *Drama im Bürgerlichem Realismus (1850–1890): Theorie und Praxis* (Frankfurt, 1973); Peter von Rüden, *Sozialdemokratisches Arbeitertheater (1848–1914): Ein Beitrag zur Geschichte des politischen Theaters* (Frankfurt, 1973); and Manfred Brauneck, *Literatur und Öffentlichkeit im ausgehenden 19. Jahrhundert: Studien zur Rezeption des naturalistischen Theaters in Deutschland* (Stuttgart, 1974). The Freie Volksbühne has attracted much scholarly attention. The best overviews are Siegfried Nestriepke, *Geschichte der Volksbühne Verein Berlin, I, 1890–1914* (Berlin, 1930); Heinrich Braulich, *Die Volksbühne: Theater und Politik in der Deutschen Volksbühnenbewegung* (Berlin, 1976); Cecil Davies, *Theater for the People: The Story of the Volksbühne* (Austin, TX, 1977); and his *The Volksbühne Movement: A History* (Amsterdam, 2000); and Andrew Bonnell, *The People's Stage in Imperial Germany: Social Democracy and Culture, 1890–1914* (London, 2005). Information on the importance of theater to avant-garde modernists and Social Democrats can be found in Peter Jelavich, *Munich and Theatrical Modernism: Politics, Playwriting, and Performance, 1890–1914* (Cambridge, MA, 1985); and Vernon Lidtke, *The Alternative Culture: Socialist Labor in Imperial Germany* (New York, 1985), 136–58. Heinrich Stümcke's *Hohenzollernfürsten im Drama* (Leipzig, 1903) is a perceptive study of how German dramatists treated the Hohzenzollern dynasty, while Roswitha Flatz's *Krieg im Frieden: Das aktuelle Militärstück auf dem Theater des deutschen Kaiserreichs* (Frankfurt, 1976) does the same for the military.

Efforts to censor German literature and the stage for political (and other) reasons are surveyed by Dieter Breuer, *Geschichte der literarischen Zensur in Deutschland* (Heidelberg, 1982); Hanns-Peter Reisner, *Literatur unter der Zensur: Die politische Lyrik des Vormärz* (Stuttgart, 1973); Frederick Ohles, "The French Occupation (1806–14) and the German Confederation (1815–71)" and my "The German Empire, 1868–1918," both in Derek Jones, ed., *Censorship: A World Encyclopedia*, II (London, 2001), 920–25. Many key documents on literary censorship can be found in Edda Ziegler, *Literatur und Zensur in Deutschland, 1819–1848: Materialien, Kommentare* (Munich, 1983), and Ludwig Leiss, *Kunst im Konflikt: Kunst und Künstler im Widerstreit mit der 'Obrigkeit'* (Berlin, 1971). Heinrich H. Houben has written several classic in-depth accounts of German literary censorship: *Der gefesselte Biedermier: Literatur, Kultur, Zensur in der guten, alten Zeit* (Hildesheim, 1973 [1924]); *Polizei und Zensur: Längs- und Querschnitt durch die Geschichte der Buch- und Theaterzensur* (reprinted as *Der ewige Zensor*, Kronbert/Ts., 1973 [1926]); and his massive handbook *Verbotene Literatur: Von der klassischen Zeit bis zur Gegenwart. Ein kritisch-historisches Lexikon über verbotene Bücher, Zeitschriften und Theaterstücke, Schriftsteller und Verleger* (Berlin, 1965 [1924]). Houben's work is particularly valuable because many government records that he used were destroyed in World War II. I discuss more recent works in "Censorship and Literary Life in Wilhelmine Germany: A Research Report," *Internationales Archiv für die Sozialgeschichte der deutschen Literatur* 17 (1992): 138–49.

The legal dimensions of nineteenth-century German theater censorship are covered in Kurt Kleefeld, *Die Theaterzensur in Preußen* (Berlin, 1905), while Oscar Blumenthal's *Verbotene Stücke* (Berlin, 1900) provides the perspective of a theater director who frequently clashed with the censors. Richard Grelling's *Streifzüge: Gesammelte Aufsätze* (Berlin, 1894) are essays by the lawyer who most frequently challenged police bans in court. Important local/regional studies on theater censorship include Wilhelm Herrmann, "Mannheimer Theaterzensur im 19. Jahrhundert," *Mannheimer Hefte* 2 (1976): 74–78; Wolfgang Schulze-Olden, "Die Theaterzensur in der Rheinprovinz (1819–1918)," inaugural dissertation (Cologne, 1965); Michaele Giesing, "Theater, Polizei und Politik in Hamburg um 1900," *Maske und Kothurn* 42 (1996): 121–63; Robin Lenman, "Censorship and Society in Munich, 1890–1914, With Special Reference to *Simplicissimus* and the Plays of Frank Wedekind," PhD dissertation (Oxford, 1975); and Michael Meyer, *Theaterzensur In München, 1900–1918: Geschichte und Entwicklung der polizeilichen Zensur und des Theaterzensurbeirats unter besonderer Berücksichtigung Frank Wedekinds* (Munich, 1982).

More focused studies of important politically motivated government interventions include Heinrich Meissner, "Monarchisches Prinzip und Theaterzensur: Eine Skizze nach den Akten," *Preußische Jahrbücher* 206 (1926): 316–36; and my essays, "La police berlinoise et la Freie Volksbühne: Une etude de l'integrétion socialist," *Revue d'Histoire du Théatre* 38 (1986): 7–19; "Freie Volksbühne, 1890–1912," *Censorship: A World Encyclopedia*, II, 886–87; and "Diplomacy By Other Means: Entertainment, Censorship, and German Foreign Policy, 1871–1918," in John McCarthy and Werner von der Ohe, eds., *Zensur und Kultur/Censorship and Culture: Zwischen Weimarer Klassik und Weimarer Republik mit einem Ausblick bis heute/From Weimar Classicism to Weimar Republic and Beyond* (Tübingen, 1995), 123–33. The state's attempts in the 1890s to suppress Gerhart Hauptman's *Die Weber* is perhaps the most notorious case of German political censorship of the nineteenth-century stage. It is discussed in my "Gerhart Hauptmann, *Die Weber*," in *Censorship: A World Encyclopedia*, II, 1036–37; Hans Schwab-Felitsch *Gerhart Hauptmann: Die Weber: Vollständiger Text des Schauspiels Dokumentation* (Frankfurt, 1963); and Helmut Praschek, ed., *Gerhart Hauptmanns "Weber": Eine Dokumentation* (Berlin, 1981), the latter two of which reproduce many of the key documents.

## Notes

1. Maria Porrmann and Florian Vaßen, "Doch die Verhältnisse, sie sind nicht so! Theaterverhältnisse im Vormärz," in Porrmann and Vaßen, eds., *Theaterverhältnisse im Vormärz* (Bielefeld, 2002), 13.
2. Friedrich Schiller, "Die Schaubühne als eine moralische Anstalt betrachtet," in Schiller, *Sämtliche Schriften*, V (Munich, 1968), 92–101. A translation, "The Stage Considered as a Moral Institution," appears in Frederick Ungar, ed., *Friedrich Schiller: An Anthology for Our Time* (New York, 1959), 263–83.
3. On the German national theater movement, see W. Bruford, *Theater, Drama, and Audience in Goethe's Germany* (Westport, CT, 1974 [1950]), 105ff.
4. Schiller, "The Stage Considered as a Moral Institution."
5. Robert Justin Goldstein, *Political Censorship of the Arts and the Press in Nineteenth-Century Europe* (New York, 1989), 113–14; Eda Sagarra, *Tradition and Revolution: German Literature and Society, 1830–1890* (New York, 1971), 79, 96;

Horst Denkler, *Restauration und Revolution: Politische Tendenzen im deutschen Drama zwischen Wiener Kongress und Märzrevolution* (Munich, 1973), 23–24.
6. Eduard Devrient, *Über Theaterschule* (Berlin, 1841), as quoted in George Brandt, ed., *German and Dutch Theater, 1600–1848* (Cambridge, 1993), 317.
7. Henry Vizetelly, *Berlin Under the New Empire: Its Institutions, Inhabitants, Industry, Monuments, Museums, Social Life, Manners*, II (New York, 1968 [1879]), 236.
8. Arthur Brehmer and Max Grube, "Der Kaiser und die Kunst," in A. Brehmer, ed., *Am Hofe Kaiser Wilhelms II* (Berlin, 1898), 360; and Wilhelm II's "Rede zu Kunstpersonal der Königlichen Schauspiele, 16 Juni 1898," in Johannes Penzler, ed., *Die Reden Kaiser Wilhelm II in den Jahren 1901–Ende 1905* (Leipzig, 1907), 98–99.
9. See, for example, Conrad Alberti [Konrad Sittenfeld], *Was erwartet die deutsche Kunst von Kaiser Wilhelm II? Zeitgemässige Anregungen von \*\*\** (Leipzig, 1888), 70; and Franz Mehring, *Gesammelte Schriften*, T. Höhle, H. Koch, J. Schleifstein, eds., Bd. 12: *Aufsätze zur ausländischen Literatur, Vermischte Schriften* (Berlin, 1976), 268.
10. Prussian Interior Minister von Rheinbaden memo, 5 December 1899, in Landesarchiv Berlin A, Pr. Br. Rep. 30 Berlin C: Polizei-präsidium Berlin, Tit. 74-Theatersachen (hereafter LAB A/74), Th 25; Wolfgang Schulze-Olden, "Die Theaterzensur in der Rheinprovinz (1819–1918)," inaugural dissertation (Cologne, 1965), 26; Robin Lenman, "Censorship and Society in Munich, 1890–1914, With Special Reference to *Simplicissimus* and the plays of Frank Wedekind," PhD dissertation (Oxford, 1975), 244. See also Kurt Kleefeld, *Die Theaterzensur in Preußen* (Berlin, 1905), 5.
11. Susanne Ghirardini-Kurzweill, "Das Theater im den Politischen Strömungen der Revolution von 1848," inaugural dissertation, Ludwig-Maximilians-Universität zu München (Munich, 1960), 22; and Max Martensteig, *Das deutsche Theater im neunzehnten Jahrhundert: Eine kulturgeschichtliche Darstellung*, 2nd ed. (Leipzig, 1924), 265.
12. Martensteig, *Das deutsche Theater*, 268ff, 384–86.
13. LAB A/74, Th 5; Gerdi Huber, *Die Klassische Schwabing: München als Zentrum der intellektuellen Zeit- und Gesellschaftskritik um 1900*, Miscellanea Bavarica Monacensia, 37 (Munich, 1973), 240.
14. Le Bon, *Psychologie der Massen*, trans. Rudolf Eisler (Stuttgart, 1982), 44.
15. See, for example, Dr. Leuthold, "Theaterpolizei," in Karl Freiherr von Stengel, ed., *Wörterbuch des deutschen Verwaltungsrechts*, II (Freiburg, 1890), 625–26; Otto Opet, *Deutsches Theaterrecht* (Berlin, 1897), 149–50; Dr. von Bar, "Rechtmäßigkeit und Zweckmäßigkeit der Theaterzensur?" *Deutsche Juristenzeitung* 8 (1903): 205–6; Wilhelm von Polenz, "Über die Grenzen des Unanständigen in der Kunst," *Das Magazin für Literatur* 62 (17 June 1893): 384–85.
16. Maximilian Harden, *Berlin als Theaterhauptstadt* (Berlin, 1888), 14; Charlotte Klinger, "Das Königliche Schauspielhaus unter Botho von Hülsen, 1869–1886," PhD dissertation (Berlin, 1954), 203–4.
17. J. Düringer and H. Bartels, *Theater-Lexicon* (Leipzig, 1841), as quoted in Brandt, 287.

18. H. H. Houben, *Der ewige Zensor* (Kronberg/Ts., 1978 [1926]), 101ff.
19. Houben, *Der ewige Zensor*, 103.
20. Houben, *Der ewige Zensor*, 101ff; Maria Sommer, "Die Einführung der Theaterzensur in Berlin," *Kleine Schriften der Gesellschaft für Theatergeschichte* 14 (Autumn 1955 / Summer 1956): 32–42; and Schulze-Olden, 1–17.
21. Dieter Breuer, *Geschichte der literarischen Zensur in Deutschland* (Heidelberg, 1982), 186.
22. Prussian interior minister to all provincial governors, 28 July 1884, cited in Schulze-Olden, 76 (see also 78, 80), and interior minister memo of 9 April 1895, LAB A/74, Th 24.
23. Frankfurt police president to administrative specialist of Erfurt, 13 June 1893, Hessisches Hauptstaatsarchiv, Abt. 407: Polizeipräsidium Frankfurt (herafter cited as HHStA/407), 25, Bd. 2. See also Frankfurt police ordinance of 25 November 1889, in *Ewald's Polizei-Verordnungen für Frankfurt am Main* (Berlin, 1906), 1; police president to director of city theater, 5 and 14 September 1891, HHStA/407, 25, Bd. 1; *Frankfurter Finanzherold*, 14 November 1891, and *General Anzeiger*, 9 December 1891; Frankfurt district administrative president to Prussian interior minister, 17 October 1904, Geheimes Staatsarchivs Preußischer Kulturbesitz, Berlin, Rep. 77: Ministerium des Innern, Tit. 1000 (hereafter GStA PK/1000), 7, Bd. 3; HHStA/407, Nrs. 408, 409; Schulze-Olden, 67–81, 95–97; and provincial governor of Hanover to Prussian interior minister, 2 July 1895, GStA PK/1000, 4, Bd. 2.
24. Dresden police instituted prior theater censorship on 24 December 1876, while Leipzig police issued their regulation on 10 March 1894. On theatrical censorship in Saxony, see Wenzel Goldbaum, *Theaterrecht* (Berlin, 1914), 67; G. Krais, "Über Theaterzensur," *Blätter für administrative Praxis* 51 (1901): 29 n. 2; and Dr. Schmid, "Theaterzensur," *Zeitschrift für die freiwillige Gerichtsbarkeit und die Gemeindeverwaltung in Württemberg* 51 (1909): 148. The Munich police censorship ordinance, which closely parallels the 1851 Berlin ordinance, is quoted in Krais, 31ff., and in Lenman, 214–15.
25. Hans Schorer, *Das Theaterleben in Münster in der zweiten Hälfte des 19. Jahrhunderts* (Emsdetten, 1935), 146, 158; Wilhelm Herrmann, "Mannheimer Theaterzensur im 19. Jahrhundert," *Mannheimer Hefte* 2 (1976): 74–78.
26. On origins of the Censorship Advisory Board, see Lenman, 247–51; Peter Jelavich, *Munich and Theatrical Modernism: Politics, Playwriting, and Performance, 1890–1914* (Cambridge, MA, 1985), 247–50; and Michael Meyer, *Theaterzensur in München, 1900–1918: Geschichte und Entwicklung der polizeilichen Zensur und des Theaterzensurbeirats unter besonderer Berücksichtigung Frank Wedekinds* (Munich, 1982), 66–74, 79–95. (Quote from Munich police director to Bavarian interior minister, in Meyer, 73–74.)
27. Heinrich Heine, *Reisebilder, Zweiter Teil: Ideen. Das Buch Le Grand* (Berlin, 1826), chapter XII; Karl Gutzkow, *Säkularbilder* (Berlin, 1846), quoted in Marianna Choldin, *A Fence around the Empire: Russian Censorship of Western Ideas under the Tsars* (Durham, NC, 1985), 172.
28. Johann Nestroy, *Freiheit in Krähwinckel* (Berlin, 1849), act I, scene 14.

29. Petra Hartmann, "Das 'dramatische' Ende des jungen Deutschland," in Porrmann and Vaßen, eds., *Theaterverhältnisse*, 246–47.
30. Ottokar Stauf von der March, *Zensur, Theater, und Kritik* (Dresden, 1905), 13; Ernst Müller-Meiningen's comments in the Reichstag, *Stenographische Berichte über die Verhandlungen des Reichstages, Haus der Abgeordneten*, Bd. 169 (7 February 1900), 3928.
31. Wedekind, "Herr von der Heydte," *Die Aktion*, 19 February 1912; and in *Werke*, II, 708–9; also reprinted in Meyer, 345; Wedekind, "Torquemada," *Gesammelte Werke*, IX, 391–95, first published in *Berliner Tageblatt*, 17 March 1912; *Berlin Börsen-Courier*, 24 March 1912; see also Artur Kutscher, *Frank Wedekind: Sein Leben und sein Werke*, III (Munich, 1922–31), 48–51; and Meyer, 266–71.
32. Mann's response to a questionnaire about theater censorship, reprinted in Robert Heindl, "Die Theaterzensur," diss. jur., University of Erlangen (Berlin, 1907), 65ff.
33. Petition of Union of German Goethe Leagues, 10–11 November 1900, in Deutsches Literaturarchiv, Marbach, Cotta Archiv, Nachl. Sudermann, XXV3. See also *Dritter Verwaltungsbericht des Königliche Polizeipräsidiums von Berlin für die Jahre 1891–1900* (Berlin, 1902), 335.
34. *Stenographische Berichte des Reichstages*, 10. Leg. Periode, II. Session, Drucksache 16 (Bd. 189, 281). On the parliamentary effort in 1901 to abolish censorship, see Andreas Pöllinger, *Der Zensurprozeß um Paul Heyses Drama "Maria von Magdala" (1901–1903)* (Frankfurt, 1989), 134–49.
35. Remarks by Ernst Müller-Meiningen, Dr. H. Pachnicke, and A. Traeger, *Stenographische Berichte des Reichstages*, 10. Leg. Periode, II. Session, Sitzung 30 January, 6 and 20 February 1901 (Bd. 180, 1016–27, 1160–61, and 1459–65; quotations from 1019, 1022, 1026–27.)
36. Heinrich Houben, *Der gefesselte Biedermier: Literatur, Kultur, Zensur in der guten, alten Zeit* (Hildesheim, 1973 [1924]), 241–42.
37. Heinrich Houben, *Verbotene Literatur: Von der klassischen Zeit bis zur Gegenwart. Ein kritisch-historisches Lexikon über verbotene Bücher, Zeitschriften und Theaterstücke, Schriftsteller und Verleger*, I (Berlin, 1965 [1924]), 567.
38. Goldstein, *Political Censorship*, 159; <http://www.albertlortzing.org/timetab2.html#1826> (accessed 20 March 2007); Eugen Mehler, "'Rienzi' und die Dresdener Theaterzensur," *Die Musik* 12 (1913): 195–201.
39. Houben, *Verbotene Literatur*, I, 381.
40. Breuer, *Geschichte der literarischen Zensur*, 174–75.
41. Berlin police ban of 24 November 1898, Berlin police president to District Administrative Council, 8 January 1899, censor's report of 10 March 1899, LAB A/74, Th 308; text with censor's markings in Landesarchiv Berlin, Pr. Br. Rep. 30 C/a: Theater-Zensur (hereafter LAB/C); and O. Schinnerer, "The Suppression of Schnitzler's Grüne Kakadu by the Burgtheater: Unpublished Correspondence," *Germanic Review* 6 (1931): 183–92.
42. *Frankfurter Zeitung*, 16 February 1918; LAB A/74, Th 36.
43. As quoted in Theodore Hamerow, ed., *The Age of Bismarck: Documents and Interpretations* (New York, 1973), 246.

44. Caprivi's speech of late February 1891, as quoted in J. Alden Nichols, *Germany After Bismarck: The Caprivi Era, 1890–1894* (Cambridge, MA, 1958), 75–76.
45. Report of Police President von Hepp, 30 July 1883, as quoted in Peter von Rüden, *Sozialdemokratische Arbeitertheater (1848–1914): Ein Beitrag zur Geschichte des politischen Theaters* (Frankfurt, 1973), 60. For detailed statistics on the total number of socialist publications and associations banned under the Anti-Socialist law, see Otto Atzrott, *Sozialdemokratische Druckschriften und Vereine verboten auf Grund des Reichsgesetzes gegen die gemeigefährlichen Bestrebungen der Sozialdemokratie von 21. Oktober 1878* (Berlin, 1886; Nachtrag 1888), v–vi.
46. Chemnitz police order, 7 December 1894, cited in Rüden, *Sozialdemokratische Arbeitertheater,* 95.
47. Police ban of 4 February 1893, LAB A/74, Th 54; Berlin police president ban of 5 August 1895, and Berlin police president to Brandeburg provincial governor, 9 August 1895, in LAB A/74, Th 55.
48. Wilhelm II's marginalia on clipping from *Allgemeine Zeitung,* 12 August 1890, and Wilhelm II to Prussian interior minister, 16 September 1890, Geheimes Staatsarchivs Preußischer Kulturbestiz, 2.2.1., Königliches Geheime Zivilkabinett (herafter GStA PK/ZK), 21012, Bl. 154, 163.
49. Supreme Administrative Court decision of 6 January 1892, reprinted in *Die Freie Volksbühne: Eine Schrift für den Verein "Freie Volksbühne"* 1 (Berlin, 1891); portions also quoted in Siegfried Nestriepke, *Geschichte der Volksbühne Verein Berlin, I. Teil: 1890–1914* (Berlin, 1930), 55–56. See also Bruno Wille, "Die Justiz als Kunstrichterin: Glossen zur Urteil des Oberverwaltungsgerichts über die 'Freie Volksbühne,'" *Allgemeine Theater-Revue für Bühne und Welt* I (8 March 1892): 1–5.
50. Berlin police president to Prussian interior minister, undated, 1895, in LAB A/74, Th 24; Berlin police report on Freie Volksbühne of 6 June 1895, in LAB A/74, Th 1100.
51. Houben, *Der gefesselte Biedermier,* I, 203; and Supreme Administrative Court decision of 29 May 1903, as quoted in Ludwig Leiss, *Kunst im Konflikt: Kunst und Künstler im Widerstreit mit der 'Obrigkei'* (Berlin, 1971), 128.
52. Decision of District Administrative Council, 7 March 1893, LAB A/74, Th 304, also quoted in Houben, *Verbotene Literatur,* I, 342–44.
53. Berlin political police to police president, 5 October 1894, police president memo, 11 October 1894, police president to provincial governor, 12 February 1895, LAB A/74, Th 594. Text of drama is in LAB/C.
54. Supreme Administrative Court decision, 9 January 1896, LAB A/74, Th 594.
55. Ban of 20 December 1897, LAB A/74, Th 65; Berlin police president to Prussian interior minister, 29 July 1903, GStPK/1000, 7, Bd. 3, Bl. 191ff. For a partial list of the many Social Democratic plays banned from Berlin stages in the late 1890s and early 1900s, see LAB A/74, Th 56.
56. Report of Division II of Hamburg police, 22 December 1896, Staatsarchiv Hamburg, Pol.S.: Polizeibehörde—Politische Polizei (herafter StAH), 2170, vol. 23; and Michaele Giesing, "Theater, Polizei, und Politik in Hamburg um 1900," *Maske und Kothurn* 42 (1996): 126–27.

57. *Bühne und Welt*, III, Pt. 1 (Berlin, 1900–1901), 214–15; Helga Abret and Aldo Keel, *Im Zeichen des Simplicissimus: Briefwechsel Albert Langen und Dagny Bjørnson, 1895–1908* (Munich, 1987), 215–16.
58. Police ban of 18 April 1900, LAB A/74, Th 672; Houben, *Verbotene Literatur*, II, 7–8.
59. See text in LAB/C; LAB A/74, Th 672; and Houben, *Verbotene Literatur*, II, 8–9.
60. Political police to police director, 27 November 1905, police director order of 1 December 1905, and various newspaper clippings in StAH, 2170, and Giesing, "Theater, Polizei und Politik," 134–35; censor's report, 22 March 1906, LAB A/74, Th 3796.
61. Berlin censor's report; police president ban of 1 May 1912; police president to provincial governor, 29 May 1912; provincial governor's decision of 4 August 1912; and Supreme Administrative Court decision of 26 January 1914, LAB A/74, Th 799. See also Nestriepke, *Geschichte*, 372–73; *Freie Volksbühne* 16 (1911–12): 9–11; and Dietmar Trempenau, *Frühe sozialdemokratische und sozialistische Arbeiterdramatik (1890–1914): Entstehungsbedingungen-Entwicklungslinien-Ziele-Funktion* (Stuttgart, 1979), 197–98.
62. Hildesheim police to Berlin police president, 23 November 1912, LAB A/74, Th 799; *Bühne und Welt*, XVI, Pt. I (Berlin, 1913–14), 189; *Berliner Tageblatt*, 4 May 1912.
63. Memo of Censor von Glasenapp, 27 September 1904, LAB A/74, Th 495. See also GStA PK/1000, 4, Bd. 1, Bl. 67–70; 5, Bd. 7, Bl. 88; and Lenman, 245.
64. Houben, *Der gefesselte Biedermeier*, 244–47.
65. Prussian Ministry of the Royal House and interior minister's decrees of 27 April 1844, GStA PK/1000, 5.
66. Prussian Ministry of the Royal House and interior minister's decrees of 27 April 1844, 3 May 1883, 28 July 1884, 20 October 1884, 27 December 1900, GStA PK/1000, 5; GStA PK/ZK, 21008–21011; LAB A/74, Th 60–62. Also Houben, *Verbotene Literatur*, I, 316–19, and II, 599; Heinrich Houben, *Polizei und Zensur: Längs- und Querschnitt durch die Geschichte der Buch- und Theaterzensur* (Berlin, 1926), 123–30; and Heinrich Meissner, "Monarchisches Prinzip und Theaterzensur: Eine Skizze nach den Akten," *Preußische Jahrbücher* 206 (December 1926): 316–36.
67. GStA PK/1000, 5, Bd. 4, Bl. 293ff.
68. GStA PK/ZK, 21013, Bl. 102–12.
69. Dagmar Walach, "Das doppelte Drama, oder die Polizei als Lektor: Über die Entstehung der preussischen Theaterzensurbibliothek," in Antonius Jammers, et al., eds., *Die besondere Bibliothek, oder die Faszination von Büchersammlungen* (Munich, 2002), 270.
70. Civil-Cabinet to Prussian interior minister, 13 December 1909, GStA PK/1000, 5, Bd. 7, Bl. 247; also GStA PK/ZK, 21011, Bl. 61; LAB A/74, Th 496 and 134; Ferdinand Bonn, *Zwei Jahre Theaterdirektor in Berlin: Ein Beitrag zur deutschen Kulturgeschichte* (Berlin, 1908), and *Mein Künstlerleben: Was ich mit dem Kaiser erlebte und andere Erinnerungen* (Munich, 1920), 71–141.

71. Robert von Landmann and Gusta Rohmer, *Kommentar zur Gewerbeordnung für das deutsche Reich,* 5. Aufl (Munich, 1907), 513; Hanseatic ambassador to Bremen mayor, 26 March 1907, Staatsarchiv Bremen, 4, 14/1—VI.D.1, and Bremen Senate to Stadttheater, 27 March 1907, Staatsarchiv Bremen, 3-S.23a, 44; *Frankfurter Zeitung,* 28 March 1907; Berlin police president memo of 24 March 1907, GStA PK/1000, 5, Bd. 4, Bl 27; Hamburg police memo of 28 March 1907, StAH, 2170, 23; Hessian interior minister to County Offices, 10 May 1907, Staatsarchiv Darmstadt, G15 Friedberg, XIX. Abt., III Abschnitt, Bd. 1.
72. Roswitha Flatz, *Krieg im Frieden: Das aktuelle Militärstück auf dem Theater des deutschen Kaiserreichs* (Frankfurt, 1976), "Stückenverzeichnis," 289–344.
73. Flatz, *Krieg im Frieden,* 4–18.
74. Berlin police president ban of 18 January 1893, District Administrative Council decision of 11 July 1893, and Supreme Administrative Court decision of 9 August 1893, in LAB A/74, Th 560. A copy of the play, with censor's markings, is in LAB/C.
75. Letter of Bremen police chief to Berlin police president, 25 March 1910, and Berlin police president to Bremen police, 27 June 1910, Staatsarchiv Bremen, 4, 14/1, VI.D.1, and Brandenburg provincial governor decision of 8 September 1910, LAB A/74, Th 434. Revised scripts are in LAB/C.
76. Flatz, *Krieg im Frieden,* 323; *Hamburger Echo,* 28 January 1897; and Alex Hall, *Scandal, Sensation, and Social Democracy: The SPD Press and Wilhelmine Germany, 1890–1914* (Cambridge,1977), 128.
77. Schulze-Olden, 92; Heinz-Dieter Hinrichs, "Das Rose-Theater: Ein volkstümliches Familientheater in Berlin von 1906 bis 1944," dissertation (Berlin, 1965), 129 n. 42.
78. Houben, *Der gefesselte Biedermeier,* 258–59; remarks by Dr. Rzepnikowski, *Stenographische Berichte über die Verhandlungen des preußischen Hauses der Abgeordneten,* 25, Sitzung am 21 February 1895, Bd. 391, 787. On the background of language disputes in this area, see Richard Blanke, *Prussian Poland in the German Empire (1871–1900)* (New York, 1981), and Richard W. Tims, *Germanizing Prussian Poland: The H-K-T Society and the Struggle for the Eastern Marches in the German Empire* (New York, 1966), 144–50.
79. See Hubert Orlowski, *Polnisches Schrifttum unter Zensur: Wilhelminische und Nationalsozialistische Zensorpolitik im Vergleich* (Frankfurt, 1988), 9–19; also Ewa Skorupa, *Polnische Druckschriften, 1850–1932* (Bd. IV of Herbert Birett, *Verbotene Druckschriften in Deutschland* [Vaduz, 1996]).
80. Gembitz police ban of 21 January 1909, District Administrative Council decision of 3 December 1909, and Supreme Administrative Court decision of 7 July 1911, LAB A/74, Th 130. For examples of other works banned or cut, see Posen police to Danzig police president, 13 September 1911, 3 September 1912, 13 September 1913, September 1914, and September 1918, GStA PK, Rep. A 209, 3; and Bochum police to Posen police, 13 December 1912, as quoted in Orlowski, *Polnisches Schrifttum,* 8–9.
81. LAB A/74, Th 36.

82. For examples of such contemporary censorship in France, see Louis Gabriel-Robinet, *La Censure* (Paris, 1965), 117, and Goldstein, *Political Censorship*, 107. For examples in Britain, where Gilbert and Sullivan's operetta *Mikado* was banned temporarily after a long run to avoid offending a visiting Japanese prince, see John Stephens, *The Censorship of English Drama, 1824–1901* (New York, 1980), 130–31; Frank Fowell and Frank Palmer, *Censorship in England* (New York, 1969 [1913]); and Goldstein, *Political Censorship*, 169. For a fuller discussion of the German Empire's censorship of public entertainments, including film and circuses, in the interests of foreign policy, see my "Diplomacy By Other Means: Entertainment, Censorship, and German Foreign Policy, 1871–1918," in John McCarthy and Werner von der Ohe, eds., *Zensur und Kultur zwischen Weimarer Klassik und Weimarer Republik* (Tübingen, 1995), 123–33.
83. Berlin police president to Prussian interior minister, 13 August 1898, and Brandenburg provincial governor deposition, 20 October 1899, GStA PK/1000, 7, Fasc. 2, Bl. 16–17, 26–31.
84. Prussian interior minister to district administrative presidents, 27 December 1913, LAB A/74, Th 28; also Schulze-Olden, 99.
85. Houben, *Der gefesselte Biedermier*, I, 314–15.
86. Schulze-Olden, 61.
87. Confidential letter of imperial chancellor to Prussian interior minister, 17 June 1875, and Prussian interior minister memo to provincial governors, 23 June 1875, GStA PK/1000, 5, Bl. 133, 135; see also Schulze-Olden, 26.
88. Berlin police president to Prussian interior minister, 23 January 1880, GStA PK/1000, 7, Bd 2, Bl. 18ff; also LAB/C.
89. Prussian interior minister to Berlin police president, 16 January 1885, and Berlin police president to Prussian interior minister, 17 January 1885, GStA PK/1000, 7, Bd. 2, Bl. 60, 57ff.
90. *Berliner Tageblatt*, 13 September 1907; GStA PK/1000, 5, Bd. 2, Bl. 285ff., 342.
91. GStA PK/1000, 5, Fasc. 2, Bl. 1–41; and GStA PK/ZK, 21001, Bl. 200–202. Also Kathy Harms, "Writer by Imperial Decree: Ernst von Wildenbruch" in Volker Dürr, et al., eds., *Imperial Germany* (Madison, WI, 1985) 143–45; Alfred Mühr, *Rund um den Gendarmenmarkt: Von Iffland bis Gründgens: Zweihundert Jahre musisches Berlin* (Oldenburg, 1965), 194–98; Berthold Litzmann, *Ernst von Wildenbruch, Zweiter Band: 1885–1909* (Berlin, 1916), 70–76; and Helene Bettelheim-Gabillon, "Wildenbruch und Grillparzer in Spiegel der Zensur," *Österreichische Rundschau* 53 (1917): 229–30. On the Leipzig performance, see Paul Raché, "Leipziger Theaterbrief: Wildenbruch's "Generalfeldoberst," *Das Magazin für Literatur* 59 (18 January 1890): 44–45.
92. GStA PK/1000, 5, Fasc. 2; and edited copy in LAB/C, 1620.
93. Foreign minister to Prussian interior minister, 27 March 1907, StA PK/1000, 5, Bd. 4, Bl. 28; and *Frankfurter Zeitung*, 28 March 1907.
94. Berlin police president to Munich police director, 31 January 1910, Staatsarchiv München, Pol. Dir. 4591.
95. Bayerisches Hauptstaatsarchiv München, Allgemeine Abteilung, MA 92, 418.

# France

ROBERT JUSTIN GOLDSTEIN

### Introduction: The Fear of the Theater

During an 1880 French parliamentary debate, deputy Robert Mitchell, in discussing censorship of caricature, noted that "drawings which displease the government are always forbidden," while those which "gained official favor are displayed in the windows of all the bookstores," thus providing knowledge of "exactly what the government fears and what it encourages" and a "clear revelation of its intimate thoughts," including important information for the "attentive observer, curious for precise information on the tastes, preferences, sentiments, hates and intentions of those who have control and care over our destinies." The same point could be—and, in fact, has been—made about nineteenth-century French theater censorship, which, like caricature censorship, mirrored broader political currents in French society to an extraordinary degree, as the exact nature of what was banned from the stage revealed with extraordinary precision what the authorities feared most, and, just as those fears changed over time, so did the drama censorship. Thus as French drama censor Victor Hallays-Dabot wrote in his 1862 memoirs, "both the banned play and the approved scene reveal the public mentality and the mentality of the government on the day of the ban and the moment of authorization." More than a century later, retired French archivist Odile Krakovitch, the leading authority on nineteenth-century French drama censorship, conveyed the same concept in writing that the massive and well-preserved French censorship archives provide "a marvelous witness to the preoccupations, mentalities, reflexes, struggles, fears, consciences and knowledge of people of the past century" and document a "strange ballet, with the appearances and disappearances of censorship, entering and leaving at more or less regular intervals." She also noted that it is "both sad and funny" to owe "the censorship, the repression, the bureaucracy and the police for having collected and preserved such eloquent and definitive proofs of the reactions and mentalities of the public and the governments," as it is a "great contradiction" that censorship, "created to impose silence," and which sought "to extinguish" materials of which it disapproved, has "conserved for eternity the very texts and the written traces of spectacles otherwise destined by their very nature to disappear."[1]

As Krakovitch suggests, not only did the nature of theater censorship at any particular time reflect the precise fears of the authorities then in power, but its very presence or absence reflected the changing political tides of a deeply divided nation with an extremely turbulent history. The sharp divisions in nineteenth-century France, above all those related to class differences and struggles for power, led to repeated upheavals and changes in regimes that were invariably accompanied by major revisions in theater censorship policies, thereby providing extraordinarily revealing insights into the authorities' shifting thoughts and fears. Thus, the 1789 French Revolution, with its slogan of "liberty, equality and fraternity," led to the 1791 abolition of drama censorship, but a reaction against the perceived excesses of the Revolution saw a return of stage censorship in 1794, and the same "strange ballet" followed all three subsequent nineteenth-century French revolutions, each also proclaimed in the name of liberty. The theater censorship was abolished following the July Revolution of 1830 (which overthrew the repressive ancien régime Restoration Bourbon monarchy [1815–30] that had been imposed on France by the European powers in the wake of Napoleon's 1815 defeat), but it was reestablished during a general counterreaction in 1835; once more terminated in the wake of the 1848 February revolution, which dethroned King Louis-Philippe, a member of the cadet Orléans branch of the Bourbons who, representing above all the rising upper-middle class of industrialists and bankers, had soon betrayed the promises of freedom and social reform that had brought him to power in 1830; restored in 1850 following the June 1848 rebellion that reflected the perceived betrayal of the urban working class after the February revolution; and terminated yet again in the aftermath of the August 1870 revolution that overthrew Emperor Napoleon III (who had emerged as a dictator soon after his free election as president in late 1848), only to be restored once more in 1871 following the eruption and brutal suppression of the Paris Commune, another working-class rebellion. The drama censorship was finally abolished for good (at least in peacetime) only in 1906 when the French legislature defunded the censors (although without repealing the laws authorizing drama censorship).

The enormous amount of energy that French authorities devoted to nineteenth-century drama censorship reflected both the extraordinary importance of the stage during this era and the particular characteristics of the theater that made its power especially feared. In an era in which a large segment of the population was illiterate (53 percent of French military conscripts in 1832 and over 20 percent as late as 1872, figures unquestionably far higher for women and older men) and in which radio, television, movies, spectator sports, the internet, and other modern forms of diversion and communications were absent, the theater was a largely uncontested focus of public interest and mass entertainment in France. Moreover, it provided the quickest road to fame and fortune for writers, was arguably the primary form of mass education before the establishment of publicly supported elementary schools in 1833 and the rise of a mass press after 1840, and, at a time when freedom of assembly and association were strictly regulated, was the only public arena aside from churches in which regular mass gatherings were authorized. If this was also true in other nineteenth-century European countries, the theater was arguably even more important in France. Thus, theater historian F. W. J. Hemmings writes that the nineteenth-century French theater provided "to a greater degree probably than for any other nation, a unique focus of collective interest," engaging "the attention of every class of people throughout the length and breadth of the land," as "the one and only purveyor of excitement, amusement and pathos that the mass of the population knew," offering "the one and only escape from their usually laborious and lackluster existence."[2]

At least until after 1840, when increasing literacy and urbanization, along with technological advances and modern advertising, reduced newspaper prices and produced the first mass press, the theater—if economically off limits to the destitute (perhaps 50 percent of the total population during the 1830s)—was far more affordable than newspapers. Around 1830 the daily circulation of the entire Parisian press was only fifty thousand, partly because newspapers could only be purchased by annual subscription, at costs averaging about 10 percent of a typical worker's annual salary. By contrast, although the more prestigious state-subsidized "legitimate theaters" were too expensive for most workers, at the popular Parisian "boulevard" theaters (so called because many were located on the Boulevard du Temple, often termed the "Boulevard of Crime" because so many dramas performed there featured violence, robbers, etc.), the cheapest seats cost less than a loaf of bread, and regularly employed workers could afford to at least periodically attend. The French theater industry truly had extraordinary vitality and public appeal: during the nineteenth century an astounding 32,000 new plays were produced; at mid century the Parisian theater industry alone employed more than 10,000 people, with almost 35,000 seats available nightly; and, during the 1880s, about 500,000 Parisians attended the theater weekly. In the words of contemporary observer Pierre Giffard, "The population of Paris lives at the theater, of the theater and by the theater." Perhaps the clearest indicator of how important the theater—and its censorship—was regarded by the authorities is that episodically ruling kings and emperors personally intervened to examine particular plays.[3]

The theater was feared by the authorities not only because it was so popular and influential in French life, but also due to some of its particular characteristics: it was seen as far more powerful and potentially threatening than the written word, as it delivered its "message" in animated visual and oral form rather than in "cool" print, because, unlike the press, it was accessible to the especially feared often-illiterate masses, and because it addressed a public, collective audience rather than isolated individuals reading in private. That fears of the theater exceeded that of print and even of caricature (whose powerful visual imagery was comprehensible by the illiterate, but usually not viewed collectively), is evident from the fact that prior press censorship was never enforced in France after 1822 and that of caricature was abolished in 1881, but stage censorship continued until 1906 (subsequently, prior censorship was imposed on the new cinema, which was viewed as even more powerful, attractive, and affordable to the poor than print, drawings or theater). In 1831 French interior minister Camille Montavilet summarized the view of many governmental officials when he declared that the theater "acted as a magician on the audience: fascinating, entrancing, passionate and dangerous," adding that "among all the opportunities for public disorder the theater could produce the most."[4]

The especial fear of the stage as far more powerful than the written word was clearly articulated by French minister of justice Jean-Charles Persil in 1835, when he successfully urged legislators to reimpose prior censorship of theater and caricature (both of which had collapsed following the 1830 Revolution) on the grounds that these media were entirely different and far more dangerous than print, and therefore not covered by the 1830 constitutional charter's promises of the "right to publish" and that "censorship can never be reestablished." According to Persil:

> This ban on the reestablishment of the censorship only applies to the right to *publish* and have *printed one's opinions;* it is the [written] press which is placed under the guarantee of the Constitution, it is the free manifestation of *opinions* which cannot be repressed by preventive measures. But there the solicitude of the charter ends. It would clearly go beyond that goal if the charter were interpreted to accord the same protection to opinions converted into actions. Let an author be content to print his play, he will be subjected to no preventive measure; let the illustrator write his thought [in words], let him publish it in that form, and as in that manner he addresses only the *mind,* he will encounter no obstacle. It is in that sense that it was said that censorship could never be reestablished. But when opinions are converted into *acts* by the presentation of a play or the exhibit of a drawing, one addresses people gathered together, one speaks to their eyes. That is more than the expression of an opinion, that is a *deed, an action, a behavior,* with which ... the charter is not concerned.[5]

The French theater censor Victor Hallays-Dabot, in an 1862 book, made the same basic argument at great length in defending prior stage censorship:

> An electric current runs through the playhouse, passing from actor to spectator, inflaming them both with a sudden ardor and giving them an unexpected audacity. The public is like a group of children. Each of them by themselves is sweet, innocuous, sometimes fearful; but bring them together, and you are faced with a group that is bold and noisy, often wicked. The courage or rather the cowardice of anonymity is such a powerful force! ... Social theories of the most false and daring nature excite an audience who, in the emotion of the drama, cannot discern the lies from the portrayals and speeches which are presented to them. When thousands of spectators, swept along by the intoxication of the drama, are subjected to a fatal influence, when the reverberations of the scandal will create a disturbed public, what safeguard could society find in the slow and methodical march of the laws [i.e., post-production prosecution of a play]?

French socialist politician Louis Blanc agreed completely, writing in the 1840s:

> To permit a private person to act at on his own caprice upon the assembled audience by the seduction of the set, the interest of the drama, the beauty of

the women, the talent of the artists, the enchantment of the decoration and the lighting, that is to deliver the souls of the people as fodder to the first corrupter who comes along; that is to abandon to him the right to poison the sources of human intelligence. In such a country, in which the government would be unworthy of the name, the state could not renounce the moral direction of society by the theater without abdicating.[6]

Fear of the theater's potential subversive power was especially marked before the introduction of free primary education (for males) in 1833 in France, because the stage was widely considered one of the most important forms of mass education, above all for the lower classes. Thus, a Restoration (1815–30) defender of drama censorship declared that it was necessary to distinguish between "the right of theatrical presentation and the right to publish one's thoughts," with the former requiring "in the name of society" the "most serious and firm attention, care and surveillance" because in France the theater had "a social importance like nothing else." It was "among the most powerful means of public instruction," exercising a "real influence on general and private morals, on relationships between the sexes, within families and with our fellow man, as well as on the sentiments, prejudices, and opinions which spread among all classes, to which they could give birth or inflame." Similarly, according to one of the Restoration theater censors, the "people" obtained their "only instruction" from melodrama, as they "no longer go to church," but rather "believe in the theater, which is for them the only thing real," so that "a dramatic representation is for them like a course in morals." During the 1830–48 reign of King Louis-Philippe, theater inspectors were directed to report in great detail what they observed in theaters "in which the coarsest classes of people gather," since such venues had "become the only school in which the lower class of society goes to learn its lessons."[7]

From the standpoint of the authorities, not only was the theater a potentially dangerous venue for the spreading of subversion, but, unlike printed matter, which was perceived as primarily consumed in private by relatively educated people who would not be immediately affected even by subversive matter (and therefore, if a publication proved dangerous, there would be time to confiscate unsold copies before its effects were evident), drama was viewed as immediate and irremediable in its impact, posing the threat that the collective audience might be stirred to immediate action when exposed to seditious words or portrayals. Thus, French author Maxime du Camp wrote in 1875 that theater censorship was necessary because dramas were "attended by gatherings of people, subject to a kind of electric current which is communicated far more intensely than with a book or journal, which only acts upon isolated individuals." Similarly, in a 1789 newspaper article, ancien regime censor Jean-Baptiste-Antoine Suard characterized theatrical freedom as more dangerous than press freedom because "one reads a book on one's own, quietly, and communicates the impression it has made only in conversation with a few individuals," while plays addressed themselves "to the imagination and the senses; they can excite every passion, and the resulting impressions acquire an extraordinary energy from the simultaneous interaction of all the impressions received by a great multitude in concourse." The impact of subversive theater could apparently be instantaneous: according to a French prison director, "When they put on a bad drama, a number of young new criminals soon arrive at my prison." For decades censorship backers cited the widespread belief that the opera *La Muette de Portici* had incited the 1830 Belgian revolution, while censor Hallays-Dabot wrote in 1862 that plays that incited political protests in the 1840s had provided "a sort of dress rehearsal" for the 1848 revolution.[8]

The threat that the stage was perceived to pose because plays were presented to a collective audience reflected the indisputable fact that, especially before about 1850, theater disturbances were common, ranging from routine outbreaks of applause, hoots, and whistles, to throwing food or even furniture, and occasionally escalating into full-scale riots that sometimes required police or military intervention with sabers or bayonets. Thus, in October 1840 when a theater audience in the provincial town of Carpentras demanded that "La Marseillaise" be played between acts, thus preventing continuation of the play, thirty soldiers were called to clear the theater. Following an 1839 disturbance, author Théophile Gautier exclaimed that the theater should not become "a boxing ring; it's not nice at all to return home with a bloody nose and an eye all the colors of the rainbow." As even an extremely hostile account of the "absurdity" and "tyranny" of the Restoration theater censorship concedes, spectators "jumped at each turn of verse to find allusions to the [Napoleonic] empire or to the Bourbons," with the result that the "theater was always ready to be transformed into a field of battle." According to a study of the Restoration theater in Nantes, "disorders were ready to surface at any time" and the "continuous nature of the disruptions and disorderly behavior" demonstrated the "extent to which the theater was the principle site at which to express discontent and political opposition under the returned monarchy." Despite the frequency of such disorders and the fear the authorities had of seditious dramas, the theater was also seen as potentially distracting the discontented from even more politically threatening behavior. Thus, during the 1820s, the Nantes prefect declared that the "theater occupies the leisure-time of large number of young people, who, denied this distraction, would perhaps work themselves up to some reprehensible disorders," and the Marseilles city council described the stage as a gathering place for those "who without honest distraction could compromise public tranquility."[9]

Not only was the theater (and other media such as caricature perceived as especially accessible to lower-class audiences) particularly strictly surveilled, but, even *within* each media category, material that the authorities viewed as particularly targeted at the "dark masses" was often more highly controlled than that aimed at a more elite, educated, and upper-class audience. As John House notes in a study of the censorship of images in France in the 1860s, while the authorities were in general "particularly wary of the potency of visual experience, in the form of a print or a stage representation or a performance of a popular café-concert song," the "question of class—of determining what types of material should be permitted for which social groups—seems to have been the most fundamental concern." Thus, in 1829 the French interior minister instructed his subordinates, concerning the proposed circulation of Napoleonic imagery, that "in general, that which can be *permitted* without difficulty when it is a question of expensive engravings, or lithographs intended only to illustrate an important [i.e., expensive] work, would be dangerous and must be outlawed when these same subjects are reproduced in engravings and lithographs at a cheap price." The French police minister similarly declared in 1852 that drawings were among "the most dangerous … means employed to shake and destroy the sentiments of reserve and morality … so essential to conserve in the bosom of a well-ordered society," since "the worst page of a bad book requires some time to read and a certain degree of intelligence to understand," but the drawing "offers a sort of personification of the thought, it puts it in relief, it communicates it with movement and life, so as to thus present spontaneously, in a translation which *everyone* can understand, the most dangerous of all seductions, that of example."[10]

Not surprisingly, therefore, the severity of the theater censorship varied with the perceived class nature of the audience. As French theater censorship historian Krakovitch summarizes, "The more modest and popular the theater, the harsher the censors' judgments and the more numerous the required modifications." Thus, plays that might be approved for "legitimate" state-subsidized theaters typically patronized by the middle and upper classes were often barred from the popular stage, an audience differentiation that was in part cultural but largely purely economic. In the

1830s, for example, the cheapest seats at the Boulevard theaters typically cost only about 15–30 percent of the price of the least expensive seats in the "legitimate" theater; put another way, the typical Parisian worker would have to toil for about three hours to buy a cheap seat in a "popular" theater, but attending the opéra would cost him fifteen hours of labor. The censors' reports repeatedly contain phrases such as "this appears to us to contain passages which could be troublesome given the [working-class] theater for which this work is destined" and "there is reason to fear that, in [a theater] currently frequented by the working class, such a spectacle would only arouse [class] animosities." The censor's report for the 1822 play *Pauline Delorme* declared that its depiction of "theft, assassination, even arson, premeditated, openly carried out in a work whose characters come from the common people" should not be presented, especially to "those who habitually frequent the Boulevard theaters." Similarly, under King Louis-Philippe, an 1837 play about the death penalty, *La Mort en loterie,* intended for the popular Gâité, was banned because, according to the censors, "if reform ideas which attack one of our penal institutions are admissible in the sphere of politics and philosophy, they are out of place in a vaudeville intended for a Boulevard theater." During Napoleon III's reign, a censor wrote, concerning *King Lear,* that "its boldness could only be presented in an essentially literary venue, before an elite public," as "before the public of the Boulevard, it would be a spectacle whose philosophical import would not be understood but in which we fear only the degradation of royalty would be perceived."[11]

## The Goals of the Censorship

The theater censorship (as well as censorship of other media) was designed above all to uphold the existing political and social order, and especially to protect the existing political regime. Thus, historian Krakovitch notes that although the censorship varied in its exact application, "whether the censors based their actions on political, religious or moral grounds, they always acted on one and the same principle: the defense of the social class in power" and "respect for the established order." Not surprisingly then, the hero in Beaumarchais's text to Salieri's opera *Tarare* was changed from king to republican ruler to constitutional monarch as French regimes changed during the nineteenth century. Victor Hugo's 1829 play *Marion de Lorme* was personally banned by King Charles X because it unfavorably depicted the latter's long-dead ancestor Louis XIII, while Alfred de Musset's *Loren-*

*zaccio*, a play about Renaissance Italy, was forbidden in 1864 because, as the censor put it, "The discussion of the right to assassinate a sovereign whose crimes and iniquities, even including the murder of the prince by his parents, cry out for vengeance, ... is a dangerous spectacle to present to the public." Similar sensitivities led to frequent bans on material that was seen as mocking even low-level governmental officials or as inciting class conflict. Thus, during the 1850s, the censors rejected a play that portrayed a postman who neglected his official duties and insisted that a customs official who was mocked be transformed into a wine taster, apparently to avoid lowering public esteem for government officials. They also banned from Victor Séjour's play *Les Aventuriers* (1860) a line that stated, "if a rich man wants to go hunting or dancing, they roll out a carpet for him on the way lest he weary his feet."[12]

In general, the same censorship principles applied to spoken drama also applied to opera, and, in far harsher form (as discussed below), to café-concerts, which became a craze after 1850 especially appealing to the feared lower classes. Thus, during the Restoration, when all references to Napoleon were banned from plays, the same rule applied to opera. Gioachinno Rossini's 1826 *Le Siege de Corinthe*, a clearly supportive allusion to the contemporaneous Greek revolt against the Ottoman (Turkish) Empire, was approved only after six separate censors' reports, which resulted in attenuating its appeals to liberal sentiment; thus, "O fatherland!" had to be substituted for "Liberty!" in the libretto text reading, "Liberty! All our sons will rise us in your name." The uncertain political situation arising from the Greek revolt also led the censors to postpone action on another similarly themed opera, *Le dernier jour de Missolonghi*, but after the Turks were soundly defeated in the 1827 battle of Navarino, it was approved. During the July Monarchy numerous modifications were enforced upon the presentation of the opera *Blois, ou le 23 décembre, 1588*, about the assassination of the duc de Guise by King Henry III; among the phrases struck was "It is the people who designate [the king] and their voice is the voice of God!" A general ban on any representations of clergy and clerical regalia on stage after 1835 was applied equally to the opera: Gabriel Donizetti's 1843 production of *Dom Sébastien* was allowed only after all religious insignia were removed and the character of Dom Antonio was transformed from a priest into a royal advisor. The government of President Louis Napoleon Bonaparte (soon to proclaim himself Emperor Napoleon III) banned an 1852 opera treating the seventeenth-century Fronde uprising in France because the censors viewed any revolutionary themes as dangerous and particularly feared that the phrase "Aux armes!" might be carried to the streets. In 1867 Napoleon III's regime banned a duet of two gendarmes in Jacque Offenbach's operetta *Geneviève de Brabant* because, the censors declared, "We cannot have the gendarmerie held up to ridicule." The duet was ultimately approved on condition that the gendarmes were reduced in rank from corporal to sergeant (a rank non-existent in the gendarmerie). A planned 1887 performance of German composer Richard Wagner's *Lohengrin* was banned by a local prefect due to protests by those still embittered over Germany's defeat of France in the 1870–71 war, while a 1901 performance of Xavie Leroux's *Astarté* was so badly mutilated by censorship demands based on "moral" reasons that, according to historian Franck Hochleitner, a production that originally had "libertine taints became an insipid sermon to the glory of pure love."[13]

Although clearly the same basic principles that generally governed the theater censorship encompassed the opera, at times the censors used their blue pencils somewhat less ferociously with regard to "grand" opera (as opposed to operetta) than to the spoken drama. The clearest example of this differentiation occurred during Napoleon III's Second Empire, when Hugo's dramas were all banned from the regular stage between 1852 and 1867, yet several operas based on his interdicted plays were tolerated (i.e., Giuseppe Verdi's *Rigoletto*, based on *Le Roi S'Amuse*, and Gaetano Donizetti's *Lucrezia Borgia*, drawn from the play of the same name). The reason for this differential treatment appears to have been twofold: first, the audience for grand opera, both due to its extremely high price and other factors, largely excluded the poor; and secondly, the authorities felt (at least at times) that the music and staging of opera overwhelmed any subversive textual messages, unlike with spoken drama (although authorities in Italy appear to have adopted the opposite view, namely that stirring music and vivid staging added to the potential incitement of a libretto, making opera especially dangerous, particularly given the considerably broader popular appeal of opera in Italy as compared to France). Thus, in approving the 1853 staging of *Rigoletto*, the censors noted that, although the libretto "reproduces the basic plot of the [banned] drama, *Le roi s'amuse*," the transformation of French King Francis I into the "Duke of Mantua" in *Rigoletto* would "naturally make disappear the historical personages which have largely motivated the ban on the French play from which it is borrowed," and especially as the opera was in Italian, the libretto, "not at all designed to excite unfortunate passions," would become "an accessory to the music which dominates the work." In an 1869 report again barring *Le roi s'amuse*, the censors declared that *Rigoletto*, although presenting "the essential plot" of Hugo's play, "bleaches and camouflages its audacity due to the needs of the special world to which it addresses itself, since ultimately the music's importance absorbs everything."[14]

According to French scholar and leading operetta authority Jean-Claude Yon, operetta, an art form developed after 1850 and made famous by Jacques Offenbach, was "much more surveilled" by the censors than was "grand" opera, because the former's audience was much larger for economic and other reasons. Although the relatively high price of opera tickets severely restricted the ability of the poor to attend, the authorities' fears about the potentially subversive romantic-democratic appeal of opera undoubtedly reflected some very real incidents in nineteenth-century French history: two 1800 assassination plots against Napoleon I (one of which left 80 people killed or wounded) were coordinated with his visits to the opera; in 1820 the duc de Berry, heir to the throne, was assassinated at the Paris Opéra (after which the authorities tore down the theater building); and in 1858 Napoleon III was the target of a bomb explosion that killed or wounded over 150 people while he was en route to hear Rossini's opera *William Tell*, which centers on Swiss resistance to medieval Habsburg oppression. In July 1830 the hero's cry of "Independence or Death" during a *William Tell* rehearsal was taken up by everyone in the theater: the audience, musicians, stagehands, and even soldiers on guard rushed into the streets and joined in the ongoing revolt that overthrew King Charles X.[15]

According to an analysis of over two hundred censorship and prosecutorial decisions involving plays, newspapers, and novels undertaken by four different regimes between 1815 and 1870, about 55 percent of such actions were based on perceived challenges to existing political/social authority; in almost all other cases, challenge to the "moral order" was cited. Sensitivity to potentially "morally" objectionable material (i.e., pornography) and to "antireligious" views (which usually meant either generally anti-clerical or specifically anti-Catholic opinions) varied considerably, but the censors' antennas were always especially attuned to political materials, and above all to direct political attacks on sitting regimes. Napoleon I expressed this attitude with great bluntness when he declared, with regard to public entertainment, "Let the people amuse themselves, let them dance, so long as they keep their noses out of government affairs." Under the Second Empire (1852–70) of his nephew, Napoleon III, officials were directed on 30 December 1852 to eliminate "attacks against the principle of authority, against religion, the family, the courts, the army, in a word against the institutions upon which society rests," and especially to "completely avoid" all scenes "imprinted with a revolutionary spirit," as well as "all forms of factionalism, based on the principle that the theater must be a place of repose and of distraction and not an overt arena of political passions." Also included in this directive was a ban on plays that presented "antagonism between the lower and upper classes in which the latter are invariably sacrificed."[16]

Despite such general guidance, it was impossible to provide the censors with rules that applied such broad principles to all potential scripts, so particular censorship decisions inevitably were often arbitrary and/or inconsistent. Thus, theater censor Jacques-Louis Florent, who served three successive regimes, testified in 1849 that the censors "never received any special instructions" and therefore,

> We have no other guide than our conscience. In seeing a scabrous passage, we would ask ourselves, "Would we take our wife and daughters to a theater to hear such things?". ... In seeing passages with a political or social significance we asked ourselves, "Does that aim at causing the different classes to rise up against each other, to excite poor against the rich, to excite to disorder?" We asked ourselves in principle if it was possible to allow the ridicule on the stage of the institutions of the country, and especially those who maintain order most effectively ... and expose them to the laughter and mockery of the crowd. We had no trouble in answering no. ... As for details and allusions, we banned that which seemed to us to threaten public tranquility and the nation's institutions.[17]

## Censorship Mechanics

Nineteenth-century French authorities devoted truly amazing amounts of time and energy to restricting expression. Whenever prior censorship was enforced, specialized censors implemented the regulations as they applied to different media. Before 1830 the censors were often fairly well-known men of letters. For example, during the Restoration, André-Polydore Alissan de Chazet, a former newspaper editor, founder of the Société des Bonnes Lettres and author of over 150 plays, served as censor. However, especially after 1830 the censors increasingly became faceless bureaucrats who, generally lacking any formal guidance, made support for their masters their prime directive, and political reliability rather than literary judgment became the key criterion for their appointment and retention. Several censors had no difficulty serving first Napoleon I and then his successor Louis XVIII; similarly, several, such as Florent, who served King Louis-Philippe, unhesitatingly later took up their blue pencils for Napoleon III. Despite the scorn and bitterness often heaped on them, their posts were often highly sought, as they were viewed as well-paid, generally secure jobs with considerable power, not to mention a variety of fringe benefits, including free theater tickets, deference from actors and directors, and perhaps even "other signs of friendship on the part of actresses."[18]

The Parisian theater censorship (which regulated drama, operas, and drinking establishments that presented songs or other popular entertainment) was controlled by a board of (typically four or five) censors under the jurisdiction of the Bureau of Theaters, which was supervised at various times by the ministries of state, interior, fine arts, and education (and, under Napoleon III, the imperial household ministry). Other individuals acting under the censors' direction, known as theater examiners, attended dress rehearsals and occasional regular performances in order, as one none-too-friendly account of the Restoration censorship puts it, "to clean one last time the phrases clothed with the approval of the censors, to assure themselves that the actors conformed to these suppressions, to approve of the costumes, the actors and the extras, to measure with the eye the length of the dancers' skirts, [and] to warn if they discovered that acts visibly hostile—anti-monarchical, revolutionary—could take birth from the combination of certain colors." In the departments, censorship decisions were ultimately made by the prefects, who could ban plays approved in Paris, but could not approve those that had been forbidden in the capital; in the unusual circumstances of plays proposed for the departments without first being examined in Paris, the prefects were on their own. Thus, in a 29 October 1850 letter to the prefects, the interior minister advised that they could forbid plays approved in Paris if "you believe that they could prove dangerous in your department," citing the example of Giacomo Meyerbeer's extremely popular opera *Les Huguenots,* about religious divisions in medieval France; although approved by the Parisian censors once the royal figure of Catherine de Médicis had been removed and other material perceived as denigrating royalty had been attenuated, the minister pointed out that it had been forbidden "where religious quarrels have left unhappy memories which could be revived" (i.e., in towns, such as Nimes, with significant Protestant populations). Adverse decisions by the drama censors could not be appealed to the courts, but usually could be administratively appealed to the head of the appropriate ministry. Ministers frequently intervened with regard to highly politically sensitive plays, and if a dramatist was famous enough or had the right connections, it was sometimes possible to have plays personally considered by the monarch. Censorship violations could, and did, lead to severe reprisals: in the department of Vaucluse a theater director was jailed for a month and fined Fr 1,000 for presenting an unauthorized play.[19]

Considerable variation in the censorship's day-to-day operation occurred, depending on the venue involved, individual censor's personalities, and, sometimes, the author's renown, since banning plays by leading dramatists was often highly publicized and embarrassing for the regime (thus, Louis-Philippe's censors generally sought to avoid angering the esteemed author Alexander Dumas père (Sr.) sometimes approving plays by him that probably would have been banned if written by an unknown author; on several occasions they even bribed him into withdrawing plays). Theater directors were required to submit scripts two weeks before a performance was planned, and the censors could accept a drama as submitted, forbid it entirely, or allow it with modifications. The censors often "negotiated" changes in scripts with the authors or theater managers and, until 1866, produced detailed written explanations of their decisions (thus providing a treasure trove for subsequent historians, much as secret police reports often provide the most detailed information about political dissidents available to future scholars). Since rehearsals and sets were typically well advanced by the time the censors acted, theater managers were effectively forced by the looming threat of financial disaster to accept and implement the censors' demands within forty-eight hours (otherwise the dress rehearsal would have to be postponed). Thus, as historian Krakovitch notes, the censors' "requests" amounted to "blackmail" for "playwrights and especially for directors," as the latter, typically financially stressed, exerted "all possible pressure on recalcitrant authors to rapidly comply" to avoid losing their production costs. Nonetheless, theater censor Hallays-Dabot maintained that at meetings between the censors and the censored the former merely "explained sincerely their objections and the others defended their thoughts!"[20]

In some celebrated cases the censors reversed their original positions or were overruled by their superiors, leading to widespread rumors that personal connections or bribes, including the sexual favors of actresses, were involved. In perhaps the most notorious such case, *La Dame aux Camélias* by Alexander Dumas fils (Jr.), the story of a courtesan, was banned in 1849 as offensive to public morality, but approved in 1851 after Dumas' friend, the duc de Morny, became interior minister. Morny simultaneously banned Honoré de Balzac's *Meracadet*, a previously approved play satirizing financial speculators, apparently reasoning, in one historian's sarcastic account, that financiers "who render the state no small service, have a right to be shielded from the darts of impertinent satirists; whereas no offense is given to any influential segment of the community by revealing that young men about town habitually frequent the houses of loose women."[21]

Until 1864, stage censorship was accompanied by the requirement that all theaters and their directors receive licenses from the state, which were both costly and normally restricted the types of plays that could be legally presented. Under the licensing rules in Paris, only the handful of state-subsidized theaters such as the Comédie-Française and the Académie de Musique (the Opéra) could legally perform "legitimate" stage works such as "serious" comedies, tragedies, and opera, while the popular theaters could officially present only pantomimes, vaudevilles, melodramas, and short skits and songs that could not easily encompass serious political critiques (although in practice such restrictions were enforced with increasing laxity after about 1830 and, as French opera historian Mark Everist notes, effectively had "unraveled" even before being abolished in 1864). Thus, when the Funambules Theater opened in 1816 it was restricted to "acrobatic displays," so when it switched to the pantomimes for which it became famous, actors were forced to enter on a tight rope that was permanently stretched across the stage; the *Almanac of Spectacles of 1822* noted that "the leading man is forbidden to take part in the action and to concern himself with affairs of the heart without having first performed a few leaps and done some cartwheels." The Panorama-Dramatique was allowed to present dramas, vaudevilles, and comedies in 1819, but only if no more than two actors appeared together on stage, a restriction that was circumvented through the use of quick-change artists and life-size marionettes, whose lines were spoken from the wings. The Pantheon Theater's 1834 license restricted it to "small comedies of manners and popular vaudeville, to the exclusion of all serious plays and especially of all political allusions." To get around such restrictions, theaters sometimes effectively invented new "genres," such as "opera de genre," "operetta," and "vaudeville avec airs nouveaux," which sometimes suspiciously resembled genres supposedly exclusively reserved for the state theaters. In addition to supposedly abiding by genre restrictions, private theater directors also had to furnish so-called "security bonds." In 1846, for example, the director of the Vaudeville Theater had to deposit Fr 300,000, the equivalent of over $60,000 in contemporary American currency. Theoretically, the licensing and bond requirements simply insured that theaters were reputable and had sufficient financial backing to meet their obligations to the state, the public, and their employees, and served as guarantees against any future fines for transgressing theatrical regulations. In practice, they allowed the authorities to ensure that theater owners were politically reliable, as they had to be reasonably wealthy and license applications had to be accompanied by letters from referees guaranteeing his (licensees were by law always male) morals, "public spiritedness," and "loyalty to the regime." Even after licenses were approved, theater owners remained subject to constant police surveillance and could have their licenses revoked at any time for virtually any reason; thus, typically, the license of the Petit Théâtre des Bouffes-Parisiens obtained in 1855 (with a Fr 10,000 caution bond) stated that its license could be withdrawn, if "by reasons of circumstances that the Minister of State reserves to determine, the [theater] director ceases to merit the confidence of the administration." The licensing and genre restriction requirements for theaters (although not for café-concerts) were finally lifted in 1864, when Napoleon III decreed that henceforth anyone (male) could open a stage, and "dramatic works of all types" could be "represented in all the theaters."[22]

## The History of French Theater Censorship

### Early French Theater Censorship to 1814

Embryonic attempts to regulate French theatrical performances date to 1398, with sporadic attempts to impose prior censorship on plays thereafter, at least partly because, as was also often the case elsewhere in Europe, the theater was widely seen as a den of inequity and vice. Thus, a French writer complained in 1588 that the stage was leading to the "ruin of families of poor artisans, who fill the cheap seats two hours before the performance, passing their time in lewd ways, playing cards and dice, publicly eating and drinking in a manner which leads to fights and quarrels." In 1666 the French writer Pierre Nicole termed playwrights "public poisoners." In 1641 King Louis XIII forbade representations of "all dishonest actions, all lascivious words and double entendres which could affect the honest public." Systematic French theater censorship began in 1701, when Louis XIV ordered that all proposed plays be submitted to the Paris police to ensure their conformance to standards of "the highest purity." Subsequently, Pierre Beaumarchais famously battled for over five years before finally gaining permission to stage *The Marriage of Figaro* in 1784 (it was originally personally rejected by King Louis XVI, who declared, "The Bastille would have to be destroyed before the presentation of this play could be anything but a dangerous folly"). Perhaps the difficulty partly stemmed from one of Figaro's remarks in the play: "They all tell me that if in my writings I mention neither the government, nor public worship, nor politics, nor morals, nor people in office, nor influential corporations, nor the opera, nor the other theaters, nor anyone who has aught to do with anything, I may print anything freely, subject to the approval of two or three censors."[23]

Amid the turmoil of the 1789 French Revolution, which proclaimed "liberty" as one of its most basic principles, theater censorship, including the existing requirement that all theaters be licensed and restrict their productions to approved genres, was abolished in early 1791. The number of Parisian theaters immediately leapt from ten in 1789 to thirty-five by 1792, leading one observer to lament, "If this craze goes on, there will soon be one theater in every street, one dramatist in every house, one musician in every cellar and one actor in every garret." The post-1792 period witnessed a return to strict controls on freedom of expression as France was convulsed by continual internal strife and war with its neighbors. Thus, major press crackdowns in 1791–94 and 1797 led to the suppression of forty-four Paris newspapers in the latter year alone; numerous journalists (almost 20 percent of those active in Paris), as well as at least two caricaturists, were executed during the 1793–94 Reign of Terror. Freedom of the stage also quickly eroded under these conditions; all references to monarchs and aristocrats soon disappeared from the theaters, to be replaced by pro-republican propaganda pieces. In 1794 theater censorship was officially reimposed and enforced with extreme harshness: in one three-month period, 33 out of 151 plays submitted were rejected and 25 others were mutilated.[24]

The end of the Reign of Terror in 1794 was followed by a modest relaxation of censorship controls (punctuated by occasional severe crackdowns), but Napoleon reintroduced the whole panoply of ancien régime restrictions after seizing power in 1799, while enforcing them with considerably more bureaucratic efficiency than the Bourbon kings had ever mustered. He reduced the Parisian press from 72 newspapers to 4, closed two-thirds of the city's printshops, and reduced the number of Parisian theaters from 33 to 8. By 1810–11 he reintroduced or continued virtually all pre-1789 censorship controls, including licensing of printers, bookshops, and theaters, prior censorship of drama and the press, and genre restrictions for theaters. Napoleon personally supervised a rigid theater censorship, for example completely banning all references to the deposed Bourbons as well as to other threatening topics such as the punishment of tyrants and (when he decided to leave his wife Josephine) divorce.[25]

## The Restoration, 1814–30

The restored Bourbon monarchy of 1814–30 largely continued that dynasty's past censorship practices. Theater censorship and licensing were continued, and, before its 1830 demise, the Restoration regime enforced theater censorship in a spirit of extraordinary pettiness, capriciousness, and narrow-mindedness. As two specialists note, the drama censorship "furnished a kind of caricature of the state of the governmental soul, with its preoccupations and its fears" and resulted in a theater of "mediocrity" and "indisputable poverty." Although, according to data from an 1891 legislative inquiry, only two dozen plays were forbidden outright during the Restoration, many others suffered forced modifications: the 7 December 1824 Paris newspaper *Le Globe* complained that the theater censors had "done such a superb job that no trace of us will remain to satisfy the curiosity of our successors." Of 50 plays (at least for which censorship reports survive) intended for a leading "legitimate" theater, the Comedie-Française, only 11 were authorized as submitted, another 11 were forbidden, and 28 were approved with changes (some quite minor). The result was that gifted dramatists such as Casimir Bonjour simply avoided writing anything with political implications, since, as historian Neil Arvin notes, "examples of the unpleasant results of ridiculing or attacking the regime were frequent enough to give pause to any but the most public-spirited writer."[26]

Theater censorship historian Krakovitch notes that the "great preoccupation" of the Restoration censorship was the treatment of royalty and "the legitimacy of royal power," which was "extreme to the point of obsession." Strict surveillance of the theaters was viewed as promising some positive benefits rather than only preventing the communication of subversion: according to an 18 March 1816 interior ministry circular, a "well-directed" theater offered the "most noble enjoyment for the educated class of society," could spread "healthy maxims and useful viewpoints," and had often been found by local authorities to be a "means of occupying, during the leisure hours, a restless population, which, left to itself, could become dangerous." In fact, the theaters often became the site of anti-government demonstrations, particularly during the 1814–30 reign of Charles X, no doubt partly because few other venues for protest existed; historian Denise Davidson writes that by the mid 1820s, the theater had "become *the* venue in which to express criticism of the Bourbon regime," since "theaters and other 'cultural' gatherings were the only places available to express oppositional political views."[27]

The censors of Louis XVIII (ruled 1815–24) forbade all theatrical allusions to Napoleon or even the sites of his great victories (such as Marengo and Austerlitz), as well as to virtually any events in French history between 1789 and 1815 or even to Enlightenment authors such as Rousseau and Voltaire. Ever sensitive to perceived attacks on the monarchy and nobility, the censors especially frowned on any dramas treating royalty, even in the distant past and in foreign countries; they declared that "the monarchy has already lost too much of its remote magic without playwrights stripping it of the remnants of its dignity" and warned against plays "infested" with the "spirit of revolt" or the "dangerous taste of democracy." They even banned one play that had the son of a count marrying the daughter of a shopkeeper (it was suggested that the shopkeeper "get rich and become a great businessman" since then "at least, there would not be a misalliance"). The Danish king and queen in *Hamlet* became a "duke and duchess" (thus, Hamlet could not express hope to "catch the conscience of the king") and the clown's remarks about class distinctions in disposing bodies of suicides was deleted from the gravedigger's scene.[28]

Under Charles X, attacks upon his close alliance with the Catholic Church led to a complete ban on any dramatic depiction of religious officials, rites, and costumes, all references to suicide or depictions of death on stage, and the censoring of an entire religious vocabulary, including "mass," "religion," "Christian charity," "Jesuit," and even "heaven bless you." The censors even insisted that a character in an 1827 comedy express passion for his mistress by offering her "centuries" rather than "eternities" of celestial happiness in order to possess her "for a moment on earth." The strict ban on Napoleonic references and a strong suspicion of all plays portraying former monarchs continued: in 1828 one of the early dramas by Alexander Dumas père, *Henri III et sa cour*, about the sixteenth-century French king, was scrubbed clean of anti-monarchial references before it was approved. Shortly before the king was overthrown by an 1830 popular revolt following years of growing general unrest, Victor Hugo's *Marion de Lorme*, about the seventeenth-century King Louis XIII, was banned because, the interior minister told Hugo, "people will see Charles X in it" and "this is not the time to expose the king to public laughter and insults." Hugo emerged a popular hero by revealing that he had rejected a royal offer, apparently designed to silence him, to triple the pension he had been receiving as a distinguished writer since 1822; he declared, "I have only asked that my play be presented. I ask nothing else."[29]

In the late 1820s the regime's highly differential handling of two works which were both based on the same mid–seventeenth-century Neapolitan revolt against Spanish rule was highly revealing both of the government's mentality and of the self-censorship that the official censorship often evoked among writers and composers. These two works were *Massaniello,* with music by Michele Carafa and words by A. Lafortelle and Charles Moreau, which opened at the Opéra-Comique in late 1827, and *La Muette de Portici,* with text by Eugéne Scribe and music by Daniel Auber, which premiered at the Paris Opéra in early 1829. The original text of *Masaniello* conveyed a real sense of revolutionary spirit among the ordinary Neapolitan fishermen who led the uprising, which was triggered by resistance to Spanish rule, and especially by opposition to new taxes. Before approving *Masaniello,* the censors required virtually a complete rewrite of the libretto, involving six separate censorship evaluations stretching over four months, and ultimately the personal authorization of King Charles X, with the result, as theater historian Olivier Bara has noted, that its "essential political content was obliterated" and a "fundamentally subversive" script was "reoriented towards a discourse overtly counter-revolutionary." No doubt learning from this experience, in contrast, the Scribe-Auber version (which was submitted to the censors in 1827, about two months after they had begun to dismantle *Masaniello*) was centered not on popular grievances, but rather upon fisherman Masaniello's desire to avenge the seduction of his deaf sister, Fanella ("*la meutte*") by a Spanish official. With virtually all revolutionary implications of the opera removed in advance, the censors approved *Muette* virtually intact, requiring only the striking of a few phrases, including one line that declared, "it is necessary to arm the people," and a scene with a choir repetitively singing, "the people are master." In general, the censors praised Scribe's libretto, especially because "the contestation of legitimate authority, the popular tumult" had been "forgotten or blended into the interest inspired" by the wronged Fanella, "the character of the fierce Masaniello" had been "softened," and "the people of Naples only rise up against this foreign [Spanish] domination" rather than against taxes or other grievances that might allude to French domestic politics. Nonetheless, *Muette* aroused in France and elsewhere considerable liberal-nationalist-oppositionist sentiment; it was originally banned in Brussels and in German cities near the French frontier, and after it was finally performed in Brussels on 25 August 1830, it was widely, if probably incorrectly, perceived as triggering the successful revolution against Dutch rule that led to Belgian independence. But perhaps at least some French elites had a premonition triggered by *Muette:* supposedly the future French King Louis-Philippe (who would come to power in the July 1830 revolutionary overthrow of Charles X), upon attending *Muette's* February 1829 Paris opening, commented, "We are dancing on a volcano," a reference to the opera's famous climax, in which Fanella throws herself into the exploding Vesusius.[30]

## The July Monarchy, 1830–48

Following the 1830 July Revolution, among the first acts of the new king, Louis-Philippe of the house of Orléans, were the annulment of all press convictions and the proclamation of a constitution that declared that "censorship can never be reestablished." This provision was generally interpreted as ending censorship of all media, including theater and caricature, as well as terminating security bond and licensing requirements for newspapers and theaters. However, that the basic orientation of the ruling class had changed little was clearly indicated by the absurdly minute 1831 legislative expansion of the wealth-based suffrage, which increased those enfranchised from 0.3 percent to 0.5 percent of the population. Rising urbanization and literacy rates combined with the hopes raised by the July Revolution to massively increase public interest in news and politics, reflected by an explosion of newspapers, reading clubs, literary societies, libraries, and bookstores. Between 1830 and 1837 the number of Parisian dailies jumped from about ten to over seventy, and their combined daily circulation quadrupled from about 60,000 to over 275,000. Despite a rising tide of urban poverty, the regime turned its back on the rising clamor for meaningful social reform; the new king's attitude was symbolized by his answer, shortly after the revolution, to one of his ministers, who chided him for joining crowds singing "The Marseillaise": "Do not concern yourself, Minister. I stopped saying the words long ago." In response to the desperate messages conveyed by a series of riots, strikes, insurrections, and assassination attempts against the king during 1830–35, the regime answered primarily with waves of political arrests and growing restrictions on freedom of assembly, association, and expression.[31]

The 1830 collapse of caricature and drama censorship spawned an efflorescence of drawings and plays that could not have been produced during the previous fifteen years: Victor Hugo wrote that "the plays that the Restoration censorship had buried alive broke out of the coffin and they scattered noisily over the theaters of Paris," while historian Krakovitch wrote in 1992 that "it is difficult today to comprehend the impact of the theater and the enthusiasm of the Parisian populace" once the stage was freed from all restrictions, as the public not only mobbed theaters seeking out previously banned material but swarmed bookstores to purchase play scripts. Among the most popular dramatic themes were paeans to Napoleon and the French Revolution, bitter attacks on the Catholic Church and the fallen Bourbons, portrayals of class exploitation and social injustice, and, increasingly, embittered attacks on the new regime, in which money and business increasingly dominated politics, culture, and society. Within months of the July Revolution, three different plays entitled "The Barricades of 1830" celebrated the popular uprising that ushered in the new regime, which quickly began considering how to restore theater censorship and instituted a backdoor version of it by seizing on an obscure 1806 law that it claimed authorized the closure of any play (after performances had begun) that threatened public order. This law was invoked over twenty times between 1831 and 1835, almost always to ban politically sensitive plays, including dramas viewed as attacking the royal family, inciting to revolt, or alluding to censorship or sensitive foreign developments (although violently anti-clerical plays and bitter social satires were left untouched). For example, Félix Pyat's 1832 *Les Romans chez eux* was suppressed after one performance, apparently because its reference to the Roman emperor Claudius as "big, fat and stupid" was viewed as an allusion to Louis-Philippe.

The 1806 law was most infamously invoked in 1832 to shut down Hugo's *Le Roi s'amuse* (1832), which depicted the sixteenth-century French King Francis I in a highly unflattering light, at the prestigious Comédie-Française. Such closures—often imposed absent any demonstrated threat to the peace—menaced theaters with ruin, as the costs of hiring actors, rehearsals, publicity, costuming, and sets had already been undertaken. Their owners therefore increasingly succumbed to governmental pressure to "voluntarily" submit advance scripts, an idea first advanced in January 1831 and officially "suggested" in a July 1834 letter to theater directors: "You can avoid all problems by submitting your manuscripts in advance to the Fine Arts Ministry. Plays not submitted will be stopped, purely and simply, if by their contents they merit the application of the [1806] decree and you will only have yourself to blame for the loss resulting from the costs of staging a production which has become useless." Hugo responded to the ban on *Le Roi s'amuse* by (unsuccessfully) suing the Comédie-Française for breach of contract, winning new fame by declaring (with considerable prescience, as he was forced into exile twenty years later by Napoleon III and civil liberties were suspended in France following 1848 and 1871 workers' revolts and Napoleon's late 1851 coup that overthrew the Second Republic): "Today, my freedom as a poet is taken by the censor; tomorrow my freedom as a citizen will be taken by a policeman. Today, I am banished from the theater; tomorrow, I shall be banished from the land. Today, I am gagged; tomorrow I shall be deported. Today, a state of siege exists in literature; tomorrow, it will exist in the city."[32]

Alarmed by a 70 percent jury acquittal rate in political cases and the growing boldness of written, drawn, and theatrical criticisms of the regime—characterized by the duc de Broglie in 1835 as having turned the stage into a "school of debauchery, a school of crimes"—Louis-Philippe seized upon a gruesome failed assassination attempt (directed at him while he was reviewing troops in the Boulevard du Temple theater district on 28 July 1835) to quickly shepherd through a compliant legislature the notoriously repressive "September Laws" of 1835, which one historian has termed so drastic that they amounted to a "change of regime." The legislation was endorsed by almost a two-thirds majority with virtually no vigorous opposition; deputy and famous poet Alphonse de Lamartine declared that the theater had "failed in its mission," prostituting "itself to money and to the low instincts of the populace," and becoming a "place of evil affairs" that every night exuded "vice, insanity and crime."[33]

The September Laws reimposed prior theater and caricature censorship along with the licensing requirement for theaters; increased the security deposit required of Paris dailies from Fr 2,400 to the fantastic level of Fr 100,000; created a vast new web of press violations and drastically increased fines for such press offences as "insulting" the king, holding him responsible for governmental acts, or "expressing the wish, the hope or the threat of the destruction of the constitutional monarchical order"; made it far easier to obtain press convictions by removing some cases from juries and reducing the required jury majority in all others; and banned newspaper accounts of press trials, the publication of jury members' names, and public subscriptions to pay press fines, techniques that had been widely and effectively used to embarrass the regime and thwart press prosecutions.

The September Laws completely changed the rules regarding the stage by reimposing prior censorship. Of 8,330 plays submitted between 1835 and 1847, only 204 (2.4 percent) were completely forbidden, and changes were formally required to another 500 (about 6 percent); however, in a very large number of additional cases, the censors seem to have informally successfully demanded changes, as is suggested by a more-detailed study of plays submitted by the Comedie-Française: of 107 plays decided upon by the censors (another 14 were referred to their supervising minister), 11 (10 percent) were banned outright, 43 (40 percent) were approved only with changes, and 53 (50 percent) were cleared as written. In 15 cases, most notoriously Balzac's *Vautrin,* plays that were originally approved were banned following their presentation. Along with official theaters, drinking and other popular establishments that presented informal entertainment were also subject to careful supervision. In Paris, where the spontaneous singing of patriotic songs as expressions of political protest became frequent in the theaters after 1835, over five hundred *goguettes* (meeting places and bars that featured group singing) were closed in 1836. In 1847 the interior minister directed his officials to limit authorizations of songs and music so that sponsoring establishments "will in the future present only romances or ditties" rather than parodies or political allusions.[34]

Political allusions to the current regime were cited as the reason for censorship modifications in 25 percent of censored dramas. Other types of political allusions accounted for another 20 percent, moral objections were cited in about one-third of the cases, and religious allusions accounted for the remaining 20 percent. A number of dramas that had been popular before 1835 were banned, notably plays featuring or even vaguely referring to "Robert Macaire," a stage character whom the great actor Frederick Lemaître had made famous in such plays as *Robert Macaire* and *l'Auberge des Adrets* by brutally satirizing the bourgeoisie, whose often unscrupulous ascendancy was so marked an aspect of the era. As Lemaître biographer Robert Baldick notes, Macaire "revealed by his example how greed and graft flourished in France under the mask of philanthropy and respectability." Censors were especially alert for any criticisms or suggestions of conspiracies against the king, the regime, and its functionaries, including legislators, prefects, judges, and notaries, as well as against past kings (especially if such acts were depicted in a favorable light or as motivated by ideological beliefs, rather than by individual desires for power). As theater historian Louis Allard writes, "like Caesar's wife, the virtue of a minister was sheltered from suspicion." The censors also banned works for directly inciting class conflict, advocating republicanism, or criticizing the concept of royalty, even if they centered on the French Revolution or the very 1830 revolution that enthroned Louis-Philippe. The censors asked with regard to *Les Trois Mousquetaires* by Alexandre Dumas père, proposed for 1845 presentation at a Boulevard theater, "Would it not be troublesome for such a subject, already presented at the Odeon [one of the 'respectable' theaters], to be presented at a stage especially frequented by the working class?" They eventually approved it, but only with the excision of the remarks of English King Charles I, facing execution, in which he asks his son to swear to let himself be crowned "only if you have a legitimate right to the crown, because otherwise, one day they will take both head and crown." Similarly, plays touching on the pre-Napoleonic period of the French Revolution were generally viewed as unsuitable for popular theaters, although they were sometimes authorized for venues primarily patronized by the middle and upper classes. The regime could never decide whether stirring up nationalist sentiments associated with Napoleon would strengthen or undermine their authority: references to him were "temporarily" banned from the stage in 1835 and again in 1840, but generally tolerated in 1839 and after 1842 (the regime also banned Napoleon's *living* relatives from visiting France, yet transferred his *remains* from St. Helena to Paris in 1840 in a widely publicized reburial).[35]

Among the victims of moral and religious censorship after 1835 were scores of plays with material viewed as violating middle-class norms, including (especially in plays destined for the popular theaters) references to suicide, rape, prostitution, incest, convicts, prisons, nudity, illegitimacy, impotency, drunkenness, and, especially, adultery. Also banned were depictions of religious characters, settings, and insignia, including (especially following an unequivocal ministerial decree of 1844) virtually any scenes portraying convents, churches, cemeteries, tombs, and even the cross. Victor Hugo's *Notre Dame de Paris* was forbidden because (among other reasons) of the repulsive nature of its central character, the priest Claude Frollo. Such religious bans caused severe problems for operas, which often heavily dealt with clerical characters or themes: Eugène Scribe's *La Favorite* was forbidden, since, the censors maintained, "one cannot tolerate in the theater an amorous priest who detests the vows he has taken, seducing a young girl, making her pregnant and clasping his child in his arms." Eugène Sue's 1840 *Les Pontons Anglais* was barred for diplomatic reasons, as the censors feared it would excite "hatred against the English" (it was approved after the English were transformed into Spaniards, who counted relatively little in European politics). Similarly, in Ludovic Halevy's 1843 opera *Charles VI*, the cry "War to the English!" was changed to "War to the tyrants!"[36]

Despite such bans, the July Monarchy's theater censorship was generally never quite as petty or pigheaded as that of the Restoration, and especially with regard to socially conscious dramas, it never approached the sternness of the subsequent Second Empire. Even after 1835, numerous plays were allowed that focused on social injustice and indirectly challenged the entire foundations of society, of which perhaps the most notorious were Sue's *Les Mystères de Paris* (although it was approved only after severe modifications demanded by the censors and ministerial intervention), *La Tour de Nesle* by Dumas père, and Félix Pyat's *Le Chiffonnier de Paris*. Regarding such plays, theater censor Hallays-Dabot complained in an 1862 book that even after 1835 "the popular theaters propagated an unhealthy and pernicious literature based exclusively on social antagonism against which the censorship unfortunately could not erect a strong enough barrier." The September Laws had promised subsequent legislation that would spell out the principles to be applied by the censors, but none was ever submitted; however, the upper chamber endorsed drama censorship in principle by 94 to 6 in 1843.[37]

## The Second Republic, 1848–52

In February 1848 Louis-Philippe was overthrown by a popular uprising partly provoked by the regime's incessant repression. As in 1830, among the first acts of the succeeding (now republican) government was to free political prisoners and abolish most restrictions on the press and the theater, including abrogating (on 6 March 1848) the September Laws, as well as ending newspaper taxes and security bonds. This action followed a 5 March 1848 convocation of about one hundred playwrights and composers, at which suppression of licensing and caution bonds was demanded along with an end to theater censorship. Subsequently, over four hundred (often ephemeral) newspapers sprouted overnight, scores of new caricature journals emerged, and the newly freed theater was rejuvenated with the reappearance of *Robert Macaire* and other banned works. However, as in 1830, the new regime soon cracked down on the press, especially after the "red scare" that ensued following the brutal suppression of the Paris workers' 1848 "June Days" insurrection, with security deposits reintroduced in August 1848 and earlier press offenses reenacted with minor changes (such as now banning attacks against republican institutions).

Three separate inquiries were quickly launched concerning regulation of the theater, one by the Council of State, another by the interior ministry, and a third by the legislative assembly. During the most extensive of these inquiries, that of the Council of State, thirty-two playwrights, composers, theater directors, actors, drama critics, and others testified in September and October 1849. Only about ten witnesses (including six of the eight dramatists who testified) opposed the stage censorship unequivocally, while the great majority supported restoring it, either as before or with certain reforms. Hugo and Dumas père were the most noted spokesmen for abolition, with both arguing that an uncensored stage would benefit society and that censorship ultimately could not block the transmission of ideas. Thus, Dumas declared that, although "very harsh" in the eighteenth century, the censorship had failed to prevent the French Revolution, while being "destructive of art and of intellectual freedom." Hugo described the theater as a "crucible of civilization," a "place of enlightenment," and "one of the branches of public instruction" that "forms the public soul," which, if subsidized and uncensored by the state, could reconcile class differences in France as "the rich and poor, the happy and unhappy, the Parisian and the provincial, the French and foreigners will meet each other every night [at the theater], mix their souls fraternally and share in the contemplation of great works of the human spirit." Hugo maintained that such theater would contribute to the "moral sentiments and instruction of the poorer classes," and thus help make "calm reign in that part of the population from which sometimes erupt fatal commotions" and lead people to "read fewer bad pamphlets, drink less bad wine, loiter less in bad places and make fewer violent revolutions." On the other hand, Eugène Scribe, by far the most prolific dramatist and librettist of the first half of the nineteenth century, who had frequently experienced censorship difficulties himself, expressed a totally opposite view, declaring that "the liberty of the theaters will ruin art, taste, industry and morals," as well as immediately foster creation of "many bad theaters" since "good theaters don't make much money while bad ones make a lot of it."[38]

The Council of State's report ultimately recommended reviving drama censorship, because "liberty without limits is condemned both by experience and reason," and at the government's request the legislature provisionally reinstated it for a year, with little debate, by a vote of 352 to 194 on 1 August 1850. Napoleon's nephew, Louis Napoleon Bonaparte, elected president in late 1848 on a "law and order" platform in the wake of the "June Days," extended the censorship for a year by decree on 31 July 1851 in the absence of a promised statute to implement it. The provincial prefects were told on 4 August 1850 by chief censor Pierre Baroche to "put an end to the moral disorder which reigned in the theater," and specifically to ensure that no play "made with an injurious or exaggerated political sentiment or attacking morals or religion" was presented in their departments, and to "eliminate from the stage those brutal personalities who have invaded it, by ending antireligious portrayals, socialist ideas and incitements to class antagonism." They were also directed to reexamine works allowed under the July Monarchy since "recent circumstances have given certain works an importance which they did not have before and which could not be presented today without danger." The revived theater censorship proved especially sensitive to material touching on class conflict or presented to a primarily working-class audience. Thus, a passage in George Sand's 1851 *Molière* was struck in which the hero toasted "the poor people of France, who pay the fiddlers for all the festivals and the trumpets for all the wars," and her 1851 *Claudie* was stripped of all references viewed by the censors as having "socialist tendencies" or otherwise portraying class conflict. Laws and decrees imposed between 1849 and 1851 required special police permission for owners of drinking establishments to present music, drama, or songs, and (under a 17 November 1849 decree) that all such presentations be approved by the censors, with any permissions valid only for a specific day and time.[39]

## The Second Empire, 1852–70

Whatever remained of freedom of expression was quickly destroyed after Louis Napoleon overthrew the regime in a December 1851 coup d'état that triggered massive rural resistance, suppressed with 25,000 arrests and over 500 killed. In the coup's aftermath, scores of newspapers were suspended or suppressed: only 14 Parisian dailies were permitted to survive (with security deposits more than doubled to Fr 50,000), while provincial dailies declined from 430 to 260 between 1851 and 1865, largely due to various forms of harassment. In a 17 February 1852 decree, Louis Napoleon reintroduced prior censorship of caricature, and in December 1852, as the newly self-crowned and self-declared Emperor Napoleon III, he indefinitely extended theater censorship. Even "La Marseillaise" was forbidden between 1852 and 1870 (as it had been between 1815 and 1830) due to its obvious appeal to republicanism. In 1870 the censors recommended that the ban continue because, although on the surface the song was simply the "French song par excellence" with an "indisputable heroic and grandiose character," it had become "the symbol of revolution" and the "war chant of demagogy," whose repeated public performance would cause "new and dangerous excitation," especially as its "exclusively revolutionary character is too universally known and accepted today to hope for the government's generosity to change this at all."[40]

The administration of restrictions on plays and drawings was extremely harsh during the Second Empire—considerably more so than during the July Monarchy, when a variety of social and political topics could at least be discussed, even if direct attacks on the regime were not tolerated. Censorship was especially strict during the period immediately following the coup: according to an 1853 report, in 1852 the censors accepted outright only 246 out of 682 submitted plays, completely rejected 59, and demanded changes in 323 (the remainder were still awaiting decisions). Many plays banned at one time or another under Napoleon III, especially those with themes of class conflict, had been allowed (in some cases with modifications) by the censorship of the July Monarchy and/or the Second Republic, including *Richard Darlington* and *La Tour de Nesle* by Dumas père, and Sue's *Les Mystères de Paris* and *Atar-Gull*. The censors reported, for example, that although *La Tour de Nesle,* one of the most famous July Monarchy dramas, was "a work of incontestable talent," to allow it would be "contrary to the government's views and interests," especially "from the viewpoint of public morality and the respect due to crowned heads," given its portrayal of the debauched life of a former French queen. The censors were especially vigilant for material hostile to the imperial regime or the Catholic Church, as well as those with themes of conspiracy and revolt or which treated republican or democratic causes. As censorship historian Albert Cahuet notes, "As a general rule, the censorship did not allow criticism of the diverse branches of the imperial administration; and the more highly placed the target the better it was protected." Due to the regime's determination not to alienate the Church, leading dramatist Victorien Sardou suffered repeated censorship difficulties, which he often went to great lengths to publicize: among his anti-clerical plays, *Candide* was banned in 1861 and *Séraphine* was severely mutilated before it was authorized in 1868. The regime reaffirmed Louis-Philippe's 1844 ban on all depictions of religious persons or objects, and the portrayal of Jews was generally banned for fear of provoking anti-semitism. A 24 April 1858 ministerial circular added a ban on the use of "argot," or popular slang, characterized as a "bad element of low comedy which shocks good taste."[41]

Perhaps the greatest scandal was provoked by the banning of all of Victor Hugo's plays, especially a drama inspired by his famous novel *Notre-Dame de Paris,* which was found especially offensive because its central character, Claude Frollo, was a debauched priest; the censors maintained that "the clergy must be treated in the theater with only the greatest respect, and his role should produce a happy impression, elevated and moralistic upon the mind of the public." Although Paul Foucher, the dramatist who adapted the play, offered to transform Frollo into an artist and to make numerous other changes, the censors felt that Hugo's novel was so well known that such modifications would fool no one and that all of those "enemies of the government which make the name of Victor Hugo a banner" of opposition would make such a presentation an excuse for "tumultuous protests." Therefore, the censors concluded in an 1868 report, allowing even the modified version of *Notre Dame* would be "doubly troublesome," since Hugo's supporters would bitterly complain about the "mutilation" of his work, yet "there would be no benefit to public order" resulting from the changes.[42]

Frank depictions of poverty, class conflict, or lifestyles that challenged bourgeois morality were not allowed by Second Empire censors. For example, *Palaisse*, a drama by Marc Fournier and Adolphe Dennery, Adrien Decourcelle's *Jenny l'ouvrière*, and Alfred de Musset's *Andrea del Sarto* all had to be "sweetened" before they could be presented, the first because of its portrayal of a child dying for lack of money to obtain medical care, the second for depicting a young woman forced into prostitution to support her family, and the third for its presentation of female adultery and other moral failings. Among plays completely rejected were Glais-Bizoin's 1865 comedy *Le Vrai Courage*, forbidden because, the censors reported, it included "scenes in which the hateful recriminations of the socialists against law and order erupt in all their violence and brutality." *Robert Macaire* was again banished, as were all plays inspired by his character, such as *L'Auberge des Adrets*. Scribe and Offenbach's 1860 operetta *Barkouf* was banned for its portrayal of a foreign ruler in the form of a dog, while Victorien Sardou's *Les Grands Vassaux*, with its depiction of the murder by the medieval king Louis XI of his brother, was also forbidden. *Uncle Tom's Cabin* was allowed only on condition that the slave master be transformed into a mulatto and former slave himself, as this would make any analogy between "Negro slaves and European workers disappear." Émile Augier's 1853 play *Pierre de Touche* could only be performed in mutilated form, including the elimination of the phrase "The rich, in God's plans, are only the treasurers of the poor," and in his libretto to the opera *Sapho*, the phrase "Mystery adds spice to pleasure," apparently viewed as too risqué, had to be changed to "Mystery is the ally of bliss." As government ministers were sacrosanct, the 1858 play *Les Doigts de fée* was allowed only after the central character became a railway director. The censors approved the 1855 play *Paris* only after, they contemporaneously reported, the theater director had, against the wishes of playwright Paul Meurice (who had been jailed for his republican sentiments), "profoundly modified it according to our requests," thus transforming a drama written as a paean to liberty into an ode to Napoleon I. Censor Hallays-Dabot later wrote that Meurice, "a republican author," had become an "imperialist agent" despite himself.[43]

Plays dealing with Napoleon I, Napoleon III's uncle, were so sensitive that the censors habitually referred all such dramas (about fifty between 1849 and 1869) for the emperor's personal scrutiny: while depictions of the earlier Napoleon's triumphs were welcome as boosting his nephew's prestige, those that depicted the former's ultimate defeat and exile and the resulting foreign occupation of France after 1814 were viewed highly skeptically. Thus, in recommending interdicting Victorien Sardou's 1862

*L'Invasion* (eventually rewritten and approved as *Les Voluntaires de 1814*), the censors declared that "under the [ruling] Napoleonic dynasty" the drama's "humiliating" depiction of "one of the most disastrous epochs in our contemporary history [under Napoleon I]" could "not be placed before" the public despite the "glorious place which Emperor Napoleon III has regained among the nations." Plays focusing on pre-Napoleonic aspects of the French Revolution were generally banned or allowed only after minute scrutiny.

Plays that featured Napoleon I at war often had foreign policy implications, since they might cast aspersions upon countries with which Napoleon III wished to maintain good relations. Thus, in response to the 1861 proposal by Alexander Dumas père to revive his 1831 play *Napoleon Bonaparte,* the censors recommended against its presentation in a "popular theater," since although it seemed to have been "composed for the glorification of Emperor Napoleon I" following the July Revolution, it included the cry "Vive la République" and "La Marseillaise," and depicted, "along with the splendors of the First Empire, the [subsequent] disasters of France," including the "betrayal" of Napoleon by his leading generals and nobility, and the "captivity and agony of the martyr of Saint Helena, attributing to the English ruling house the opprobrium of his death." Such a play, according to the censors, raised several questions of "great gravity," because it was "important to cover with the veil of forgetfulness" past domestic quarrels and, from the standpoint of "international relations with an allied country [England], it would be perhaps inopportune to recall our past grievances." Anti-Russian and anti-Prussian plays were forbidden when the regime sought accommodation with those countries, but when diplomacy failed and wars ensued (against Russia in 1854 and Prussia in 1870), plays that violently attacked those regimes were suddenly authorized or even encouraged. In 1865, when French troops were still occupying Rome (as they had since 1849) and relations with the papacy were extremely delicate, the censors banned Charles Gounod's opera *Les Deux reines de France,* at least partly because it dealt with the twelfth-century power struggle between France's King Philip Augustus and the pope. In general, as theater censorship historian Alberic Cahuet has noted, Napoleon III's theater "had to make considerable concessions to diplomatic proprieties" and these "changed according to the variations of imperial politics and gave rise to the most contradictory decisions."[44]

By 1857 Second Empire censors had forbidden at least 180 plays, including all of Hugo's works, and a large percentage of authorized plays suffered enforced modifications (although there was a significant censorship relaxation after 1855 and especially after 1867, when Hugo's dramas, with the major exception of *Notre Dame de Paris,* were again permitted). Vaudevilles, like those by Eugène Labiche, a leading dramatist in that field, were routinely censored, especially any scenes that challenged bourgeois values, such as representations of adultery or marriage difficulties. Thus, the amorous indiscretions of the leading character in Jacques Offenbach's smash 1864 hit, *La Belle Hélène,* were toned down: at one point, for instance, she could be found only "with" rather than "in the arms" of her lover. The emperor personally approved Émile Augier's play *Les Lionnes pauvres* only after the author publicly declared that the censors' request that his adulterous heroine die of smallpox suggested to him that it be retitled, "On the Usefulness of Cowpox." Only similar intervention by Princess Mathilde with her cousin, the emperor, saved *Les Mohicans de Paris,* by Dumas père, from interdiction in 1864. Another Dumas play, *La Jeunesse de Louis XIV,* was banned in 1853 for supposed adverse allusions to the emperor's marriage, but Dumas rewrote it in record time and obtained censorial approval for a retitled *La Jeunesse de Louis XV,* which, he assured his brother, would not have "a single line or situation" intact from the earlier play.[45]

In one significant liberalization, the regime ended theater licensing, with its attendant genre restrictions, in 1864; the number of Parisian theaters, which had slowly grown from about 10 in 1815 to about 40 in 1864, exploded to about 55 by 1866 (although many of the new theaters were apparently very short-lived, as the number of Parisian theaters sharply declined to about 30 by 1890). However, physical changes that drastically affected the Paris theater clearly reflected the regime's fear of mass disturbances among the poor at the theater. Most popular stages on the Boulevard du Temple were physically destroyed during the 1860s reconstruction of Paris and remaining theaters were required to dispense with the notorious *parterre* (pit), where spectators of all classes were jammed together standing up or on overcrowded benches, in favor of assigned seats. This led to both a decrease in the sense of crowd collectivity and an increase in prices that helped drive the poor away from large theaters into small café-concerts (which one government minister described approvingly as "houses of tolerance ['maisons de tolerance,' revealingly, a term also used for brothels] which shelter the people and prevent them from thinking about politics"). During the so-called 1860s "liberal empire," slightly relaxed political controls were accompanied by an eruption of anti-regime demonstrations at theaters, as audiences regularly chanted forbidden songs such as "La Marseillaise."[46]

With regard to opera, in 1854 the regime imposed the new requirement that general rehearsals, attended by a theater inspector, had to include all costumes and décor, apparently to avoid subversive allusions slipped into the librettos by such means. Although café-concerts generally featured far more frivolous material than that presented at regular theaters and the opera, their appeal to the popular classes made them subjects of especial surveillance. In December 1851 Louis Napoleon decreed that all popular drinking establishments, which often served as centers of working-class socializing and organization, could be closed at will; by 1855 their number had been reduced from 350,000 to 291,000. Under a 30 December 1852 decree, all political songs were banned from such locales, as well as from any other venue in which cheap political literature was distributed; and the prior censorship of all entertainment presented in such settings first required in 1849 was continued. Songs intended for such venues had to be presented daily before noon to the Bureau of Theaters, which in 1867 assigned a censor specifically to supervise café-concerts; any demanded modifications had to be accepted before the Bureau closed at 4:00 PM, or else the café-concert had to remain closed until the following night. Interior ministry figures for 1852, the year following the coup, indicate that of over 600 songs submitted to the censors for performance in café-concerts and similar venues, almost 10 percent were completely forbidden and another 40 percent underwent enforced changes. During the entire Second Empire, 800 out of around 6,000 submitted songs were banned, generally for "moral" reasons, but sometimes for political motives, such as ridiculing the English when they were allied with the French, or denouncing class oppression.[47]

## The Third Republic, 1870–1914

### *The Commune and Its Aftermath: The "Monarchist Republic," 1870–77*

With the revolutionary overthrow of the Second Empire in 1870 amid the fiasco of the Franco-Prussian War, a provisional government quickly abolished most restrictions on the press (including security bonds, newspaper taxes, and colportage regulations), caricature, and the stage, and restored jury trials for remaining press offenses. However, during 1871–77 the new regime, the so-called "monarchist Republic," was dominated by monarchists and conservative republicans haunted by memories of the 1871 Paris Commune, a working-class insurrection that was suppressed with the deaths of 25,000 Parisians (the vast majority of whom were slaughtered in cold blood) along with the imprisonment or exile of another 50,000. The 1871 legislature approved new press laws that restored security bonds, newspaper taxes, restrictions on colportage, and prior censorship of caricature, and which contained numerous provisions designed to suppress the left-wing press. Theater censorship was reimposed by an 18 March 1871 executive decree, and after being maintained for three years as an emergency measure while Paris remained under a state of siege, was regularized by the 1874 legislature. Until the state of siege was lifted in 1875, ultimate authority over drama censorship lay with the military governor of Paris, who relied upon the theater censors for advice but was not bound by their recommendations.

Fears of Commune-like working-class upheavals and of the growth of liberal republican sentiment were the driving forces behind the extremely harsh regulation of all media until the monarchists were defeated in the 1877 legislative elections, leading to the so-called "republican Republic." The interior minister declared in 1878, concerning the 1870–74 period, that censorship had "never been more severe" for the "repertoire of theaters and especially for those of café-concerts." A February 1872 directive to the prefects warned them against lax theater censorship, especially with regard to political matters, and declared that while the "administration does not intend to proscribe political allusions in an absolute manner, it has the duty to forbid all works which strike at the political order and at morality as well as those which, owing to local circumstances, could cause disorder." A strict ban was enforced on all theatrical depictions of religious costumes or objects, and all references to the Commune were excluded from the stage.   Several dramas that had been allowed under the July Monarchy and/or the Second Empire were forbidden, including Felix Pyat's famous pre-1848 play of social criticism, *Le Chiffonnier de Paris*. Hugo's *Notre Dame de Paris* was again banned in 1872 (it was finally approved for the stage only in 1885), and the ban on Hugo's *Le roi s'amuse*, originally imposed in 1832, was reaffirmed in 1873 (it was finally allowed in 1882). In the latter case, the military governor of Paris overturned the censors' recommendation, apparently largely because one of the "popular theaters" had proposed its presentation. The censors had futilely argued that any dangers posed by *Le roi s'amuse* would largely be "discounted" by its existing notoriety, especially as the opera *Rigoletto*, based on it, had made its essential plot well known, and because "everyone has read it and knows it," allowing its stage representation would "cause less trouble for the government than the uproar that would be provoked in the press" by another interdiction. The continued ban on *Le roi s'amuse* did provoke considerable journalistic criticism: in early July 1873 *Le Siècle* described the interdiction as absurd because "all of France knows the play and can recite the words by heart," while *Le Rappel* asked how that which was "good" concerning *Rigoletto* was "bad" when the "same events" were presented in spoken form. An adaptation of Hugo's *Les Misérables* was banned in 1874, but approved four years later, while several of his other less overtly political plays, including *Marion Delorme* and *Marie Tudor*, were approved as early as 1873. *Marion Delorme* was apparently approved without difficulty because it was proposed for the "respectable" Théâtre Française, a venue the censors reported was "generally so calm" and whose patrons would probably not apply its historical material to contemporary events, while they advised that although *Marie Tudor* was proposed for a "popular" theater, it would require the "most intense efforts" for an audience to find in it "allusions" that "are not there." Subsequent reports indicated that spectators had "seized with enthusiasm" several passages in *Marie Tudor* and sought "the least excuse to express their opinions." However, the censors advised against further action, especially because, following the *Le roi s'amuse* affair, censoring *Marie Tudor* would "present the appearance" of persecuting Hugo and, as the play's script was "in everyone's hands," suppressing passages would "doubtless lead audiences to insist upon them in a manner which would disrupt the presentation" and produce "a demand for the play," while audiences would otherwise soon find it "long and boring."[48]

In November 1872, café-concert proprietors were informed that all political allusions were "strictly forbidden"; of at least thirty plays banned between 1870 and 1874, over two dozen were intended for that venue, and in 1876 alone twenty café-concerts were closed in Paris (about 10 percent of all such establishments) for presenting unauthorized programs. In general, political, social, and "immoral" songs were systematically eliminated from café-concerts, including those that expressed sympathy for the poor or denounced the repression of trade unions. Altogether, between 1870 and 1906 (when stage censorship was abolished) almost 9,000 café-concert songs, from over 90,000 submitted to the censors, were interdicted, sometimes for "moral" offenses but very often for their political allusions. About 80 plays destined for regular theaters were also banned. In December 1871 the military governor of Paris banned the sale or display of "all illustrations, photographs or emblems" that might "trouble the public peace," including specifically pictures of "individuals prosecuted or condemned for their participation in the recent insurrection." This decree led to months of what press historian Fernand Drujon has termed "incessant searches and seizures" and an "almost incalculable" number of prosecutions, involving medals, statues, coins, pipes, cigarette cases, and even tapioca boxes. Caricatures faced especially minute scrutiny (during 1875 alone, 225 were banned) leading the caricature journal *L'Eclipse* (a major target) to lament on 22 December 1872 that despite three revolutions (1830, 1848, and 1870) that supposedly had "crushed censorship," the "phoenix of arbitrariness has been reborn—not from its own cinders, but from the cinders it creates from books, drawings, our rights and our freedoms!"[49]

## *The Republican Republic, 1877–1914*

Although the republican-controlled legislature elected in 1877 quickly established a commission to draft a new press law, the "republican Republic" at first maintained theater and caricature censorship and continued to prosecute the written press, primarily simply switching primary targets from republicans, socialists, and radicals to the monarchists. Despite a liberal new press law in 1881 that ended caricature censorship, continuing fears that French political elites retained of the "dark masses" was reflected in the maintenance of theater censorship until 1906, although its implementation gradually atrophied after 1875. During the next thirty years, fewer than sixty plays intended for the legitimate stage were banned (only nine after 1891), mostly on moral rather than political grounds, although several others were suppressed after their first performance, thereby regularly provoking political uproars that eventually doomed the censorship. In order to insure that enforced censorship modifications were honored, after mid 1874 final approval of plays was given only following special so-called "censorship rehearsals" rather than simply upon reading scripts: a government circular of 31 July 1874 informed theater directors that the rehearsal "must take place with scenery, costumes, properties and complete lighting of the stage," in a manner "that does not conceal any of the effects of the performance," and if modifications were then required, "a second partial or full dress rehearsal may take place at the demand of the administration." However, the range of acceptable political criticism on the stage broadened considerably compared to past regimes—for example, unflattering accounts of judges, police, soldiers, ministers, and parliamentary life became commonplace. Yet, even between 1880 and 1893 four of eight plays that dealt with the Commune were forbidden; in the 1887 play *Jacques Damour*, exactly why the heroes of the play were returning to France from New Caledonia (where many Communards had been exiled) was left a mystery due to censorship excisions. References to the Commune were still periodically banned from the stage into the twentieth century; thus, the censors eliminated such allusions in a 1903 drama, while declaring, "The words Commune, communards, no longer exist."[50]

The decreasing frequency of politically motivated censorship reflected ministerial instructions of 26 February 1879, in which the censors were directed to, "in matters political, provide all liberty compatible with maintenance of the public peace and preserve your severity for licentious songs and immoral plays, remembering that the two principles of the Republic are dignity and liberty." Dramas viewed as exacerbating contemporary domestic or foreign political conflicts were still occasionally forbidden or censored, however, as with three plays centering on class conflict by the former Communard exile Louis Michel, whose *Nadine* (1882), *Le Coq rouge* (1888), and *La Grève* (1890) all suffered significant excisions. In the latter play references to the Commune were eliminated, as were numerous passages about exploitation of workers, such as the phrase "The right of free workers is no different than that of slaves, except that free workers die of hunger while dreaming of justice, while Blacks and dogs graze peacefully in their abandonment." The censors were also sensitive to plays that revived memories of the 1870 Franco-Prussian War: *La veillée allemande*, which had been presented in 1864, could only be revived in the 1880s if the setting was transported from Germany to Switzerland. The left was outraged when *Germinal*, by Émile Zola, was banned in 1885 for, as the censors put it, the play's "socialist tendency" and especially for depicting "troops firing at striking miners in revolt." The censors not only insisted on deletion of the latter scene before finally approving *Germinal* in 1888, but also struck out virtually all words even remotely suggesting class conflict, including "capital," "property," "stockholder;" "comrade," and "strike." Additionally, all overt appeals to strike or revolt were eliminated, mine owners became the "powerful" instead of the "rich," workers were required to "labor" rather than "work themselves to death," and the mine owners "jostled" their employees rather than treating them as "brutes." Following the massively publicized *Germinal* affair, bitter parliamentary debates over theater censorship erupted almost annually, with attempts to cut off censorship funding defeated 329 to 163 in 1887 after the minister of public education warned, specifically referring to the opera, that it would be "too late" to act after the presentation "before 3,000 spectators of a song, a manifestation" that might provoke possibly "irrevocable" international consequences.[51]

During the 1880s several plays that were feared to wound German or Russian sensibilities were banned, while in 1890 Henri de Bornier's drama *Mahomet* was forbidden by special action of the Council of Ministers due to protests by the Ottoman government. Ottoman Sultan Abdul-Hamid personally thanked the French government for a "wise decision" concerning a play that "could only have wounded" the "feelings of your Muslim subjects." A huge political uproar was ignited in 1891 when two plays were closed soon after their opening performances within a four day period: *La Fille Élisa,* a realistic depiction of prostitution based on Edmund de Goncourt's novel, and Sardou's *Thermidor,* banned after its alleged defamation of Robespierre and French Revolution by its depiction of the Reign of Terror provoked loud, apparently pre-planned, audience protests. During subsequent legislative debate, the government fine arts minister declared, concerning *Élisa:* "Short of opening a brothel on stage, one could not penetrate the conditions of prostitution more deeply than the play had, and therefore it was not possible to authorize its performance." As a result of the controversy, a print-run of 300,000 copies of the *Élisa* script quickly sold out. The *Thermidor* affair produced the odd specter of leftists, who normally attacked the censorship (as with *Germinal*) defending it, thus switching positions with conservatives, who wanted *Germinal* banned but attacked the closure of *Thermidor.* The 1891 *Thermidor* debate also elicited one of the most famous comments in French history: deputy Georges Clemenceau, leader of the radical republicans and a future prime minister, defended the government's action by declaring that the French Revolution was a "bloc from which you cannot subtract anything [i.e., the reign of terror]" and that "we will not let the French Revolution be soiled by any speculation whatever, we will not tolerate it." Deputy Joseph Reinach attacked the ban on *Thermidor,* however, accusing the government of condemning Sardou for *"lèse-majesté"* against Robespierrre and for abandoning its "principle, which is and must always be liberty!" The *Thermidor* ban was effectively endorsed by a legislative vote of 315 to 192.[52]

The 1891 uproar led to the formation of a legislative commission to examine the entire question of theater censorship. The commission heard testimony from fifteen playwrights, theater directors, and others, who were about evenly divided; for example, a spokesman for the Society of Dramatic Authors expressed support for continued prior censorship (primarily to protect theaters against losing their production costs if plays were suppressed following their presentation), while Zola termed it "shameful that after 20 years of republican rule, we still lack freedom of the theater." Committee *rapporteur* Gaston Guillemet told the legislature that no epoch had ever developed "satisfying censorial legislation, since no one has ever been able to lay his hands on a fixed principle of direction, since each generation undoes the work of predecessors while anticipating that the next generation will do the same to its own." A "compromise" proposal urged by the committee to end the censorship on a trial basis for three years was never voted on after conservatives fought it as too far-reaching and liberals opposed it as inadequate. In 1893 government minister Charles Dupuy defended the ban on the play *L'Autumne* because of its depiction of what he termed "an unhappy conflict between soldiers and the population" during a strike, on the grounds that "art does not consist in reopening, before an audience, wounds all too recent from which all the world here is suffering." While parliamentary debates on the censorship continued, the censors were increasingly overwhelmed by the sheer amount of material presented to them: in 1900, for example, 9,000 plays and songs were submitted to them for proposed presentation in over 160 theaters, café-concerts, music halls, and other venues. No doubt partly for such purely logistical reasons, surveillance of café-concerts substantially loosened after 1881 and censorship approval of songs became valid for a week, instead of only for one day, which was usually previously the case. Moreover, in at least some cases, plays banned by the censors were apparently nonetheless performed: the author of one drama about prostitution banned in 1897 claimed several years later to have presented it over three hundred times without interference.[53]

The banning of several plays between 1900 and 1902 touched off another uproar, inspiring leading caricature journals such as *Le Rire*, *L'Assiette au beurre*, and *Courrier français* to devote entire issues to attacking the drama censorship and triggering a November 1901 petition against the censorship signed by most of France's leading literary lights. Among the plays banned during this period were Georges Ancey's anti-clerical *Ces Messieurs*, Albert Guinon's anti-Semitic *Décadence* (especially unwelcome in the wake of the Dreyfus Affair), Jean Drault's *La Question des Huiles* (an attack on parliamentary corruption and thus a reminder of the 1890s Panama scandal), Urbain Gohier's *Le Ressort* (characterized by the censors as a "thinly-disguised apology for anarchism" appealing to "hatred, violence and revolt"), and Louis Marsolleau's bitterly anti-business *Mais quelqu'un troubla la fête* (which the authorities found unacceptable for portraying French society as "corrupt, blind, cowardly and coarse, pitiless towards the weak"). Renewed opposition to the censorship was above all incited by the 1901 ban on *Avaries* by Eugène Brieux, perhaps the most talented playwright of his time, which dealt frankly with syphilis, and which the censors found "perhaps salutary" if presented to medical students, but likely to cause "legitimate offense" by its use of "crude, precise and detailed" medical language before a "regular" audience. During a 1902 parliamentary debate, Minister of Public Instruction Georges Leygues defended the censorship by the long-standing argument that "the power of the theater to offend is infinitely greater than that of the book," and the legislature rejected ending it by 328 to 124. However, beginning in 1903, reflecting a leftward political shift during the so-called 1902–5 "Radical Republic," the legislature, led by deputy Maurice Couyba, reduced for four straight years the Theater Bureau's budget by an amount equivalent to the salary of one of the four censors; following a bitter 1905 debate, the government's request for full funding was rejected 329 to 217 and the reduced amount was approved by voice vote in the Chamber of Deputies. After a final Senate vote on 9 April 1906 (no longer resisted by the government), the theater censorship was effectively killed via the stage door, so to speak, by a complete legislative defunding (the 1874 law that authorized theater censorship remained on the books but there were no censors left to enforce it).[54]

Even after 1906, however, local officials maintained they could still legally halt any theatrical performances deemed immoral or prejudicial to public order and, even as the curtain fell on prior stage censorship, local authorities simultaneously, and with little challenge, began applying prior censorship to the wildly popular new medium of cinema. They cited as a legal basis for these positions an arcane 1790 law authorizing local officials to license "public spectacles" and an 1884 law giving local police the power to ban spectacles that could trouble public order, thereby creating what film historian Richard Abel has termed a "crazy quilt of standards and wild fluctuations in censorship practices" until a standardized and centralized national cinema censorship system was implemented in 1916. Because cinema's impact was considered even greater than that of the stage, whose importance had in any case relatively declined by 1906, and because the far cheaper movies had a much larger and more popular audience, the authorities saw no contradiction in introducing film censorship shortly after ending that for drama. As censorship historian Odile Krakovitch writes, it was the "blossoming cinema which inherited the distrust and the fear, and then the censorship" formerly accorded the stage. But even prior stage censorship was not entirely dead: perhaps because the law authorizing it had never been repealed, the French government was able to restore theater censorship without serious challenge in August 1914, with the outbreak of World War I, and the resurrected censorship was not again reinterred until October 1919, a full year after the war's end.[55]

## The Impact of Restrictions on Freedom of the Stage

The obvious impact of theater censorship and licensing and genre restrictions on the content of plays and the number of theaters and their repertoire has been discussed above. The censorship had far subtler, but extremely serious, impacts upon the ability of dramatists to freely express or even freely think their thoughts, and frequently and almost necessarily they censored themselves rather than submit material that obviously would not be approved. Thus, Alexander Dumas likened theater censors to "customs officers of thought," while Edmond de Goncourt referred to the "homicidal" pencil wielded by the censors. Victor Hugo, perhaps the leading literary nineteenth-century spokesman for freedom of the theater, compared the censorship to the Inquisition, terming it "detestable" and a "prison" for writers, which "like the other Holy Office," had its "secret judges, its masked executioners, its tortures and mutilations and its death penalty." In a famous preface to the printed version of his play *Le Roi S'Amuse,* suppressed in 1832 after one performance, Hugo declared, "The ministerial suppression of play is an assault on liberty by censorship, and an assault on property by confiscation." When stage censorship was reimposed in 1850 after two years of dramatic freedom, Hugo declared, "It brought sobs to the depths of my heart." Eugène Sue, in a letter concerning the modifications enforced on his famous play *Les Mystères de Paris,* complained that his work had been "mutilated" by "repulsive" and "unbelievable" demands "against which the conscience and dignity of a writer revolt" and that "made a complete abnegation not only of self-love but of literary thought." Sue added that he made the changes only to avoid financial disaster for the theater that planned to present his play and because its censored production would, for future history, "at least provide useful and good information, and hopefully raise grave and serious reflections concerning the theater [censorship] law." Gustave Flaubert, who was famously prosecuted in 1857 (on moral grounds) for his novel *Madame Bovary,* termed censorship "a monstrosity, something worse than homicide: attacking thought is a crime of soul destruction (*lèse-âme*)."[56]

Dramatists (and caricaturists) especially resented their continued subjection to prior censorship long after the written word was freed. Thus, Edmond de Goncourt demanded in 1892, "Speech is free, newspapers are free, the book is free, only the theater is not. Why this anomaly under a Republic which has liberty for its motto?" Similarly, Zola, who compared the drama censors to a "torturer" and the censorship to an "abortion of liberty" and the "old Bastille [prison]," declared, "Books have been freed, periodicals have been freed. Why is the theater condemned to eternal servitude?" He complained that if he printed his thoughts he was "a citizen like everyone else, subject only to the common law," but "everything changes upon writing a play, when I become subject to an absolute power and have to submit to the whims of prior censorship." Zola declared that "sadness squeezed my heart" when the legislature voted to continue the censorship in 1887, and termed it both "astonishing and comic" that "a republican government maintains the censorship after having attacked it under all other regimes!" He bitterly wrote in 1887 that only "militant journals of the extreme left" opposed the censorship and that the "truly guilty" parties were dramatists, journalists, and other men of letters who supported it and, were a legislative inquiry to be convened, would "come on their knees, their hands trembling, sobbing, 'Please, we are so happy enchained, don't take our chains away! What would we do, what would become of us, without these good chains with which we protect ourselves?'" He concluded, "One day the censorship will be suppressed and everyone, filled with shame, will be indignant that the pig was not strangled earlier." French dramatist Albert Guinon complained in 1901: "If I understand correctly the functioning of the censorship, its role is to forbid all work of social satire which would tend to move the audience and thus cause a certain effervescence judged dangerous. But, if a work of social satire does not affect the public, it is clearly an inferior work. ... From which it follows, a little humiliating for the institution of the censorship, that its role is to let pass social satires which are weak and faded and to stop those which are strong and intense." Another argument against the censorship was that, since all stage presentations had to be approved by the government, inevitably everything that was allowed had the government's implicit endorsement. As one observer noted, "With the censorship, it's the government which sings smutty songs, it's the government which dances the can can."[57]

## Resistance to Theater Censorship

Opponents of nineteenth-century French drama censorship went far beyond words in fighting it: they also repeatedly defied or evaded it at the risk, not only of the suppression of their material, but of prosecutions, fines, and jail terms. As Victor Hugo told an 1849 French legislative inquiry into the theater censorship, the means by which it could be resisted were virtually innumerable and "of all sorts," including those which authors can commit voluntarily in writing in a play something against the law. ... There are also the offences of the actor; those which he can commit in adding to words by gestures or inflections of voice a reprehensible sense not meant by the author. ... There are the offences of the director who arranges a display of nudity on the stage; then the offenses of the decorator who exposes certain seditious or dangerous emblems mixed in with the decor; then those of the costumer, then those of the hairdresser. ... Finally there are the offences of the public, an applause which accentuates a verse, a whistle which goes beyond what the actor or author intended.[58]

If the means of resisting the theater censorship were thus enormously varied, nonetheless they can be divided into two categories: (1) overt or outright defiance of the censorship regulations, such as presenting an unauthorized play or including censored dialogue in a performance; and (2) technical evasions, which complied with the letter of the law while subverting its spirit, such as highlighting censored material while publishing the text of expurgated or plays, or presenting plays to a supposedly "private" audience. Although it is certain that, especially in small venues such as café-concerts that offered numerous short presentations, plays were sometimes performed without having been submitted to the censorship, such occurrences are difficult to document (although in at least a couple of cases, the leading theater in Rouen, for example, is known to have defied censorship bans between 1835 and 1837). The practice of violating the censorship rules by gradually and surreptitiously restoring forbidden material was far more common at the regular theaters. The theater censorship bureaucracy usually had neither the manpower nor the time to attend each performance to ensure that their instructions were carried out or that no offences of the sort Hugo described occurred. Although, especially after 1874 at least, censors supposedly attended special rehearsals (and sometimes opening performances) and/or made spot checks, especially if a complaint had been lodged or newspaper reviews aroused concern, the inevitably spotty censorship enforcement opened up plenty of opportunities for evasion by actors willing to risk the consequences of improvising or restoring expurgated text and at least a sprinkling of performers did so. Thus, theater historian F. W. J. Hemmings writes that under Napoleon III, "at the dress rehearsal and for the first few performances, the passages that had been blue-pencilled would be obediently omitted; but as performance succeeded performance, the cuts would be imperceptibly restored by the players, or the author would even add new matter that the censor had never seen." This practice became so common that in 1861 an office of "Commissioner-Inspector of Parisian theaters and Spectacles" was created to supposedly monitor play performances more closely. However, at least one Parisian theater, the Porte Saint-Martin, soon worked out a system whereby when an inspector was sighted the actors would be signaled, so they could revert to the approved text.[59]

Far more common than outright defiance of the theater censors were a variety of other techniques, many of which Hugo referenced in his 1849 testimony, which clearly violated the spirit of the laws while technically remaining within their boundaries. During the "Golden Age" of pantomine during the 1820s, for example, the government was at a loss in its inability to censor silent performances that transmitted subversive messages solely via gestures. During the Restoration, when all references to Napoleon were banned from the theaters, one actress wore a bouquet of violets, a Bonapartist symbol, on stage, and in an 1821 production the famous actor Talma wore a mask that made him look like Napoleon. In an especially notorious similar instance, Balzac's play *Vautrin*, which had been cleared by the censors on its fourth revised submission, was banned in 1840 after one performance because famous actor Frederick Lemaître appeared in a costume that made him resemble King Louis-Philippe. During the 1849 theater censorship inquiry, the well-known actor Bocage recalled how he had similarly subverted the censorship under Louis-Philippe by a simple dramatic pause: his response to a query as to whether his character was generous was, "As the King ... of Spain." Similarly, café-concert performers imaginatively alluded to forbidden material by, as one scholar described it, "a game of evocative words, repetitive or frankly absurd, by a comic 'visual code,' a gesture, a cry, a whistle, a game of body language, a mask, a costume or make-up."[60]

Even more frequent than such technically legal "alterations" to the approved text by actors were audience interventions by applause or hooting that underlined particular passages and attributed to them often unintended political connotations. This form of audience intervention became so common that it was given the name of "making applications," characterized by historian Nicholas Harrison as "a creative act on the part of the audience, pressing words into a political service for which they had not been intended by the playwright." During the late 1820s "making applications" became so common that the Paris prefect of police directed his subordinates in 1827 to report on "any political or other allusion upon which the subversive might seize," including "the nature of the applause or expressions of disapproval it has provoked," as it was "particularly in places of assembly which are as heavily frequented as theaters are nowadays that subversion endeavors to influence public opinion" and it was "vital" for the "authorities not to be unaware of anything that you may have occasion to observe." Many (or perhaps all) French theaters posted detailed rules outlawing "making applications." Thus, according to "regulations for the policing of spectacles" issued in 1838 by the mayor of Angoulême, it was "expressly forbidden" to "trouble or interrupt" theatrical presentations by "cries, clamor, harmful reprimands, hoots or whistling" or to "make any signs of approval or disapproval which create tumult and lead to disorder"; otherwise the "curtain will be lowered and the police will order all those in the auditorium to immediately leave."

Despite such regulations, "making applications" was a common, if not constant, feature in French theatrical life. For example, the play *Edward in Scotland*, which dealt with an exiled ruler, was approved by both the Napoleonic and Restoration censors as inoffensive, but was applauded under Bonaparte as a royalist piece and then subsequently hailed as a pro-Bonapartist piece during the Bourbon Restoration. At a time when all references to Napoleon were strictly forbidden, the Nantes prefect reported in 1820 that a score of Bonapartist sympathizers had effectively gained control over the theater there, seizing "on every allusion favorable" to Napoleon and opposing the "display of any sentiment to the contrary." In a variant of "making applications," during the late 1820s, when King Charles X was intent upon reinforcing the power of the Catholic Church, theater audiences in numerous cities responded to bans on performances of Molière's bitterly satirical anti-clerical comedy *Tartuffe* by demanding that it be performed, a phenomenon dubbed "Tartufferie." In 1826 spectators at the Clermont-Ferrand theater even succeeded in having a bust of Molière crowned on stage. Such "subversion" continued even during the brief lifting of prior theater censorship between 1830 and 1835; thus, the prefect of Limoges informed the interior minister on 20 January 1834 that the theater had become a "school of scandal and immorality" and "a sort of arena in which passions are expressed, often with violence, between the acts, and in which allusions are also often seized with an extreme animosity." Under Louis Philippe, the massive applause that greeted the phrase (referring to a king of Spain) "down with Philippe" in Lemercier's 1834 play *Pinto* led the authorities to close it, while after drama censorship was reimposed in 1835 theater audiences took to spontaneously singing patriotic songs as a form of political protest. When a censored version of Victor Hugo's *Hernani* was allowed in 1867 (after being banned, along with all of

Hugo's other works, for fifteen years) to celebrate a Parisian international industrial exhibition, crowds greeted it with delirious acclaim, turning performances into anti-regime demonstrations, and responding to omissions by shouting out the correct words.[61]

Another means of evading theater censorship laws was the perfectly legal practice of printing censored plays, often accompanied by bitter denunciations of the censors (although prior stage censorship continued until 1906, printing was not subject to prior censorship after 1822). Thus, the Restoration press delighted in informing its readers exactly which lines had been deleted, sometimes by printing the original lines next to a censored version. When Nepomucene Lemercier's play *La Démence de Charles VI* (The Madness of Charles VI), an unflattering portrayal of an insane fourteenth-century French king, was banned from the Odéon theater in 1820 on the personal orders of King Louis XVIII, even the royalist newspaper *Le Drapeu blanc* wrote a sympathetic account, adding that "curious readers" can "buy the play; it is published and sold at the Barba bookstore, Palais-Royal, stone gallery, behind the Theater Français, number 51."[62]

An additional legal means of evading theater censorship was the presentation of plays at so-called "private clubs," which were theoretically only open to members who paid annual subscription fees, thus avoiding any charge at the door and technically avoiding the censorship, which applied only to dramas that charged admission fees and/or were open to the general public. The most famous such "private club" in France, the Théâtre Libre of Paris, flourished under the direction of André Antoine, a former gas company clerk, between 1887 and 1894, and closed for financial reasons in 1896 after presenting a total of 62 programs with 184 plays and attracting over 50,000 subscribers.[63]

## Conclusion

It is extremely difficult to disentangle cause and effect in seeking to determine what impact theater censorship had upon broader aspects of nineteenth-century French life, society, and politics, especially since restrictions on dramatic presentations were part of a much larger web of political controls. Until the introduction of universal male suffrage in 1848 voting rights were restricted to less than 1 percent of the population, until 1864 strikes were illegal, trade unions were legalized only in 1884, the press was subject to severe controls (including prior censorship of caricature) until 1881, and full freedom of assembly and association was not guaranteed until 1901.

The "strange ballet" of the coming and going of theater censorship referred to by historian Krakovitch, as well as the particular issues reflected in specific censorship decisions during different eras, clearly *reflected* broader political currents and therefore studying this subject can provide invaluable information about the especial fears and concerns of the numerous regimes that ruled France between 1815 and 1914. However, to what degree censorship significantly *contributed* to specific or broad political currents and developments is virtually impossible to determine—even if the extraordinary amount of time and energy devoted by French authorities to controlling the theater clearly expressed their deeply held convictions that the stage had the power to decisively influence the course of political events.

Certainly the drama censorship was never entirely effective in its goals of stifling the stage as a venue for political dissent: as discussed above, the theater was frequently the site of political protests and demonstrations, censorship rulings were sometimes ignored or sidestepped, seemingly "subversive" plays such as *Les Mystères de Paris* (during the July Monarchy) were sometimes approved, and particular censorship bans often had the primary effect of drawing attention to forbidden plays and/or igniting general attacks upon the censorship itself and the regimes that sought to enforce it. Beyond that, perhaps the only major conclusion that can be safely drawn is that, despite such resistance and evasions, the theater censorship substantially impoverished the nineteenth-century French stage and French culture more generally. Thus, during an 1897 legislative debate, a former director of the government's fine arts ministry declared, "If we don't have the social works that we ought to, the blame lies largely with the censorship." Émile Zola, along with Victor Hugo probably the leading nineteenth-century literary opponent of the drama censorship, eloquently explained both the impact of censorship and the difficulty of measuring such in his 1879 brochure "La République et la Littérature":

> A well-meaning man said to me, "Cite for me the works of talent that the censorship has prevented from playing." I replied to him, "I cannot tell you the titles of the masterpieces of which the censorship has deprived us, precisely because these masterpieces have not been written." That is the whole issue. If the censorship does not play a very active role, it has the inhibiting effect of a scarecrow: it paralyzes the evolution of dramatic art. Everyone knows the plays he shouldn't write, those which couldn't be performed, and no one writes them.[64]

## Bibliographical Essay

Two good general introductions to nineteenth-century French history are Roger Magraw, *France, 1815–1914: The Bourgeois Century* (Oxford, 1983), and Robert Tombs, *France, 1814–1914* (London, 1996). English-language readers are extremely fortunate to have a plethora of accessible material related to nineteenth-century French theater and theater censorship. By far the most useful materials are two volumes by F. W. J. Hemmings, both published by Cambridge University Press: *Theater and State in France, 1760–1905* (1994) and *The Theater Industry in Nineteenth-Century France* (1993). Together they comprise a comprehensive overview of nineteenth-century French theater, with the former volume providing considerable information about theater censorship. Two other surveys of nineteenth-century theater, Harold Hobson, *French Theater Since 1800* (London, 1978), and Marvin Carlson, *The French Stage in the Nineteenth Century* (Metuchen, NJ, 1972), have only scattered information about censorship. There are, additionally, an amazing number of specialized books on the nineteenth-century French theater, at least four of which devote a chapter to censorship or related matters: John McCormick, *Popular Theaters of Nineteenth-Century France* (London, 1993); Sheryl Kroen, *Politics and Theater: The Crisis of Legitimacy in Restoration France, 1815–1830* (Berkeley, CA, 2000); Angela Pao, *The Orient of the Boulevards: Exoticism, Empire and Nineteenth-Century French Theater* (Philadelphia, 1998); and Sally Charnow, *Theater, Politics and Markets in Fin-de-Siècle Paris* (New York, 2005). There is also useful information on theater censorship in three dissertations and theses: Nancy Nolte, *Government and théâtre in Nineteenth-Century France: Administrative Organization for Control of the Comedie-Française Repertoire*, PhD dissertation, University of Akron (Akron, OH, 1984); Thomas Sudik, *The French Administration of Fine Arts and the National Theaters (1882–1906)*, MA thesis, University of North Carolina (Chapel Hill, NC, 1972); and Edward Hopkins, *Theater and State in France, 1789–1914*, MA thesis, University of Virginia (Charlottesville, VA, 1978). There is nothing in English that focuses specifically on opera censorship, but there is some useful information in André Spies, *Opera, State and Society in the Third Republic, 1875–1914* (New York, 1988); Mark Everist, *Music Drama at the Paris Odéon, 1824–1828* (Berkeley, CA, 2002); Anselm Gerhard, *The Urbanization of Opera: Music Theater in Paris in the Nineteenth Century* (Chicago, 1998); and Jane Fulcher, *The Nation's Image: French Grand Opera as Politics and Politicized Art* (Cambridge, 1987). David Charlton, "The Nineteenth Century: France," in Roger Parker, ed., *The Oxford Illustrated History of Opera* (Oxford, 1994), 121–68, has a lengthy and useful summary of nineteenth-century French opera, but nothing significant about censorship.

There are numerous specialized English-language articles that focus on nineteenth-century French theater censorship. Among those that center on particular time periods are Nicholas Harrison, "Colluding with the Censor: Theater Censorship in France After the Revolution," *Romance Studies* 25 (1995): 7–18; F. W. J. Hemmings, "Applause for the Wrong Reasons: The Use of Applications for Political Purposes in Paris Theaters, 1780–1830," *Theater Research International* 14 (1989): 256–70; Marvin Carlson, "The French Censorship Enquiries of 1849 and 1891," *Essays in Theater* 5 (1986); Natalie Isser, "Napoleon III and Human Rights Censorship and the Theater," unpublished paper presented to the 1990 meeting of the Western Society for French History at the University of California, Santa Barbara; and Neil Carruthers, "Theatrical Censorship in Paris from 1850 to 1905," *New Zealand Journal of French Studies* 3 (1982): 21–41. Case studies of individual dramatists or plays include Dawn Sova, *Banned Plays* (New York, 2004); Sheryl Kroen, "Ushering in the Reign of *Tartuffe:* Practicing Politics in an Age of Counterrevolution, 1815–1830," in Michael Adcock, et al., eds., *Revolution, Society and the Politics of Memory* (Melbourne, 1996), 228–36; Charles O'Neill, "Theatrical Censorship in France, 1844–1875: The Experience of Victor Séjour," *Harvard Library Bulletin* 26 (1978); Eugene Weber, "About *Thermidor:* The Oblique Uses of a Scandal," *French Historical Studies* 17 (1991): 330–42; Barbara Cooper, "Censorship and the Double Portrait of Disorder in Lemercier's *La Demence de Charles VI,*" *Orbis Litteratum* 40 (1985): 300–316; and Mary Ann Smart, "Mourning the Duc d'Orléans: Donizetti's *Dom Sébastien* and the Political Meanings of Grand Opera," in Roger Park and Mary Ann Smart, eds., *Reading Critics Reading: Opera and Ballet Criticism in France from the Revolution to 1848* (Oxford, 2001). Since virtually every significant nineteenth-century French dramatist, actor, and director encountered censorship, most English-language biographies on them include at least some scattered information on the subject. For example, see Karin Pendle, *Eugène Scribe and French Opera of the Nineteenth Century* (Ann Arbor, MI, 1979); Alexander Faris, *Jacques Offenbach* (London, 1980); Mark Everist, *Giacomo Meyerbeer and Music Drama in Nineteenth-Century Paris* (New York, 2005); Claude Schopp, *Alexandre Dumas* (New York, 1988); Albert Halsall, *Victor Hugo and the Romantic Drama* (Toronto, 1998); Robert

Baldick, *The Life and Times of Frédérick Lemaître* (Fair Lawn, NJ, 1959); Lawson Carter, *Zola and the Theater* (New Haven, CT, 1963); and Jean Chothia, *André Antoine* (Cambridge, England, 1991).

The best of several available French-language general studies of the nineteenth-century theater is Gérard Gengembre, *Le théâtre frança022 au 19e siècle* (Paris, 1999); as with Gengembre, there is a section on censorship in Michel Autrand, *Le Théâtre en France de 1870 à 1914* (Paris, 2006). The field of nineteenth-century French theater-censorship studies is dominated by recently retired French national archivist Odile Krakovitch, whose most important work is *Hugo Censuré: la liberté au théâtre au XXe siècle* (Paris, 1985). Her other two leading works are inventories of the censorship archives, accompanied by lengthy introductions that summarize or update her work: *Les Pièces de théâtre soumises a La Censure (1800–1830)* (Paris, 1982) and *Censure des Répertoires des Grands Théâtres Parisiens (1835–1906)* (Paris, 2003). Krakovitch has also produced a steady, almost innumerable stream of articles, some of which largely summarize her work, such as "La mise en pièces des théâtres: la censure des spectacles au XIXe siècle" in *Maintien de l'ordre et polices en France et en Europe au XIXe siècle* (Paris, 1987), 287–300; and "Les Ciseaux d'Anastasie: Le Théâtre au XIXe Siècle" in *Censures: de la Bible aux l'armes d'eros* (Paris, 1987), 258–67. Other articles mostly center on particular time periods, dramatists, or plays, such as "Le théâtre sous le Restauration et la monarchie de Juillet," in Alain Vaillant, ed., *Mesure(s) du Livre* (Paris, 1992), and "'Le Plus Refusé des Auteurs Dramatiques': ou les Démêlés de Balzac avec la Censure," *L'Année Balzacienne* (1994): 273–307. Most of her many other works are cited in individual endnotes and not repeated here.

Beyond Krakovitch, the key works for studying nineteenth-century French theater censorship include two nineteenth-century volumes published by theater censor Victor Hallays-Dabot: *Histoire de la censure théâtrale en France* (Geneva, 1970 [1862]) and *La Censure dramatique et le* théâtre, *1850–1870* (Paris, 1871); and the unjustly neglected 1902 study by Albert Cahuet, *La Liberté du Théâtre en France et a l'Etranger* (Paris), which, very unusually, includes some comparative information. Janice Best, *La subversion silencieuse: Censure, auto censure et lutte pour la liberté d'expression* (Montreal, 2001), includes a number of case studies of censored plays and operas, and is the single most informative source on opera censorship. Other useful French studies for musical stage censorship include Olivier Bara, *Le théâtre de l'opéra-comique sous la restauration* (Hildesheim, 2001); Odile Krakovitch, "L'Opéra-Comique et la censure," in Herbert Schneider, ed., *Die Opéra Comique und ihr Einfluß auf das europäische Musiktheater im 19. Jahrhundert* (Hildesheim, 1997), 211–34; Anselm Gerhard, "La 'Libérté inadmissible à l'Opéra," *Avant-Scene Opera* (1989): 69–71; and Franck Hochleitner, "La Censure à l'Opéra de Paris aux Débuts de la IIIe République," in Pascal Orly, ed., *La Censure en France* (Paris, 1997), 233–50. Concetta Condemi has published several important books and articles with information about café-concert censorship: *Les Cafés-Concerts* (Paris, 1992); "La Chanson de café-concert en France (1848–1920): Censure et liberté d'expression d'un loisir de masse," in Herbert Schneider, ed., *Chanson und Vaudeville: Gesellschaftliches Singen und unterhaltende Kommunkation im 18. Und 19. Jahrhundert* (St. Ingbert, 1999), 233–47; and "Les spectacles dans les cafés de Paris entre 1848 et 1881," in *Théâtre et Spectacles Hier et Aujourd'hui: Epoque Moderne et Contemporaine* (Paris, 1991), 303–11. Also important on this subject is Eva Kimminich, "Chansons étouffées: Recherche sur le café-concert au XIXe siècle," *Politix* 14 (1991): 19–26.

Important articles that focus on particular time periods include two articles by Louis Allard: "La Censure Théâtrale Sous La Restauration," *Harvard Studies and Notes in Philology and Literature* 14 (1932): 197–217; and "Un Épisode de la Censure Dramatique: La Comédie et la Censure sous Louis-Philippe," *Romanic Review* 34 (1943). Other such studies include Jean-Marie Thomasseau, "Le Mélodrame et La Censure sous le Premier Empire et la Restauration," *Revue des sciences humaines* 162 (1976): 171–82; Claude Gevell and Jean Rabot, "La Censure Théâtrale sous la Restauration," *Revue de Paris* 120 (1913): 339–61; Gilles Malandain, "Quel Théâtre pour la République? Victor Hugo et ses Pairs Devant le Conseil d'État en 1849," *Société et Représentations* 11 (2001): 205–27; François Lesure, "Un débat sur les théâtres lyriques en France en 1849," in Henri Vanhulst and Malou Haine, eds., *Musique et Société* (Brussels, 1988), 11–20; Silvia Desegni, "Les Censeurs de Théâtre en Hommes de Lettres sous le Second Empire," *Micromégas* 25 (1998): 167–83; Jean-Claude Yon, "La légende napoléonienne au théâtre, 1848–1869," in *Napoléon de l'histoire à la légende* (Paris, 2000), 315–44; Josette Parrain, "Censure, théâtre et Commune (1871–1914)," *Mouvement Social* 79 (1972); Madeleine Rebérioux, "Roman, théâtre et chanson: Quelle Commune?" *Mouvement Social* 79 (1972); Philippe Ivernel, "Censure théâtrale sous la République: le cas du théâtre d'inspiration anarchiste," *Revue d'histoire du théâtre* 56 (2004): 9–21; Michel Autrand, "Idéal Démocratique et Censure Théâtrale sous la Troisième République," *Revue d'histoire littéraire de la France* 105 (2005): 301–12; Philippe Baron, "La censure théâtrale sous le government de Waldeck-Rousseau (1899–1902)," in Peter Brockmeier, ed., *Zensur und Selbstzensur in der Literatur* (Würzburg, 1996), 143–55; and Odile Krakovitch, "De Thermidor aux Paravents: La liberté théâtrale, objet de débat politique à l'Assemblée," *Théâtre/Public* 181 (2006): 6–18. Most of the useful case studies and studies of individual dramatists are in the Best book cited above or in studies by Krakovitch, but see also: Jean-Pierre Galvan, "*Les Mystères de Paris* sous les Ciseaux d'Anastasie," *Rocambole* 20 (2002): 39–49; Marin Kanes, "Zola, 'Germinal' et la Censure dramatique," *Les Cahiers Naturalistes* 29 (1965): 35–42; Clélia Anfra, "*Germinal* en rouge," *Théâtre/Public* 181 (2006): 18–22; Paule Adamy, "De Quelque Oeuvres des Frères Goncourt Censurées et Parfois de l'Autocensure," in Jacques Domenech, ed., *Censure, auto censure et art d'écrire* (Paris, 2005), 219–41; Michael Autrand, "La Censure au théâtre à fin du XIXe siècle: *Thermidor* de Victorien Sardou," *French Studies in Southern Africa* 10 (1991): 1–27; James Sanders, "Zola et la censure théâtrale," *Les Cahiers Naturalistes* 51 (1977): 141–48; and Paule Salvan, "Le *Tartuffe* de Molière et l'Agitation Anticléricale en 1825," *Revue d'histoire du théâtre* 12 (1960): 7–16.

## Notes

1. *Journal Officiel de la République Française* (hereafter *JO*), 8 June 1880, 6214; Victor Hallays-Dabot, *Histoire de la censure théâtrale en France* (Paris, 1862), vi; Odile Krakovitch, "La mise en pièces des théâtres: la censure des spectacles au XIXe siècle," in *Maintien de l'ordre et polices en France et en Europe au XIXe siècle* (Paris, 1987), 299; Krakovitch, "Les Ciseaux d'Anastasie: Le Théâtre au XIXe Siècle," in *Censures: de la Bible aux l'armes d'eros* (Paris, 1987), 56, 63; Krakovitch, "Éphémère de la Fête, Pérennité des Archives: Le Fonds de la Censure Théâtrale," in *Memoires de l'Éphémère: Fêtes et Spectacles dans le Patrimoine Écrit* (Lyon, 1998), 127, 143. For inventories of archival material on the nineteenth-century French theater censorship, as well as useful introductory essays on the subject, which summarize much of her research published elsewhere, see Odile Krakovitch, *Les Pièces de théâtre soumises a La Censure (1800–1830)* (Paris, 1982); and Odile Krakovitch, *Censure des Répertoires des Grands Théâtres Parisiens (1835–1906)* (Paris, 2003), quotation from page 35. See also Elizabeth Barlet, "Archival Sources for the Opéra Comique and its Registres at the Bibliothèque de l'Opéra," *Nineteenth-Century Music* 7 (1983): 118–28; and Lesley Wright, "A New Source for 'Carmen,'" *Nineteenth-Century Music* 2 (1976): 61–71.
2. F. W. J. Hemmings, *Theater and State in France, 1760–1905* (Cambridge, 1994), 1.
3. F. W. J. Hemmings, *The Theater Industry in Nineteenth-Century France* (Cambridge, 1993), 2; Harold Hobson, *French Theater Since 1800* (London, 1978),

4–5; Hemmings, *Theater and State*, 1; Dominique Leroy, *Histoire des Arts du Spectacle en France* (Paris, 1990), 136–91; Steven Huebner, "Opera Audiences in Paris, 1830–1870," *Music and Letters* 70 (1989): 218–24.
4. Sally Charnow, *Theater, Politics and Markets in Fin-de-Siècle Paris* (New York, 2005), 56, 58.
5. *Archives Parlementaires de 1787 à 1860* (hereafter *AP*) 98 (1898): 257–58 (emphasis in original).
6. Krakovitch, *Pièces*, 14; Hallays-Dabot, *Histoire*, 116; Odile Krakovitch, *Hugo Censure: la liberté au théâtre au XXe siècle* (Paris, 1985), prologue.
7. Krakovitch, "Mise," 294; Louis Allard, "Un Épisode de la Censure Dramatique: La Comédie et la Censure sous Louis-Philippe," *Romanic Review* 34 (1943): 331–32; Olivier Bara, *Le théâtre de l'opéra-comique sous la restauration* (Hildesheim, 2001), 208; Krakovitch, *Censure*, 88.
8. Jean-Claude Yon, "La censure dramatique au XIXe siècle: La règne d'Anastasie," *L'Avant-Scène Opéra* 225 (2005): 85; Alberic Cahuet, *La Liberté du Théâtre en France et a l'Etranger* (Paris, 1902), 348; Hemmings, *Theater and State*, 52; Albert Delpit, "La Liberté des Théâtres," *Revue des deux mondes* (1878): 623; Allard, "Épisode," 332.
9. Hemmings, *Theater Industry*, 113; Louis Allard, "La Censure Théâtrale Sous La Restauration," *Harvard Studies and Notes in Philology and Literature* 14 (1932): 201; Denise Davidson, "Controlling Urban Amusements: The Police and Provincial Theater, 1800–1830," *Proceedings of the Western Society for French History* 27 (2001): 144; Davidson, *France after Revolution: Urban Life, Gender and the New Social Order* (Cambridge, MA, 2007), 103–30; Claude-France Hollard, "L'administration, partenaire de la vie théâtrale en province au XIX siècle, l'exemple du départment de Vaucluse," in *Théâtre et Spectacles Hier et Aujourd'hui: Epoque Moderne et Contemporaine* (Paris, 1991), 319.
10. John House, "Manet's Maximilian: Censorship and the Salon," in Elizabeth Childs, ed., *Suspended License: Censorship and the Visual Arts* (Seattle, WA, 1997), 187; Archives Nationales, Paris, F18 2342 (emphasis added).
11. Odile Krakovitch, "Robert Macaire ou la Grande Peur des Censeurs," *Europe: Revue litteraire mensuelle* (1987): 55–56; Leroy, 145–47, 178–84; Jean-Marie Thomasseau, "Le Melodrama et La Censure sous le Premier Empire et la Restauration," *Revue des sciences humaines* 162 (1976): 179; Krakovitch, *Hugo*, 114, 131, 140; Nicholas Harrison, "Colluding with the Censor: Theater Censorship in France After the Revolution," *Romance Studies* 25 (1995): 12. See also, generally, John McCormick, *Popular Theaters of Nineteenth-Century France* (London, 1993); and Krakovitch, "L'Opéra-Comique et la censure," in Herbert Schneider, ed., *Die Opéra Comique und ihr Einfluß auf das europäische Musiktheater im 19. Jahrhundert* (Hildesheim, 1997), 211–34.
12. Krakovitch, *Hugo*, 150, 241; W. Howarth, *Sublime and Grotesque: A Study of French Romantic Drama* (London, 1975), 306; Charles O'Neill, "Theatrical Censorship in France, 1844–1875: The Experience of Victor Séjour," *Harvard Library Bulletin* 26 (1978): 434.
13. Karin Pendle, *Eugène Scribe and French Opera of the Nineteenth Century* (Ann

Arbor, MI, 1979), 19; Henry Raynor, *Music and Society Since 1815* (New York, 1976), 10; Anselm Gerhard, "La 'Libérté inadmissible à l'Opéra," *Avant-Scene Opera* (1989): 70–71; Mark Everist, *Music Drama at the Paris Odéon, 1824–1828* (Berkeley, CA, 2002), 118–19; Jane Fulcher, *The Nation's Image: French Grand Opera as Politics and Politicized Art* (Cambridge, 1987), 26–32, 201; J. Walsh, *Second Empire Opera* (London, 1981), 21; Albert Boime, "The Second Empire's Official Realism," in Gabriel Weisberg, ed., *The European Realist Tradition* (Bloomington, IN, 1982), 39; Alexander Faris, *Jacques Offenbach* (London, 1980), 144–45, 157–58; Franck Hochleitner, "La Censure à l'Opéra de Paris aux Débuts de la IIIe République," in Pascal Orly, ed., *La Censure en France a l'ère démocratique* (Paris, 1997), 238–40; Gilles de van, "De Triboulet à Rigoletto," *Les Cahiers Comédie-Française* 2 (1992): 21–28.

14. Odile Krakovitch, "Hugo Censuré: Encore et Toujours sous la Troisieme République comme sous le Second Empire," *L'Echo Hugo* 6 (2006): 9, 15; Janice Best, *La subversion silencieuse: Censure, auto censure et lutte pour la liberté d'expression* (Montreal, 2001), 65–88.
15. Yon, "Censure," 85; James Billington, *Fire in the Minds of Men* (New York, 1980), 151–55, 561; Winston Dean, "French Opera," in Gerald Abraham, ed., *The Age of Beethoven, 1790–1830* (London, 1982), 105, 112; Ruth Bereson, *The Operatic State: Cultural Policy and the Opera House* (London, 2002), 42, 45, 48.
16. James Allen, *In the Public Eye: A History of Reading in Modern France* (Princeton, NJ, 1991), 94; Krakovitch, *Hugo*, 224–25, 227; Krakovitch, *Censure*, 15; Cahuet, 217.
17. Cahuet, 206.
18. Krakovitch, *Hugo*, 75. Nancy Nolte, "Government and Theater in Restoration France," *Proceedings, Consortium on Revolutionary Europe* 1985 (1986): 419–40, offers considerable biographical information on a number of the theater censors; Krakovitch, *Censure*, 38–41, also provides such information.
19. Allard, "Censure," 199–200; Marc Precicaud, *Le théâtre lyrique à Limoges, 1800–1914* (Paris, 2001), 36; Pendle, 20–21; Hollard, 314–16, 327. On *Les Huguenots*, see Best, *La subversion silencieuse*, 89–115.
20. Hallays-Dabot, *La Censure dramatique et le théâtre, 1850–1870* (Paris, 1871), 6; Krakovitch, *Pièces*, 21.
21. F. W. J. Hemmings, *Culture and Society in France, 1848–1898* (London, 1971), 48–49. See generally on *Camélias*, Best, *La subversion silencieuse*, 145–48, 157–62.
22. Krakovitch, "Mise," 289; Hemmings, *Theater and State*, 163; Mark Everist, *Giacomo Meyerbeer and Music Drama in Nineteenth-Century Paris* (New York, 2005), 6, 310, 326; Everist, "Theaters of Litigation: Stage Music at the Théâtre de la Renaissance, 1838–1840," *Cambridge Opera Journal* 16 (2004): 133–61; Jean-Claude Yon, "La Creation du Théâtre des Bouffes-Parisiens (1855–1862) ou La Difficile Naissance de l'Operette," *Revue d'histoire moderne et contemporaine* 39 (1992): 575–600; Marvin Carlson, "The Golden Age of the Boulevard," *Drama Review* 18 (1974): 29–30; John Lough, *Writer and Public in France: From the Middle Ages to the Present Day* (Oxford, 1978), 339.

23. Cahuet, 43, 52; Jonas Barish, *The Anti-theatrical Prejudice* (Berkeley, CA, 1981), 199; Glynne Wickham, *A History of the Theater* (Oxford, 1985), 11; Edward Hopkins, *Theater and State in France, 1789–1914* (University of Virginia MA thesis, 1978), 5; John Hohenberg, *Free Press/Free People* (New York, 1971), 72.
24. Hemmings, *Theater and State*, 61; Beatrice Hyslop, "The Theater during a Crisis: The Parisian theater during the Reign of Terror," *Journal of Modern History* 17 (1945): 332–55.
25. On Napoleon's regulation of the theater, see Leroy, 86–87, 109; David Chaillou, *Napoléon et l'Opéra* (Paris, 2004), 184–245.
26. Claude Gevell and Jean Rabot, "La Censure Théâtrale sous la Restauration," *Revue de Paris* 120 (1913): 339, 343, 351; Alan Spitzer, *The French Generation of 1820* (Princeton, NJ, 1987), 253; Neil Arvin, "Casimir Bonjour and the French Theater during the Restoration," *French Review* 17 (1944): 207.
27. Krakovitch, "Opéra," 222; Thomasseau, 178, 180; Nolte, "Government," 437; Jean-Claude Yon, "La Politique Théâtrale de la Restauration," in Jean-Yves Mollier, et al., eds., *Repenser la Restauration* (Versailles, 2005), 286; Davidson, *France*, 105, 128.
28. Allard, "Censure," 205; Allen, 90; Krakovitch, *Hugo*, 36; F. W. J. Hemmings, *Culture and Society in France, 1789–1848* (Leicester, 1987), 141.
29. Allard, "Censure," 208; Gevell and Rabot, 358; Jacqueline de Jomaron, *Le théâtre en France*, vol. II (Paris, 1989), 39; Odile Krakovitch, "Alexandre Dumas et la Censure," in Ferdnande Bassant and Claude Schopp, eds., *Les Troise Mousqeutaires: Cent Cinquante ans Apres* (Paris, 1995), 166–67; Claude Schopp, *Alexandre Dumas* (New York, 1988), 108; Florence Naugrette, *Le Théâtre romantique* (Paris, 2001), 80; Fernande Bassant, "La Création de *Marion de Lorme*," *Revue d'histoire du théâtre* 48 (1996): 430–46; Albert Halsall, *Victor Hugo and the Romantic Drama* (Toronto, 1998), 73.
30. Extensive discussions of *Masaniello* and *La muette de Portici* can be found in Fulcher, 25–46; Best, *La subversion silencieuse*, 39–64; and Bara, 259–79.
31. John Merriman, "Contested Freedoms in the French Revolutions, 1830–1871," in Isser Woloch, ed., *Revolution and the Meanings of Freedom in the Nineteenth Century* (Stanford, CA, 1996), 179.
32. Halsall, 111–16; Hopkins, 29, 35; Odile Krakovitch, "Le théâtre sous le Restauration et la monarchie de Juillet," in Alain Vaillant, ed., *Mesure(s) du Livre* (Paris, 1992), 148; Cahuet, 203; Jean-Claude Yon, "Le Revolution de 1830 au théâtre ou le triomphe de la Barricade imprimée," in Alain Corbain and Jean-Marie Mayeur, eds., *La Barricade* (Paris, 1997), 94; Dawn Sova, *Banned Plays* (New York, 2004), 235; Best, *La subversion silencieuse*, 65–88. On the explosion of plays about Napoleon, see Sylvie Vielledent, "Le retour du 'petit chapeau' en 1830," in *Napoléon de l'histoire à la légende* (Paris, 2000), 351–71.
33. Allard, "Épisode," 335; J. Talmon, *Romanticism and Revolt: Europe, 1815–1848* (New York, 1967), 74; Hopkins, 37.
34. Krakovitch, *Hugo*, 88, 286–87; Krakovitch, *Censure*, 25; Nancy Nolte, *Government and théâtre in Nineteenth-Century France: Administrative Organization for Control of the Comédie-Française Repertoire*, PhD dissertation, University of

Akron (Akron, OH, 1984), 206; Odile Krakovitch, "'Le Plus Refusé des Auteurs Dramatiques': ou les Démêlés de Balzac avec la Censure," *L'Année Balzacienne* (1994): 273–307; Robert Baldick, *The Life and Times of Frédérick Lemaître* (Fair Lawn, NJ, 1959), 178–81; Concetta Condemi, *Les Cafés-Concerts* (Paris, 1992), 24; Eva Kimminich, "Chansons étouffées: Recherche sur le café-concert au XIXe siècle," *Politix* 14 (1991).

35. Krakovitch, *Hugo*, 155, 286–87; Allard, "Épisode," 337–45; Odile Krakovitch, "Robert Macaire ou la Grande Peur des Censeurs," *Europe: Revue littéraire mensuelle* (Paris, 1987), 49–60, 703–4; Baldick, 142; Odile Krakovitch, "La Révolution à travers le théâtre de 1815 à 1870," in *Le XIXe siècle et la Révolution française* (Paris, 1992), 61–67. Krakovitch summarizes the July Monarchy drama censorship in two identical articles that appear under the same title, "Les romantiques et la censure au théâtre," in *Romantisme* 28 (1982): 33–43, and *Revue d'histoire du théâtre* 36 (1984): 56–68.

36. Krakovitch, *Hugo*, 130, 141, 153, 165; Odile Krakovitch, "Eugène Sue, Auteur Dramatique Censuré," *Rocambole* 28/29 (2004): 35–36; Yon, "Censure," 85; Best, *La subversion silencieuse*, 124–27.

37. Jean-Pierre Galvan, "*Les Mystères de Paris* sous les Ciseaux d'Anastasie," *Rocambole* 20 (2002): 39–49; Hallays-Dabot, *Histoire*, 319.

38. On the 1849 theater inquiry, see Krakovitch, *Censure*, 14–16; Gilles Malandain, "Quel Théâtre pour la Republique? Victor Hugo et ses Pairs Devant le Conseil d'État en 1849," *Société et Représentations* 11 (2001): 205–27; Marvin Carlson, "The French Censorship Enquiries of 1849 and 1891," *Essays in Theater* 5 (1986): 5–8; François Lesure, "Un débat sur les theaters lyriques en France en 1849," in Henri Vanhulst and Malou Haine, eds., *Musique et Société* (Brussels, 1988), 11–20; Odile Krakovitch, "La Société des Auteurs et Compositeurs dramatique, pour ou contre la censure?" *Nineteenth-Century French Studies* 18 (1988–90): 370–73; Hopkins, 66. On Scribe and the censorship, see Diana Hallman, *Opera, Liberalism and Antisemitism in Nineteenth-Century France* (Cambridge, 2002), 63; and scattered material in Jean-Claude Yon, *Eugène Scribe: La Fortune et La Liberté* (2000).

39. Hallays-Dabot, *Histoire*, 7; Cahuet, 217; Gay Manifold, *George Sand's Theater Career* (Ann Arbor, MI, 1985), 64, 77; Odile Krakovitch, "George Sand et la Censure," *Bulletin de la Société de l'Histoire de Paris et de l'Ile de France* 131 (2004): 10–11; Edgar Newman, "The End of Allusions, or Why the Mouchards Could Finally Smile: Policing Poetry and Song during the July Monarchy and the Second Republic," *Proceedings of the Western Society for French History* 18 (1991): 594.

40. Maurice Mauron, *La Marseillaise* (Paris, 1968), 161–64; Frédéric Robert, "La Marseillaise Pendant la Deuxième République ou d'une Nouvelle Renaissance a une Nouvelle Proscription," *Revue Internationale de Musique Française* 1 (1980): 321–28.

41. Krakovitch, *Hugo*, 224; Allen, 90; Ferdnande Bassan, "L'Accueil fait à *Richard Darlington*," *Oeuvres et Critiques* 21 (1996): 60; Cahuet, 225; Krakovitch, "Dumas," 177; Odile Krakovitch, "Sardou et la censure, ou le contestataire con-

testé," paper delivered at a colloquium on Sardou at the University of Strasbourg in 2005; Odile Krakovitch, "Le Silence des Théâtres sur la Drogue et l'Alcool: Autocensure ou Censure," *Sociétés et Représentations* (1995): 161. Generally, on Second Empire theater censorship, see Odile Krakovitch, "Censure," in Jean Tulard, ed., *Dictionnaire du Second Empire* (Paris, 1948), 254–60.

42. Krakovitch, "Hugo," 10–13; Best, *La subversion silencieuse*, 124–27.
43. Hallays-Dabot, *Censure*, 75–76; Best, *La subversion silencieuse*, 173–79, Krakovitch, *Hugo*, 233; Krakokvitch, *Censure*, 62, 66; Krakovitch, "Hugo," 10–12; Natalie Isser, "Napoleon III and Human Rights Censorship and the theater," paper presented to the 1990 meeting of the Western Society for French History at the University of California Santa Barbara; Neil Carruthers, "Theatrical Censorship in Paris from 1850 to 1905," *New Zealand Journal of French Studies* 3 (1982): 22, 25; McCormick, 108; Hervé Lacombe, *The Keys to French Opera in the Nineteenth Century* (Berkeley, CA, 2001), 26; Angela Pao, *The Orient of the Boulevards: Exoticism, Empire and Nineteenth-Century French Theater* (Philadelphia, PA, 1998), 75; Silvia Desegni, "Les Censeurs de Théâtre en Hommes de Lettres sous le Second Empire," *Micromégas* 25 (1998): 170; Odile Krakovitch, "Paul Meurice et la censure: l'affaire *Paris*," paper delivered at a colloquium on Meurice held in Paris in 2005.
44. Jean-Claude Yon, "La légende napoléonienne au théâtre, 1848–1869," in *Napoléon de l'histoire à la légende* (Paris, 2000), 315–44; Odile Krakovitch, "La Révolution à travers le théâtre de 1815 à 1870," in *Le XIXe siècle et la Révolution français* (Paris, 1992), 67–72; Odile Krakovitch, "Censure et Autocensure des livrets: le Théâtre Lyrique et son directeur, Carvalho," in Georges Zaragoza, ed., *Le Livret d'opéra* (Ivry-sur-Seine, 2002), 325–26; Cahuet, 242.
45. Odile Krakovitch, "Labiche et la censure ou un vaudeville de plus!" *Revue Historique* 576 (1990): 341–57; Jean-Claude Yon, "Hélène censurée: le liberté et le théâtre à Paris en 1864," *Les Cahiers des Amis du Festival* (Aix-en-Provence, 199), 9; Krakovitch, *Hugo*, 241; Schopp, 273–74, 404–5.
46. Leroy, 91, 382; Harrison, 13; Krakovitch, *Censure*, 59.
47. Walsh, 48; Odile Krakovitch, "La Censure des Spectacles sous le Second Empire," in Orly, ed., *La Censure en France*, 71–72; Concetta Condemi, "La Chanson de café-concert en France (1848–1920): Censure et liberté d'expression d'un loisir de masse," in Herbert Schneider, ed., *Chanson und Vaudeville: Gesellschaftliches Singen und unterhaltende Kommunkation im 18. Und 19. Jahrhundert* (St. Ingbert, 1999), 233–47; Condemi, "Les spectacles dans les cafés de Paris entre 1848 et 1881," in *Théâtre et Spectacles*, 303–11.
48. *JO* (1878), 4042; Krakovitch, *Hugo*, 249; Krakovitch, *Censure*, 75; Hopkins, 52; Robert Herbert, "Courbet's 'Mère Gregoire,'" in Klaus Gallwitz, ed., *Malerei und Theorie* (Frankfurt, 1980), 80; Krakovitch, "Hugo," 16–27; Pierre Langlais, "1873: Défense de Jouer *Le roi s'amuse*," *L'Echo Hugo* 4 (2004): 36–55.
49. Josette Parrain, "Censure, théâtre et Commune (1871–1914)," *Mouvement Social* 79 (1972): 330; Condemi, *Café-Concerts*, 39; Allen, 90; Krakovitch, "Censure des Spectacles," 71–72, 77.
50. Parrain, 330, 338; Madeleine Rebérioux, "Roman, théâtre et chanson: Quelle

Commune?" *Mouvement Social* 79 (1972): 277–78, 281; Wright, 67; Condemi, "Spectacles," 309–11; Condemi, "Chanson," 242–43.

51. Philippe Ivernel, "Censure théâtrale sous la République: le cas du théâtre d'inspiration anarchiste," *Revue d'histoire du théâtre* 56 (2004): 13–17; Best, *La subversion silencieuse,* 225, 227–51; Carruthers, 38; Janice Best, "L'actionnaire dormait la nuit ... *Germinal,* et d'autres contest nihilistes," *Nineteenth-Century French Studies* 25 (1996–97): 131–53; Marin Kanes, "Zola, 'Germinal' et la Censure dramatique," *Les Cahiers Naturalistes* 29 (1965): 35–42; Clélia Anfra, "*Germinal* en rouge," *Théâtre/Public* 181 (2006): 18–22; Lawson Carter, *Zola and the Theater* (New Haven, CT, 1963), 136–42; Michel Autrand, "Idéal Démocratique et Censure Théâtrale sous la Troisième République," *Revue d'histoire littéraire de la France* 105 (2005): 301–12.

52. On *La Fille Élisa,* see Charnow, 70–76, Paule Adamy, "De Quelque Oeuvres des Frères Goncourt Censurées et Parfois de l'Autocensure," in Jacques Domenech, ed., *Censure, auto censure et art d'écrire* (Paris, 2005), 225–27; Jean Chothia, *André Antoine* (Cambridge, 1991), 115. On *Thermidor,* see Eugene Weber, "About *Thermidor:* The Oblique Uses of a Scandal," *French Historical Studies* 17 (1991): 330–42; and Michael Autrand, "La Censure au théâtre à fin du XIXe siècle: *Thermidor* de Victorien Sardou," *French Studies in Southern Africa* 10 (1991): 1–27.

53. Thomas Sudik, *The French Administration of Fine Arts and the National Theaters (1882–1906),* MA thesis, University of North Carolina (Chapel Hill, NC, 1972), 58–68; Charnow, 77–80; Allen, 102; Odile Krakovitch, "Silence Consenti, Silence Imposé? L'Evolution de la Legislation de l'Exercice de la Censure Théâtrale au XIX Siècle," *Bulletin de Société d'Histoire de la Révolution de 1848* 10 (1994): 48; Carlson, 8–13; James Sanders, "Zola et la censure théâtrale: sa déposition du 11 mars 1891 à la Chambre des députés," *Les Cahiers Naturalistes* 31 (1985): 181–86; Carter, 137; Michale Autrand, *Le Théâtre en France de 1870 à 1914* (Paris, 2006), 42; Krakovitch, *Censure,* 21, 80; Hochleitner, 246.

54. Philippe Baron, "La censure théâtrale sous le government de Waldeck-Rousseau (1899–1902)," in Peter Brockmeier, ed., *Zensur und Selbstzensur in der Literatur* (Würzburg, 1996), 143–55.

55. On the parliamentary debates that eventually led to the end of French theater censorship in 1906, see Odile Krakovitch, "De Thermidor aux Paravents: La liberté théâtrale, objet de débat politique à l'Assemblée," *Théâtre/Public* 181 (2006): 6–18; Charnow, *Theater,* 80–84; and Thomas Sudik, *The French Administration.* On subsequent developments, see Richard Abel, *French Cinema* (Princeton, NJ, 1984), 38; Odile Krakovitch, "Le censure des théâtres durant la grande guerre," in *Théâtre et Spectacles,* 331–53.

56. Barry Daniels, *Revolution in the Theater: French Romantic Theories of Drama* (Westport, CT, 1983), 193; Krakovitch, *Hugo,* 43, 69, 219; Anselm Gerhard, *The Urbanization of Opera: Music Theater in Paris in the Nineteenth Century* (Chicago, 1998), 40; Odile Krakovich, "Liberté du roman-feuilleton et censure au théâtre: le cas Eugène Sue," in Anne-Simon Dufief and Jean-Louis Cabanès, eds., *Le roman au théâtre: Les adaptations théâtrales au XIXe siècle* (Paris, 2005),

35; Roger Berthet, *Anastasie, Anastasie: Groupemente textes sur la censure* (Reims, 1992), 18.
57. Carter, 141; James Sanders, "Zola et la censure théâtrale," *Les Cahiers Naturalistes* 51 (1977): 141–48; Krakovitch, *Hugo*, 245; Cahuet, 281, 339.
58. Krakovitch, *Hugo*, 84.
59. Claude Millet and Florence Naugrette, "Un Faubourg de Paris? Le Vie Théâtrale à Rouen sous la Monarchie de Juillet," in *Province/Paris: Topographies Littéraires de XIXe Siècle* (Rouen, 2000), 422; Hemmings, *Culture*, 50.
60. Carolyn Johnston, "Censoring Silence: The Theater of the Funambules and the Politics of Pantomime, 1820–1830," *Proceedings of the Western Society for French History* 24 (1997): 278–88; Nolte, *Government*, 117–18; Krakovitch, *Hugo*, 84–85, 87; Graham Robb, *Balzac* (London, 1994), 321–22; Condemi, 57.
61. Harrison, 16; Krakovitch, *Hugo*, 55; Sheryl Kroen, *Politics and Theater: The Crisis of Legitimacy in Restoration France, 1815–1830* (Berkeley, CA, 2000), 229–84; Kroen, "Ushering in the Reign of *Tartuffe*: Practicing Politics in an Age of Counterrevolution, 1815–1830," in Michael Adcock, et al., eds., *Revolution, Society and the Politics of Memory* (Melbourne, 1996), 228–36; Paule Salvan, "Le *Tartuffe* de Molière et l'Agitation Anticléricale en 1825," *Revue d'histoire du théâtre* 12 (1960): 7–16; Jean-Claude Yon, "Du droit de sifflet au théâtre au XIXe siècle," in Philippe Bourdin, ed., *La Voix & Le Geste: Une Approche Culturelle de la Violence Socio-Politique* (Paris, 2005), 322; Precicaud, 28, 39; F. W. J. Hemmings, "Applause for the Wrong Reasons: The Use of Applications for Political Purposes in Paris Theaters, 1780–1830," *Theater Research International* 14 (1989): 256–70; Corbain, *Time Desire and Horror: Towards a History of the Senses* (New York, 1995), 39–52; Hollard, 319.
62. Barbara Cooper, "Censorship and the Double Portrait of Disorder in Lemercier's *La Demence de Charles VI*," *Orbis Litteratum* 40 (1985): 300, 306.
63. On Antoine and Le Théâtre-Libre, see Samuel Waxman, *Antoine and The Théâtre Libre* (New York, 1926); Chothia; and John Henderson, *The First Avant-Garde, 1887–1894: Sources of the Modern French théâtre* (London, 1971), 44–73.
64. André Spies, *Opera, State and Society in the Third Republic, 1875–1914* (New York, 1988), 127, 129.

# Russia

### Anthony Swift

## Introduction

The heavy hand of the Russian censorship fits easily into the popular stereotype of repressive tsarist Russia, "the prison of peoples," to use Lenin's phrase. The stereotype does not differ greatly from the opinions expressed by those Russian artists who had to live with the restrictions imposed by the censors. "In Russia," according to avant-garde theater director Vsevolod Meyerhold, "they always begin by saying it's forbidden." Anton Chekhov remarked that writing with the censorship in mind was like "writing with a bone in your throat." At the onset of the 1905 Russian revolution, Moscow Art Theater director Konstantin Stanislavsky complained that the Russian theater was "being choked by the regulations, surveillance, and arbitrary actions" of the authorities responsible for censoring plays.¹ A few months after the October 1905 Manifesto, in which the tsar was forced to concede some civil liberties to his subjects, the First Congress of Drama and Music Writers condemned the censorship for violating writers' rights, catering to the capricious demands of government officials, failing to stop the production of aesthetically and morally offensive works, and for placing dramatic literature in a separate category from all other literature. The writers called for the abolition of the preliminary theater censorship and the establishment of the principle that writers and theater owners would be responsible to the courts for legal offences in productions.[2] Their call fell on deaf ears. Although prior censorship of most publications ended in 1906, prior censorship of drama lasted until the 1917 end of the Old Regime (and was soon resurrected by the new regime, with the 1922 creation of Glavlit).

Russia censored the stage with greater severity than it did the press because, as elsewhere in Europe, the theater's potent mix of visual impressions and spoken words was believed to have a greater impact than mere printed words. Moreover, as the stage was accessible even to the illiterate and less educated populace, theater performances could spread ideas to a much wider public than could the press, and thus potentially threaten public order if audiences were incited by subversive or immoral works. In censoring plays, the authorities were concerned not only with the texts, but also tried to imagine how audiences would interpret and react to performances. As liberal and radical opposition to the autocracy grew after 1850, the state especially feared that the stage would infect the masses with subversive political ideas and began to subject plays destined for "popular" theaters to even more stringent controls than those performed in theaters attracting the middle and upper classes. Thus, in 1868 Minister of Court V. F. Adlerberg warned that a popular theater would be "the most powerful and easiest means to cultivate in the people ideas hostile to the existing order," and "no censorship will be able to forestall that harmful influence just as it is not able to control the press, with the difference that while the press influences only the educated class, which is capable of discerning the truth and is not easily carried away, the theater can distort the comprehension of the simple folk and instill in them the germs of disorder by a mere trick or simply a scene."[3]

## The Origins of Theater Censorship

Professional theater and literary drama arrived comparatively late in Russia, in the mid seventeenth century, although a number of proto-theatrical entertainments existed previously. The state was the primary force behind theater's development in Russia: it founded theaters, trained actors, and sought to control what was performed on the stage. Secular drama appeared during the reign of Tsar Alexis (ruled 1645–76), who began holding drama performances at court with foreign and Russian actors. Peter the Great (ruled 1682–1725) established Russia's first public theater in

Moscow in 1702 as part of his program to Westernize his subjects. It lasted for only five years, but under Peter's successors theatrical entertainments gradually took root, as troupes of foreign actors came to Russia and native Russians began to hold performances of comic sketches and dramatic interludes. Empress Elizabeth (ruled 1741–62) founded the first imperial theater in St. Petersburg in 1756, and by the end of the eighteenth century a modest repertoire of Russian comedies and dramas coexisted on the stage with foreign imports in the original or translation. Besides the imperial theater, a few privately owned public theaters existed, as well as private theaters where serfs performed dramas for the pleasure of their masters.[4]

A rudimentary stage censorship developed alongside the emergence of Russian theater in the eighteenth century, although formal censorship institutions and regulations were established only in 1804, early in the reign of Alexander I (ruled 1801–25). In 1750 a police edict permitting performances in private homes forbade the representation of clergymen, and in 1782 the police were tasked with monitoring performances to ensure that they contained nothing "against the law and morality." Censorship of St. Petersburg's imperial theater was the responsibility of its directorate, while other theaters were censored by local committees or the police. Influenced by the European Enlightenment, eighteenth-century Russian monarchs viewed theater as having an essentially didactic function. As Catherine the Great (ruled 1762–96) famously remarked, "Theater is the school of the people and it should be under my direct supervision, for I am the senior teacher in that school and answer to God for the morals of my people." The moralistic neoclassical dramas of the period, mostly French imports or their Russian imitations, were well suited to this didactic vision of the theater.[5]

Under Catherine, who wrote several satirical comedies and two adaptations of Shakespeare, theater censorship policy was quite liberal by the standards of the following century. Social and political criticism was tolerated so long as it was not directed at the empress or Russia's social and political institutions. Comic operas such as Alexander Ablesimov's *The Miller, Sorcerer, Cheat, and Matchmaker* poked fun at social snobbery, while Dmitrii Fonvizin's brilliant satire on the ignorance of the provincial gentry and the abuses of serfdom, *The Minor* (1781), was performed at court and in theaters throughout Russia. The only evidence that *The Minor* encountered difficulties with the censorship was an attempt by a Moscow censor to strike out some offending passages, which Fonvizin refused to countenance; the unaltered play premiered in Moscow in 1783. Although nineteenth-century and Soviet critics tendentiously interpreted *The Minor* as an attack on the institutions of serfdom and autocracy, its content is typical of the moralizing neoclassical comedies of the period, which often denounced ignorance and the misuse of authority, and contemporaries did not see anything subversive in the play. Catherine herself attacked the mistreatment of serfs (although not serfdom per se) in her comedy *What Tricks Are These?* and intervened on occasion to protect plays from overly vigilant censors. When in 1785 the commander of the Moscow garrison halted performances of Nikolai Nikolev's new tragedy *Sorena and Zamir* (a Russian adaptation of Voltaire's *Alzire*) because it criticized religious fanaticism and tyranny, Catherine reprimanded him and reinstated the play, pointing out that it condemned tyrants rather than her own rule.[6]

The French Revolution's ideological challenge to monarchy caused theater censorship to tighten its grip throughout Europe. In Russia Catherine outlawed the Freemasons and suppressed virtually all political or social criticism. The most famous casualty of the more repressive attitude toward the theater was Iakov Kniazhnin's tragedy *Vadim of Novgorod* (1789), whose plot (borrowed from Corneille's *Cinna* and relocated from imperial Rome to medieval Russia) centers on the failed rebellion of a Novgorod military leader against the newly elected Scandinavian prince, Riurik, who generously forgives the rebel and orders a plebiscite in which the citizens vote to retain the prince as their ruler. Although the play endorses monarchy and depicts the prince as a virtuous, enlightened ruler, Kniazhnin realized that its depiction of a popular uprising and discussion of the virtues of republican versus monarchical rule were too close for comfort to contemporary events in France, and in 1790 therefore abandoned plans to stage it in St. Petersburg's imperial theater. The play was published with the approval of the censors by Catherine's old and trusted friend Princess Dashkova in 1793, after Kniazhnin's death. When the empress was told by a courtier, however, that the work was subversive, she immediately ordered all copies to be confiscated and destroyed, ignoring Dashkova's entreaty to at least read it before making a decision. Repression gave *Vadim* an undeserved notoriety and the text circulated surreptitiously for decades. In another well-known case, Catherine's successor, Paul I (ruled 1796–1801), ordered Vasily Kapnist's *Chicane*, a verse comedy attacking judicial corruption, banned after four performances in 1798 and exiled the playwright. Purportedly, on seeing the play for himself in a private performance Paul reversed his opinion, called Kapnist back to St. Petersburg and rewarded him, although the prohibition of the play remained in force.[7]

## The Early Nineteenth-Century Censorship

At the beginning of the reign of Alexander I there were three imperial theaters in St. Petersburg, the privately owned Maddox theater in Moscow, and several provincial theaters scattered around the Russian Empire. The state took over the Maddox theater in 1806 and established another imperial theater in Moscow, the Bolshoi, in 1825. In the course of the first half of the century the Directorate of Imperial Theaters gradually gained a de facto monopoly on public performances in St. Petersburg and Moscow that lasted until 1882. The monopoly protected its imperial theaters from competition and effectively placed virtually all theatrical life in Russia's two capitals under the total control of the state, although private clubs were permitted to stage plays for their members. The imperial theaters were by far the most important and influential in Russia, and the provincial theaters generally followed their lead in matters of repertoire.

The censorship statute of 1804 established the principle of preliminary censorship for all publications as well as plays to be performed in any theater in the country, including the imperial and court theaters. The task of censoring plays was initially assigned to the Ministry of Education. The 1804 statute, generally considered to be the most liberal of tsarist Russia's censorship laws, instructed the censors to ensure that publications and performances contained nothing against "god's law, the government, morality, or the personal honor of any citizen." No criteria applied specifically to works performed on stage, for, although the law was interpreted as requiring that all manuscripts or published texts of plays had to be approved before performances by censorship committees where these existed, or by educational authorities and local officials where they did not, censorship practice was left to the personal interpretation of the censors and decisions were sometimes determined by the interventions of government officials and clerics. The literal text of the censorship law called only for drama scripts to be censored, implying that published plays could be performed without the permission of the theater censors, but in 1805 the minister of education decided that all plays had to be vetted by the censors before they could be performed, including those that had been already deemed acceptable for publication. In a sign of the government's increasing vigilance over what was performed on stage, theater censorship was transferred from the Ministry of Education to the Ministry of Police in 1811. Seven years later the Ministry of Police was incorporated into the new Ministry of Internal Affairs, which assumed its censorship duties. Under Alexander I, plays that contained anything immoral, depicted religious figures, or could be interpreted as challenging the principle of autocracy were the main targets of the censors. St. Petersburg's German theater, for example, was prohibited from staging Goethe's *Egmont* in 1823 because the tragedy dealt with the sixteenth-century uprising of the Dutch against their Spanish rulers, a subject that "instead of teaching audiences obedience to the government could arouse in them the opposite feeling."[8]

## The Zenith of Censorship under Nicholas I

Alexander's death in 1825 was followed closely by the Decembrist uprising, in which a secret society of young army officers tried to overthrow the autocracy and establish a constitutional republic. Having put down the revolt, the new tsar, Nicholas I (ruled 1825–55), was determined to root out any trace of sedition and protect Russia from western political ideas. During his reign Russian censorship reached its oppressive zenith. Nicholas introduced new laws on censorship that were more detailed than the previous legislation and frequently took on the role of censor, most famously in personally censoring Alexander Pushkin's work. In 1826 the so-called "cast-iron statute" on censorship was adopted, according to which one censor remarked that "even the Lord's Prayer could have been considered a Jacobin speech." The new law forbade anything to be published or performed that did not contain "moral, useful or at least harmless ideas." Its detailed regulations instructed censors to forbid historical works that showed sympathy for opponents of legal authority as well as works that contained hidden subversive meanings, unfavorable comments on monarchical rule, or even bad grammar or impure language.[9]

The cast-iron statute gave the censors an extremely broad remit to judge works and root out sedition, but it was replaced within two years by the statute of 1828, which instructed the censors not to judge the quality of works or try to direct public opinion, but simply to prohibit works that were "harmful with respect to faith, the throne, morality, and the personal honor of citizens." Although the 1828 censorship statute was progressive by contemporary European standards, it was soon supplemented by directives, corrections, and new regulations according to the government's concerns of the moment. Political upheavals abroad, such as the 1830 revolution in France and the anti-Russian Polish uprising of the same year, resulted in a tightening of censorship controls, as did the European revolutions of 1848. According to the censor Alexander Nikitenko, by 1830 the censorship statute had been "completely overturned" by the mushrooming restrictions on the press. The tsar constantly intervened in the minutest details of government, including censorship. As the autocratic ruler of the Russian Empire, Nicholas was not bound to observe any restraints: his will was law and his interventions often determined the boundaries of the permissible. The 1828 censorship statute, like its predecessors, did not contain any specific rules applying to the stage. In practice, however, theater performances were subjected to a harsher regime than were literary publications. While published works were censored by committees under the Ministry of Education, the task of judging whether foreign and Russian plays could be performed in theaters was assigned to the tsar's secret political and moral police, the Third Section of His Majesty's Own Chancery, headed by Count Alexander Benckendorff.[10]

Obtaining permission to produce a play or opera was an arduous and time-consuming process unless one had official or imperial connections. In 1829 St. Petersburg and Moscow each had one imperial theater devoted to Russian drama and one where plays were performed in French. St. Petersburg also had German and Italian theaters, while in the provinces there were seventeen theaters, eleven of which staged Russian works, as well as performances given by traveling companies of actors. The Directorate of Imperial Theaters dispatched to the Third Section a copy of the play it wished to stage. The censor marked passages that he felt violated the regulations and wrote a short summary of the plot, which he submitted to the head of the Third Section, who decided whether the play could be staged. If approved, the play was returned to the Directorate with the censor's cuts. The title was entered in an alphabetical catalog and the deletions entered in a separate registry. Provincial theaters submitted plays through the local governor, who in turn sent them to the Third Section. Each new production of a play had to receive the censor's approval, even if it had been previously approved and staged at another theater. Russian theaters staged dozens of plays every season, and the four theater censors had the Herculean task of examining several hundred plays each year.[11]

Nicholas was keen to protect the Russian theater from anything he considered to be a harmful political, moral, or even aesthetic influence. He personally read many plays to decide their fate, a practice that benefited Nikolai Gogol enormously. His magnificent comedy *The Government Inspector*, a biting satire of official corruption, should have been banned according to the usual rules because of its satirical mockery of Russia's corrupt and ignorant officialdom. The tsar, however, read and approved it personally, after which it was staged with the deletion of a few phrases deemed disrespectful to religion (such as "Oh God!" and "My sainted mother!"). Gogol enjoyed the tsar's protection and financial support, and his other comedies were handled with kid gloves by the censors due to their author's imperial patronage. Pushkin's dramas, in contrast, were less kindly received by his imperial censor. He was permitted to publish his historical tragedy *Boris Godunov* with a few changes in 1830, but the play was not allowed to be performed, a prohibition that remained in force until 1866. Still, some of Pushkin's plays on topics less sensitive than the dynastic struggles of the late-sixteenth-century's "Time of Troubles" were permitted. His "little tragedy" *Mozart and Salieri* was performed in 1832 and *The Stone Guest* would have premiered in February 1837 had it not been canceled due to Pushkin's death at the end of January from a wound received in a duel. His unfinished folklore drama *Rusalka* premiered in 1838.[12]

The censors prevented other leading Russian authors from seeing their works performed, and a number of works that have since become classics did not appear in theaters until after Nicholas's death in 1855. Alexander Griboedov's *Woe from Wit* (1824), a comic masterpiece satirizing upper-class society, was kept off the stage for years despite the fact that it circulated in manuscript form and was familiar to most educated Russians. In the aftermath of the Decembrist uprising, its political debates and sarcastic references to secret societies were much too provocative for the censors. *Woe from Wit* was finally permitted to appear on the imperial stage in 1831, after the censors had deleted any references that could be interpreted to be political, as well as some sexually suggestive remarks, but the prohibition remained in force for provincial theaters until 1863. The complete version was published and performed only in the reform era of the 1860s, and ever since it has been a favorite of Russian audiences. None of Mikhail Lermontov's plays were allowed to be published or staged during his lifetime. His romantic masterpiece, *Masquerade* (1835), was banned for years despite Lermontov's repeated revisions for the censors, due to its harsh portrayal of aristocratic moral depravity. Not until 1852 were some scenes allowed on stage, and the complete work was not performed until 1862.[13]

The severity of censorship may account for the decline in plays submitted to the censors under Nicholas, which dropped from 659 in 1838 to 275 in 1846. A pre-revolutionary theater historian estimated that the censors prohibited 12 to 19 percent of the plays they examined. Ivan Turgenev's *The Houseguest*, a short play about a sponging nobleman, was banned in 1849 because the censor found it "equally offensive to morality and the nobility." Nicholas's censors struck out references to God and religious figures, language deemed uncouth, depictions of immoral behavior, and representations of or references to public officials. Most works that dealt with controversial historical subjects or included former Russian rulers were forbidden. Mikhail Pogodin's tragedy *Peter I* was not even permitted to be published in 1831 because it depicted the tsar on stage. In 1837 Nicholas ruled that no tsar could appear in an opera, and only pre-Romanov tsars were to be allowed in dramas (it was explained decades later to composer Nikolai Rimsky-Korsakov, with regard to the opera ban, that were a tsar to "suddenly sing a ditty, well, it would be unseemly"). Nonetheless, theaters were sometimes allowed to stage historical tragedies that portrayed tsars if they were considered to have a sufficiently clear patriotic message. Nestor Kukolnik's immensely popular patriotic drama *The Hand of the Almighty Has Saved the Fatherland* (1832) encountered no obstacles even though it dealt with rebellions, pretenders, and tsars. Nikolai Polevoi's jingoistic *The Grandfather of the Russian Navy* (1838), which celebrated Peter the Great's rule, enjoyed great success in the imperial theaters, as did his melodramatic *Parasha the Siberian Girl* (1840), the tale of a girl who journeys on foot to St. Petersburg to beg Catherine the Great's pardon for her father. A number of foreign historical tragedies were also approved, including Friedrich Schiller's *Maria Stuart* and *Don Carlos*, Victor Hugo's *Angelo*, and Shakespeare's *King Lear, Hamlet,* and *Coriolanus*. Of course, the censors deleted anything that could possibly be interpreted as subversive. In *Coriolanus,* for example, they softened the social conflict between the Roman plebeians and patricians. Two foreign operas presented in the 1830s that originally had revolutionary themes, Giaccomo Rossini's *William Tell,* about a Swiss revolt against Habsburg rule during the middle ages, and Daniel Auber's *La Muette de Portici,* about a seventeenth-century Italian uprising against Spanish rule, were each allowed only with significant alterations: the themes of struggles for liberty were completely eliminated and even the plays' names were changed (moreover *Portici,* retitled *Fenella,* could only be performed in German in 1834 rather than the original French, since even well-educated Russians were generally unfamiliar with the former language—it was later presented in Italian in 1847, but in Russian only in 1857, after the death of Nicholas I). *William Tell* was first presented in its original form in Russia only in 1932.[14]

Even under the draconian censorship of Nicholas I, a few plays were produced which dealt with important contemporary social issues. Aleksei Potekhin's *Men's, Not God's, Judgment,* which examines the relations between serfs and their masters, managed to overcome the censors' objections thanks to the support of Grand Duke Konstantin and was produced in Moscow in 1854. Pavel Lenskii's enormously successful vaudeville about the torments endured by provincial actresses at the hands of their gentry patrons, *Lev Gurych Sinichkin,* was a perennial favorite after its premiere in 1840. Russian vaudeville, which became very popular during Nicholas's reign, was one of the few genres in which mild social criticism was tolerated. The tsar was particularly fond of it and interceded to stop the censors from deleting inoffensive references to the police in Pavel Karatygin's vaudeville *The Bakery, or A Petersburg German.*[15]

It is difficult to assess the impact of Nicholas's reign on Russian theater. Censorship was probably at its most restrictive under him, and even if plays were not banned outright they were usually subjected to niggling "corrections" and cuts of anything the censors might deem offensive or subversive. Although the provincial theaters sometimes ignored, or were ignorant of, the rules and staged uncensored plays, the most important theaters in Russia were the imperial theaters of St. Petersburg and Moscow, where it was impossible to avoid the vigilance of the tsar and his censors. The last seven years of Nicholas's reign, which followed Europe's 1848 revolutions, was an era of "censorship terror" for the press, literature, and the theater, as the tsar and his police attempted to stamp out any suspected or imagined criticism. Yet, paradoxically, despite the restrictions and repression, the thirty years that Nicholas occupied the throne witnessed great achievements in Russian drama and literature, and it was in this period that a distinctly Russian theater repertoire began to take shape. As Bruce Lincoln has observed: "To portray the Nicholas era as a time of oppression and intellectual sterility is to tell only one side of the story. ... Nicholas's reign was, after all, the Golden Age of Russian literature; it saw the emergence of some of Russia's major composers; and it marked the development of the Russian theater to a point where it assumed a complete identity of its own and was no longer a mere copy of the West as it had been in the eighteenth century."[16]

## The Reforms of Alexander II

Nicholas died in 1855, in the midst of Russia's disastrous performance in the Crimean War, which called into question the strength of Russia's autocratic system. His son, Alexander II (ruled 1855–81), soon made it clear that he was intent on restoring the autocracy's prestige by undertaking fundamental reforms of Russia's social and administrative institutions, reforms that included the abolition of serfdom. Although Alexander relaxed controls on the press in order to encourage public support for his reform program, the secret police remained in charge of theater censorship during the first decade of his reign, and the censors went about their business much as they had under Nicholas. During the preparations of the reforms censors were anxious to keep government officials from being portrayed on the stage lest they be caricatured. Historical plays dealing with the topic of rebellion were almost always prohibited during the early years of Alexander's reign, although sometimes the censors examined the motifs for rebellion and permitted plays in which an uprising aimed to restore the legitimate authority. The government continued to view theater as a dangerous weapon that could easily be used to attack the existing order. In 1858 a proposal to abolish the imperial theater monopoly in the capitals was vetoed due to the minister of court's argument that privately owned theaters would promote seditious influences:

> Those who desire a revolution will discover a reliable means to have a powerful and rapid effect on all classes, especially the common people. ... Even at the beginning the government will be unable to protect itself from works that are hostile, if not in their entirety, then in particular episodes, one of which will be enough to refute everything written in the spirit of the government. No censorship and no police will prevent this. It should not be forgotten that in all revolutions privately owned theaters served as a means for arousing passions, and that their proliferation in France and Germany is the fruit of revolutions.

The minister's association of theater with revolutionary unrest would not have been out of place during the reign of Nicholas I.[17]

The fate of Alexander Ostrovsky's early dramatic works reveals the fundamental continuity in theater censorship between the last years of Nicholas's reign and the first years of Alexander's. The talented and prolific author, who enriched the Russian national repertoire with nearly fifty plays during his long career, had severe difficulties with the censors at the start of his career. Ostrovsky achieved one of his first literary successes with the publication in 1847 of his one-act comedy *A Family Picture*, which was quickly scheduled for performance in Moscow's imperial Little Theater, but it was prohibited for the stage by the Third Section due its portrayal of the unsavory business practices of Moscow merchants. His first full-length play, *It's All in the Family* (1850), another comedy about merchants' nefarious schemes, was not only banned from performance after having been published, but subsequent publication was forbidden and Ostrovsky was placed under police surveillance for several years. His translation of Shakespeare's *The Taming of the Shrew* was also barred from the stage in 1850, while *The Poor Bride* (1852), about a young woman with no dowry who is forced to marry a corrupt official twice her age, was only approved after the censors had removed many of the colloquial expressions that pepper its dialogue. Not all of Ostrovsky's plays were forbidden, however. It has been suggested that he softened the tone of his work in an effort to get it through the censors, and perhaps that is why the moralistic plays *Sit in Your Own Sled, Poverty Is No Vice,* and *You Can't Live as You Please,* which celebrate old-fashioned Russian virtues, were approved without any fuss. Indeed, after seeing *Sit in Your Own Sled,* Nicholas is said to have approvingly commented, "That's not a play but a moral lesson." Even after Alexander II came to the throne, the Third Section's censors showed no sign of changing their negative opinion of Ostrovsky's talent for scathing social comedy. *A Lucrative Position,* a satire on official corruption, was prohibited on the day of its premiere in 1857, while in the same year *It's All in the Family* was banned for a second time.[18]

The Great Reforms that began with the abolition of serfdom in 1861 and subsequently embraced the judiciary, local government, universities, and the military, affected censorship, too. It was reorganized and removed from the secret police in 1865, when the Main Administration for Press Affairs, attached to the Ministry of Internal Affairs, was given responsibility for censoring the press, literature, plays, and operas. The Main Administration was to remain the primary institution of theatrical censorship until 1917. Works produced on the stage continued to require a special authorization independent of their approval for publication, but the censorship process was simplified and became less burdensome. Previously censors only reported on plays and the head of the Third Section made the final decision. Each theater that wanted to stage a play had to obtain approval, regardless of whether the play had been performed previously at another theater. Under the new rules, the censors could decide to grant plays "unconditional approval for the stage" merely by placing an official seal on the copy of the text submitted. The titles of published plays passed by the censors were published in *The Government Herald,* which indicated the edition that had been approved. The government also periodically issued lists of plays that it had authorized for performance. Once the published text received the censor's approval any theater could stage it. When a play had been approved on the condition that some passages were deleted, theaters were allowed to use only the corrected text bearing the censor's seal. Enforcement of the censorship regulations was left entirely to local authorities, who were supposed to verify that all plays performed in the area under their jurisdiction were either on the official list of unconditionally approved plays or, if the play was approved with excisions, that the script to be used bore the censor's seal of authorization for the stage. Local authorities could also prohibit a play if they thought its performance might result in "disorders."[19]

Under the 1865 "Statute on Censorship and the Press" the censors were "to prohibit offence to the respect due to the teachings and rituals of Christian faiths, protect the inviolability of the Supreme Authority and its attributes, and insure respect for members of the reigning house, the steadfastness of the basic laws, popular morality, honor and the domestic life of each person." Works forbidden included those that "expound the harmful teachings of socialism and communism, which lead to the undermining or overthrow of the existing order and to the introduction of anarchy," that "arouse the enmity and hatred of one class towards another," or that "offensively ridicule entire classes or officials in the state or public service." Works dealing with historical or political topics were to contain "nothing offensive to the Russian government or to those governments friendly to Russia." The guidelines contained in the new censorship statute applied equally to the press, scientific works, literature, drama, and opera, yet a separate theater censorship division of the Main Administration for Press Affairs was responsible for examining dramas, even if they had already been approved for publication. The rules specifically applying to theater performances were not elaborated in the statute, but were contained in various circulars, directives, and informal instructions that were issued on an ongoing basis by the Main Administration in response to the policy needs of the moment. For example, theaters were forbidden to stage works depicting members of the clergy or the Romanov dynasty, but there is no mention of this prohibition in the censorship statute itself. Sometimes permission to stage a play was given only to a particular theater.[20]

The 1860s and 1870s were turbulent decades in Russia. Disappointment with the limitations of Alexander's reforms led some radicals to call for the autocracy to be abolished altogether, and one group in the underground revolutionary movement that emerged in the wake of the reforms tried several times to assassinate the tsar before achieving its goal in 1881. The easing of restraints on the press in the late 1850s led to increased criticism of government policies, which frightened officials and led them to attempt to suppress it. Yet as the government's fear of radicalism grew, moderate criticism became "more palatable," as Daniel Balmuth points out in his study of press censorship during the period. With respect to theater, this tendency resulted in a somewhat more liberal censorship that tolerated plays critical of Russian society, provided they did not espouse revolutionary ideas, attack the institution of monarchy or its officials, or focus on social conflict. Even a major Soviet history of pre-revolutionary drama concedes that after 1860 "the theater could develop its repertoire more freely than earlier."[21]

The censors became less concerned with uncovering subversive allusions in every line and tried to judge the overall direction of the ideas expressed in the works they examined, and several plays that had been prohibited earlier were permitted to be staged with some changes in the 1860s and 1870s. Ostrovsky's *It's All in the Family* appeared on the stage in 1861, after the author softened some of the language and added a final scene in which misdeeds were punished. Pushkin's *Boris Godunov* finally premiered in 1870, the censors having deleted clerical characters and religious rites from the script. Previously forbidden foreign plays such as Schiller's *Love and Intrigue* and Beaumarchais's *The Marriage of Figaro* were also now permitted. Pavel Shteller's *Errors of Youth,* which contains a depiction of a contemporary student commune, was prohibited in 1868, but two years later the ban was lifted and it premiered in St. Petersburg's imperial drama theater. Several important plays, however, were published but kept off the stage by the theater censors. Aleksandr Sukhovo-Kobylin's dark comedies *The Case* (1861) and *Tarelkin's Death* (1869) were banned due to their caustic treatment of official corruption. The first drama of Aleksei Tolstoi's historical trilogy, *The Death of Ivan the Terrible* (1866), was performed to great acclaim in 1867, but the censors vetoed productions of the sequels, *Tsar Fedor* (1868) and *Tsar Boris* (1870), because they were set in the political upheavals of the seventeenth-century Time of Troubles and allegedly did not depict the tsars with sufficient respect. *Tsar Fedor* was eventually performed in 1881 (with numerous excisions), but the prohibition on performances of *Tsar Boris* remained in effect for nearly thirty years.[22]

Almost any educated Russian was familiar with *Tarelkin's Death, Tsar Boris,* and other prohibited plays that had been published. In evaluating plays for the stage, however, the censors aimed to prevent actors and audiences from giving performances political interpretations that were not apparent in the text, and were well aware that the Russian public knew how to read between the lines to find associations with contemporary political issues. Beginning in the 1860s it became common for literature and literary criticism to employ Aesopian language to discuss political issues that could not be directly addressed. The radical critic Nikolai Dobroliubov famously used Ostrovsky's play *The Storm,* which premiered in 1859, to criticize serfdom and the autocracy. In the play, Katerina, a young wife, who seeks refuge from her husband's cruel and ignorant family in an adulterous liaison is driven to suicide. In a tendentious review of the published text, Dobroliubov made Katerina into a symbol of the masses' desire for freedom and interpreted her suicide as an act of rebellion against social and political oppression. Theaters occasionally became forums for expressions of anti-monarchical sentiment. At an 1876 performance of Lope de Vega's *Fuenteovejuna* at Moscow's imperial drama theater, for instance, the renowned actress Maria Ermolova, in the role of the peasant girl Laurencia, drew attention in her performance to the play's denunciation of tyranny. The audience responded with such stormy applause that the authorities temporarily banned the drama.[23]

## Censorship under Alexander III and Nicholas II

The reign of Alexander III (ruled 1881–94), who acceded to the throne following his father's assassination by revolutionary terrorists, was notable for its reactionary policies and political repression, but he also finally abolished the imperial theater monopoly in St. Petersburg and Moscow in 1882, and permitted the establishment of privately owned public theaters in the capitals. Censorship was particularly harsh during the 1880s and early 1890s: between 1882 and 1891 about one-third of the 3,947 Russian plays examined by the theater censors were banned for performance. In 1887 Lev Tolstoy's *The Power of Darkness* was in the last stages of rehearsal at St. Petersburg's imperial Aleksandrinskii Theater when Alexander III, offended by its grim depiction of peasant immorality and infanticide, intervened to order it withdrawn. But the tsar did not succeed in keeping the play off the stage entirely. One of the actors, Vladimir Davydov, organized an amateur performance in a private home, where Anton Chekhov, the actress Maria Savina, and other members of the artistic community saw it. Savina later selected the play for one of her benefit performances, in which she played Akulina. The censors lifted the ban in 1895.[24]

Authors were sometimes able to negotiate or even bargain with the censors in order to preserve certain scenes or bits of dialogue. According to director and playwright Pavel Gnedich, some playwrights even intentionally inserted scenes and remarks that were clearly in violation of the rules in order to make others appear less censorable and save them from excision. When Stanislavsky adapted Dostoevsky's *The Village of Stepanchikovo* for his Society of Art and Literature in 1888, the censors prohibited its performance. He then reworked it slightly, changed the names of the characters, retitled it *Foma*, and resubmitted it to the censors in 1889. This time they approved it, on the condition that Stanislavsky was identified as the author. Stanislavsky refused, and when the play was performed no author was credited.[25]

In 1888, concerned by the growth of popular theaters that aimed to attract lower-class audiences, Minister of Internal Affairs Dmitrii Tolstoi issued an administrative order requiring plays performed in theaters with low ticket prices to get special approval, even if the censors had already approved them for performance in other theaters. The issue, as Tolstoi explained, was whether the common people might be corrupted by material that was harmless when performed before more educated audiences:

> In examining plays the censor has in view the more or less educated public that attends theater performances, but not exclusively any one social class. Due to his level of mental development, his outlooks and conceptions, the common man will often interpret in an utterly wrong sense something that would present no temptation for a somewhat educated person, and thus a play containing nothing blameworthy from a general point of view may be unsuitable and even harmful for him. Since the theater unquestionably has an important educational significance, it would seem necessary to ensure that the people receive from it sober and beneficial impressions and nothing that would promote their moral corruption.[26]

The special censorship provisions for popular theaters lasted until 1917 and resulted in the prohibition of many plays that had long been permitted on the legitimate stage, particularly those that depicted rulers or authority figures, dealt with sensitive historical subjects such as rebellion or serfdom, portrayed social antagonisms, or showed sexual immorality or unpunished crimes. Thus, monarchs generally could not be depicted on the popular stage, even if approved for other venues, as with Aleksei Tolstoy's *Death of Ivan the Terrible*. *The Marriage of Figaro*, although approved for the imperial theaters in 1896, was banned from the popular theaters because, the censors declared, it was "spotted with witty escapades against the nobility"; and Lev Tolstoy's 1886 play *The Power of Darkness*, an unvarnished portrayal of misery and poverty in a peasant household, although originally banned for all theaters, was subsequently approved for all venues except for the "popular" stage in 1895. In considering the latter for translation into Latvian in 1899, the censor declared that Tolstoy's play "must create disagreeable feelings for educated theater audiences" and would "create a really debauched image" among "uneducated audiences."

A version of Rossini's opera *William Tell* was approved only for one theater, where the censor reported the audience consisted mainly of "officers, officials and people like them or otherwise well off" and in the back seats where ordinary people might be able to afford a seat, "it is impossible to make out the words."[27]

For the growing numbers of legitimate theaters in the capitals and the provinces, censorship started to become less harsh in the 1890s, and by the 1900s many earlier prohibitions had been reversed. Nonetheless, censors continued to prohibit plays whose content could be interpreted as critical of Russian political and social institutions, for Nicholas II (1894–17) was no less determined than his father to preserve the autocracy, despite growing opposition. The Moscow Art Theater (MAT), founded in 1898, was relatively successful in its dealings with the censors, as Stanislavsky was on fairly good terms with them. Aleksei Tolstoy's *Tsar Fedor*, prohibited for nearly thirty years, was approved for the MAT in 1898, with a few cuts to satisfy the ecclesiastical authorities. The Theater also got permission to stage the radical celebrity Maksim Gorky's *The Philistines*, *The Lower Depths*, and *Children of the Sun*, although the censors subjected these plays to many cuts. The chief censor, Prince Shakhovskoi, insisted on attending the general rehearsal of *The Philistines* to make sure that it contained nothing provocative, even after the censors had gone over the text. In contrast, Chekhov's plays, staged to acclaim at the MAT, had only minor phrases deleted. For example, in *The Cherry Orchard*, the censors had Chekhov replace two of the student Petya's phrases concerning the poverty of factory workers and the legacy of serfdom with less provocative comments.[28]

The MAT did lose some of its encounters with the censorship, however. At the beginning the Theater tried to make itself accessible to the working poor by distributing blocks of tickets for sale at a reduced price at local factories, but the police forced them to stop because some of the plays they were performing had not been approved for lower-class audiences. The main practical concern was that the censors might rescind approval for a play after considerable money and creative effort had already been invested in the production. The MAT had already started work on Gerhardt Hauptmann's *Hannelle* when the play was prohibited on the eve of the dress rehearsal due to the intervention of Moscow Metropolitan Vladimir, who found the play blasphemous. Stanislavsky and his partner, Vladimir Nemirovich-Danchencko, attempted to explain to the metropolitan that the censored text did not contain any of the passages that he found objectionable, but their efforts were in vain. Stanislavsky later estimated that the ban cost the theater 30,000 rubles. Leonid Andreev's *Anathema* had already been staged thirty-seven times when the play was suddenly banned in 1909. The censors retracted their earlier approval due to the intervention of the head of the Holy Synod, Konstantin Pobedonotsev, who had heard that one of the actors in the play was made up to resemble Christ. Still, Stanislavsky and Nemirovich were able to stage most of the plays they wanted, and the critical success of the Art Theater suggests that they were not hamstrung by the censors in their effort to create a new kind of naturalistic theater that challenged contemporary staging conventions.[29]

Others were less fortunate, although few were as unlucky as Vera Kommissarzhevskaia, whose Dramatic Theater was forced to close due to the financial losses incurred when director Nikolai Evreinov's production of Oscar Wilde's *Salomé* was suddenly prohibited in at the behest of the ecclesiastical authorities. Evreinov, however, went on to achieve fame for his modernist productions of old liturgical plays and dramas that posed no problems for the censors. Meyerhold, too, was prevented by the censors from presenting *Salomé*, now at the imperial Aleksandrinskii Theater. Most of his theatrical experiments, however, such as the innovative productions of Molière's *Don Juan* and Richard Strauss's opera *Elektra*, aroused little interference from the censors.[30]

Directors and writers usually complained that the censors damaged plays with their cuts and rewrites, but most of the censors' interventions after 1900 did not do much to change the character of the plays. In Gorky's *Philistines*, for example, the censors struck out phrases that could be interpreted as social criticism, referred to the hard lives of workers, or suggested that the oppression of the honest by the dishonest would someday end. To give one example, the censors deleted the statement, "The boss is he who toils," with its socialist undertones. The play was a smash hit in any case, and audiences eagerly consumed its socially critical message. The most common complaint about the Russian censorship after 1865 was its arbitrariness, which, of course, characterized the Russian state as a whole. Thus, the governor-general of Odessa once told a newspaper editor there, "If something appears in your paper that does not please me, or if it should bore me when I read it, or if I just feel like it, or if perhaps my stomach aches, I will close your paper down immediately." Sometimes, as previously noted, plays were prohibited by government officials even after the censors had approved them. Alexander Sanin, an actor and director at the imperial Aleksandrinskii Theater, got permission to stage Gorky's *The Lower Depths* in 1903. A big hit when it had premiered at the Moscow Art Theater in 1902, Sanin was already rehearsing the play when Tsar Nicholas II intervened to stop the play from being performed on the imperial stages. The actors then held a reading of the play at the columned hall of the Noble Assembly in St. Petersburg. Later that year the reactionary Minister of Internal Affairs Viacheslav Plehve issued an unofficial ban on the play on the basis that it was too immoral. Plehve was responding to a complaint by St. Petersburg municipal Governor Kleigels that *The Lower Depths* glamorized "the dregs of society, depicting scoundrels as heroes." Nonetheless, Gorky's play was still being performed in popular theaters and summer stages in 1903 and 1904. The censors rescinded the ban during the upheavals of the 1905 revolution, reasoning that there was little point in keeping the play off the stage as it was by now familiar to audiences throughout Russia. Ecclesiastical authorities also sometimes meddled in theatrical affairs. In 1907 authorities in the provincial town of Saratov were instructed by the Ministry of Internal Affairs to halt performances of Frank Wedekind's *Spring Awakening* due to complaints from the local bishop about its allegedly immoral treatment of adolescent sexuality.[31]

Operas, like plays, often suffered from the capriciousness of the censorship. Modest Mussorgsky gained approval to present his opera *Boris Godunov* (based on Pushkin's forbidden play of the same name) only by the personal decision of Tsar Alexander II and after agreeing to suppress a variety of monks and other ecclesiastics who appeared in the original text (the opera censorship rules imposed a general ban on depicting clerics, leading an Italian journalist to note in 1862 that "monks are changed into pilgrims, or even magistrates or procurators"). Peter Tchaikovsky had to make drastic changes in *The Oprichnik* (1873), which dealt with political abuses during the medieval reign of Ivan the Terrible, with the result that, according to Russian opera historian Rosa Newmarch, the opera failed because "in order to comply with the demands of the censor," Ivan, the central figure, "had to be reduced to a mere nonentity." The great composer Nikolai Rimsky-Korsakov had repeated tangles with the censors. He had to pull strings to avoid a complete ban on *The Maid of Pskov,* but was forced to remove all references to republicanism and self-government in sixteenth-century Russia. Rimsky's 1894 *Christmas Eve* was first forbidden as violating the 1837 ban on depicting a tsar (or tsarina) in an opera, because of its semi-disguised portrayal of Catherine the Great (earlier, Tchaikovsky suffered the same fate with his opera *Vakula the Smith,* based on the same story by Gogol that inspired *Christmas Eve*). However, Rimsky again pulled strings and succeeded in gaining the personal approval of Tsar Nicholas II to present *Christmas Eve* intact. Nonetheless, after two influential members of the imperial household complained about the depiction of Catherine upon attending a final rehearsal in late 1895, Rimsky was forced to change the empress into a "most serene highness," thus completely gutting the plot and leading him to write bitterly to a friend that the authorities had forgotten the saying, "Don't give your word unless you intend to keep it." His final opera, *The Golden Cockerel,* an allegory on the decay of the Russian aristocracy based on a well-known poem by Pushkin, was delayed for two years by the censors, no doubt partly because of Rimsky's overt support for democratic reforms during the 1905 revolution, which led to his temporary dismissal from his faculty position at the St. Petersburg Conservatory. Soon afterward, when the presentation of his opera *Kashchei the Immortal* on 27 March 1905 in St. Petersburg became the excuse for a political demonstration, all of Rimsky's works were banned for two months; largely due to public protests, Rimsky regained his position eight months later. *The Golden Cockerel* was eventually allowed in 1909 (after Rimsky's death), but only in a mutilated version: for example, the original libretto's tsar was transformed into the "Mighty Tsar's General" and a key choral verse asking, "What will the new dawn bring?" was changed to refer to a "white dawn," which was apparently viewed by the authorities as less threatening.[32]

After 1850, as the theater increasingly became a focus for the self-expression and aspirations of Russia's national minorities, the authorities frequently imposed especially strict censorship and sometimes complete bans on productions in their languages. Thus, for twenty-five years beginning in 1883, all theater productions in Yiddish were completely forbidden (although Yiddish publications were tolerated). Performances in Ukrainian were entirely banned for five years after 1876 and thereafter strictly controlled until 1905, because, according to the so-called "Ems Decree," "stage performances, lyrics to music and public readings" had "the character of Ukrainophile manifestations." In 1885, the governor of Bessarabia refused to allow a Romanian-language troupe to perform in the capital of Kishinev on the grounds that such a performance might incite Romanian separatism. Polish plays were subjected to extremely strict censorship, especially after the 1863 uprising in Russian Poland, and in what were deemed other "sensitive" areas of the Russian Empire, such as the Caucasus, local officials were required to individually approve any productions presented in non-Russian languages, even if they had been previously approved for presentation in Russian by the St. Petersburg censors. Thus, *The Haunted Manor,* the leading Polish composer Stanislaw Moniuszko's operatic masterpiece, was banned by tsarist authorities after being hailed in its first three productions, as part of the post-1863 censorship crackdown, and was not performed again in Warsaw until 1914.

Rossini's opera *William Tell* was rejected amid the ferment of the 1905 revolution for popular audiences partly because, "especially in border areas with foreign populations," its story of Swiss revolt against the Habsburgs might "present agitators an additional opportunity and free material for igniting the various tribes and arousing revolt." With regard to the 1883 Yiddish ban, Minister of Internal Affairs D. A. Tolstoy informed local governors that the regime had difficulty in "controlling" the Yiddish theater because there were not enough police and other authorities who understood the language and because it had become "evident that Jewish entrepreneurs were abusing the ignorance of the language on the part of the local authorities and putting on the stage" material that was "directly forbidden," including scenes "insulting to the Christian religion." In at least some cases, these restrictions on performances in minority languages were far less strict in practice than in official policy: thus, hundreds of Yiddish plays were in fact presented during the period when they were officially banned, often under the thinly disguised pretense that they were being performed in German.[33]

Implementation of the so-called 18 May 1876 Ems Decree, which banned all theater performances in Ukrainian (as well as tightening restrictions on publications in that language which had been first introduced in 1863), was slightly eased in 1881, but until it was rescinded in 1906, Ukrainian theater was subjected to a whole variety of niggling restrictions. Although after 1881 Ukrainian language dramas were allowed "with the special permission of the governors-general," they were still forbidden in most Ukrainian-majority regions, while in Ukrainian areas where they were allowed they could only be presented by traveling theater companies (i.e., no resident Ukrainian theaters were allowed until the Decree was rescinded) and they were required to accompany any presentations in Ukrainian with plays in Russian with the same number of acts: the result was that performances often lasted for five hours and exhausted actors had to play numerous roles during the same evening; although the Ukrainian performances were packed, the Russian plays were often presented to empty chairs and policemen. The content of Ukrainian plays was strictly censored, with no satires, histories, or depictions of middle- and upper-class characters tolerated, so that in practice only mundane presentations about ordinary peasant lives were possible. On one occasion, according to the daughter of a Ukrainian playwright whose drama was forbidden, the censors informed her father that his play might be approved for Russian performances but it was "not desirable that people see plays in the language which they understand." The slight easing of restrictions in 1881 may have reflected a memorandum prepared that year by the governor of a Ukrainian-speaking region, who declared that the "prohibition of stage performances and the singing of national songs" in the Ems Decree "not only has not reached any purpose whatsoever, but has caused great consternation and disapproval even among all the [Ukrainian] supporters of a union with Russia," while "directly" aiding "the Ukrainophile party's authority by giving it an opportunity to point out the suppression of even such innocent manifestations of the popular spirit and creativity." Bizarrely, Ukrainian productions were actively welcomed in St. Petersburg and Moscow, since, as the governor of one Ukrainian speaking area explained, "there it is only theater," but "here it is politics." Even after the Ems Decree was rescinded in early 1906 and the first resident Ukrainian theater company was founded (in Kiev in 1907), it was subjected to intense censorship and harassment. Despite everything, the theater was the only form of Ukrainian high culture tolerated at all during the last part of the nineteenth century and it played a critical role in maintaining and reviving Ukrainian culture and sentiments generally: thus, the 1910 death of the leading Ukrainian playwright Marko Kropyvnytsky triggered a tremendous outpouring of grief, and his coffin was decorated with a crown of thorns and a banner reading, "To a fighter, for his dreams."[34]

The government's attempts to regulate the theaters brought mixed results at best. As with other branches of the Imperial civil service, the censorship was hampered by a lack of coordination among the agencies responsible for ensuring adherence to its decisions. The censorship regulations were routinely ignored, and since their enforcement depended entirely on the vigilance of the police, there was little the Main Administration could do beyond sending out innumerable circulars calling for closer adherence to the rules. Although a high percentage of plays submitted for presentation in the popular theaters were officially rejected—about 10 percent to 15 percent—such rulings apparently were only sporadically enforced. Even the popular theaters funded by the government's temperance organizations failed to adhere to censorship restrictions: in 1901 the Main Administration reported that, of 196 plays staged recently by the theater of the St. Petersburg temperance organization, 75 were not approved for performance in popular theaters. Moreover, many had been expressly prohibited, such as Schiller's *The Robbers* and Leo Tolstoy's *The Power of Darkness*. A 1913 investigation revealed that 80 percent of the repertory of one popular theater in Saratov consisted of plays not approved for popular venues.[35]

The censorship was often circumvented because the Main Administration had little control over performances. Focusing on the written text rather than on its performance, the censors were unable to regulate gesture, ad-libbing, intonation, makeup, or audience response. As a result, the text as performed might differ considerably from the text as the censor had read it, and could contain things that would have been banned had they been visible to the censor when he approved the text. In 1915, responding to complaints in the conservative press accusing them of excessive leniency, the censors noted that unless they were actually present at performances they could do little to prevent directors and actors from violating both the letter and the spirit of censorship rulings. Since there were only four censors at the time, it was, of course, impossible for them to monitor performances even in St. Petersburg alone.[36]

An official who was briefly assigned to report on the Moscow theaters emphasized this point in 1901. In letter to the head of the Main Administration, Prince Shakhovskoi, he justified his assignment by arguing that the censorship office could fulfill its mission only by monitoring theater performances: "In the continual struggle with the demands of the censorship, the theater disposes of a quite wide arsenal of weapons that are perfected from year to year. Actors have at their disposal weapons in the form of the methods by which they realize their roles: diction, mimicry, makeup, gestures and costume. ... With this arsenal there can be no doubt in the outcome of the struggle, of course under the condition that the censorship limits itself to only controlling the text, neglecting to control the performance." Ad-libbing by either inserting topical references into their lines or presenting material that the censors had struck was another way performers could circumvent censorship, although they risked punishment if caught. Thus, Pavel Orlenov, performing in Edmond Rostand's *L'Aiglon* during a spate of student demonstrations, uttered the censored words, "Students who start shouting in the streets are ordered to be immediately drafted into the army." In 1912 an actor was brought before a Poltava court for pronouncing a phrase the censors had deleted in Lev Tolstoy's *The Living Corpse* ("And you, earning twenty kopecks for dirty tricks, don a uniform"). Ad-libbing was a widespread habit among actors working in the provincial and popular theaters, who often went on stage after only two or three rehearsals and relied on improvisation when they forgot their lines.[37]

Actors at times simply ignored the censors and stuck to the original text. This was especially common in theaters that specialized in farce and light comedies spiced with sex. Censor Mikhail Tolstoi, attending the performance of a farce at a St. Petersburg theater in 1907, was shocked to find that the actors paid no heed to the censors' deletions and with their gestures "impart a pornographic sense to the most ordinary of scenes." The censors, he complained, could not possibly divine what would become of a text once it reached the theater, since all depended on the actors' "adherence to decency" in their performance. "This condition, however," he concluded, "lying entirely within the jurisdiction of the police inspectorate, is constantly violated, just as is adherence to the censored text." Alexander Briantsev, who worked briefly at a St. Petersburg people's theater, recounts in his memoirs that the actors never adhered to the censors' deletions and always performed the full texts of plays. According to Briantsev, the censors themselves suggested possibilities for tendentious interpretations, for their deletions drew the actors' attention to the very parts of the texts that were crossed out.[38]

Censorship did not prevent theater performances from becoming an important public forum for the expression of political discontent in the turbulent 1890s and 1900s, marked by strikes, student demonstrations, and the formation of underground political parties. "For us," one drama critic remarked in 1899, "plays and theaters are the same things as, for example, parliamentary events and political speeches are for a Western European." When the notoriously anti-Semitic melodrama *Smugglers* was staged in St. Petersburg in 1900 it sparked a riot in which dozens were arrested and led to strikes by university students. The police viewed the unrest as a protest "against the government regime and the powers that be," and they were right, for Alexander III and his son Nicholas II had placed increasingly severe restrictions on their Jewish subjects throughout the 1890s. Performances of *Smugglers* in other cities were accompanied by further demonstrations and arrests, leading the minister of internal affairs to forbid other plays that contained negative depictions of Jews lest they provide opportunities for more public disorders. The MAT's 1901 performance of Henrik Ibsen's *An Enemy of the People* in St. Petersburg, which followed a day of student clashes with police on the city's streets, became an anti-government demonstration. The students in the audience responded to the play's theme of protest against arbitrary authority with cries of approval. When Stanislavsky, playing Dr. Stockman, proclaimed, "One must never put on a new coat when going out to fight for freedom and truth," students interrupted the performance with applause and cheers and even climbed onto the stage to embrace the surprised actor.[39]

During the 1905 revolution, when the state's authority came under assault throughout Russia, the censorship's ability to control what took place on the stage was further weakened and political demonstrations frequently erupted in the theaters. In November 1905, as the urban revolution began to fizzle out in the wake of the civic freedoms promised by the tsar's October Manifesto, Saint Petersburg's Nevsky Farce staged an enormously successful topical review called *Days of Freedom*, which criticized the government for failing to carry out its promises, contained ditties referring to the plight of political prisoners, and referred to the martial law that was in force in Poland. Despite warnings from the censorship board and visits by the police, the theater continued staging the review with no adverse consequences. The censors even complained that the police were not enforcing the law, but admitted that, since the political criticism expressed in *Days of Freedom* was nothing compared to the articles and caricatures then appearing in the newspapers, it was rather pointless to crack down on the theater. Attempting to restore order in early 1906, the Main Administration demanded that theaters and actors adhere to its guidelines, complaining that "by the deletion of separate expressions and whole phrases, a play is intentionally given a tendentious character that it does not actually have." For example, during an early 1906 performance of *Antigone*, the line "a free land cannot belong to one person" provoked an enormous outburst of enthusiasm from the audience. If anything was potentially subversive, there was little the censors could do.[40]

Censorship policy did change over time. Although the theater censorship was not abolished in 1905, as was preliminary censorship of publications, it did become a bit less repressive. For the popular theaters, this meant that a number of previously forbidden classics and literary plays could now be staged. Among the works approved for the popular theaters in 1905–6, for example, were *The Cherry Orchard*, *Uncle Vanya*, *Faust*, *Maria Stuart*, *A Winter's Tale*, *Hamlet*, *Don Giovanni*, *The Barber of Seville*, *An Enemy of the People*, and *The Lower Depths*. Certainly fewer plays were prohibited out of fear that they could be interpreted as criticism of the authorities or social injustice, although works touching, even obliquely, on religion or class conflict were still at the mercy of the censor's judgment and subject to the possible intervention of ecclesiastical authorities. The most common reason for plays to be prohibited or cut after 1905 was for moral objections. This is probably due to the shift in theater away from naturalistic socially critical drama after the 1905 revolution.[41]

## Conclusion

The Russian censorship statutes in force between 1865 and 1917 did not differ greatly from those of other European countries. In Russia, however, the application of the rules remained more stringent for a longer period of time than most, if not all, other European countries. While constitutions and civil rights were slowly granted to most Europeans during the nineteenth century, Russia remained an autocracy until the 1905 revolution forced some concessions from the tsar, and the harsh Russian censorship was a product of Russia's autocratic order. In 1906 the censorship of publications and the press eased somewhat in Russia, but the theater continued to be subject to the rules established in 1865 until the overthrow of the autocracy in 1917.

What was the impact of censorship on Russian theater? To be sure, the burden of censorship was heavy, especially for writers, who were forced to self-censor themselves if they wanted their plays to be staged. As Lev Tolstoy once wrote, "What matters is not what the censor does to what I have written, but what I might have written." Still, Russian drama developed considerably in the last decades of tsarist rule, when playwrights such as Ostrovsky, Chekhov, and Gorky created works that even today have not lost their resonance. After the tsarist regime collapsed in 1917 there was a widespread expectation that the abolition of censorship would result in the appearance of many previously banned plays, but this did not happen, although the complete uncensored texts of some plays could now be performed. (Similar expectations after the collapse of the Communist Party's rule in the 1990s also turned out to be unfounded.)[42] For Russian directors, the problem centered on getting permission to stage the works they wanted and, once permission was obtained, being able to actually present their plays without a sudden intervention by the authorities. Censorship, however, did not stifle the innovations of Stanislavsky, Meyerhold, Evreinov, and other experimenters. The text, after all, is only one of the raw materials that the director uses to craft a performance. To be sure, censorship did have a negative impact on Russian theater, as it did elsewhere in Europe, but that impact should not be overstated. Tsarist Russia's theatrical culture was innovative, and left behind a vital legacy.

## Bibliographical Essay

For general background reading on nineteenth-century Russian history, see Nicholas V. Riasanovsky and Mark Steinberg, *A History of Russia* (New York, 2004); John Westwood, *Endurance and Endeavour: Russian History, 1812–2001* (Oxford, 2001); and Roger Bartlett, *A History of Russia* (New York, 2005). Good general histories of the Russian theater with some material on the censorship include B. V. Varneke, *History of the Russian Theater: Seventeenth to Nineteenth Centuries* (New York, 1951), and Robert Leach and Victor Borovsky, eds., *A History of Russian Theater* (Cambridge, 1999). Early private Russian theaters are discussed in Robert Stites, *Serfdom, Society and the Arts in Imperial Russia* (New Haven, CT, 2005), while Nick Worrall's *The Moscow Art Theatre* (London, 1996) studies a late experimental theater.

There is only limited material specifically centered on nineteenth-century Russian theater censorship in English, although there are several good sources that focus on press censorship, above all Charles Ruud, *Fighting Words: Imperial Censorship and the Russian Press, 1804–1906* (Toronto, 1982), and Marianna Tax Choldin, *A Fence Around the Empire: Russian Censorship of Western Idea under the Tsars* (Durham, NC, 1985). Ruud includes a few pages about theater, opera, and music censorship in his general survey of nineteenth-century Russian censorship, "Russia," in Robert Justin Goldstein, ed., *The War for the Public Mind: Political Censorship in Nineteenth-Century Europe* (Westport, CT, 2000), 259–65. Simon Karlinsky's *Russian Drama from Its Beginnings to the Age of Pushkin* (Berkeley, CA, 1985) contains insightful discussions of how drama and opera were censored under Catherine II, Alexander I, and Nicholas II. While Varneke, cited above, emphasizes the harshness of tsarist censorship from a Soviet perspective, Murray Frame provides a more balanced view in his *School for Citizens: Theater and Civil Society in Tsarist Russia* (New Haven, CT, 2006), and also has some information on censorship in his *The St. Petersburg Imperial Theaters: Stage and State in Revolutionary Russia, 1900–1920* (Jefferson, NC, 2000). The censorship of popular theater is covered in E. Anthony Swift, "Fighting the Germs of Disorder: The Censorship of Russian Popular Theater, 1888–1917," *Russian History* 18 (1991): 1–49; Swift, *Popular Theater and Society in Tsarist Russia* (Berkeley, CA, 2002); and Gary Thurston, *The Popular Theater Movement in Russia, 1862–1919* (Evanston, IL, 1998). Hubertus Jahn touches on wartime drama censorship in his *Patriotic Culture in Russia During World War I* (Ithaca, NY, 1995).

The censorship history of Pushkin's drama *Boris Godunov* is examined in Chester Dunning and Caryl Emeron, *The Uncensored Boris Godunov: The Case for Pushkin's Original Comedy* (Madison, WI, 2006). Both Pushkin's tragedy and Modest Mussorgsky's opera of the same title are the subject of Robert William Oldani's "Boris Godunov and the Censor," *Nineteenth-Century Music* 2 (1978): 245–53; on Rimsky-Korsakov and his struggles with the censorship, see Gerald Abraham, *Rimsky-Korsakov* (London, 1945), and his "Satire and Symbol in the *Golden Cockerel*," *Music and Letters* 52

(1971): 46–54. An article in French treats Russian opera censorship generally: Walter Zidaric, "Traduction/adaptation des livrets d'operas: la rôle de la censure en Russia aux XIXe et XXe siècles," in Gottfried Marschall, ed., *La Traduction des Livrets* (Paris, 2004), 494–504. Little in English focuses on the censorship of non-Russian plays, with the notable exceptions of John Klier, "Exit, Pursued by a Bear: The Ban on Yiddish Theater in Imperial Russia," in Joel Berkowitz, ed., *Yiddish Theater: New Approaches* (Oxford, 2003), 159–74; and Valerian Ruvutksy, "The Act of Ems (1876) and Its Effect on Ukrainian Theatre," *Nationalities Papers* 5 (1977): 67–78.

Many biographies of Russian dramatists and directors examine their dealings with the censors, but plays tend to get less attention than books. Biographies with some information on theater censorship include David Magarshack, *Pushkin* (London, 1967); T. J. Binyon, *Pushkin: A Biography* (London, 2003); Leonard Schapiro, *Turgenev: His Life and Times* (Oxford, 1978); Jean Benedetti, *Stanislavskii: A Biography* (London, 1988); Konstantin Rudnitsky, *Meyerhold the Director* (Ann Arbor, MI, 1981); and Ronald Hingley, *A New Life of Chekhov* (New York,1976). Hingley has a chapter on censorship, with some attention paid to drama, in his *Russian Writers and Society, 1825–1904* (New York, 1977). Some information on the Moscow Art Theater's dealings with the censors can be found in Constantin Stanislavsky, *My Life in Art* (New York, 1956), and in Vladimir Nemirovich-Danchenko, *My Life in the Russian Theater* (New York, 1968).

The best Russian-language account of the theater censorship is N. V. Drizen, *Dramaticheskaia tsenzura dvukh epoch, 1825–1881* (Petrograd, 1917), although it only deals with the reigns of Nicholas I and Alexander II. E. G. Kholodov, et al., eds., *Istoriia russkogo dramaticheskogo teatra v semi tomakh*, 7 vols. (1977–87), is an invaluable source of information on theaters, plays, censorship, and performances. For a good overview of the changing censorship regulations, see S. S. Danilov, "Materialy po istorii russkogo zakonodatel'stva o teatre," in S. S. Danilov, and S. S. Mokul'skii, eds., *O teatre: Sbornik statei* (Leningrad, 1940), 177–200. An excellent analysis of the Third Department's censorship activities during the first years of Alexander II's reign is O. Iu. Abakumov, "Dramaticheskaia tsenzura i III otdelenie (konsta 50-x – nachalo 60-x godov xix veka," in *Tsenzura v Rossii: istoriia i sovremmenost': Sbornik nauchnyh trudov*, 1 (St. Petersburg, 2001), 68–74. The Main Administration for Press Affairs, the key censorship organ, is described in Iu. A. Nelidov, "Teatralnaia biblioteka im: A. V. Lunacharskogo," in *Teatral'noe nasledie: Sbornik pervyi* (Moscow, 1934), 11–43. On censorship during the 1905 revolution, see S. Dreiden, "Teatr 1905–07 godov i tsarskaia tsenzura," *Teatr* 12 (Moscow, 1955);

A. Ia. Al'tshuller, ed., *Pervaia russkaia revoliutsiia i teatr* (Moscow, 1956); and *Russkii teatr i dramaturgiia epokhi revoliutsii 1905–1907 godov: Sbornik nauchnykh trudov* (Leningrad, 1987). The struggles of Ostrovsky with the censors are discussed in A. I. Revkina, "A. N. Ostrovskii i tsenzura," *Stranitsy istorii russkoi literatury* (1971): 348–53. The censorship of Gorky's plays is examined in S. D. Balukhatyi, "Dramaturgiia M. Gor'kogo i tsarskaia tsensura," in *Teatral'noe nasledie: Sbornik pervyi* (Moscow, 1934). For a post-Soviet Russian revisionist approach to the imperial censorship, one that challenges the myth of the artist in combat with the repressive state, see Anastasiia Kasumova, "Nikolai I. Gogol: 'Revizor,'" *Peterburgskii Teatral'nyi zhurnal* 32 (2003): 34–38.

## Notes

1. David Magarshack, *Stanislavsky* (New York, 1951), 276; Ronald Hingley, *A New Life of Chekhov* (New York, 1976), 212; K. S. Stanislavskii, *Stat'i Rechi Besedy Pis'ma* (Moscow, 1953), 174.
2. *Zolotoe runo* 3 (1906): 106–7.
3. E. Anthony Swift, "Fighting the Germs of Disorder: The Censorship of Russian Popular Theater, 1888–1917," *Russian History* 18 (1991): 11.
4. Simon Karlinsky discusses the origins of Russian drama and its development in the eighteenth and early nineteenth centuries in *Russian Drama from Its Beginnings to the Age of Pushkin* (Berkeley, CA, 1985). On Russian theater censorship in the eighteenth century, see Catriona Kelly, "The Origins of the Russian theater," in Robert Leach and Victor Borovskyin, eds., *A History of Russian Theater* (Cambridge, 1999), 18–40, and N. V. Drizen, *Materialy k istorii russkogo teatra*, part 3 (St. Petersburg, 1905), 93–120.
5. S. S. Danilov, "Materialy po istorii russkogo zakonodatel'stva o teatre," in S. S. Danilov and S. S. Mokul'skii, eds., *O teatre: Sbornik statei* (Leningrad/Moscow, 1940), 184–85; Drizen, *Materialy*, 98.
6. Karlinsky, 81, 159–76; Drizen, *Materialy*, 99–100.
7. Karlinsky, 136–49, 172–76; Drizen, *Materialy*, 108–19.
8. G. V. Zhirkov, *Istoriia tsenzury v Rossii XIX–XX vv* (Moscow, 2001), 42; *Istoriia russkogo dramaticheskogo teatra v semi tomakh*, II (Moscow, 1977), 39–41; Drizen, *Materialy*, 125.
9. V. P. Pogozhev, *Stoletie organizatsii Imperatorskikh Moskovskikh teatrov: Opyt istoricheskogo obzora*, I, book 3 (St. Petersburg, 1908), 88; T. J. Binyon, *Pushkin: A Biography* (London, 2003), 243–44; K. Sivkov, "S. N. Glinka," *Russkii biograficheskii slovar'* V (1916): 294; W. Bruce Lincoln, *Nicholas I: Emperor and Autocrat of All the Russias* (London, 1978), 237–38; Danilov, 188; Zhirkov, 57–58.
10. Zhirkov, 58–61; Sidney Monas, *The Third Section: Police and Society in Russia under Nicholas I* (Cambridge, MA, 1961), 139–45.

11. *Istoriia russkogo,* III (1978), 23–24, 28. O. Iu. Abakumov, "Dramaticheskaia tsenzura i III otdelenie (konsta 50-x - nachalo 60-x godov xix veka," in *Tsenzura v Rossii: istoriia i sovremmenost'. Sbornik nauchnyh trudov,* I (St. Petersburg, 2001), 67. The censors examined 659 plays in 1838, 493 in 1840, and 590 in 1842. The imperial government spent far more money on the imperial French theaters than it did on the Russian theater in the first half of the nineteenth century.
12. Anastasiia Kasumova, "Nikolai I. Gogol: 'Revizor,'" *Peterburgskii Teatral'nyi zhurnal* 32 (2003): 34–38; *Istoriia russkogo,* III (1978), 29.
13. Karlinsky, 305; *Istoriia russkogo,* III (1978), 21, 29–30.
14. N. V. Drizen, *Dramaticheskaia tsenzura dvukh epokh (1825–1881)* (Moscow, 1905), 77, 144–45; Zhirkov, 70; *Istoriia russkogo,* III (1978), 36–38, 54–61; Walter Zidaric, "Traduction/adapation des livrets d'operas: la rôle de la censure en Russia aux XIXe et XXe siècles," in Gottfried Marschall, ed., *La Traduction des Livrets* (Paris, 2004), 496–97.
15. B. V. Varneke, *History of the Russian Theater: Seventeenth to Nineteenth Centuries,* (New York, 1951), 194–95, 397; Drizen, *Materialy,* 146–47.
16. Lincoln, 238.
17. Drizen, *Dramaticheskaia,* 197–212; Abakumov, 68–74; E. Anthony Swift, *Popular Theater and Society in Tsarist Russia* (Berkeley, CA, 2002), 49.
18. A. I. Revkina, "A.N. Ostrovskii i tsenzura," *Stranitsy istorii russkoi literatury* (1971): 348–54; Kate Sealey Rahman, "Aleksandr Ostrovsky, Dramatist and Director," in Leach and Borovsky, 168; Abakumov, 71.
19. "Ustav o tsenzure i pechati. O tsenzure dramaticheskikh sochinenii, naznachennykh k predstavleniiu na teatrakh," articles 83–92, 128, 135, in *Svod zakonov Rossiiskoi imperii,* part 2, XIV (St. Petersburg, 1904), columns 55, 80.
20. "Ustav o tsenzure i pechati. Pravila v rukovodstvo tsensure," articles 93, 94, 95, 96, 102, in *Svod zakonov Rossiiskoi imperii,* part 2, XIV, column 56.
21. Daniel Balmuth, *Censorship in Russia, 1865–1905* (Washington, 1979), 140; *Istoriia russkogo,* V (1980), 43.
22. *Istoriia russkogo,* V (1980), 43, 422, 445, 511; Oleg Pivovarov, "Minuvshee ob"emlet zhivo," *Sovetskaia dramaturgiia* 2 (1988): 251–52; Cynthia Marsh, "Realism in the Russian theater, 1850–1882," in Leach and Borovsky, 155–57.
23. Rufus Matthewson, *The Positive Hero in Russian Literature* (Stanford, CA, 1975), 54–62; I. F. Petrovskaia, *Istochnikovedenie istorii russkogo dramaticheskogo teatra* (Leningrad, 1971), 29; Varneke, 375.
24. Murray Frame, "Freedom of the theaters: The Abolition of the Russian Imperial theater Monopoly," *Slavonic and East European Review* 83 (2005): 254–89; *Istoriia russkogo,* VI (1980), 59; A. la. Al'tshuller, "Russkii teatr i obshchestvennoe dvizhenie," in Al'tshuller et al., eds., *Russkii teatr i obshchestennoe dvizhenie (konets XVIII–nachalo XX veka)* (Leningrad, 1984), 14–15; Arkady Ostrovsky, "Imperial and Private Theaters, 1882–1905," in Leach and Borovsky, 240; A. P. Kugel, *Teatral'nye portrety* (Leningrad, 1967), 152.
25. P. P. Gnedich, "Moi tsenzurnye mytarstva: Iz 'Knigi zhizni,'" in A. C. Polianov, ed., *Ezhegodnik Petrogradskikh Gosudarstvennykh teatrov: Sezon 1918–1919 gg.*

(Petrograd, 1920), 198; Jean Benedetti, *Stanislavski: A Biography* (London, 1988), 30, 39–40.
26. Russian State Historical Archive (RGIA), f. 776, op. 25, d. 340, l. 8.
27. Swift, *Popular*, 88–130; Murray Frame, *The St. Petersburg Imperial Theaters: Stage and State in Revolutionary Russia, 1900–1920* (Jefferson, NC, 2000), 87; Frame, *School for Citizens: Theater and Civil Society in Tsarist Russia* (New Haven, CT, 2006), 142; Gary Thurston, *The Popular Theater Movement in Russia, 1862–1919* (Evanston, IL, 1998), 150, 175, 179; Swift, "Germs," 43, 46.
28. B. Rostotskii and N. Chushkin, *"Tsar' Fedor Ioannovich" na stene MKhT* (Leningrad, 1940), 215–19; K. S. Stanislavskii, *Stat'i. Rechi: Besedy; Pis'ma* (Moscow, 1953), 154, 169, 706–7; A. P. Chekhov, *Polnoe sobranie sochinenii i pisem v tridtsati tomakh*, vol. 13 (Moscow, 1978), 472–73.
29. Vladimir Nemirovich-Danchenko, *My Life in the Russian Theater*, trans. John Cournos (New York, 1968), 175–82; K. S. Stanislavskii, *Stat'i. Rechi. Besedy. Pis'ma* (Moscow, 1953), 169.
30. Spencer Golub, "The Silver Age, 1905–1917," in Leach and Borovsky, 277–301.
31. M. Gor'kii, *Sobranie sochinenii v tridtsati tomakh*, vol. 6 (Moscow, 1950), 516–17; Petrovskaia, *Teatr i zritel' rossiiskikh stolits*, 143-45; RGIA, f. 776, op. 25, d. 702, ll. 32–44 ob., d. 27, ll. 6-11 ob.; D.I. Zolotnitskii, "Akademicheskii teatr dramy im. A.S. Pushkina na podstupakh k Gor'komu," in *Teatr i dramaturgiia: Trudy Gosudarstvennogo teatra, muzyki i kinematografii* (Leningrad, 1959); Al'tshuller, 15.
32. Chester Dunning and Caryl Emeron, *The Uncensored Boris Godunov: The Case for Pushkin's Original Comedy* (Madison, WI, 2006); Robert William Oldani, "*Boris Godunov* and the Censor," *Nineteenth-Century Music* 2 (1978): 245–53; Gerald Abraham, *Rimsky-Korsakov* (London, 1945); Abraham, "Satire and Symbol in the *Golden Cockerel*," *Music and Letters* 52 (1971): 46–54; V. V. Yastrebtsev, *Reminiscences of Rimsky-Korsakov* (New York, 1985), 102–3, 128–31, 350–77; Lynn Sargeant, "*Kaschei the Immortal:* Liberal Politics, Cultural Memory and the Rimsky-Korsakov Scandal of 1905," *Russian Review* 64 (2005): 22–43.
33. John Klier, "Exit, Pursued by a Bear: The Ban on Yiddish Theater in Imperial Russia," 159–74, and Barbara Henry, "Jewish Plays on the Russian Stage," 61, both in Joel Berkowitz, ed., *Yiddish Theater: New Approaches* (Oxford, 2003); Thurston, 181; Jim Sampson, "East Central Europe: The Struggle for National Identity," in Sampson, ed., *The Late Romantic Era: From the Mid-Nineteenth Century to World War I* (London, 1991), 224.
34. David Saunders, "Russia's Ukrainian Policy (1847–1905)," *European History Quarterly* 25 (1995): 181; Serhy Yekelchyk, "The Nation's Clothes: Constructing a Ukrainian High Culture in the Russian Empire, 1860–1900," *Jahrbücher für Geschichte Osteuropas* 49 (2001): 239; Alexei Miller, *The Ukrainian Question: The Russian Empire and Nationalism in the Nineteenth Century* (Budapest, 2003), 227, 241, 267; Irena Makaryk, *Shakespeare in the Undiscovered Bourn: Les Kurbas, Ukranian Modernism and early Soviet Cultural Politics* (Toronto, 2004), 10–14; Valerian Ruvutksy, "The Act of Ems (19876) and Its Effect on Ukrainian

Theatre," *Nationalities* Papers 5 (1977): 67–78; Michael Hamm, *Kiev: A Portrait, 1800–1917* (Princeton, NJ, 1993), 99, 148–50.
35. RGIA f. 776, op. 26., d. 42, ll. 19, 24, 33, 39, 51, 57–58, 62, 64, 77, 97, op. 25, d. 633, ll. 12–13; Swift, *Popular*, 116-20; Thurston, 215.
36. RGIA, f. 776, op. 25, d. 1179, ll. 17–18.
37. RGIA, d. 624, l. 4; GARF, f. 102 OO, d.13, l. 42; Al'tshuller, 17; B. Glagolin, "Akterskaia otsebiatina," *Teatr i iskusstvo* 27 (2 July 1906): 425–27.
38. RGIA, f. 776, op. 25, d. 624, ll. 26–29, d. 911, l. 1; A. A. Briantsev, "Vospominaniia," in Briantsev, ed., *A. N. Gozenpud* (Moscow, 1979), 51–52. For example, in Aleksandr Griboedov's *Woe from Wit* (Gore ot uma) the censors deleted a phrase referring to lions: "Whatever you say, even if they're animals, they're still tsars!" Had the phrase not been crossed out, suggests Briantsev, "no one would have paid any attention to it."
39. I. Ivanov, "O sovremennom nevrastenii i starom geroisme," *Teatr i iskusstvo* 50 (12 December 1899): 900–901; Laurence Senelick, "Anti-Semitism and Tsarist Theater: The Smugglers Riots," *Theater Survey* 44 (2003): 68–101 (citation on 88); Constantine Stanislavski, *My Life in Art* (New York, 1956), 378–79.
40. RGIA, f. 776, op. 25, d. 826, ll. 2–39; D. I. Zolotnitskii, "'Dni svobody' Russkogo farca," in A. A. Ninov, ed., *Russkii teatr i dramaturgiia epokhi revolution, 1905–1907* (Leningrad, 1987), 131–42; Glavnoe upravlenie po delam pechati, "Tsirkuliar No. 758" (25 January 1906), RGIA, f. 776, op. 25, d. 858, l. 1; *Teatr i iskusstvo* 7 (12 February 1906), 97; Frame, *St. Petersburg*, 125–27; Murray Frame, "Censorship and Control in the Russian Imperial Theatres during the 1905 Revolution and Its Aftermath," *Revolutionary Russia* 7 (1994): 164–91.
41. A. Chargonin, "Neskol'ko slov o repertuare narodnykh teatrov," *Teatr i iskusstvo* 32 (7 August 1905): 513–15; RGIA, f. 776, op. 26, d. 57, ll. 93–121.
42. Robert Justin Goldstein, *Political Censorship in Nineteenth-Century Europe* (London, 1989), 199; Anthony Swift, "Kul'turnoe stroitel'stvo ili kul'turnaia razrukha? Nekotorye aspekty teatral'noi zhizn' Moskvy i Petrograda v 1917 g.," in V. Iu. Chernaev, et al., eds., *Anatomiia revoliutsii: 1917 god v Rossii: Massy, partii, vlast* (Moscow, 1994), 401–4.

# Spain

## David T. Gies

### A Century of Conflict

Spain experienced a startling series of political and social upheavals during the nineteenth century, some of which were imported and some of which resulted from internal forces. Between the War of Independence (1808–14, called the "Peninsular War" by the British) and the embarrassment of the Spanish-American War of 1898 (which resulted in the loss of Spain's last colonies in the New World—Cuba, Puerto Rico, and the Philippines), the country dealt with at least seven internal uprisings (at the Aranjuez Palace in March 1808; Rafael de Riego's successful overthrow of Fernando VII in 1820; the aborted coup attempts of Francisco Espoz y Mina and J. M. Torrijos in 1830 and 1831, respectively; Ramón de Narváez's coup of 1844; Leopoldo O'Donnell's uprising against the government in 1854; and the Glorious Revolution of September 1868, which forced Queen Isabel II into exile, temporarily ending the Bourbon monarchy that had ruled Spain since 1700), two foreign kings (José Bonaparte in 1808–12 and Amadeo de Savoy in 1871–73), two civil wars (the so-called Carlist Wars of 1833–39 and 1870–75), two French invasions (Napoleon's troops in 1808 and the Quadruple Alliance–backed forces of 1823), dozens of street skirmishes against the government, no fewer than six constitutions (1812, 1834, 1837, 1845, 1869, 1876), one failed Republic (1873), and several political assassinations (the most momentous being those of General Juan Prim in 1869 and of Prime Minister Antonio Cánovas del Castillo in August 1897). It is therefore no surprise that anxiety about what the people read, heard, saw, and thought ran high in official circles and that censorship, as a tool to control such matters, was everpresent. As Adrian Shubert writes, "Censorship legislation during the nineteenth century was abundant, diverse, and contradictory, and thus faithfully mirrored the country's turbulent political history as censorship laws changed repeatedly and frequently along with governments and even regimes. There was only one constant: with the sole exception of the revolutionary interlude of 1868–74, there was always censorship of some kind."[1]

Throughout the century, Spanish authorities viewed the theater as a dangerous enterprise, one whose spontaneity, power, and free expression needed to be supervised, curtailed, and/or completely muffled as deemed necessary. This belief, a powerful residue built up from centuries of seeing the theater as a subversive and immoral activity,[2] dominated thinking during the entire century, whose chaotic and conflictual history was frequently reflected on stage. Political instability, military threats and intervention, church moralizing, and ideological conflict marked Spain's nineteenth century,[3] so it is hardly unexpected that the theater, which captured both the anxiety of the literate classes and the aspirations of the masses, would be subject to rigorous control. Writer and critic Ventura García Escobar, writing in *La Luneta* in 1847, noted that certain phrases and ideas that might seem innocuous or innocent when read silently, if declaimed from the stage in front of a live audience could have a more "powerful" impact. This impact (*efecto*) was something that the authorities struggled to minimize. The conservative newspaper columnist Cándido Nocedal warned of the theater's "perverse social tendencies and terrible moral teaching" in a 2 December 1856 statement. Seeking to find a way to bring the theater permanently into line, Nocedal continued: "The theater, which can greatly influence human feelings, should not offer the slightest example of offense to good habits" and "should offer to all [social classes] innocent entertainment."[4] In this view, "innocent entertainment" was to be prized above all else, and anything deemed provocative or immoral or not upholding "good habits" was to be eschewed. Such beliefs confirm theater historian Joaquín Álvarez Barrientos's statement that "the role of censorship should be kept foremost in our minds when we study nineteenth-century Spanish theater, since its influence was noteworthy and seen in all areas."[5]

## Censorship and the Theater

Playwrights faced multiple obstacles in their attempts to publish and stage their plays. Theatrical censorship came in multiple forms, all of them legitimated by the weight of history and custom, and backed by law. Both civil and ecclesiastical authorities had accrued the power, through years of struggle and negotiation, to force playwrights to submit works for prejudgment. If the playwright was a woman—and, granted, there were few enough of them—an additional censorship could be exercised by her husband or father, who had the "right" to approve or veto any literary activity leading toward publication or public performance.[6]

If church and civil authorities had always attempted to control theatrical activity through censorship, in the aftermath of the cataclysmic upheavals of the 1789 French Revolution, Spanish authorities redoubled their efforts to prescribe what could and could not be seen on the country's stages. Dozens of successful attacks on freedom of the theaters had been carried out during the eighteenth century,[7] but as the new century dawned, concern over the power of the theater to influence not only the literary tastes of theatergoers but also their moral compasses and ideological leanings increased. Actors, acting companies, impresarios, and dramatists tried to circumvent the insidious restrictions of the censors, and critics like Mariano José de Larra (1809–37) railed mightily against the arbitrary nature of official censorship, but few inroads were made against it until the early twentieth century. Even then, when it looked as though such censorship might abate (if not end entirely), the Franco Regime (1939–75) reinstated it in all its brutality, inconsistency, and vigor.

Censorship of all media was an active business. Throughout the eighteenth century, dozens of royal decrees limited the publication of essays, scientific tracts, poetry, narrative, newspapers, and even images. The Royal Decree of 18 May 1785, for example, fixed the size of newspapers at four to six pages, and delegated censorship rights to the Juez de Imprentas (publication judge), who was permitted to name two officials to carry out censoring activities. Anyone interested in publishing a newspaper needed to apply for a permit, and even then individual issues had to be submitted for prior approval. Approval was granted so long as nothing that the censors considered to be improper, salacious, satirical, or ad hominem appeared anywhere, and so long as there were no references to the government (monarchs or ministers) or to church dogma.[8] This standard procedure produced what Spanish press historian Iris Zavala has called a "semiology of silence."[9]

That theater censorship similarly had an ideological and moral component was clear to all. As historian Emilio Palacios Fernández reminds us about the years of the "enlightened" King Carlos III (specifically 1777),

> We can verify that the censor exercised his duties with the utmost diligence, always careful to control the ideological and social nature of the plays: he systematically defends the institution of the monarchy (including the King and Queen's habits), protects the nobility and its privileges, demands rigorous respect for the principles of religion and of ecclesiastical authorities, keeps the moral values of social customs in check (overly aggressive women, criticism of suicide, daring scenes), submitting the plays at times to a crude cutting of the texts themselves. "Approve it and put it on, keeping in mind the censor's comments as well as the crossed out or underlined items" was the standard formula that we read just before the definitive approval of the Protective Judge is issued for any stage performance.[10]

Significantly, the censor was called a "Juez *Protector*" (*protective* judge; emphasis added), implying in his very title that the position carried social weight far beyond the confines of "mere" literary activity. In 1807 a Reglamento General sobre teatros (General Regulation on the Theaters) emphasized the special role of the censor, who had the power to modify or ban works destined either for publication or stage presentation. The censor was charged with examining all new dramas as well as works not performed during the previous ten years, in order to root out all offenses against "religion, laws, and customs."[11] The Reglamento granted him (it was always a "him," of course) not only de facto autonomy over the theater, but also free tickets and a special box from which to watch the plays that were approved for staging (to insure that nothing was changed at the last minute).

## Changes in Censorship Laws

Political upheaval frequently brought in its wake changes in censorship laws. While the War of Independence (1808–14) allowed for some relief from tight censorship, the return of the tyrannical King Fernando VII to the throne triggered its intensification, and newspapers, broadsheets, engravings, printed pictures, and theater once again all became subject to prior scrutiny. All dramatic works to be staged or published passed through the censor's hands, but that was not enough for Fernando's nervous government: actors were warned not to add unscripted words or phrases to their performances, and any incidents of "disorder, impiety, or licentiousness" would cost them fines or even imprisonment.[12] It seemed essential to avoid the "absolute freedom" that had reigned—so governing officials thought—during the king's absence. Even plays such as those by the country's dominant neoclassical playwright Leandro Fernández de Moratín, including his classic *El sí de las niñas,* which opened in 1806 to an unprecedented reception and seemed hardly designed to offend anyone, was by 1815 subject to the Inquisition's censorship.[13] In 1817 in Seville, his play *El viejo y la niña* (The Old Man and the Girl) was banned because "its plot is provocative, obscene, and consequently not in line with healthy morals and good habits."[14] At the same time, a rather innocuous one-act play, Juan Ignacio González del Castillo's *El desafío de la Vicenta* (Vicenta's Challenge), was shut down because one of the characters, a pregnant woman, goes to the theater, an activity deemed too racy and inappropriate for young women, particularly one in her delicate condition.[15]

In contrast, on 22 October 1820, following the liberal uprising by the military leader Rafael de Riego ten months earlier, prior censorship for newspapers and prints ended, although such publications still needed to beware of publishing material that could be considered seditious, obscene, or libelous. The abolition of censorship encompassed the theater also, but that open window slammed shut in May 1823 when, following the French invasion by the so-called 100,000 Sons of St. Louis (backed by the Quadruple Alliance in order to restore the reactionary King Fernando VII to the Spanish throne), officials reinstated prior censorship of all published and performed works. This restraint was confirmed on 15 October 1823, when the king decreed that "all of the acts, of any type or nature, of the so-called Constitutional Government that dominated my country from March 7, 1820 until today, are hereby declared null and void." The censors were a mixed bag of clerics, military types, politicians, and loyalists (including the king's private doctor), and the rules they laid out provide us with details of their concerns. For example, authors were expressly banned from using pseudonyms, but the names of the censors themselves were kept off their critiques for fear of reprisals. All books and papers that mocked or criticized "our holy and one-and-only Catholic Religion" were banned, as were any works critical of the king and the government. Penalties could be as light as monetary fines, or as severe as exile or even the death sentence for serious transgressions of the rules.

## The Rebirth of the Theater

Following the French invasion, Jean-Marie Grimaldi, a French adventurer and soldier who had entered Madrid with the invading troops of the French Duke of Angoulême (who spearheaded the 100,000 Sons of St. Louis) in 1823, brashly requested that the city council hand over the capital's two failing theaters to him. It was a bold and perhaps foolish move, since Grimaldi had neither experience as a theater director nor a solid knowledge of the Spanish language. Yet city hall, desperate to find a solution to the financial burden that the theaters represented to the city's coffers, agreed to put Grimaldi in charge of the Príncipe Theater and the Cruz Theater. Grimaldi's immediate goal was to provide entertainment in French for the invading forces, but it slowly dawned on him that he might be able to make a go of the enterprise, and he began to contract local talent to rekindle theater in Spanish. Without the express approval of the city's appointed theater censor, no plays could be staged, so Grimaldi worked with officials in order to bring a safe mix of reworked classics, comedies, translated plays, Italian operas, and melodramas to the two theaters. He began slowly and cautiously, staging works that had been approved in prior years, in order to placate Father Fernando Carrillo, the head censor, who guarded the "decorum" of the theater. Among the works that were performed were Rossini's *Tancredi*, a French farce translated as *El sordo en la posada*, Dionisio Solís's reworking of Tirso de Molina's *Don Gil de las calzas verdes*, Moratín's *El viejo y la niña*, a magical comedy entitled *A falta de hechiceros lo quieren ser los gallegos*, Lope de Vega's *El mejor alcalde, el rey*, a short musical play by José María Carnerero titled *La noticia feliz*, Spanish versions of plays by the French dramatist Pixérécourt, and so on. Still, as he gained in confidence—and as he improved the theaters' physical spaces, signed on more actors and trained them better, hired painters and set designers, and identified writing talent such as Larra, José María Carnerero, Manuel Bretón de los Herreros, and Ventura de la Vega—Grimaldi, now hispanized into Juan de Grimaldi, became a major force in Spanish intellectual circles. Within less than thirteen years he would become Spain's most powerful impresario and director, and the man responsible for staging many of the country's now-canonical romantic plays.[16] Yet even Grimaldi had limited powers in the Spain of Fernando VII. It was during this period (1826–27) that the edition of Moratín's works that was being prepared for publication was subjected to severe censorship; in fact it was "ruined by censorship" according to a contemporary writer, Ramón de Mesonero Romanos.[17]

Since opera was viewed as a theatrical performance, librettos underwent censorial scrutiny along with dramatic texts, although the lack of a home-grown Spanish opera (until the second half of the century, when it appeared in the indigenous form called the *zarzuela*) generally made the librettos less troublesome than drama per se. However, this had not always been the case. While the first Italian operas were performed in Spain in the early eighteenth century, by the end of the century they were banned from the country's stages, not due to questionable content, but to the simple (xenophobic) fact that theater censors rejected any works not spoken or sung in Spanish.[18] But by the early 1820s Italian opera was all the rage (the ban of 1799 was lifted in 1821 by the new liberal—if temporary—government), and indeed the "furor" provoked in the capital by the arrival of works by Rossini threatened to shove legitimate theater right off the stage.[19] In his first year as theater impresario, Grimaldi successfully staged operas by Rossini (*La Cenerentola*), Giovanni Mayr (*La rosa blanca y la rosa encarnada*), and Saverio Mercadante (*Elisa y Claudio*).[20] This "delirium, fever, fanaticism"[21] produced substantial income for theater owners, and works like *La Straniera, La bella tabernera, L'Esule di Roma, I Capuleti ed i Montechi, Anna Bolena, Otelo, La Cenerentola, Chiara di Rossemberg,* and *El barbero de Sevilla* excited the crowds nightly. Opera, while more expensive to produce because of the elaborate scenery and costumes it demanded, was safer in a way since the texts were pre-approved and relatively well known. Attempts to suppress the opera during these years came not from political or religious censorship, but from actors, who viewed its popularity as a threat to their livelihood. In one document they wrote: "As long as a company of Italian singers is working in the theaters in Madrid, Spanish actors will be scorned, poorly paid, relegated to second-class status ... and Spanish theater, already in decline, will find itself in complete ruin."[22] On that front nothing changed, however, since the king himself was a huge opera fan and mandated the existence of an Italian opera company in Madrid from 1827 onward.[23]

While a slight loosening of the censorship rules occurred in 1828—an opening that allowed Larra to publish the first of his numerous newspaper articles, many of which would attack the very institution of censorship—a more fundamental change occurred five years later when (following the death of Fernando VII on 29 September 1833) the Inquisition, weakened by years of internal conflict and set to disappear completely in 1834, abandoned religious censorship. The end of the Inquisition did not mean the termination of censorship, however, since controls by lay authorities continued. The king's widow, Queen Regent María Cristina, asked several leading writers (Manuel José Quintana, Francisco Martínez de la Rosa, Alberto Lista) to draw up some guidelines that would help her new government think about the issues of theatrical freedom, writers' rights, and the conduct of actors. In November 1833 theater censorship was temporarily formally abandoned, but the state still found a need to "control" the theater, so a bewildering series of regulations, suggestions, ideas, strictures, and prohibitions spilled forth for the next several decades. In fact, while not necessarily intending to do so, state regulators merely took over the job of the Inquisitors with "a continuous wavering, in agreement with whatever politics [the government] wished to impose,"[24] that is, with the same arbitrariness and inconsistency as before. While some censorship breakthroughs occurred as early as 1834 (Larra's play *Macías* and Bretón's comedy *Elena*, both of which had been banned in 1833, were now readied for staging by Grimaldi), the church continued to pressure civil authorities to ban work it regarded as improper or that contained scenes, moments, objects, characters, or words that could even remotely offend the hierarchy's conservative sensibilities (for example, the church protested the title of Mariano Pina y Bohigas's 1848 comedy, *La mujer del Obispo* [The Bishop's Wife]), and lobbied to have the play banned). On 30 April 1856, the church succeeded in having enacted into law a ban on any play that represented the Holy Trinity or the Holy Family, a move that created enormous confusion around Christmas, when traditionally parishioners were treated to tableaux representing scenes from the birth and passion of Christ.[25]

## Inconsistency and Chaos

This arbitrary chaos was the model that would remain in effect throughout the rest of the century. Some continued to support ecclesiastical censorship, arguing that although civil authorities made the laws, church authority should trump civil law when necessary. Thus, *El Pensamiento Español* of 11 June 1863 defended ecclesiastical censorship in response to an article published in the progressive newspaper *Las Novedades*, which questioned the church's right to interfere with secular laws when censorship was concerned (at stake was the furor provoked by the recent translation of Victor Hugo's *Les Miserables*). Novelist and playwright Francisco Navarro Villoslada similarly voiced his conviction that "the permission granted to a book by government agents does not prevent, cannot prevent, the disapproval and banning by diocesan authorities." The explosion of publications—of novels, poetry, essays, newspapers, and plays—that erupted following Fernando VII's death proved too much for an informal censorship apparatus to handle, so in 1836 the official job of theater censor (that is, of someone whose sole responsibility was to inspect and censor plays for publication and performance) was created. Quintana wanted the job, but the queen regent thought him much too prestigious for such a prosaic position, and gave it to a minor intellectual and lawyer named Tomás Sancha.

Larra was perhaps theater censorship's most vitriolic and articulate critic.[26] His intense distaste for government and church intervention in the right of authors to express themselves freely, combined with his acerbic wit, made him a formidable adversary. In his article "Don Cándido Buenafé o el Camino de la Gloria" (Cándido Buenafé or the Road to Glory), published in the *Revista Española* on 2 April 1833, he was already complaining about the government's theatrical restrictions. He complained about how slow the process was for a play to make it to the stage: the first censors lost the manuscript, which required the author to re-create it and send it in again; six months elapsed, then the second censors demanded cuts. When it was finally ready for production, one of the actors refused to play his part, so it was sent to another company, and so on. Larra despaired, yet he frequently outsmarted the authorities by writing with such subtlety, clever allusions, and circumlocution that much of what probably should have been excised from his articles by alert censors in fact survived in print. The newspaper *Correo Literario y Mercantil* also protested the strictures of censorship—both formal and informal—by publishing on 15 May 1833 Bretón's hilarious piece that listed the numerous censorships (more than thirty-one are given) that dramatists needed to pass through on the way to having a play staged in Madrid. Bretón (who intimately knew the subject at hand) included among the "censors" not only the official ones (magistrates and random government bureaucrats) but also friends, copyists, theater directors, actors, printers, and others who at any moment claimed the right to change the author's text to suit individual needs.[27] In short, censorship had again become a sticky substance that spread over the whole of literary activity in Spain.

While in theory censorship became less restrictive after 1833, its reality it was very much alive and on Larra's mind. On 2 February 1834, in his review of Moratín's *La mojigata*, published in the *Revista Española*, Larra issued a broadside against literary censorship, declaring: "The majority of works written by our authors that have passed through and pass through our hands constantly would never have seen the light of day if they had been subjected at the outset to the partisan and oppressive censorship with which a suspicious and weak group in our times has kept the door to knowledge closed."²⁸ In "Lo que no se puede decir, no se debe decir" (What Can't Be Said Shouldn't Be Said), published in *El Observador* in October 1834, Larra complained ironically about demanding people who are never satisfied, people who want wars to stop, who want factional fighting to end, who want the press to be free, who complain about their leaders, etc. He claimed to support docility, then went on to mock mercilessly the new laws of censorship that turned writers into self-censoring cowards. What should "independent" writers do in "times like this," he asked, and ironically answered his question by suggesting that they do nothing, other than study the law, follow it, and stop complaining. Larra then quoted the laws themselves, whose very absurdity was revealed as he continued. Thus, noting that the laws banned conspiracies against religion, he declared, "Now, should an idea ever occur to me that tries to destroy religion, I shall keep it quiet, not write it out, chew it up and swallow it."²⁹ Having been criticized previously for "allusions" in his articles, he repeated the words "keep it quiet" several times, underscoring his frustration with his inability to write freely. "If I don't write it, they can't ban it," he observed, adding: "I don't write anything; better for me; better for him [the censor]; better for the Government: let them find allusions in what I don't write. … I look at my paper; I haven't written anything, I haven't done an article, it's true. But on the other hand I have carried out the law. This will always be my *modus operandi*: good citizen, I shall respect the whip that governs me and I will always conclude with: What can't be said, shouldn't be said."³⁰

Shortly thereafter, in "Un periódico nuevo" (A New Newspaper), published in *La Revista Española* on 26 January 1835, Larra returned to the topic and stated with ironic joy that a new "system of freedom" had been announced in Madrid and had been extended "even to the press." Heavily borrowing from the complaint of the hero of French dramatist Beaumarchais's originally censored play, *The Marriage of Figaro*, Larra expressed ironic comfort in the fact that as long as he did not write about "the authorities, or the Church, or politics, or morals, or public servants, or corporations, or actors, or anyone who belongs to anything, I can publish everything freely, after, of course, submitting it to the inspection and revising of two or three censors."³¹ This was a constant complaint in Larra's writing, and his conflicts with the authorities led him in turn to be funny, ironic, daring, nervous, or pessimistic. In "La alabanza, o que me prohiban este" (Praise, or Let Them Ban This One),³² published in *La Revista-Mensajero* on 16 March 1835, he aggressively mocked the weight of censorship and swore not to write for the censors (or with the censors in mind). His opposition revealed itself to be due not only to some intense affinity for personal freedom, but because he believed that censorship was a leading cause of the low quality of the theater of his day. Opposition was not easy, and even Larra—one of the highest paid, most powerful, and most daring writers in nineteenth-century Spain—was forced into silence or self-censorship with alarming frequency.

Larra's anger was understandable, since the hypocrisy of the government's stance concerning censorship was patent. Larra did not live to see the ratification of the Constitution of 1837 (he committed suicide in February of that year, at age 28), a document that ostensibly guaranteed all Spaniards the right to publish their ideas freely, a "right" in practice always curtailed by the inability of the government—and the church—to allow truly free speech to reign.[33] The catch was the clause that modified that freedom to include only works approved "within the limits permitted by law," thereby enabling the authorities to ban works, even if "prior censorship" was eliminated by the Constitution. The confirmation of the constitutional clause on free speech that was issued by the Moderate government on 9 April 1844 was an equally hollow rhetorical exercise. Still, Larra's resistance contrasted starkly with the attitude of conformity and passivity displayed by the newspaperman Ramón de Mesonero Romanos, more typical than Larra in his stance,[34] and by most playwrights of the day. Scholar Jesús Rubio Jiménez reminds us that censorship is always about power,[35] and the fear, whether expressed during a strict dictatorship or during periods of more openness, was that the theater, as a "school for morals," could unduly influence society; hence its designation as a dangerous enterprise that needed to be controlled. Thus, Tomás Sancha, the Madrid theater censor in 1836 and 1837, declared that society had to be protected, so that "the school of customs not become a house of prostitution."[36]

## Playwrights and the Censors

No playwrights—not even famous writers like Bretón, Antonio García Gutiérrez, and Antonio Gil y Zárate—were exempt from censorship. For example, even seemingly innocuous pieces like Bretón's 1827 rewrite of Calderón de la Barca's *No hay cosa como callar* (Nothing Beats Keeping Quiet) had become caught in the web of censorship under Fernando VII and had suffered important modifications;[37] Bretón fought many battles with the censors (in particular, with the fierce Father Carrillo). Later, Grimaldi had planned to stage Bretón's *Elena* in the early 1830s, after the death of the king, but it was stalled by the censors and not performed until 1834. Just as the authorities had persecuted newspapers for publishing articles deemed too political,[38] so too they similarly harassed plays whose content was perceived as touching on sensitive political topics. In 1844, just as the Moderados (in reality, a conservative coalition led by the reactionary upstart Ramón de Narváez) were grabbing power from the Progressive government, the dramatist Eusebio Asquerino provoked a considerable national scandal by writing an overtly political play called *Españoles sobre todo* (Spaniards Above All), the performances of which caused riots, closings, and endless commentary in the daily press.[39] This same year saw the republication of the *Índice general de los libros prohibidos* (Index of Banned Books), first published by the Inquisition in 1805; four years later, an extension of that document was issued as *Apéndice al Índice general de los libros prohibidos*, a failed attempt to reinvigorate the book banning that had been canceled when the Inquisition went out of business in 1834. The mere attempt to revitalize these two works reveals much about the official mentality of church and state at mid century.[40] On 16 May 1847, Tomás Rodríguez Rubí, one of the country's most prolific and admired playwrights (he had already enjoyed success with *Bandera negra* [Black Flag, 1844][41] and the two parts of *La rueda de la fortuna* [The Wheel of Fortune, 1843 and 1845]), wrote to the government to complain of the arbitrary closing of his play *Alberoni*, which had premiered successfully at the Príncipe Theater in 1846, but which, for reasons no one could explain satisfactorily, was shut down by Madrid's Chief of Police, Pedro Sabater, after one performance. He pointed out that as a dramatist his livelihood depended on his ability to have his plays performed and demanded some compensation for his efforts.[42]

Since none of the efforts at controlling or censoring the theater had worked to official satisfaction (nor that of the theater professionals), a Royal Decree of 7 February 1849 created a Junta Consultiva de Teatros del Reino designed to watch over theater matters, including which works were most appropriate—or not—for public viewing. The putative purpose of this Junta was to support the theaters by designating certain theaters as exclusive venues for different genres (tragedy, comedy, etc.), and people intimately involved in the theaters were conscripted to serve on the board (the playwright José María Díaz and the critic Manuel Cañete, among others). Eugenio Ochoa was named censor of the kingdom's theaters, but the position was purely honorific. Each year, the Junta published a list of plays pre-approved for performance, in an attempt to streamline the cumbersome mechanism of censorship; the list was published in the daily press, and it included, oddly, titles of plays that had been performed for years, although not always without controversy (for example, Asquerino's *Españoles sobre todo* appeared on the list published in *La Nación* on 13 May 1849). By 1853 the experiment was declared a failure and was abandoned.[43]

Newspaper accounts from 1850 can help track the difficulties faced by dramatists at mid century. *El tesorero del rey* (The King's Treasurer), written by two well-known playwrights, Antonio García Gutiérrez (whose smash hit *El trovador* had catapulted him to fame in 1836) and Eduardo Asquerino (brother of the author of the controversial *Españoles sobre todo*, 1844), was approved for performance in early November, as reported in *La España* on 4 November 1850. Yet only two days later, the press reported that the censors had experienced second thoughts, and would not allow the play to be performed unless a reference to the *Book of Kings* was excised (apparently the authors had put words that rightfully belonged elsewhere into the mouth of a Jew, Samuel Levi; such sins against dogma and biblical accuracy were viewed with some alarm and, consequently, banned). García Gutiérrez's *Los hijos del tío Tronero* (Uncle Tronero's Children) was also banned in 1850. All playwrights faced similar inspection; some, more than others, faced constant hostility from the censors. José María Díaz, whose strong views on issues such as capital punishment kept him in constant conflict with the authorities, fought numerous battles with the censors over plays such as *Catalina* (1856), *Luz en la sombra* (Light in Shadow, 1860), and *Mártir siempre, nunca reo* (Always a Martyr, Never a Defendant, 1863), all three of which finally were produced, but only after significant rewriting. According to the newspaper *El Contemporáneo* (19 April 1863), *Mártir* "has been amply mutilated by censorship." Authors could, of course, fight such "mutilation," but often the results were problematic or inconclusive. When voices were raised, as was the case with Vicente Rodríguez Varo's protest against the banning of his play, *La rama torcida* (The Twisted Branch, 1860), a commission was created to pass final judgment (here, the commission was formed by Rodríguez Rubí, García Gutiérrez, and Manuel Catalina).

A detailed "Real Decreto de 1852 sobre el ejercicio de la libertad de Imprenta" (Royal Decree of 1852 On the Exercise of the Freedom of the Press) laid out specific items that would be banned from overt criticism anywhere; these included the king and his family, issues of state security, public order, "society," religion or public morality, "authority," foreign sovereigns, or "individuals." These sweeping generalizations left the authorities effectively in charge of what was written in the press or seen on stage. The process for making sure that the spirit and letter of the law was followed was cumbersome in the extreme. As the *Gaceta de Madrid*, quoting from the Royal Decree, explained on 31 July 1852:

> When a work needs to be looked at by the censors, two copies must be sent to the designated Governor [of the province], and this individual will send them on to the censor. When the work has been examined, the Governor will return to the author [or director] one of the two copies, signed by the censor on every one of its pages, conceding or denying permission to be staged, or pointing out the modifications needed in order to be so. The second copy, attached to the censor's report, and signed by him on the first and last pages, will be kept in the archives of the provincial government.

Following the so-called Liberal Biennium of 1854–56, more conservative men forced additional censorship on the theaters (Nocedal's comments, cited in the first section of this chapter above, are emblematic). Not surprisingly, 1857 was one of the strictest years for theater censorship.

## The Censors

Being a theater censor carried some prestige and could lead to higher government posts, although most of the censors aligned themselves with the more conservative governments (the socialist writer Fernando Garrido put it more simply: for him, censorship was always in the hands of reactionary elements[44]). After the dramatist and writer Ceferino Suárez Bravo gave up his job as censor in January 1857, he was named Spanish Consul in Genoa. Antonio Gil y Zárate, a dramatist who had been persecuted in the early 1820s, and whose *Carlos II el hechizado* (Charles II the Bewitched) caused considerable tongue-wagging over the years, became under secretary in the Ministry of Government in 1857, and was apparently responsible for the promulgation of a regulation concerning the theater that was, in the words of his critics at *La Época*, a throwback to the dictatorial times of Fernando VII: "Now—and here is where the anachronism of this measure gets absurd—since this censorship, newly centralized in the hands of one person, is retroactive, it turns out that the very works of Mr. Antonio Gil y Zárate ... would be prohibited by Mr. Antonio Gil y Zárate, Under Secretary of the Government in 1857!!" The article's author continued in this ironic vein, finally concluding that censorship might have a salutary effect if it could save Spanish theater from some of the bad, boring, or useless plays that had been put on recently: "We welcome censorship, therefore! We welcome it, since it brings us an excuse to not die of shame!"

Between 1857 and 1863, the noted author Antonio Ferrer del Río served as official censor, and issued reasoned, if strict, judgments on plays submitted for approval. In 1864, one of the most popular and prolific playwrights of his time, the now-forgotten Narciso Serra,[45] took over as Censor de Teatros (theater censor), a post that he occupied for four years (with the exception of a short hiatus, taken for health reasons, in 1866, when Luis Fernández-Guerra became interim censor, and during the final year, when Luis Eguílaz filled in). Many of the printed texts used today carry Serra's seal of approval on the last page, where he assured readers that the play contained nothing offensive or against the rules of decorum. Serra proved to be a particularly obdurate censor, a revelation that surprised his peers, although his well-known conservative views hardly suggested that he would act otherwise. As the newspaper *La Discusión* wrote on 29 November 1864, "The new theater censor, Narciso Serra, has begun his job seriously, which he demonstrates by banning works that do not go against morals. And it is surprising that it is he, author of *El amor y la gaceta*, a play which some critics claim to be immoral, who is being so severe." Theater historian Carlos Cambronero described him as "indolent" and "dreamy" in his work as censor.[46]

As new plays arrived for approval, Serra's task was to examine them, then appoint a select committee to review them (each committee consisted of a president and several voting members). When García Gutiérrez's *Juan Lorenzo* was submitted in 1865, Serra first banned it (*La Democracia*, 27 October 1865), then, following considerable public outcry, appointed a committee comprised of the playwrights Juan Eugenio Hartzenbusch, Tomás Rodríguez Rubí, Adelardo López de Ayala, and Francisco Villegas, all highly regarded and active literary figures of the day. *La Iberia* called the ban "violent and ridiculous," but the committee sought to investigate what the newspaper *El Contemporáneo* (27 October 1865) referred to as the play's "marked political tendencies," which is precisely what had made Serra uncomfortable in the first place. As historian Cantero García writes, Serra, as an ex-military man, was particularly concerned that the theater not become a hotbed of political passion and subversive activity, fears not entirely unfounded in the years leading up to the Revolution of 1868.[47] García Gutiérrez could hardly be accused of harboring any socialist tendencies (the great fear of the conservatives at mid century), so *Juan Lorenzo* finally opened at the Príncipe Theater on 20 December 1865, although to tepid response. Ironically, Serra himself had been the target and recipient of the censor's ire: his own play, *Un hombre importante* (An Important Man), had been banned in the provincial city of Pamplona in 1858 (*El*

*Fénix*, 4 May 1858). Most of the time Serra defended his censorship on ideological and moral grounds, but sometimes he was forced to bow to public pressure. When a letter-writing campaign of parents protesting the performance of a musical comedy called *Un tenor modelo* (A Model Tenor) came to his attention in November 1864, he and the provincial governor, Gutiérrez de la Vega, pulled the play until rewrites could be made that satisfied all parties (*El Contemporáneo*, 30 November 1864).

One of Serra's most ignoble fights involved José María Gutiérrez de Alba, a figure on the Spanish literary scene since the early 1850s, when the latter's satirical comedies—many of which took the pulse of current events and issues (*Una mujer literata* [A Writerly Woman], from 1851, is a good example)—provoked laughter and resistance in Madrid. Gutiérrez de Alba wrote a short skit that chronicled the horrific events of what has become known as the Noche de San Daniel (Night of St. Daniel), 10 April 1865, when government troops shot and killed several students who were protesting the removal of some of their favorite professors from their university posts. *Revista de 1865* addressed the events (allegorically, of course), and was consequently banned by Serra for its "political allusions and depictions of politicians," even after the author protested and made significant changes to his original text. Only after the piece had undergone enough changes as to be practically unrecognizable did Serra give his approval on 12 January 1866.[48] Like the church, the military establishment kept a close watch on the theater and protested vigorously all negative depictions of its members or what it perceived to be attacks on its "honor." The ill-considered war in Africa, which erupted in 1859 when General Leopoldo O'Donnell landed at Ceuta, stimulated a large number of plays that addressed both sides of the issue; those that were critical of the government, not surprisingly, were challenged by the authorities, cut, modified, or simply banned.

## The Theater after 1868

Serra lost his job when the government inaugurated by the Revolution of 1868 eliminated all theater censorship—a period of "unprecedented freedom," according to scholar Nancy Membrez[49]—but he returned for a second term in August of 1875, when the restored Bourbon monarchy reinstated it (*La Época*, 23 August 1875). Prime Minister Antonio Cánovas del Castillo, while supporting the theater and developing regulations that helped it flourish, nevertheless at the same time defended strict censorship on moral and political grounds; he was supported, as always, by the church and the military. The two most common forms of censorship—prior censorship and on-the-spot closings—became the norm during the period called the Restoration (1874–1923), when the Bourbons, ejected from the country in 1868, again claimed power. Even newspapers called for censorship of plays, as happened following the performances of José de Echegaray's *En el pilar y en la cruz* (On the Column and on the Cross) in 1878: "Newspapers demand theater censorship so that plays like Echegaray's last one cannot be performed" (*La Iberia,* 2 March 1878). Suspected "political tendencies" resulted in the banning of performances of Ricardo de la Vega's *La quinta de la esperanza* (Villa of Hope, 1879), although it quickly sold out in two printed editions (*La Correspondencia de España,* 5 October 1879). Echegaray himself joined a group of writers from the Círculo Literario Artístico in 1887 to protest the ban of Marcos Zapata's play, *La piedad de una Reina* (A Queen's Mercy), then presided over a major meeting of playwrights in 1897 to voice dismay to the mayors of two Spanish cities, San Sebastián and Palma de Mallorca, who had banned the performances of various dramatic works.

These years witnessed the proliferation of new theatrical genres—one-act plays performed in bars and canteens (*teatro por horas*), *zarzuelas*, *revistas* (reviews), a rebooting of the one-act *sainete*, the *juguete cómico* (comic plaything), etc.—which were treated as regular plays for censorship purposes, but which were much more difficult to control because of their often ephemeral nature. Three types of performances were treated as a seamless whole, and their scripts/libretti inspected (or not) as time and circumstance allowed. Plays could be verse or prose performances (without a musical component), operas or *zarzuelas* (with music), or *teatro por horas* (with or without music).[50]

## Inconsistencies

Some plays approved during one time period were banned in another. Even though the censor Jerónimo de la Escosura had approved the translation of French playwright Alexander Dumas' *Richard Darlington* for performance in Madrid in the 1830s, when Andrés Fontcuberta (also known as J. A. Covert-Spring, a translator of Dumas) tried to stage it in Barcelona, local authorities shut the production down. Antonio Gil y Zárate's wildly romantic play, *Carlos II el hechizado,* when performed in 1837 startled everyone—"leaving the public in shock because of its daring nature"[51]—but still became an immediate hit in spite of its perceived "immorality" and political connotations. However, when a producer attempted to revive it in Cádiz in 1868, the censors tried (successfully for a while) to ban it (*La Época,* 3 December 1868). Hartzenbusch's *Doña Mencía,* first performed in 1839 to good reviews and a positive reception, was banned in Valencia in 1857 when that city's theater censor deemed it unacceptable (*La Discusión,* 22 January 1857). Likewise, although Ventura de la Vega's immensely popular comedy *El hombre de mundo* (Man of the World) had transformed the unknown writer into one of the true stars of the Madrid stage when it was first performed in 1845, when five actors from one of the capital's dramatic societies recited several scenes from the innocuous play in September 1848 (a time of panic and upheaval in European politics, it must be noted), they were arrested and jailed for three days (*El Clamor Público,* 21 September 1848). Even stranger, the newspaper *La Discusión* reported on 13 December 1859 that the censors in Chile (!) had banned Vega's play "because it is immoral." According to *El Clamor Público,* 24 October 1848, Rafael Villalobos' play *Intrigas* (Intrigues) could not be performed at the Cruz Theater in Madrid because it had somehow been "semi-filed away" in the government ministry. Even the silly *Los amantes de Chinchón* (The Lovers from Chinchón), a parody of Juan Eugenio Hartzenbusch's now-classic romantic tragedy, *Los amantes de Teruel* (The Lovers from Teruel), was banned in December, 1848.

In 1839, José María Díaz saw two of his plays banned or cut by the censors. The first, a hyper-romantic historical play entitled *Laura o la venganza de un esclavo* (Laura, or a Slave's Revenge), never made it to the Madrid stage because of its putative "immorality" (this word is repeated ad nauseam by the censors). When it was finally performed in Murcia in 1841, the public greeted it with less than overwhelming enthusiasm; it was received "with repugnance," closed down, and accused of the same "immorality" that had got it banned in Madrid.[52] This "immorality" centered on the young lovers' passion and adulterous love affair (Laura is married to someone else), but the play is clearly a morality tale since Laura dies at the end for her obvious sins. Still, the unacceptable "sin" (that privileged romantic love over the sacrament of marriage) unnerved critics and public alike. An even stronger reaction awaited Díaz's *Baltasar Cozza* (1839), which was not performed in Madrid or in the provinces (although it was read in manuscript form and eventually published), accused of being "highly immoral" and "indecent." The presence of a character who in the first act is a common pirate and in the second a cardinal of the church and, eventually, a pope (Juan XXIII) could hardly have endeared it to the censors or the church fathers (it was formally banned by the Junta de Censura in 1849, although that ban was overturned the following year).[53] Years earlier, Hartzenbusch had warned of the excessive zeal of censors as he defended some of the works of the Spanish classical repertory: "But we must take into account that in Lope's times dramatists could write anything, from casual comments to blasphemy, from social sayings to direct attacks on power—because there did not seem to be any Inquisition or censorship for the theater—leading to more recent times when in the most innocent joke an offense against morality was seen, and the simple act of bringing from history to the stage a crowned head was interpreted as an attack on the dignity of the throne."[54]

These few examples demonstrate the arbitrary nature of theater censorship, which Larra had protested for years. The examples are legion. Even José Zorrilla's *Don Juan Tenorio* (1844), an ultra-Catholic and ultra-conservative play that quickly became the most important drama of the Spanish nineteenth century, was the target of senseless attacks. As the newspaper *El Heraldo* reported on 11 February 1846, "*Don Juan Tenorio* debuted in Mahón, with great success. But it has been banned in subsequent performances because it is immoral and contrary to good customs." A similar fate befell the play in 1863 in Madrid, when following a series of complaints from the newspaper *El Diario Español*, the play was pulled from the performance lineup, and an unknown piece entitled *Don Juan Arana* replaced it (*La Discusión*, 9 December 1863). As late as 1910 the work appeared in Father Amado de Cristo Burguera y Serrano's catalog of plays that should be banned as "bad" (as did Vega's *Hombre de mundo* and Asquerino's *Españoles sobre todo,* along with hundreds of other dramatic works).[55]

The ironies of censorship accumulated, including that Larra's son, a prolific (but understudied) playwright named Luis Mariano de Larra, participated in the censoring of works in the early 1860s. *Cora, o la esclavitud* (Cora, or Slavery), in a translation by Miguel Morayta, grappled with the uncomfortable topic of slavery in the Spanish colonies and produced great disquiet in official circles. The play was originally banned by the censor, sent to a committee (comprised of Eugenio Rubí, Luis de Eguílaz, Fernando Martínez Pedrosa, and Luis Mariano de Larra) in December 1864, stalled, and then was approved only following some excisions and only in Spanish lands where slavery was not an issue (the country that caused the most discomfort was Cuba, whose anti-slavery uprisings would cause continued trouble for Spain until the century's end).[56] As with other playwrights, however, Larra (the son) himself was subjected to censorship.

In 1861 his play *La primera piedra* (The First Stone) was scheduled at the main theater in Valencia, but was canceled at the last minute "by censorship."

## A Gradual Loosening of Control

Near the end of the century censorship was more difficult to impose and playwrights and directors demonstrated less patience in obeying what they considered to be arbitrary and unfair restrictions. The clearest examples are Joaquín Dicenta's *Juan José* (1895) and Benito Pérez Galdós's *Electra* (1901). Both plays were admittedly and demonstrably provocative, the first a fervent defense of workers' rights against the oppression of the oligarchy and the second a ferocious attack on the clergy; both, naturally, provoked strong reactions on both the left and the right. *Juan José* had precedents in plays by early socialist or progressive writers such as Sixto Sáenz de Cámara (*Jaime el barbudo* [Bearded Juan], 1853), Fernando Garrido (*Un día de revolución* [A Day of Revolution], 1855), or even Eugenio Sellés, Enrique Gaspar, and Angel Guimerà, but the former playwrights experienced such problems with the conservative censors that their plays hardly ever made it to the stage. A minor work by a minor playwright—*Nobleza republicana* (Republican Nobility), by Francisco de Paula Montemar—became entangled in debate when one theater censor banned its performance but a subsequent one approved it (*El Clamor Público*, 5 November 1848). Dicenta's play, however, is the most instructive. Dicenta very clearly wanted to cause a reaction (he had written against social injustice and class division as early as 1890) and with this angry play he succeeded; the authorities clearly underestimated the play's power to instigate action among its viewers. Local politicians in particular had a vested interest in having the play banned, but instead of disappearing, it quickly became a symbol for downtrodden workers, and was revived every 1 May (International Workers Day) for years. The church likewise worked to ban it, because church fathers could hardly approve of a play whose two main protagonists, Juan José and Rosa, lived together without benefit of marriage. In fact, following Zorrilla's canonical *Don Juan Tenorio* (which was performed yearly on All Soul's Day), *Juan José* was the most frequently performed play in the Spanish repertory between 1895 and 1939 (some 100,000 performances have been documented by the Sociedad de Autores in Madrid). In 1895 the newspaper critic and novelist Leopoldo (Clarín) Alas scandalized Spanish society with *Teresa*, a one-act play that revealed similar socialist tendencies, but its failure to capture an audience—the public found it to be "crude, revolting, and producing an awful effect" (*Almanaque del Diario de Barcelona para 1895*)—enabled the authorities to ignore it rather than persecute the play or the author.

Galdós's *Electra* did, however, produce a monumental scandal similar to (perhaps even more so than) Dicenta's *Juan José*. The details have been told elsewhere:[57] the great novelist's attack on the clergy—which he had referred to as a "bacillus mística" (mystical germ) in another play—outraged the censors, the church hierarchy, and the viewing public. Riots broke out in the streets of Madrid, Seville, Córdoba, and Málaga; bishops specifically prohibited parishioners from seeing the play (*El Heraldo de Madrid*, 9 April 1896). The church had no legal authority to take such a stance, but it had enormous moral authority to cajole, persuade, or threaten the faithful through publications and preaching. Nothing, however, could stop the play's popularity, and the chaotic attempts to stifle it failed miserably. It ran for more than 80 nights in Madrid, an additional 180 in Paris, 32 in Rome, and dozens more in Buenos Aires (where it played in four theaters consecutively), Chile, Peru, Venezuela, and even Russia. The published edition sold 30,000 copies in the first month. Later, in his play *Casandra* (1910), Galdós posited an even more radical solution to what he perceived to be obscurantist clericalism: violence. When Casandra stabs doña Juana, who had been associated with the Church throughout the play, she proclaims, "I have killed the poisonous serpent that laid waste to the land. ... Humanity, you may now breathe freely." One of Galdós's correspondents reacted in typical fashion: "Your play *Casandra* is false, stupid, abominable. Go to Hell, sir."

## Conclusion

The foregoing look at theatrical censorship in nineteenth-century Spain helps open up what scholar Leonardo Romero Tobar has termed the "secret galleries of Spanish culture."[58] The socialist Fernando Garrido and his cohorts of like-minded progressives believed that, "Dramatic literature, like all manifestations of intelligence, needs to breathe in the gentle breeze of freedom,"[59] but such beliefs were not widely shared. Even at the dawn of the twentieth century, attempts to censor the theater continued unabated, although without the same success or rigor as one hundred years before. Books like Antonio González's *La inmoralidad del teatro moderno* (The Immorality of the Modern Theater; Madrid, 1899), Víctor Espinos

Moltó's *Influencia moral y social del teatro contemporáneo en la clase obrera* (Moral and Social Influence of Contemporary Theater on the Working Class; Santander, 1910), or Amado de Cristo Burguer Serrano's *Representaciones escénicas malas, peligrosas y honestas* (Bad, Dangerous and Honest Scenic Performances; Barcelona, 1911) confirmed that, at least in some quarters, theater was still—and would be for some time—viewed as a dangerous enterprise.[60]

## Bibliographical Essay

Reliable English-language sources for the general history of nineteenth-century Spain include Raymond Carr, *Spain, 1808–1975*, 2nd. ed. (Oxford, 1982); Adrian Shubert, *A Social History of Modern Spain* (London, 1990); and José Alvaro Junco and Adrian Shubert, eds., *Spanish History since 1808* (London, 2000). The only recent major English-language survey of the nineteenth-century Spanish stage is David T. Gies, *The Theatre in Nineteenth-Century Spain* (Cambridge, 1994); an overview of theater censorship is included in Adrian Shubert's excellently researched and engaging article, "Spain," in Robert Justin Goldstein, ed., *The War for the Public Mind: Political Censorship in Nineteenth-Century Europe* (Westport, CT, 2000), 175–209. For a specialized study, see David T. Gies, *Theater and Politics in Nineteenth-Century Spain: Juan de Grimaldi as Impresario and Government Agent* (Cambridge, 1988).

In Spanish, the most comprehensive works on literary censorship are now rather dated, but still provide excellent source materials and general guidelines for further discussion. Essential starting places include J. E. de Eguizábal's *Apuntes para una historia de la legislación española sobre la imprenta desde el año 1480 al presente* (Madrid, 1879); Carlos Cambronero's brief "Cosas de antaño: apuntes para la historia de la censura dramática," *Revista Contemporánea* 116 (1899): 594–609; Ángel González Palencia's three volume *Estudio histórico sobre la censura gubernativa en España, 1800–1833* (Madrid, 1934–41); Antonio Rumeu de Armas's *Historia de la censura literaria gubernamentiva en España* (Madrid, 1940); Antonio Sierra Corella's *La censura de libros y papeles en España y los índices y catálogos españoles de los prohibidos y expurgados* (Madrid, 1947); and Emilio Cotarelo y Mori's *Bibliografía de las controversias sobre la licitud del teatro en España*, edición facsímil, José Luis Suárez García, ed. (Granada, 1997). Additional information can be found in Víctor Cantero García's "El oficio de censor en nuestra historia literaria (siglos XVII–XIX): estudio y consideración de la censura dramática en la España decimonónica," *Letras de Deusto* 32 (2002): 63–89.

The best modern pieces on censorship in eighteenth-century Spain include Lucienne Domergue's *Tres calas en la censura dieciochesca (Cadalso, Rousseau, prensa periódica)* (Toulouse, 1981) and René Andioc's study of the theater, *Teatro y sociedad en el Madrid del siglo XVIII* (Madrid, 1976); his "La *Raquel* de Huerta y la censura," *Hispanic Review* 43 (1975): 115–39, is a detailed study of García de la Huerta's signature play. A clear and helpful discussion of censorship and theater in the final years of the eighteenth century and the initial years of the nineteenth is provided by Emilio Palacios Fernández in "Teatro y política (1789–1833)" in *Se hicieron literatos para ser políticos: Cultura y política en la España de Carlos IV y Fernando VII*, Joaquín Álvarez Barrientos, ed. (Cádiz, 2005), 185–242. John Dowling studies the classic *El sí de las niñas*, by Leandro Fernández de Moratín, in "The Inquisition Appraises *El sí de las niñas*," *Hispania* 44 (1961): 237–44. I have not seen del Río Barredo, "Censura Inquisitorial y teatro de 1707 a 1819," *Hispania Sacra* (1986). The censorship of both centuries is characterized by Iris Zavala as suffering a "semiology of silence" in "La censura en la semiología del silencio: siglos XVIII y XIX," in Manuel Abellán, ed., *Censura y literaturas peninsulares* (Amsterdam, 1987), 147–57.

One of the richest sources of information (and complaint) about censorship in Spain in the early part of the nineteenth century is the work of Mariano José de Larra, Carlos Seco Serrano, ed., *Obras de Mariano José de Larra [Fígaro]*, 4 vols. (Madrid, 1960), a work studied by, among others, Gregorio Martín in "Larra y el teatro: censura, crítica e historia," *Romance Quarterly* 34 (1987): 345–60. Larra's position concerning Ramón de Mesonero Romanos is examined by Amparo Medina-Bocos Montarelo in "Larra y Mesonero: Dos actitudes ante la censura de prensa," *Epos* 5 (1989): 183–99. For an overview of the issues involved, see Montserrat Puyol Rodríguez, "La cultura prohibida en España, 1805–1846: Análisis bibliográfico," in Pablo Fernández Albaladejo and Margarita Ortega López, eds., *Antiguo Régimen y liberalismo: Homenaje a Miguel Artola*, III (Madrid, 1994), 563–81; and Joaquín Álvarez Barrientos, "El mundo teatral desde la muerte de Fernando VII," in Guillermo Carnero, ed., *Historia de la literatura española*, VIII (Madrid, 1997), 254–67. For insight into one specific period in a provincial city, see Piedad Bolaños Donoso, "Sainetes y censura teatral: Cartelera sevillana en los inicios del siglo XIX (1815–1819)," in Alberto Romero Ferrer, ed., *Juan Ignacio González del Astillo (1763–1800): Estudios sobre su obra* (Cádiz, 2005), 169–96.

Individual playwrights receive spotty attention, but a good study of Bretón's troubles with censorship in his rewrite of a Golden Age play is provided by Javier Vellón Lahoz in "Moralidad y censura en las refundiciones del teatro barroco: *No hay cosa como callar,* de Bretón de los Herreros," *Revista de Literatura* 115 (1996): 159–68. Likewise, David T. Gies, "Rebeldía y drama en 1844: *Españoles sobre todo,* de Eusebio Asquerino," in *De místicos y mágicos, clásicos y románticos: Homenaje a Ermanno Caldera* (Messina, Italy, 1993), 315–32. On the playwright José María Díaz—one dramatist among many who had numerous run-ins with the censoring apparatus—the best source is José María González Subías, *Un dramaturgo romántico olvidado: José María Díaz* (Madrid, 2004). Literary censorship at mid century is the subject of Brigitte Journeau, "Problèmes de censure entre 1844 et 1854," in Claude Dumas, ed., *Culture et société en Espagne et en Amérique Latine au XIXe siècle* (Lille, 1980), 63–76. Leonardo Romero Tobar provides valuable documentation in two pieces, "Sobre censura de periódicos en el siglo XIX: Algunos expedientes gubernativos de 1832 a 1849," *Homenaje a Don Agustín Millares Carlo,* I (Las Palmas, 1975), 465–500; and "Textos inéditos de escritores españoles del XIX relacionados con la censura gubernativa," *Cuadernos Bibliográficos* 32 (1973): 89–108.

The opera and *zarzuela* in Spain have been studied by Luis Carmena y Millán, *Crónica de la ópera italiana en Madrid* (Madrid, 1878); José Subirá, *Historia de la música española e hispanoamericana* (Barcelona, 1953); Antonio Peña y Goñi, *España, desde la ópera a la zarzuela* (Madrid, 1967); Antonio Cid-Fernández, *Cien años de teatro musical en España (1875–1975)* (Madrid, 1975); and Pilar Espín Templado, *El teatro por horas en Madrid, 1870–1910* (Madrid, 1995), although a thorough and modern study of the relationship between Spanish romantic theater and Italian opera remains to be written.

The most detailed archival research has been carried out by Jesús Rubio Jiménez, who has published a number of significant books and articles on the Spanish theater in the second half of the century. Worthy of mention here are "La censura teatral en la época moderada, 1840–1868: Ensayo de aproximación," *Segismundo* 18 (1984): 193–231, and "El teatro en el siglo XIX (II) (1845–1900)," in José María Díez Borque, ed., *Historia del teatro en España,* II (Madrid, 1988), 625–762. See also Nancy Membrez's "The Bureaucratization of the Madrid Theater: Government Censorship, Curfews and Taxation, 1868–1925," *Anales de Literatura Española Contemporánea* 17 (1992): 99–123. Lisa Surwillo touches on censorship in her excellent analysis of theater copyright: *Stages of Property: Copyrighting Theatre in Spain* (Toronto, 2007).

Lists of plays banned in the end of the nineteenth and beginning of the twentieth centuries, as well as commentary on the rules and regulations that weighed on the theaters, are available in three publications by Amado de Cristo Burguera y Serrano: *Representaciones escénicas malas, peligrosas y honestas* (Barcelona, 1911), *Resumen de ambos tomos publicados en que se califican moralmente unas 6.000 obras* (Barcelona, 1915), and *Suplemento a esta obra calificando cerca de 2.750 comedias, tragedias, dramas* (Barcelona, 1915). Likewise, see Santiago Arimón and Alejo García Góngora's *El código del teatro: Compilación metódica anotada y comentada, de todas las disposiciones legales relacionadas con el teatro y demás espectáculos públicos con un juicio crítico de Jacinto Benavente y prólogo de Octavio Cuartero* (Madrid, 1912).

## Notes

1. Adrian Shubert, "Spain," in Robert Justin Goldstein, ed., *The War for the Public Mind: Political Censorship in Nineteenth-Century Europe* (Westport, CT, 2000), 178.
2. For a discussion of censorship prior to the nineteenth century, see José María Alegre Peyrón, "La censura literaria en España en el siglo XVI," *Revue Roman*, 25 (1990): 428–441; Víctor Cantero García, "El oficio de censor en nuestra historia literaria (siglos XVII–XIX): estudio y consideración de la censura dramática en la España decimonónica," *Letras de Deusto* 32 (2002): 63–89; and Rafael Vargas-Hidalgo, "Censura teatral en la España de 1600," *Revista de Literatura* 117 (1997): 129–36.
3. See, for example, Raymond Carr, *Spain, 1808–1975* (Oxford, 1982); Adrian Shubert, *A Social History of Modern Spain* (London, 1990); Angel Bahamonde Magro and Jesús Martínez, *Historia de España, siglo XIX* (Madrid, 1994); Carolyn Boyd, *Historia Patria: Politics, History and National Identity in Spain, 1875–1975* (Princeton, NJ, 1997); and José Alvaro Junco and Adrian Shubert, eds., *Spanish History since 1808* (London, 2000).
4. Cited by Jesús Rubio Jiménez, "El teatro en el siglo XIX (II) (1845–1900)," in José María Díez Borque, ed., *Historia del teatro en España*, II (Madrid, 1988), 709.
5. Joaquín Álvarez Barrientos, "El mundo teatral desde la muerte de Fernando VII," in Guillermo Carnero, ed., *Historia de la literatura española*, VII (Madrid, 1997), 263.
6. Catherine Jagoe, "La misión de la mujer," in Catherine Jagoe, Alda Blanco, and Cristina Enríquez de Salamanca, eds., *La mujer en los discursos de género: Textos y contextos en el siglo XIX* (Madrid, 1998), 38.
7. Years went by when the theaters were simply closed and the actors banished to the ranks of the unemployed; other moments witnessed monumental struggles

between authors and the authorities. For a discussion of censorship of theater in the eighteenth century, see René Andioc, *Teatro y sociedad en el Madrid del siglo XVIII* (Madrid, 1976). In "La *Raquel* de Huerta y la censura," *Hispanic Review* 43 (1975): 115–39, Andioc details the battle waged against Huerta's controversial play, *La Raquel.*

8. María José Rodríguez Sánchez de León, "Teoría y géneros dramáticos en el siglo XIX," in Javier Huerta Calvo, ed., *Historia del teatro español,* II (Madrid, 2003), 26.
9. Iris M. Zavala, "La censura en la semiología del silencio: siglos XVIII y XIX," in Manuel Abellán, ed., *Censura y literaturas peninsulares* (Amsterdam, 1987), 147–57.
10. Emilio Palacios Fernández, "Teatro y política (1789–1833)," in Joaquín Álvarez Barrientos, ed., *Se hicieron literatos para ser políticos: Cultura y política en la España de Carlos IV y Fernando VII* (Cádiz, 2005), 189. All translations are by the author.
11. Victor Cantero García, 66.
12. Antonio Rumeu de Armas, *Historia de la censura literaria gubernamentiva en España* (Madrid, 1940), 162.
13. John Dowling has studied the controversy in "The Inquisition Appraises *El sí de las niñas*," *Hispania* 44 (1961): 237–44.
14. Piedad Bolaños Donoso, "Sainetes y censura teatral: Cartelera sevillana en los inicios del siglo XIX (1815–1819)," in Alberto Romero Ferrer, ed., *Juan Ignacio González del Castillo (1763–1800): Estudios sobre su obra* (Cádiz, 2005), 177.
15. Bolaños Donoso, 180.
16. For a study of Grimaldi and his activities in Spain, see David T. Gies, *Theatre and Politics in Nineteenth-Century Spain: Juan de Grimaldi as Impresario and Government Agent* (Cambridge, 1988).
17. Ramón de Mesonero Romanos, "Memorias de un setentón," in Carlos Seco Serrano, ed., *Obras de Ramón de Mesonero Romanos,* V (Madrid, 1967), 185. For additional information, see C. Eguía, "Moratín, censor censurado," *Razón y Fe* 85 (1928): 119–35.
18. Antoni Peña y Goñi, *España, desde la ópera a la zarzuela* (Madrid, 1967), 38.
19. See David T. Gies, "Entre drama y ópera: La lucha por el público teatral en la época de Fernando VII," *Bulletin Hispanique* 91 (1989): 37–60.
20. Dionisio Chaulié reported, "The people of Madrid took to the opera enthusiastically, and attended performances eagerly, paying high prices for scalped tickets (even though scalping was strictly prohibited)" in *Cosas de Madrid* (Madrid, 1886), 55.
21. Luis Carmena y Millán, *Crónica de la ópera italiana en Madrid* (Madrid, 1878), 51.
22. Archivo Histórico Nacional, Consejos 11.411, n. 35.
23. Archivo de Protocolos, 23799.
24. Montserrat Puyol Rodríguez, "La cultura prohibida en España, 1805–1846: Análisis bibliográfico," in Pablo Fernández Albaladejo and Margarita Ortega López, eds., *Antiguo Régimen y liberalismo: Homenaje a Miguel Artola,* III (1994), 563.

25. Jesús Rubio Jiménez, "La censura teatral en la época moderada, 1840–1868: Ensayo de aproximación," *Segismundo* 18 (1984): 208.
26. Gregorio C. Martín, "Larra y el teatro: censura, crítica e historia," *Romance Quarterly* 34 (1987): 345–60.
27. Bretón also wrote an article for the newspaper *La Abeja* in which he commented on the restrictions playwrights encountered under Fernando VII: "Apuntes curiosos para la historia de la censura de obras dramáticas en la década calomardina," *La Abeja*, 2 November 1835.
28. Mariano José de Larra, *Obras de Mariano José de Larra (Fígaro)*, Carlos Seco Serrano, ed., I (Madrid, 1960), 341.
29. Larra, II, 48.
30. Larra, II, 49.
31. Larra, I, 450.
32. Larra, II, 60.
33. Brigitte Journeau, "Problèmes de censure entre 1844 et 1854," in Claude Dumas, ed., *Culture et société en Espagne et en Amérique Latine au XIXe siècle* (Lille, 1980), 64.
34. See Amparo Medina-Bocos Montarelo, "Larra y Mesonero: Dos actitudes ante la censura de prensa," *Epos* 5 (1989): 183–99, for additional details.
35. Rubio Jiménez, 194.
36. Cited by Rubio Jiménez, 197.
37. Javier Vellón Lahoz studies this issue in "Moralidad y censura en las refundiciones del teatro barroco: *No hay cosa como callar,* de Bretón de los Herreros," *Revista de Literatura* 115 (1996): 159–68.
38. Information on press censorship for the 1832–49 period is provided in Leonardo Romero Tobar, "Sobre censura de periódicos en el siglo XIX (Algunos expedientes gubernativos de 1832 a 1849)," in *Homenaje a Don Agustín Millares Carlo*, I (Las Palmas, 1975), 465–500.
39. This story is told by David T. Gies, "Rebeldía y drama en 1844: *Españoles sobre todo*, de Eusebio Asquerino," in *De místicos y mágicos, clásicos y románticos: Homenaje a Ermanno Caldera* (Messina, Italy, 1993), 315–32.
40. See Puyol Rodríguez.
41. Interestingly, when *Bandera negra* was filmed in the mid-1950s, the director was fined for filming it without official permission, the film was cut by the censors and then it was banned from distribution. See Carlos Aguilar, *Guía de Video-Cine*, 4th. ed. (1992), 123.
42. Leonardo Romero Tobar, "Textos inéditos de escritores españoles del XIX relacionados con la censura gubernativa," *Cuadernos Bibliográficos* 32 (1973): 104.
43. Madrid, Archivo Histórico Nacional, Consejos, Legajo 11.405.
44. Fernando Garrido, *La España Contemporánea,* II (Barcelona, 1865–67), 973.
45. On Serra, see Gies, *The Theater in Nineteenth-Century Spain* (Cambridge, 1994), 262–270.
46. Carlos Cambronero, "Cosas de antaño: apuntes para la historia de la censura dramática," *Revista Contemporánea* 116 (1899): 603.
47. Cantero García, 88.

48. Rubio Jiménez, "La censura teatral," 223–30, provides a discussion of the play.
49. Nancy J. Membrez, "The Bureaucratization of the Madrid Theater: Government Censorship, Curfews and Taxation, 1868–1925," *Anales de Literatura Española Contemporánea* 17 (1992): 99.
50. See Espín Templado, *El teatro por horas en Madrid (1870–1910)* (Madrid, 1995); and Antonio Fernández-Cid, *Cien años de teatro musical en España (1875–1975)* (Madrid, 1975).
51. Ramon de Valladares y Saavedra, *Nociones acerca de la historia del teatro, desde su nacimento hasta nuestros dias* (Madrid, 1848), 135.
52. José María González Subías, *Un dramaturgo romántico olvidado: José María Díaz* (Madrid, 2004), 245.
53. González Subías, 253.
54. Ma José Rodríguez Sánchez de León, "Teoría y géneros dramáticos en el siglo XIX," in Javier Huerta Calvo, ed., *Historia del teatro español* (Madrid, 2003).
55. Amado de Cristo Burguera y Serrano, *Representaciones escénicas malas, peligrosas y honestas* (Barcelona, 1911).
56. See David T. Gies, "Historia patria: El teatro histórico-patriótico en España (1890–1910)," in Serge Salaün, Evelyne Ricci, and Marie Salgues, eds., *La escena española en la encrucijada (1890–1910)* (Madrid, 2005), 57–75.
57. E. Inman Fox, "*Electra*, de Pérez Galdós (Historia, literatura y polémica entre Martínez Ruiz y Maeztu)," in *Ideología y política en las letras de fin de siglo (1898)* (Madrid, 1988), 65–93; Gies, *Theatre*, 344–48. For further information concerning the ideological implications of censorship at the turn of the century, see Antonio Castellón, *El teatro como instrumento político en España (1895–1910)* (Madrid, 1994).
58. Romero Tobar, "Textos inéditos," 90.
59. Garrido, II, 974.
60. I would like to thank Paul Begin for providing some of the archival materials used in the preparation of this study.

# Italy

JOHN A. DAVIS

## Introduction

In Italy, as elsewhere in Europe, the history of nineteenth-century theater censorship closely tracks general political developments, but also more specifically the changing nature and powers of the state, which in these years were undergoing profound and unprecedented change. It is also obviously inseparable from the history of the theater, which was simultaneously experiencing changes that in many parts of Europe, and not least Italy, made it a central focus of social and cultural life. All of these changes were closely related to broader developments that transformed the entire social, economic, political, and cultural fabric of the European Ancien regime. The history of censorship in these years, therefore, marks not only an important chapter in the longer history of political attempts to control ideas but also in the wider history of the politics of culture.

For Italy (which before 1860 was usually divided into about ten states), this was a period of particularly rapid political change that witnessed an often bewildering rise and fall of different forms of government. Beginning with absolutist monarchies in the final decades of the eighteenth century, Italy had a brief experiment in republican democracy under French domination, then a longer return to autocracy, first in Napoleonic and then legitimist guise, before proceeding to the political struggles that foreshadowed Italian independence and unification in the mid nineteenth century, eventuating in the establishment of the type of limited constitutional government which became the norm in much of western Europe by the century's end. Behind this often confusing maze of political events, however, the emergence and gradual consolidation of the modern, centralized, and bureaucratic state provided a constant thread. Immeasurably more powerful than any preceding form of government, the centralized bureaucratic administration that emerged from the French Revolutionary upheavals eliminated the competing authority of the feudal nobility and powerful corporations (and to a lesser extent that of the church) and concentrated power in the hands of state officials.

In one sense the history of censorship is simply one dimension of the emergence of the modern European bureaucratic state. But censorship acquires an added interest and importance because it also enables us to reconstruct the different ways in which political authority attempted to respond to the cultural, social, and political changes that were profoundly transforming the old European order in this period. It was a critical instrument in state attempts to control ideas and opinions and to deny the freedoms of speech and assembly that in the century following the American Declaration of Independence came to be considered the natural rights of all citizens. Not surprisingly, the more energetically censorship was deployed to silence opponents of authority, the more important a target it became for those advocating change and reform. Indeed, even the most ardent opponents of change gradually came to acknowledge that censorship was often counterproductive.

Italy offers a very rich field for the historian of censorship in these years, most clearly during the Risorgimento, which featured the recovery of a sense of Italian national identity and a growing desire for freedom from foreign rule. Originating in earlier periods, by the 1830s opposition to the autocratic legitimist rulers who had been restored to the multiple Italian states by the Congress of Vienna (1814–15) and by Austria, which directly ruled the northern Kingdom of Lombardy-Venetia and indirectly was the power behind every Italian ruler, took the form of nationalist aspirations and projects. But censorship was about more than politics. Even the most inveterate opponents of political change were aware of the scale of changes that were reshaping the economic, social, and cultural fabric of Europe in these years. There was no more tangible indicator of the wider implications of these changes than the increasing significance of public opinion. In part an indicator of wider social and cultural changes, the emergence of new forms of public opinion also directly resulted from technological innovations that during the early decades of the nineteenth century facilitated the production of printed matter at relatively low costs. The circulation of newspapers and illustrated journals marked a new print revolution that made it possible to transmit news and information with unprecedented speed and to reach audiences far beyond the narrow confines of the older educated elites.

The theater had an important role to play in this cultural revolution, as the most important and vibrant cultural institution of the age, one which played a critical role in shaping the identity of the new bourgeois Europe. The theater had never been just a place of entertainment, and in the Italian states, as in the rest of Europe, its political functions acquired a new importance in these years. The theaters first emerged center-stage in the politics of the eighteenth-century absolutist rulers, before the French Revolution cast them in new, no-less important roles. Like Robespierre and the French Jacobins, Italian revolutionary sympathizers viewed the theater as a key instrument for propagating democratic and patriotic values, while under the autocratic regimes imposed on Italy, first by Napoleon and then by the legitimist rulers restored to their thrones by the Congress of Vienna, the theater acquired quite different but still important political functions. Not surprisingly, nationalists struggling for political change and emancipation also sought to harness the theater to disseminate their cause.

These struggles to control the theater clearly reflected its popularity and importance as the venue where at least the wealthier and better educated, and above all city-dwelling people, met and socialized. Going to the theater was as much a social as a cultural event, and for much of the year it was the principal site of social life and sociability. Wealthy families rented theater boxes for the entire season, which in most Italian capitals ran from December to Easter. The boxes were designed for multiple uses, with mirrors hung on the rear walls to allow the occupants to follow what was happening on stage while they dined and drank, played cards or, it was often asserted, made love. Alexander Dumas père described how a Neapolitan aristocrat in the 1840s typically passed the day: playing cards in the morning, riding in his carriage in the afternoon, to the theater in the evening, and then back to the gaming tables. But that did not mean leaving the theater, since, following the example set by the great theatrical impresario Domenico Barbaja, first at La Scala in Milan and than at San Carlo in Naples, the principal theaters opened their own banqueting halls and gaming houses, which generated profits to help offset the growing, and sometimes devastating, costs of staging major operas.[1]

Paradoxically, in an age of political reaction and repression, the Italian theater was synonymous with modernity, the venue where artistic and cultural fashions were set. That had been true in the eighteenth century and remained so in the revolutionary and Napoleonic periods, but was even more the case in the age of Romanticism, for which the theater proved to be the ideal medium of representation and expression. This was true for Europe as a whole, but especially in Italy, whose early nineteenth-century cultural identity was inseparable from the European renown of two generations of writers, playwrights, and composers. The first included Vittorio Alfieri and Ugo Foscolo, the second Alessandro Manzoni, Silvio Pellico, Giambattista Niccolini, but above all the great Italian *maestri*—Gioacchino Rossini, Gaetano Donizetti, Saverio Mercadante, Vincenzo Bellini, and Giuseppe Verdi, whose music and Romantic melodramas conquered the European stages in the first half of the century. The works of the Italian *maestri* won acclaim across Europe, but their success in Italy was no less sensational, reflecting the central role then played by the theater in the daily lives of most wealthy and educated city dwellers. The rulers' attempts to control and filter what appeared on Italian stages in these years therefore constitute an important chapter in the broader history of censorship, one that enables us to explore the complexities and contradictions of cultural politics.[2]

## The Ancien Regime

Italian theater censorship dates back to the 1545 Council of Trent, which established a system of dual censorship, enforced by both ecclesiastical censors and secular authorities, which survived until the end of the Ancien regime. Since it had the potential to reach wider audiences, the authorities considered that the theater should be subject to even closer control than the press. Although the Jesuits were great promoters of the theater, which they considered to be a valuable medium for popular religious instruction, the church generally remained more skeptical, and as late as 1748 Pope Benedict XIV declared that "we are willing to tolerate theaters, but with regret, and they will be subject to the strictest controls." His views were echoed in an eighteenth-century religious treatise, which warned that "the theater is an inheritance from paganism, a school of the language of passion and impurity and not just because of what is heard but above all for what is seen, because the stage presents in a seductive and entertaining atmosphere all the pomp, pleasure and license of worldly things."[3]

In the eighteenth century, Europe's secular rulers began to systematically challenge and erode the church's jurisdictions in civil affairs, and took a very different view of the political and cultural missions of the theater. This was clearly evident in Italy, where the long peace that followed the close of the long wars of the French, Spanish, and Polish succession brought the Italian states and their rulers an unprecedented period of freedom from war and foreign invasions. In the years preceding the 1789 French Revolution and the political upheavals that followed, the leading Italian princes—the Bourbon rulers of the Kingdom of the Two Sicilies, the Austrian Grand Dukes of Tuscany, the House of Savoy in Piedmont and, under Pius VI, even the Papacy—began to imitate the absolutist policies pioneered by other European rulers. Like their European counterparts, the Italian princes courted the support of philosophers and intellectuals in their efforts to reform their Ancien regime states, making their capitals, such as Milan, Turin, Florence, and Naples, important centers of the Enlightenment, while Rome and Venice also benefited from the new taste for travel acquired by the European elites. There were no clearer symbols of the dynastic ambitions that underpinned the Italian age of Enlightenment than the new court theaters: La Fenice in Venice, Il Teatro del Re and La Scala in Milan, the Teatro Carignano in Turin, the Pergola in Florence, the San Carlo in Naples. These lavishly equipped theaters became an extension of the court where the ruler and his or her family regularly displayed themselves with their courtiers to a wider public. The theater was explicitly designed to exhibit the body politic in microcosm, its spatial organization and seating accurately reflecting the complex but carefully observed hierarchies of the Ancien regime. But its audiences were also treated to the works and music of the period's most highly acclaimed artists and performers; indeed the quality of the performances and productions was a measure of the ruler's grandeur.[4]

The theater was also a site of social control. In Naples, for example, it was widely rumored that King Charles III had built the magnificent San Carlo theater in order to keep a closer eye on what his nobles were doing after dark. But the court theaters were above all designed to reflect the glory of the ruling dynasty, as well as its commitment to contemporary secular values. Not only was this part of a broader struggle against the church's pretensions to dictate cultural norms, but it reflected the Enlightenment partnership between the absolutist princes and the "republic of letters" composed of writers, philosophers, artists, and composers.[5]

The growing rivalry between the secular and the church authorities threatened to seriously undermine the system of dual censorship that had originated in the sixteenth century. The secular rulers did not relax censorship, but they now sought to marginalize the ecclesiastical censors, and often deliberately approved works that had been placed on the papal Index as a sign of their independence from religious authorities. However, their concern to sponsor and promote the most fashionable artists and composers of the day did not dull their sensitivity to anything that might directly or indirectly challenge the principles of monarchy, the established order, religion, or morality.

## Republican and Napoleonic Italy

Ancien regime Italy did not survive the political upheavals that began with the French Revolution and quickly spread throughout Europe. After several earlier incursions, the armies of the French Republic invaded northern Italy in 1796, and following an astonishing sequence of battles won by the Republic's young Corsican general, Napoleon Bonaparte, the Austrians were forced to withdraw, although under the 1797 Treaty of Campoformio they did retain the former Republic of Venice. Throughout northern and central Italy, French armies set up republics under the watchful eye of French officers, the last being the Roman (January 1798) and the Neapolitan (January 1799) republics. The Republican interlude in Italy proved short-lived. In 1799 a joint Austro-Russian army drove the French out of northern Italy, precipitating the fall of the Italian republics and, in France, marked the beginning of the crisis that led to the November 1799 coup that would bring Bonaparte to power. In Italy, the collapse of the Republics was the cue for widespread and violent popular counterrevolutions and the restoration of the former rulers, triggering violent and often bloody persecution of former supporters of the Republics, many of whom fled to France. But in the spring of 1800 Bonaparte, now France's first consul, returned to Italy and, after again defeating Austria, began reorganizing the Italian states. The largest of these was initially the Italian Republic (the former Cisapline Republic of 1796) with its capital in Milan. Following the proclamation of the French empire, in 1805 the Italian Republic was renamed the Kingdom of Italy and ruled on the emperor's behalf by his stepson Eugene Beauharnais. Early in 1801, French troops invaded the southern mainland and placed the emperor's brother Joseph upon the throne of Naples. Two years later, the former Grand Duchy of Tuscany and the Papal States were occupied and annexed to France. Until the fall of the Napoleonic empire in 1814, all of Italy save Sicily and Sardinia was under direct or indirect French rule.[6]

During the brief republican era of 1796–99, Italians enjoyed an unprecedented, if brief, era of free speech that would not be repeated until the revolutions of 1820–21 and 1848–49. Not surprisingly, these three years were ones of remarkable activity and creativity, especially in the theater. In Milan, the Cisalpine Republic's administrative center, Italian supporters of the revolution enthusiastically shared the French Jacobin's belief in the theater's political importance and educational mission. The exiled Italian playwright Vittorio Alfieri had already won acclaim in Paris, and in 1796 his play *Virginia* (a classical drama set in Republican Rome) was performed in Napoleon's presence, and then again in Rome in 1798 to celebrate the declaration of the Republic. *Virginia* and *Brutus* were performed in Naples the following year, with the famous actor Paolo Belli Blanes playing the lead roles. The repertoire quickly expanded to include plays written by other Italian sympathizers with the Revolution, including Francesco Saverio Saffi, Ugo Foscolo, Melchiorre Gioja, Matteo Galdi, Giuseppe Ranza, and Giovanni Pindemonte.[7]

In Naples, Eleanora Fonseca Pimental was one of the strongest advocates of a republican theater that would use popular dialect and reach the masses, while Republican Minister of the Interior Francesco Conforti argued that the theater provided "a form of public instruction of the greatest importance, not only for the young but also for adults who have been subject to the stultifying effects of long lasting despotism. Here instruction can be presented to the citizen in the guise of entertainment." However, he did not share Robespierre's belief that in a Republic censorship was unnecessary, because once the theaters were freed they would become schools for sound principles, good behavior and patriotism. Instead, Conforti insisted on the need for close censorship, maintaining that, "Since the theater can as easily portray vice as virtue … it should be the subject of rigorous scrutiny by the public authorities, who must ensure that the people are not moved by sentiments other than patriotism, virtue and sound morality."[8]

The republican moment in Italy was too brief and insecure for broader experiments in the reorganization of theaters and their funding along the lines attempted by the French Jacobins between 1793–94. But when the French returned to Italy after the fall of the Republics, Bonaparte had, in any case, personally taken in hand the reorganized French theaters in ways designed to extinguish the liberties they had briefly acquired in the Jacobin years and to make government controls more effective. Like their French counterparts, the Italian theaters now became primarily instruments of imperial propaganda, staging plays celebrating the glories of the Empire and its emperor: what took place both on the stage and in the audience became subject to minute censorship and control. The impact of the new order was illustrated in the changing fortunes of the "Patriotic Theater of Milan," which had been founded during the Cisalpine Republic in 1796. It reopened after Napoleon's victory at Marengo in 1800, but in 1805 was renamed the theater of the Philodramatists. The authorities were willing to authorize performances only of Alfieri's works, because of their international fame, whereas other plays with Jacobin sympathies or Italian nationalist overtones were either banned or likely to incur official anger. Napoleon took the theater very seriously and personally, and in 1805 he summoned the Italian playwright Monti to a meeting in which he stressed the empire's need, above all, for great tragic works. The result was a series of rather sycophantic dramas designed to glorify the emperor and curry official patronage, which was always the most effective form of censorship, albeit indirect. Those like Ugo Foscolo who were disaffected by the new regime preferred to write novels or poetry rather than plays since they were unlikely to get permission to perform them. When in 1811 Foscolo's drama *Ajax* was staged in Milan, after the first night the police immediately denounced it as a covert attack on Napoleon, arguing that Agamemnon represented Napoleon, Ajax the conspirator General Moreau, and Ulysses Napoleon's disloyal police chief Fouché. All further performances were banned, and although Foscolo protested to Viceroy Eugène Beauharnais (who was an enthusiastic sponsor of the theater in Milan) that his work was purely dramatic and carried no political allusions, the ban remained.[9]

As in France, the Napoleonic regimes in Italy introduced a number of important institutional and organizational innovations. Under the supervision of Beauharnais, a French permanent theater company (something unknown in Italy) was established in Milan in 1808. In Milan, impresario Domenico Barbaja transformed La Scala into a commercial venture, introducing banquet facilities and gaming tables to generate profits to meet the growing costs of theatrical—and especially operatic—productions. In 1808, Joachim Murat, who had succeeded Joseph Bonaparte as King of Naples, invited Barbaja to Naples, where he stayed on and used the same commercial innovations to make San Carlo one of the most successful theaters in Europe in the 1820s. These innovations placed the opera theater at the center of an increasingly complex set of financial and commercial operations that Italian opera historian John Rosselli has aptly termed an "industry." However, French rule accentuated rather than weakened the close, and indeed exclusive, managerial links between the principal theaters and the rulers of the individual states.[10]

# Restoration Italy

After the fall of Napoleon's empire, the Congress of Vienna restored the Italian rulers to their thrones. But this was not just a matter of restoring the Ancien regime, and there were significant changes in Italy's political geography. The old republics of Venice and Genoa were not revived, but rather incorporated, respectively, into the new Habsburg Kingdom of Lombardy-Venetia (the continuation of Napoleon's earlier Kingdom of Italy, without the former papal territories), and the Kingdom of Piedmont-Sardinia ruled by the House of Savoy. The pope's dominions in central Italy were completely restored, as were the small duchies of Parma, Lucca, Modena, and Guastala. In the south, the Bourbons were restored to their capital in Naples, and in 1816 Sicily lost its centuries-old autonomy to become a part of a new united Bourbon monarchy, named the Kingdom of the Two Sicilies. Despite Italy's apparent political fragmentation, Austria dominated the entire peninsula, and from the forbidding quadrilateral of fortresses in the central Po Valley, Austrian troops could be dispatched to its remotest corners. Thus, Austrian bayonets crushed the constitutional revolution in Naples in 1821 and the 1831 rising in the Papal States, and, as demands for political change grew, even its most moderate advocates viewed Austria as their principal obstacle.[11]

The legitimist 1814–15 restorations marked the beginning of a period of great contradictions. The restored rulers gladly retained the French administrative and institutional changes that had made state authority more powerful and destroyed that of the nobility, but they opposed further political change. Censorship was subsequently deployed with unprecedented energy, although rarely very effectively, to extirpate the ideas that were believed to have given rise to the revolutionary upheavals. Panicked by the revolutions and their legacies, the Italian legitimist rulers looked to mend their bridges with the church, acknowledged that the anti-clerical policies of the previous century had damaged both throne and altar, and in general returned to the church much of the power it had lost in the age of absolutism, with the result that the church once again exercised control over education and cultural affairs in general. The church's influence regarding censorship increased and the former dual system of ecclesiastical and secular controls was retained, creating tensions similar to those previously experienced.

Despite this bleak and repressive background, the Restoration coincided with a great flourishing of the Italian theater, as was most evident in the success of the new Romantic melodramas that were the vehicles for the great works of Rossini, Donizetti, Marcadante, and Bellini. As theater historian Carlotta Sorba has demonstrated, these were also years in which a remarkable and unprecedented number of new theaters were built, although it was an era of prolonged economic depression and political reaction. The principal theaters were those of the previous century: La Fenice in Venice, La Scala and the Teatro del Re in Milan, the Teatro Carignano in Turin, La Pergola in Florence, the Teatro Valle and the Teatro Argentino in Rome, San Carlo in Naples, and the San Carlino in Palermo. But new theaters were built at an unprecedented rate, especially as smaller towns vied to possess what was universally recognized as an essential mark of progress. These were important indicators of the wider social and political changes that gave the provinces a new sense of identity and autonomy vis-à-vis the state capitals.[12]

Without exception, the Italian rulers viewed flourishing theaters as an important sign both of the power and status of the ruler and of the prosperity and well-being of their subjects. Even the most reactionary rulers actively promoted their court theaters, whose audiences were now much more varied in composition than earlier. In Turin, for example, the reactionary king Victor Emanuel I founded one of the first permanent theater companies in Italy, the Compagnia Reale Sarda, and even in the immediate aftermath of the failed insurrection in Piedmont in 1821, the company was permitted to perform two of Alfieri's plays (*Agamemnon* and *Orestes*), whose clear republican sympathies were widely acknowledged. Victor Emanuel was succeeded by the equally reactionary Carlo Felice, but throughout the 1820s the Teatro Carignano continued to stage plays by Alfieri and other authors whose liberal leanings were well known, including *Francesca da Rimini* by Silvio Pellico, one of the Milanese conspirators arrested by the Austrians in 1821 and jailed in the terrible Spielberg prison in Bohemia for a decade. The repertoire of the other permanent theater companies, the Teatro Ducale in Modena (1826–30), the Mascherpa company in Parma (1827–46), patronized by the Archduchess Maria Luisa (Napoleon's former empress), and the Compagnia Reale (1818–26) in Naples, was more traditional and relied heavily on eighteenth-century comedies, especially those of Goldoni.[13]

There were many reasons why rulers sought to promote the theater. As in the previous century, that they were still considered as instruments of social control was made very clear by the chief minister of Lombardy-Venetia, who shortly after the attempted revolution of 1821 in Milan, insisted La Scala theater should be kept open because "it attracts to a place open to observation during the hours of darkness a large part of the educated population." In Rome the authorities also believed that the theater kept peoples' minds off mischief. But there were much broader considerations, as was made clear by a leading minister of the Neapolitan government in 1820: "Theaters are at once the sign and cause of civil progress (*incivilmento*): once merely places for idle curiosity, in great capital cities they have now become a political and moral necessity that keeps the multitude from engaging in more pernicious gatherings and in Naples in particular the theater has for many years now brought our city the renown of a great metropolis and hence an important and profitable attraction for foreign visitors, too."[14]

The theater was both a sign of prosperity and a potential source of profit, as well as a political and moral necessity: this reasoning captured well the inner ambiguities and contradictions of the Restoration's cultural politics and was frequently repeated elsewhere and at other times. Caught uneasily between nostalgia for the past and an awareness of the ways in which power needed to adapt to the political and commercial realities of post-feudal Europe, Italy's autocratic Restoration rulers were eager to pose as new national monarchies, as the paternalist representatives and defenders of their subjects.

Because of its popularity, the theater offered the rulers of the different Italian states unique opportunities to identify more closely with their subjects and indeed to pose, albeit on a very local stage, as the paternalist representative of a broader nation. Like all cultural politics, this was play-acting, but that did not make it any less effective. It also reveals that contemporaries had a relatively broad understanding of the political significance of the theater, as was spelled out very explicitly by one Habsburg official when he acknowledged that La Scala was the key to Austrian control of Lombardy. The theater's dazzling repertoire and international renown not only kept the Milanese busy and entertained, but brought glory to their city, making its citizens grateful to the Habsburg rulers for their generous and enlightened patronage.[15]

The French writer Stendhal had earlier made much the same point when he claimed that nothing did more to ensure the popularity of the King of Naples after the Restoration than his decision to rebuild the San Carlo theater immediately after it had burned in 1816. For Stendhal, this was a political masterstroke that had won the king more love and loyalty from his subjects than even the concession of a constitution could have done: he declared, "San Carlo is definitely a political matter for the Neapolitans whose national pride it has restored."[16] The Italian rulers took their theaters seriously and by today's standards the levels of sponsorship and scale of productions were very lavish. Theater historian John Rosselli calculated that between 1809 and 1844 the San Carlo and the Teatro del Fondo in Naples (a city with an additional four other major theaters) both staged at least 100 productions each year (138 in 1824–25) between 1809 and 1844, an astonishing figure by standards then or today. Indeed, one reason why Italian theater became less dynamic (in terms of new productions) after the 1830s was simply that the money ran out, which was also the principal reason why Italy's great composers (Verdi being the exception) made their way to Paris.[17]

The importance and the popularity of the theater made control of what audiences saw and heard on stage especially critical, but it was acknowledged that this was much more difficult than with the printed word. The instructions given to the Milanese censors, for example, pointed out that "theatrical performances can exercise the strongest impressions on those who watch them, are frequented by every sort of person and are organized by individuals who are eager to win applause and therefore inclined to bow to the tastes and opinions of the multitude without being scrupulous about how they may achieve this." The authorities believed, probably rightly, that they had little to fear from the main body of theatergoers, and they were prepared to make a trade-off: no political liberties, but some degree of artistic freedom. The problem was finding not only the balance but also the means, since even in this relatively privileged milieu the censorship machinery was quite cumbersome. Each state had its own censorship regulations, although they were variants on a common theme, owing much to the models introduced by the Napoleonic rulers before 1814. In 1808, for example, the Neapolitan government established a Royal Commission for the Theaters under the Ministry of Police that was responsible for supervising and policing all theaters, all theatrical works and presentations, every costume that appeared on stage, and the names and background of the actors, composers, and other artists. The scripts of all plays had to be registered first with the police and no variations on the written text were permitted on stage. This was the norm in other states, too, where theatrical productions and performance were sometimes subject to multiple censorships. Written texts were subject to the press laws and any improvisation was strictly banned. Permission for performance had to be obtained from the police and police agents were present at all performances to keep order and ensure that there were no variations from the approved script. After the Restoration, Pope Pius VII instituted a Commission of six Cardinals and one prelate, assisted by nine police assessors and the Cardinal Vicar, to oversee the Roman theaters: the censor had to sign every page of each script, thus granting permission to perform subject to observation of the regulations and without omissions or additions.[18]

In Tuscany, all plays were subject to prior censorship and none could treat "history or events concerning the Church." There could be no allusions to the Old Testament or to the Church in any form of dance sequence. In addition, the censors were instructed to ban any play that was based on "an evil theme that seeks to weaken respect for Religion or the Throne, that incites ideas contrary to either, or contains material of bad taste or represents crimes or terrible deeds like assassinations, premeditated murders, suicides brought on by despair, and similar subjects." The Tuscan censors were especially concerned that historical plays should not "cause offense to the conscience and principles of modern times"; "sentimental dramas which are generally translated from German or French" might be tolerated, but could not be approved if they portrayed "dangerous or overheated passions" or incited depravity. Such criteria were widely followed. The Neapolitan censors insisted, for example, that the heroine of *La Dame aux Camelias* should not be described as a courtesan, to avoid offending the monarchy.[19]

Reference to the recent past, and in particular to Napoleon, was another obsession. In 1822 the Florentine censors banned Giambattista Niccolini's play *Nabucco* because it was seen as an allusion to Napoleon. The same author's *Sicilian Vespers* was permitted only under the title of *Joanna of Procida* (but that was subsequently banned as well when the French ambassador complained that the play was anti-French). When in 1844 the Tuscan police seized copies of Niccolini's play *Arnold of Brescia*, which had been published in Marseilles, the Tuscan censor reported with horror that "the theme of the play seems to be that the Holy Pontiff should not exercise temporal power in the Papal States, and in other places claims that the power of sovereignty rests only with the people and other such maxims of liberalism!" The Lombard censors banned Ugo Foscolo's play *Ajax*, earlier banned in the Napoleonic period because it was considered critical of Napoleon, on the grounds that it "insinuates a spirit of freedom that is directed against Austria."[20]

Generally the censors were more strict with stage plays than novels, and both the Tuscan and the Lombard censors agreed that works like the *Pazzi Conspiracy* (dealing with the unsuccessful 1478 attempt by the Pazzi family to prevent Lorenzo de Medici from taking control of the Florentine Republic) could be permitted in print but not on the stage where they could reach a much wider audience. The censors' constant, petty interference reflected the Restoration regimes' desire to monopolize and regulate every form of secular public life, but censorship was most oppressive in those states where relations between church and state was closest: Piedmont before 1848, the Papal States, the Duchy of Modena, and the Kingdom of the Two Sicilies. In Modena, the words *emperor, king, prince,* and *duke* could not be used on stage. In Rome, the word *Dio* (God) could not be used, so *cielo* (heaven) was substituted, and the censors refused to allow Bellini's *Norma* be performed under that title because *norma* was a technical theological term. Where rulers held to the eighteenth-century principles of secular autonomy, notably in the Tuscan Grand Duchy, but also in the Austrian territories, there was greater tolerance. But even there, powers granted to the censors were subject to little control. Moreover, direct censorship was only one means of controlling what appeared on the stage. In the court theaters, the rulers took decisions on every aspect of performances, choosing subjects, reading and approving the libretti, and deciding on presentation and even costumes. Since opera impresarios were dependent on the patronage of the ruling class, like publishers they were keen to avoid giving offense. Bearing out Michel Foucault's analysis of the interdependence of censorship and self-censorship, theatrical producers, composers, and librettists generally endorsed the criteria of the censors and did their best to comply.[21]

## Censorship and the Risorgimento

Censorship of the theater as well as censorship of the press was a dominant feature of the Italian states during the Risorgimento. Following Italian unification, popular imagery portrayed the theater as one of the earliest sites in which nationalist sentiment found expression, as the supporters of Italian independence pitted themselves against the reactionary censors. But this is more than a little fanciful, and retrospectively the political role of the Italian theater in the decades before unification became oversimplified. Certainly no Italian audience in the 1840s could miss the explicit reference to Italy's subject status conveyed in the chorus "Va pensiero su ali dorate" in Verdi's *Nabucco* (first performed at la Scala in 1842), and as political tensions and nationalist aspirations grew stronger in the Italian states, so too did the frequency of nationalist allusions on stage and the enthusiasm with which theater audiences responded to them. This was evident, for example, in the rapture that greeted the crusader's chorus "Signore, dal tetto natio" in Verdi's opera *The Lombards in the first Crusade* (1843), the aria "Si ridesti il leon di Castiglia" from *Ernani,* or the slaying of a tyrant in *Attila* (1846). But this did not mean, as opera historian David Kimble has claimed, that the Italian theater was "a kind of spiritual Trojan horse" of the Risorgimento. As Roberto Leydi has shown, none of the Italian composers in this period made any attempt to draw on the wider repertoire of popular music, reflecting the relatively enclosed world not only of theater audiences but of the politics of the Risorgimento. As Italian nationalist Giuseppe Mazzini noted, these coded nationalist allusions were not only extremely elusive, but above all they were totally disconnected from clearly defined political programs. Indeed, the central appeal of the key themes of Romantic melodrama—sacrifice, honor, duty, patriotism—lay in their eclecticism and lack of specificity. As with all texts, they could be read in many different ways and their appeal was by no means confined to nationalist sympathizers, although as support for the nationalist cause in Italy grew it is hardly surprising that audiences should have reacted positively to whatever they took to be allusions to Italy's political subjection.[22]

The relationship between the Romantic sensitivities that were the stuff of Risorgimento melodrama and the political movements that resulted in Italy's unification is simply too complex and elusive to be reduced to a simple formula of cause and effect. Such an argument would in any case fail to take sufficient account of the reservations advanced long ago by opera historian Rosselli, who pointed out that Rossini, Donizetti, and Bellini went to great lengths to conceal any form of political commitment, and insisted on the very conservative tastes of Italy's predominantly wealthy and more aristocratic than bourgeois theatergoers. It also must be remembered that until unification Italian theaters were financed and run primarily by the rulers, whose choice of works and productions was determined by what pleased the public most, while the critical literature of the time suggests overwhelmingly that what determined the success or failure of a work was the quality of the music and the singing, not the librettos or the plots.[23]

The Risorgimento's politics in the theater is more complicated than might first appear. While the theaters certainly played a part in shaping new national identities, before the 1840s identities were essentially local and focused primarily around the existing states. Nonetheless, the theaters were influenced by outside events, especially the liberalizing impacts of the 1830 French Revolution and the 1846 election of Pope Pius IX as new ruler of the Papal States. The theaters also continued to be an arena in which Italian rulers sought to identify themselves with their subjects, but as pressures for change grew, the theaters exposed the contradictions on which the politics of the Restoration in Italy were based. It is easily forgotten that before 1830 rigid political censorship was the norm throughout Europe, and Rossini, Donizetti, and Bellini found much the same conditions and constraints whether in Rome, Naples, Milan, Paris, or Vienna, while after the Karlsbad Decrees of 1819 the German states were scarcely more liberal than Tsarist Russia. However, pressures for political change and at least some concessions to liberal principles, even at the local level, increased everywhere in Italy following the 1830 revolution and subsequent establishment of a more liberal constitutional monarchy in France. Just as other European states were becoming more liberal, the Italian rulers were shaken by political uprisings in the Papal States in 1831 and then by the 1832 founding of Mazzini's revolutionary association "Young Italy," which was dedicated to their downfall and the creation of an independent Italian Republic. Contrasting with the French example, the Italian rulers' refusal to make political concessions made all forms of censorship more visible and irksome, which was compounded by their increasingly confused and contradictory attempts to respond to the new situation. The censorship became increasingly random and unpredictable, often reflecting bitter conflicts among the rulers' advisers, with some counseling moderate reform and others urging intransigence. This also further accentuated the contrasts between censorship in the different Italian states, with Tuscany always the most tolerant, Piedmont the most reactionary, the Austrian territories the most vigilant, Rome the least predictable, and Naples the most incoherent. Thus, in 1835, Bellini who had long since abandoned Naples for Paris and was notorious for concealing his political views, commented jokingly to a friend that his new opera *I Puritani* would be perfect for Neapolitan performances because "it contains no religion, no nefarious love-affairs, and no politics whatsoever."[24]

Especially damaging for the rulers was that censorship decisions often revealed the contradictions of their pretensions to autonomy. Increasingly, the censors were forced to respond to complaints from representatives of foreign governments among whom, for obvious reasons, the Austrian and papal envoys were the most sensitive. The censors' actions also often revealed the extent to which the Restoration rulers had surrendered control of cultural politics to the church. This was especially evident in Naples, for example, where the relatively liberal climate that accompanied the 1830 accession of King Ferdinand II was dramatically reversed following his second marriage in 1836 to the bigoted and pious Austrian Archduchess Maria Teresa. The new queen immediately replaced the civil censors with hand-picked priests who were to ensure that the dictates of the new order of moral rectitude were reflected on the Neapolitan stage.[25]

In the early 1840s the situation changed again. The collapse of the commercial boom of the previous decade brought hardship and social unrest to much of Europe, reawakening fears of political upheaval. In Italy, despite the censorship, a public debate on political change erupted for the first time as moderates openly began to call on their rulers to make concessions to stave off the threat of revolution. A remarkable circulation of political pamphlets and texts revealed the limits of press censorship, and following the election of Pope Pius IX in 1846 the situation quickly got out of control. Hopes that the new pope would be sympathetic to liberal reforms seemed to be realized when Pius IX issued an amnesty for political prisoners and relaxed censorship in his own state.

Demands for a free press and a free theater now spread everywhere, but the grand duke of Tuscany was the only ruler to follow the pope's lead: other rulers held steady until, in early 1848, they were forced to concede constitutions in the aftermath of revolutionary outbreaks in Paris and Naples. While press controls became increasingly difficult to maintain, in the theaters the rulers tried to hold firm. In a moment of growing political tension they had no desire to shut the theaters, which they again tried to turn to their own purposes by making concessions on the stage that they would not make in politics and by renewing their efforts to identify with their subjects' nationalist aspirations. In Turin, for example, the Teatro Carignano staged new plays glorifying the House of Savoy (such as Achille Montagnini's drama *Adalberto allo Assedio di Rochella*), as well as comedies with more direct nationalist allusions.[26]

This reflected the double game that other Italian rulers were playing with press censorship, secretly encouraging publications that they could not officially acknowledge for fear of offending the Austrians. That was not an issue in the Austrian territories, of course, but even there the authorities preferred to compromise, as became evident in their dealings with Verdi, whose rapidly growing popularity posed difficult challenges. Their main concern was to keep La Scala full, which meant that they could not do without him. Verdi displayed an intuitive understanding of the invisible lines that separated the permissible from the impermissible (it was generally recognized that Austrian censorship, although severe, was at least consistent). Hence, although the chorus of the Hebrew slaves in *Nabucco* (1842) clearly alluded to Italy's slavery, Verdi was careful to acknowledge his loyalty by dedicating both *Nabucco* and *I Lombardi* (1843) to the Austrian Emperor. This was purely an act of political expediency, since he was frequenting the salons of the Countess Maffei and other meeting places of the Milanese liberals where it was said that the revolution of 1848 was planned, but it proved sufficient to keep a dialogue with the authorities open. But that could have unexpected repercussions and despite (or perhaps because of) the success of *Nabucco,* in 1843 the archbishop of Milan threatened to make an official complaint to the emperor when the censors gave the green light to Verdi's new opera, *The Lombards on the First Crusade,* on the grounds that the libretto contained "religious processions, churches, the Valley of Jehosophat and a baptism." On this occasion, when Verdi and the producer declared that they would not present the opera if the libretto was substantially changed, the police chief agreed to approve the production and merely required that the words "Ave Maria" be changed to "salve Maria." But even with his popularity, Verdi was dogged by interference from the censors, who invariably insisted that his original titles be changed, as well as demanding changes to plots and librettos, with the result that the same opera often played under different titles in each state. Verdi abandoned two projected new works on historical themes with obvious allusions to the Italian struggle for independence, *The Fall of the Lombards* and *Cola di Rienzo,* because he knew the censors would not approve them (at least not without massive butchery).[27]

As nationalist aspirations escalated following Pius IX's 1846 election, divisions within the legitimist governments deepened and censorship became increasingly confused. In this climate, when moderates like Massimo d'Azeglio referred to public pressure for reform and independence as a "conspiracy in open daylight," censorship was generally ineffective and counterproductive. This was well illustrated when the censors approved Verdi's new opera, *Attila,* which was interpreted as an unambiguous denunciation of foreign tyranny and received a rapturous reception in Venice in 1846. But Verdi could not openly declare his nationalist sympathies until the outbreak of the 1848 revolutions, when his new work, *The Battle of Legnano,* was presented in Milan and Rome in a fury of nationalist expectation shortly before the 1849 declaration of the Roman Republic.[28]

## Censorship and the 1848–49 Revolutions

Especially in the months immediately prior to the granting of constitutions in early 1848, the Italian theaters frequently became sites for patriotic displays and acclamations despite the supposed best efforts of the authorities and the police (many believed that these demonstrations were often deliberately organized by police agents and anti-liberal *agents provocateurs* who were seeking to force the authorities to crack down). Following the relaxation of censorship in Rome and Florence, rulers throughout Italy decided to permit plays with nationalist themes—most notably the classical dramas of Alfieri, in particular *The Pazzi Conspiracy, Brutus, Virginia*, and *Orestes*. A rush of new plays on historical themes or figures who could be associated with the cause of Italian independence, including *Masaniello, Bianca Capello, Pietro Micca, The Lombard League,* or with stirring titles like *We're All Brothers,* were all performed. In Austrian Lombardy, the Theater of the Philodramatists in Milan staged *Moving House,* a drama written about the 1831 Roman insurrections that was an open invitation to the Austrians to depart. When the famous Austrian ballerina Fanny Essler refused to dance in Milan at La Scala with a chorus wearing medals bearing the face of Pope Pius IX, she was booed off stage.[29]

Once the revolutions began, the theaters in Turin and Milan became venues for popular rallies and engaged in sustained propaganda backing the struggle against Austria, and this was repeated in numerous dialect theaters. The favored works were still the classical plays of Alfieri and the historical dramas of Pellico and Niccolini, although a mass of new plays with more contemporary themes were also hurriedly written and performed. When the pope finally abandoned the pretext of supporting constitutional government and fled from Rome in November 1848, his departure quickly became the subject of many scurrilous and satirical works. The production of Verdi's *Battle of Legnano* in Rome at the Teatro Argentina on 31 January 1849 was undoubtedly the high point of the revolution in the Italian theater, and the Roman Republic drew the support of many of Italy's leading actors, including Gustavo Modena and Tommaso Salvini, who came to work in the city's theaters. But by the spring of 1849, the days of the Italian revolutions were already numbered. In May 1848 King Ferdinand of Naples had already launched an effective counterattack, and in the spring of 1849 Neapolitan troops put down the revolution in Sicily. In response to the appeals of Pius IX, France, Spain, and Naples all sent armies to restore the pope to Rome, which was eventually besieged by a French army which returned Pius to power in June 1849. In March 1849 the Austrians defeated the Piedmont army and reoccupied Lombardy and then Tuscany. Afterward, the theaters in Piedmont worked to raise funds to support the families of the defeated soldiers and volunteers. In July 1849 Garibaldi led the retreat of the defenders of the Roman Republic and in August the last of the Italian revolutions finally collapsed in Venice.[30]

In general, the revolutions were not a good time for the theaters, and apart from occasional use for public rallies and special performances it was very difficult to keep them going financially. In the autumn of 1848, for example, the senior Bourbon official in Sicily warned the government in Naples of the great danger this posed, especially in Palermo, where the revolution had bankrupted the contractor for the San Carolino theater, which as a result had been closed for months. He declared: "In all civilized countries theaters exist and are maintained in the interest of the government and public morality. The theaters provide a living for many artists, painters, singers, as well as a mass of other workers, and they are an essential means of educating the public. No matter what the political, moral or economic situation, theaters in all parts of the world are created by and maintained by their respective governments, which have always been solely responsible for every aspects of their management and their productions." The official concluded by stressing that the theater's closure for four months had greatly discredited the government and posed a real political threat. He advised that as a matter of political expediency the theater should be reopened as soon as possible, but warned that it must resume productions of the highest quality or audiences would stay away. Such arguments may explain why Italian rulers were quick to reopen the theaters and relaunch even truncated theater seasons as soon as the revolutions were over. Above all, this was intended to signify that life was returning to normal, and therefore the works of the most popular composers and writers were presented: in Naples, for example, San Carlo reopened with a performance of Verdi's *The Two Foscari* six weeks after the army had massacred liberal demonstrators barely twenty meters from the theater entrance.[31]

## After the Revolutions

Not surprisingly, after the 1849 collapse of the Italian revolutions the theater was subjected to even tighter censorship, and except in Piedmont its function as "the focus of the social life of the upper classes" went into deep decline.[32] In Rome, for example, after the restoration of Pius IX the theaters came under new and extremely rigid regulation. In Tuscany the powers of the censors were increased and the office of public censor was created in 1853. In Austrian Lombardy and Bourbon Naples, the climate after 1849 was one of darkest reaction: all supporters of the revolutions were in jail or exile, and the dominant climate was that of a suffocating police state. Police spies were everywhere and especially watched the educated and propertied classes. But by then autocracy was an even greater anachronism that it had been before 1848, and although Piedmont was the only constitutional regime on the peninsula, its presence was an increasingly open challenge to the reactionary and obscurantist policies of the other Italian rulers. In these circumstances, theater censorship in particular verged increasingly on the absurd and served mainly to discredit the rulers and their agents.In Naples, the censors were especially energetic in excising every allusion that might be interpreted as a criticizing authority, endorsing rebellion, or causing moral or religious offence. Plots and librettos were, as a result, often mangled beyond recognition. In 1855, for example, the censors retitled Verdi's *Traviata* to *Violetta*, while *Rigoletto* (1851) was retitled *Lionello* before it could be staged at San Carlo. *Trovatore* (1853) did appear in its original title, but the great hit of 1855 in Naples was Giacomo Meyerbeer's *Roberto il Diavolo* (1831), which the censors renamed *Robert of Picardy*, after the religious censor rejected mentioning the devil and the royal censor noted that Robert of Normandy was an ancestor of the king of Naples, hence the substitution of Picardy.[33]

Verdi cited censorship as the principal reason for declining the offer of the impresario Vincenzo Torelli to premier a new work (*King Lear*) at San Carlo in 1856, while in 1858 he called off a performance of *Un Ballo in Maschera* (which the censors had renamed *Gustav III*) for the same reasons. But censorship was only one of many factors that explained the declining attendance at San Carlo in these years, when Neapolitan theatergoers began to show a preference for the city's prose theaters. The principal reason lay in the monarchy's financial difficulties, which meant that San Carlo no longer enjoyed the primacy of earlier years. The theater in San Carlo held fewer premieres and the quality of its productions declined due to its inability to meet the escalating costs of new productions; this factor, rather than political allusions, shaped audience reactions. For example, in 1856 productions of long time favorites like Donizetti's *Anne Boleyn* (1830), *Adelia* (1841), and Bellini's *I Puritani* (1835) at San Carlo had very hostile receptions, yet Verdi's *Trovatore* met with huge acclaim. In 1858, responses were similarly unpredictable: Bellini's *Somnabula* (1831) was almost booed off the stage, while Donizetti's *Lucrezia Borgia* (1840) was a huge success, although the censors changed its title to *Elisa Fosco* to avoid upsetting the Pope (the Borgias were a papal family)—then, for reasons no one could fathom, changed the title again to *Elisa Tosca*.[34]

## Piedmont, 1848–60

Meanwhile, under the leadership of Count Benso Camillo di Cavour, Piedmont was being transformed into a liberal constitutional monarchy in the

1850s. Cavour's reforms promoted economic growth and foreign investment, and made Turin a haven for political exiles from all over Italy. The institutional and jurisdictional framework of the future Italian state was in large part established in this decade, since when Italy was unified in 1860 (save for Rome and Venice, still under respective French and Austrian occupation), Piedmont's 1848 constitution was extended to the other Italian states along with most of the liberal legislation introduced in the Savoyard kingdom after 1849, including laws on press freedom and those regulating the theaters. Like their counterparts elsewhere in Europe, Piedmont's liberals jealously sought to preserve constitutional guarantees of freedom of speech and association and agreed that censorship must be abolished. Cavour was especially determined that Piedmont should not become, as he characterized nineteenth-century Spain, "liberal today, reactionary tomorrow." But Piedmont's liberals also insisted that freedom should not be confused with license. The principles that guided the application of censorship in the new liberal state were clearly set out in 1857 by L. C. Farini, who declared, "The principle of liberty must be the premise for all our laws: you must never adopt the system of prevention and must allow liberty in all things; you can make laws to repress and punish crimes, but never to prevent them."[35]

These principles had been anticipated in Piedmont's press laws, which abolished all forms of preventive or prior censorship for published material, but established forms of repressive censorship (*censura repressiva*) that penalized any material that, once printed, "offends against, or instigates offense against religion, the person of the Sovereign and the ruling family, against representative institutions, the heads of foreign powers and diplomatic corps, or against other religious followings, public morality and property rights." For the theater, a General Directorate was established in the Ministry of the Interior in April 1849, which was specifically responsible for ensuring that prior drama censorship (which was retained in contrast to the end of preventive press censorship) was "judicious, temperate and fully in harmony with our new political institutions." Many of the pre-1848 censors were retained, but new guidelines were issued by the ministry in 1852: "Control over what appears on the stages of the theaters should be guided by moral rather than political criteria. Genuinely liberal government will win greater support by demonstrating that it is based on foundations that are too strong to be shaken by the radical aspirations of a play." The guidelines added, however, that special attention be directed to "popular theaters and their repertory, from which we should seek to remove anything that might incite sympathy for crime and hatred for the punitive activities of the State."[36]

Theaters and all forms of public performance continued to be subject to a variety of different controls. Plays were subject to the press laws and regulations, and all performances were also subject to the public security (or police) laws regarding public meetings and buildings. No play could be performed without prior script approval by the police or without the presence of a police officer, and the possible exercise of police powers went a long way to threatening the freedoms of speech and association enshrined in the constitution. What all this meant in practice depended upon how the various censorship and police powers were applied. Piedmont's censors were especially active in banning foreign-language (particularly French) plays, and Piedmont's companies were encouraged to perform only Italian dramas. In 1856 controls were tightened, and in 1857 the government circulated a list of 250 banned plays, many of which were fiercely anticlerical, while others were guilty only of celebrating Garibaldi (a Risorgimento hero who had repeatedly criticized Piedmont's government for failing to oust the French from Rome and unsuccessfully sought over official opposition to lead his own troops against that city in 1862 and 1867). Cavour was especially insistent that children's theater and dialect puppet theaters should be particularly carefully watched and censored. When in 1859 Piedmont went to war against Austria in alliance with France, the censors banned any play that seemed hostile or critical toward France, but when news of the armistice with Austria reached Turin, all dialect plays that were hostile or disrespectful toward Austria were also banned. The censors also remained alert against offending religious sensibilities; Niccolini's ill-fated *Arnald of Brescia* was once again banned on the grounds that "it is not permissible to authorize works that set on the stage scenes that depict Popes, Priests and August, sacred and Holy Rites." Due to frequent disturbances in the theaters in Turin, each was assigned an inspector to help maintain order.[37]

Given the high state of political tension that continued through the 1850s, which were marked by continuous conspiracies by the nationalists, and repeated possibilities of renewed war between Piedmont and Austria and intervention by France, it is hardly surprising that political considerations continued to weigh heavily in Piedmont's theater censorship. But even so, the nature of the censors' interventions became very different from the past and much closer to the concerns that governed theater censorship in other European constitutional regimes. The refusal to allow discussion of contemporary events or living characters reflected broader European trends, while the attention devoted to dialect plays and other forms of popular theater made it clear that the authorities were especially concerned that the theater could transcend the literacy barrier, thus crossing the divide between elite and popular culture and reaching outside the domain dominated by the new liberal consensus. In this, as in other respects, Italy's new liberal order followed models that were well established in the older constitutional states.

## Liberal Italy: The First Decade, 1860–70

In 1859, Piedmont, in secret alliance with French Emperor Napoleon III, went to war with Austria. After a series of victories, the French emperor unilaterally declared an armistice that left Austria in control of Venice, but enabled Cavour and his allies to organize the annexation of Lombardy, Tuscany, the central duchies, and the northern parts of the Papal States to the Kingdom of Piedmont. In May 1860, Garibaldi's fabled expedition to Sicily brought about the collapse of the Bourbon Kingdom of the Two Sicilies, and in 1861 Victor Emanuel II of the Piedmontese House of Savoy was crowned king of the newly unified Italian state. Rome, where Pope Pius IX remained under the protection of the French emperor, and Venice remained outside the new state. In 1866, Italy acquired Venice, following Austria's defeat by the Prussians, but Rome proved more complicated. In 1862, Garibaldi's attempt to overthrow the papal government was blocked by Italian troops and the hero of Italian unification was seriously wounded. Another attempt in 1867 finished in a disastrous rout when Garibaldi's volunteers were defeated by the pope's troops at Mentana. It was not until Napoleon III was defeated by the Prussians in September 1870 that Pius IX lost his last remaining powerful protector: two weeks later Italy was finally united after Italian troops entered Rome through the Porta Pia and the pope and his cardinals withdrew across the river Tiber to become self-proclaimed prisoners of the Vatican.

The political climate in the first decade of Italy's independence remained tense. In the south, the government attempted to disguise the scale of resistance to the new state by describing it as brigandage, but more troops were involved in restoring order in the south and Sicily between 1861 and 1864, and more lives were lost, than in all the wars of independence. The new state was also threatened by attempts of nationalists to regain Rome, which could easily have led to war with France, while many who had participated most enthusiastically in the independence struggles were profoundly opposed to the narrowly conservative Piedmont regime that had emerged. Mazzini, who died in 1872, still under sentence of death in the country he had devoted his life to creating, was unsparing in his criticism of the reactionary monarchy of Victor Emanuel, and the authorities were zealous in their attempts to track and silence his followers. Along with dissent from republicans and democrats, Italy was also faced by intransigent opposition from supporters of Pope Pius IX, who denounced the new regime as the "negation of God." Even before the first signs of anarchist and revolutionary conspiracies became evident, the new Italy's political foundations were fragile. Perhaps inevitably in these circumstances, the liberal freedoms of speech and public assembly endorsed in the constitution were in practice only conditionally tolerated. This was primarily achieved by exploiting contradictions between the freedoms affirmed in the 1848 Piedmont constitution (which became the constitution of the new kingdom of Italy in 1860 without modification) and the wide discretionary powers exercised by the police under the Piedmont public security laws.

Although the fragile and even precarious state of the new kingdom in the first decade after unification put liberal principles to the test, the consequences were less negative when it came to regulation of the theater than in other areas, such as the press and the rights of association and public assembly. The main innovation with regard to the theater was the Royal Decree of 14 January 1864 that made the local prefects responsible for approving theatrical performances in their jurisdictions, with a right of appeal to the Ministry of the Interior. In February 1864 Interior Minister Silvio Spaventa reaffirmed his ministry's 1852 theater directive, while in 1865 a new set of public security laws included two new clauses (articles 32 and 35) that effectively overrode the notion that censorship should be moral rather than political. It declared: "No theatrical performance may be presented or declaimed without the written permission of the provincial Public Security officials. Not withstanding that this permission be granted, the Public Security officials may forbid any theatrical performance or declamation if some local circumstance leads them to believe that it would be inappropriate, or liable to cause commotion or disorder." As a result, the authorities had at their disposal very wide-ranging and ill-defined powers of theater censorship. Although Bettino Ricasoli's government in 1867 again underlined the moral character of the criteria censoring theatrical performances, it also declared that plays should not contain matter "contrary to public morality and the sense of public decency, or anything that may tend to incite hatred between the social classes, or be offensive to Sovereigns, Parliament, the representatives of friendly Powers, or show disrespect for law or public institutions or be liable to disturb public order, or give offense to, or defame, the private lives of members of the Royal Family even by allusion." An 1874 law banned actors from showing disrespect to the army, and an 1879 law stated that plays presenting "deeds that may on account of their wickedness cause offense to public opinion will be subject to the attention of the magistrates" and were to be banned.[38]

In political terms, the most important and most debated issues posed by the theater after unification related to the closely linked questions of the funding and promotion of an Italian national theater. The post-unification decision to make local administrations responsible for funding theaters that had been financed by the previous rulers was seen by many as the principal cause of what by the century's end was generally considered to be the crisis of the Italian theater. Both the political structure of the new state and the strength of local cultural identities, combined with the lack of funds, prevented the realization of a national theater project. However, Italy's difficult unification did little to dampen enthusiasm for the theater; indeed, the reverse was true. According to the 1869 census, there were 930 theaters, public arenas, and concert halls in the new kingdom, situated in about 700 cities, towns, and villages. Of these, 300 were publicly owned, and 220 theaters had been created after unification (often carrying the name of Garibaldi or Victor Emanuel). Italy could claim more theaters in proportion to population than any other state in Europe. By the 1870s, the Italian theaters were presenting over 300 new plays every year, in addition to between 40 and 50 musical productions. Politically, the theater had powerful voices in the new kingdom, as novelist Alessandro Manzoni and opera composer Giuseppe Verdi were senators, while many musicians, writers, journalists, and theater critics sat in the Chamber of Deputies, to which Italy's most famous living actor, Gustavo Modena, was elected in 1860.[39]

The law proclaimed that theater censorship was essentially a matter of public morality, while clearly defining what liberals believed to be the wider mission of the new state. It declared, "The public authority of a liberal Government, which must seek in every way possible to educate, is obliged to ensure that the theater performs its proper function, which is to correct bad behavior and at the same time give examples that will inspire all to greater civility." As a result, entire subjects were deemed unsuitable for the stage, including acts that gave offence to religion and anything that seemed to endorse bad behavior (including dueling and suicide) or lauded depravity or vice or attacked the sanctity of marriage. The list of banned subjects did not leave Italy's post-unification theater censors short of work. Until 1864, censorship was organized from four centers: Turin,

Florence, Naples, and Palermo. The censors were not well paid and many had worked for the former rulers, although they were gradually replaced by new men, including prominent patriots like the playwright and theater critic Giovanni Sabbatini. Following enactment of the 1864 law that made the prefects in each province responsible for theater censorship, censorship was applied at the regional level, resulting in what many claimed were glaring disparities.[40]

In the years immediately after 1860 the activities of the censors inevitably reflected the very tense post-unification political climate. The government was particularly concerned that the theaters not be turned into sites for pro-Garibaldi demonstrations and the censors were warned to ensure that the huge wave of plays that were hurriedly being written to celebrate unification patriotism not serve as a pretext for a "host of barbarities." Thus, following the uprisings in southern Italy and Sicily in the early 1860s against the new state, any reference to brigandage or brigands on stage or in the title of plays was banned. Between October 1859 and March 1861, the climactic years of Italian unification, 110 plays were rejected by the censors, while in the three following years another 205 manuscripts were refused. The reasons most frequently cited were that they contained reference to living personages, most often Garibaldi and King Victor Emanuel II, and any play that dealt directly or indirectly with Garibaldi's famous expedition to Sicily in 1860 was almost certain to be banned. But the censors were also hostile to works that described or seemed to incite partisan loyalties, and to those that attacked or criticized the institution of Parliament or the National Guard or referred to class conflict or hatred. They also banned *The Origins of a Great Banker,* a play by Enrico Mantazio whose subject was the struggles of a Frankfurt Jew with good and evil, i.e., between the duty of an honest man and the greed for money, on the grounds that it was anti-Semitic.[41]

In these early years of the new state, the censors were particularly alert to anything that might offend Italy's powerful neighbors, especially France and Austria. An even greater problem was the Papacy, which was further complicated by the censors' determination to ban anything that might offend religious principles from the stage. The regulations on this subject were absolutely clear, but if they had changed little since earlier in the century they also reflected wider European norms. In Italy, however, the strict regulation of religious references set the censors in opposition to hordes of writers who were rapidly penning new and very often highly scurrilous anti-clerical plays, many of which focused on the Inquisition's iniquities or the debauchery of earlier papal courts. Others had more contemporary settings, for example Luigi Gandolfi's *Village Priest*, which the censor described as "a vile little farce that is quite unsuitable to be shown in any theater, because of the revulsion that would be felt at the spectacle of a young peasant girl seducing the village priest. Among the many other disgraceful things it contains is a scene in which the priest and his moll sit on a bed to eat their supper so that they more easily take their repose afterwards." Texts like these failed the censors' morality tests for fairly obvious reasons. The post-unification censors also found the original texts of two of Verdi's great operatic successes, *The Force of Destiny* and Victor Hugo's *Le Roi s'amuse* (on which *Rigoletto* was based), too immoral for dramatic performance, although they made an interesting distinction in commenting that they could still be presented as musical works since such appealed to the senses rather than the intellect.[42]

On 20 September 1870, two weeks after French Emperor Napoleon III was defeated by the Prussians at the Battle of Sedan, Italian troops finally occupied Rome. This spurred a new wave of provocatively anti-clerical dramas, many of which, like *The Mysteries of the Spanish Inquisition*, *Sixtus V and the Abbess of Castro*, and *The Nun of Cracow*, were so crude that even the liberal press protested at the "disgraceful immorality of which the theaters have become a school, with performances that not only offend good taste but are downright obscene and through sensual excitement encourage young persons to abandon piety and give themselves over to vice, licentiousness and adultery." In 1872, Pius IX protested in his Easter sermon against the daily insults to the Church on the Roman stage, and later that year the Cardinal Vicar wrote a formal protest to the Italian prime minister, Giovanni Lanza. But Lanza replied in a much more confident tone than his predecessors, rejecting the Cardinal Vicar's protests in a manner that places interesting light on the government's views of its theater censorship: "Permit me, Your Eminence, to reject the harsh and unjust criticisms you make of the Italian government, which has done everything that is possible within the limits of the law to curb abuses in the theater, since I do not believe that there is any other civilized country in Europe that enforces censorship of the theater with greater severity than we do." According to Lanza, many plays allowed in France and Belgium, "countries that Your Eminence will surely not wish to rank among the barbarous or irreligious," were banned in Italy. Acknowledging that it was not always easy to keep a close eye on what actually occurred on the stage, Lanza ended by suggesting that even the authorities doubted the effectiveness of censorship: "Past experience provides ample evidence that even the most absolute censorship and the most arbitrary forms of prohibition are on their own of little avail when it comes to protecting morality and religion, encouraging good behavior and stamping out errors."[43]

## Toward the Fin de Siècle

Italy survived the trials and challenges of its first decade, even though its political troubles were by no means over. Nonetheless, the absence of any major public debate on theater censorship (unlike censorship of the press) in the decades that followed can be taken as a measure of the bourgeois consensus that had taken shape around the new state and its institutions. Indeed, as has often been noted, the triumph of the Italian middle classes was celebrated above all in the theaters, which, when they were delegated to local administration, were run by the local parties and factions that had come to power as a result of unification. Apart from Milan, Italy's theaters were now essentially regional and municipal, as was evident in the huge success of the new bourgeois comedies that filled the Italian stages in these years, works that carefully avoided politics and focused instead on the apparently endless merry-go-rounds of marital infidelity and other tribulations of urban life and manners. These were unlikely covers for subversion, and, as earlier in the century, self-censorship was far more important than external censorship.[44]

Among the educated public, there was a degree of consensus that censorship was necessary in a society where the majority was still illiterate and therefore allegedly easily misled. When in 1864 responsibility for theater censorship was delegated to the prefects, this was criticized mainly because it risked making censorship less effective by undermining uniformity and giving too much discretion to local officials. But ten years later, Italy's leading theater critic, Yorick, could claim that he was proud to live in a country that "leads all others on the road to progress" and where theater was subject to "the most tolerant, fair and liberal regulations to be found anywhere in Europe." If anything, the complaint was that the state needed to do more to support the theater and that its intervention should not be limited simply to censorship. The only subsequent attempt to change the law on theater censorship came in 1888, when the public safety laws were revised and the government of Francesco Crispi sought to widen the existing powers of the prefects and local police chiefs to ban theatrical performances that might pose problems of public order to encompass the interest of "the health and safety of the nation." The revised measure presented to parliament in 1889 proposed, without any qualifications or justification, that "operas, dramas, choreographic representations and all forms of theatrical performance may not be presented or declaimed in public without the prior approval of the Prefect." Only two deputies expressed reservations, with one arguing that since censorship had not saved any of Italy's pre-unification rulers it was not needed now, while another protested that the criteria of moral censorship had simply become a means for the government to exercise political censorship. In a characteristically robust response, Crispi contemptuously dismissed both arguments, maintaining:

> The state must be an educator. It is not enough to have schools, gentlemen, if we do not have education. The example of the Governments of the past that have been frequently cited in this debate are of no relevance whatsoever to the present condition of our country and it is quite unjust that they should be compared with the present Government which owes its being to popular election and is responsible before this parliament. In very advanced European countries ... and you would not wish to deny that England is one of these, the theater is subject to censorship because all recognize that censorship is a social and political necessity.

The government ultimately conceded that the prefects should provide justification when a play was banned, with the law amended to read, "The Prefect may prohibit any play or declamation for reasons of morality and public order."[45]

The 1889 public security laws continued what in practice was a three-tier system of censorship for the theater: plays remained subject to the press laws and the laws regulating public performances, and might additionally be subject to censorship for infringing either the criminal law or public morality, or both. Writing in the *Nuova Antologia* in 1912, critic V. E. Imperatori lamented that such controls had subjected the provincial theaters to "capricious but constant censorship, which is not an insignificant illustration of the incomplete political unification of our country." But without any apparent sense of self-contradiction, Imperatori also joined the clamor for stricter controls over popular theater, claiming that the authorities consistently refused to take action even in cases of gross indecency. This complaint suggested that new forms of naturalist drama were finally finding a path to the Italian stage in ways that were beginning to challenge, from a different perspective, the comfortable bourgeois consensus that had prevailed in the Italian theaters in the decades after unification. As that consensus came under increasing threat, as it did during and above all after World War I, political censorship of the theaters would be revived in new and unprecedentedly aggressive forms.[46]

## Conclusion

The censorship wars in Italy's nineteenth-century theaters followed patterns similar to those during the same years in many other European states. Although the sensitivity shown by Italian theater audiences to nationalist allusions later came to be exaggerated, this phenomenon clearly reflected the central place of the theaters in the social lives of wealthy and educated Italians. The theaters' popularity inevitably made them the targets of many different and often conflicting political ambitions; no one rebuked Italy's nineteenth-century composers and playwrights more severely than Mazzini, who accused Italy's composers in particular of failing to produce works that truly promoted the nationalist mission. But Italy's pre-unification rulers also looked on the theater as an important, indeed even a critical instrument of power, which for that reason they sought both to promote and to control. Censorship therefore played an important role in the cultural politics of the Italian autocracies, although it was only one of many factors that influenced what audiences saw and heard on stage in these years, which was determined as much by audience tastes and values as by the preferences of rulers or the interventions of censors and police. Indeed, only when censorship strayed beyond the confines of what audiences found acceptable was it likely to become irksome and counterproductive. The increasingly uncertain and random application of censorship in the Italian theaters in the decade after the defeat of the Italian revolutions of 1848–49 clearly reflected the internal political uncertainties and divisions that accelerated the collapse of those absolutist rulers who rejected the path of constitutional government and political representation.

After unification, Italian law and theater censorship and the manner in which these were allied in practice came closer to the situation in other European constitutional states. Censorship continued but was in theory informed by moral rather than political criteria. This distinction was always fuzzy, and the theater censorship powers enjoyed by both the Italian prefects and the police gave them wide discretion. Yet these powers were deployed much less often than those relating to public assembly, association, and organization, or even the press. The reason for this was that after unification the theater became the quintessential institution of Italy's new ruling classes, who—as contemporaries liked to point out—preferred to spend local government funds on building or subsidizing theaters rather than on hospitals or drains. Unification did not make the Italian theaters any less financially dependent than before, but their masters had changed.

Nonetheless, the governments of liberal Italy did not remove the extensive discretionary powers of intervention exercised by the prefects and the police, which were extended in Zanardelli's 1889 Penal Code. The three-tier system of censorship, which subjected the theaters to the laws on press censorship, those regulating public assembly, and those specifically relating to theatrical and other public performances, quite deliberately maintained a degree of uncertainty that gave the authorities wide discretionary powers. This reflected the political organization of the new Italian state more generally, but also the considerable regional and cultural differences that persisted well beyond Italy's political unification. The decentralized and discretionary nature of the censorship powers allowed different criteria to be adopted to suit local conditions and cultural values: a performance acceptable in Milan, for example, might not be permitted in Bari or Palermo. Those powers also reflected tensions between the educational mission that many liberals attributed to the new state and their belief in the freedom of speech. But those tensions were certainly not unique to liberal Italy in the late nineteenth century; it was not by chance that Italian politicians frequently pointed to the censorship powers of Britain's Lord Chamberlain to argue that Italian censorship was less severe and more transparent.

## Bibliographical Essay

For introductions to Italian history, politics, and culture in this period see Nicholas Doumanis, *Italy* (London, 2001) and the chapters by Alexander Grab, David Laven, Roland Sarti and Raymond Grew in John A. Davis, ed., *Italy in the Nineteenth Century* (Oxford, 2000). Christopher Duggan's *Force of Destiny: A History of Italy Since 1796* (Boston, 2008) offers an excellent and recent general overview of the period with some references to opera but not to censorship. Far and away the best book on culture and politics in nineteenth century Italy, with focus on opera (but little about censorship) is Axel Körner's *Politics of Culture in Liberal Italy: From Unification to Fascism* (New York, 2009). Censorship in general in Italy is discussed in my contribution in Robert Justin Goldstein, ed., *The War for the Public Mind: Political Censorship in Nineteenth Century Europe* (Westport, CT, 2000), and in "Opera and Absolutism in Restoration Italy 1815–1860," *Journal of Interdisciplinary History* 36 (Spring 2006): 569–94.

Most of the English studies on censorship focus exclusively on opera and the Risorgimento, to which reference can be found in the following:

William Ashbrook, *Donizetti and his Opera* (Cambridge, 1982); Ashbrook, "The Nineteenth Century: Italy," in Roger Parker, ed., *The Oxford Illustrated History of Opera* (Oxford, 1994), 169–205; Lorenzo Bianconi and Giorgio Pestelli, eds., *The History of Italian Opera*, 4 vols. (Chicago, 1998–2003); Julian Budden, *The Operas of Verdi* (London, 1984); Jane Phillips Matz, *Verdi: A Biography* (Oxford, 1993); Michael Robinson, *Naples and the Neapolitan Opera* (Oxford, 1972); John Rosselli, *The Italian Opera Industry in Italy from Cimarosa to Verdi: The role of the Impresario* (Cambridge, 1984); Rosselli, "Opera Production 1780–1880," in Lorenzo Bianconi and Giorgio Pestelli, eds., *Opera Production and its Resources* (Chicago, 1998), 81–164; Hebert Weinstock, *Donizetti and the World of Opera in Italy, Paris and Vienna in the First Half of the Nineteenth Century* (New York, 1963); Weinstock, *Rossini: A Biography* (New York, 1968); Carlotta Sorba, "To Please the Public—Composers and Audiences in Nineteenth-Century Italy," *Journal of Interdisciplinary History*, 36 (2006), 595-614; Peter Stamatov, "Interpretive Activism and the Political Uses of Verdi's Operas in the 1840s." *American Sociological Review*, 67 (2002), 345-366; and Gary Tomlinson, "Italian Romanticism and Italian Opera: An Essay in Their Affinities," *19$^{th}$-Century Music,* 10, (1986), 43-60.

On opera censorship generally see John Rosselli, "Censorship," in Stanley Sadie, ed., *New Grove Dictionary of Opera* (London, 1992); David Kimbell, *Verdi in the Age of Italian Romanticism* (Cambridge, 1981), 23–32, 256–79; Andreas Giger, "Social Control and the Censorship of Giuseppe Verdi's Operas in Rome," *Cambridge Opera Journal* 11 (1999): 233–66; and Amanda Holden, ed., *The New Penguin Opera Guide* (London, 2001). On social-political dimensions of nineteenth-century theater history, see Axel Körner, "The theater of social change: nobility, opera industry and politics of culture in Bologna between papal privilege and liberal principles," *Journal of Modern Italian Studies* 8 (2003): 341–56. David Laven's *Venice and Venetia under the Habsburgs 1815–48* (Oxford, 2003) has much information on censorship in the Austrian territories.

General literature on the history of the Italian theater is sparse in English. Joseph Farrell and Paolo Puppa, *A History of Italian Theatre* (Cambridge, 2006) offers a good guide to theatrical productions, playwrights and actors, but has no reference to censorship for this period. On Italian Romanticism, see Giovani Carsaniga's excellent essay, "The Age of Romanticism, 1800–70," and David Kimbell, "Italian Opera since 1800," both in P. Brand and L. Pertile, eds., *The Cambridge History of Italian Literature* (Cambridge, 1996). See also Kimbell's *Italian Opera* (Cambridge, 1991). In Albert Ascoli and Krystyna von Henneberg, eds., *Making and*

*Remaking Italy: The Cultivation of National Identity around the Risorgimento* (Oxford, 2001), see Adrian Lyttelton's essay, "Creating a National Past: History, Myth and Image in the Risorgimento," for an exploration of historical imagery in Italian nationalism; and Mary Ann Smart, "Liberty on (and off) the Barricades: Verdi's Risorgimento Fantasies," for debates on the theater and the Risorgimento. See also Philip Gossett, "Becoming a citizen: the Chorus in the Risorgimento opera," *Cambridge Opera Journal* 1 (1990): 41–64; Roger Parker, *"Arpa d'or dei fatidici vati": The Verdian Patriotic Chorus in the 1840s* (Parma, 1997); Parker, *Leonora's Last Act: Essays in Verdian Discourse* (Princeton, NJ, 1997); and Roberto Leydi, "The dissemination and popularization of opera," in Lorenzo Bianconi and Giorgio Pestelli, eds., *Opera in Theory and Practice, Image and Myth* (Chicago, 2003), 287–376.

For a broader understanding of both censorship and theater history, the Italian literature is indispensable. The starting point remains the essays in the *Enciclopedia dello Spettacolo,* 12 vols. (Rome, 1956), especially those by Italo Cubedden, "State e spettacolo," IX, 314–23; Silvio D'Amico, "Morale e teatro," VII, 807–14; and Carl Vincent, "Censura," III, 399–435. See also Carlo Di Stefano, *La Censura Teatrale in Italia (1600–1962)* (Bologna, 1964); Benedetto Croce, *I teatri di Naples dal Rinascimento alla fine del secolo decimottavo* (Bari, 1947); and Federico Doglio, *Teatro e Risorgimento* (Bologna, 1972), which deals with the theater more generally. For the years after unification see, in addition to Di Stefano, V. E. Imperatori, "Teatri e libertà: La censura in Italia del secolo XIX," *Nuova Antologia,* series V, 157 (1912): 318–28.

These older studies must be supplemented by more recent works by Carlotta Sorba: *I Teatri: L'Italia del melodrama nell'e del Risorgimento* (Bologna 2001), "Il Risorgimento in musica: l'opera lirica nei teatri del 1848," in Alberto Banti and Roberto Bizzochi, eds., *Immagini della Nazione nell'Italia del Risorgimento* (Rome, 2002), 134–36, and "Il 1848 e la melodrammatizzazione della politica," in Paul Ginsborg, et al., eds., *Il Risorgimento* (Turin, 2007), 481–508. See also, in Sorba, ed., *Scene di Fine Ottocento: L'Italia di fin de siècle* (Rome, 2004), the essays by Francesco Socrate, "Commedia borghese e crisi di fine secolo," 21–60, and Irene Piazzoni, "Il governo e la politica per il teatro: tra promozione e censura (1882–1900)," 61–100. The latter's earlier study, *Spettacolo: Istituzioni e Societé nell'Italia post-Unitaria (1860–1882)* (Rome 2001), is now the principal guide to theater and state politics in unified Italy.

On Mazzini and the theater, see Giuseppe Mazzini, *La Filosofia della Musica* (1836); on the "conspiracy in open daylight" see Massimo D'Azeglio,

*Gli Ultimi Casi di Romagna* (1846). On La Scala and the politics of opera in Habsburg Lombardy, see Bruno Saepen, "Governare per mezzo dell Scala: L'Austria e il teatro d'opera a Milano," *Contemporanea: Rivista di Storia dell'1800 e del'1900* 6 (2003): 593–620. For San Carlo (Naples), see especially Philip Gossett, "La fine dell et borbonica, 1838–1860," in *Il Teatro di San Carlo* (Naples, 1987), and three studies in the multi-authored volume *Il Teatro del Re: Il San Carlo da Naples all'Europa* (Naples, 1988): Franco Carmelo Greco, "Il teatro del re: dall'istituzione alla legittimazione," 9–37; Gaetana Cantone, "Il teatro del re dalla corte alla città," 45–77; and Luciana Di Lernia, "La Visita al San Carlo del Viaggiatore Straniero," 159–71. On Neapolitan society and the theater, see H. Beyle (Stendhal), *Rome, Naples, et Florence* (Paris, 1817), and Daniela Luigia Caglioti, *Associazionismo e sociabilità d'elite a Naples nel XIX secolo* (Naples,1996). On Naples in the 1830s, see Pietro Calà-Ulloa, *Il Regno di Ferdinando II* (Naples, 1967), and, for after 1848, Raffaele De Cesare, *La Fine di Un Regno: Il Regno di Ferdinando II* (Rome, 1909). On theaters in Rome, see Philippe Boutry, "La Restaurazione, 1814–1848," in Giorgio Ciucci, ed., *Rome Moderna* (Bari, 2000), and V. Gorresio, *Risorgimento Scommunicato* (Florence, 1958). For Cavour and the Piedmont theaters, see Rosario Romeo, *Cavour e il suo tempo 1854–1861,* III (Bari, 1984). On bourgeois Italy, see Alberto Maria Banti, *Storia della Borghesia Italiana* (Rome, 1996).

## Notes

1. Alexandre Dumas, *Il Corricolo* (Milan, 1843), cited in Daniela Luigia Caglioti, *Associazionismo e sociabilità d'elite a Naples nel XIX secolo* (Naples, 1996), 3; on opera audiences see also John Rosselli, *The Italian Opera Industry in Italy from Cimarosa to Verdi: the role of the Impresario* (Cambridge, 1984).
2. See especially Giovanni Carsaniga, "The Age of Romanticism 1800–70," in P. Brand and L. Pertile, eds., *The Cambridge History of Italian Literature* (Cambridge, 1991) 399–449.
3. Carlo Di Stefano, *La Censura Teatrale in Italia (1600–1962)* (Bologna, 1964), 25–26.
4. Also important were the Teatro Argentino and Teatro Valle in Rome, and the Teatro Ducale in Modena. La Scala, which opened in 1778, seated up to three thousand spectators. See Marco Santoro in Carlotta Sorba, ed., *Scene di Fine Ottocento: L'Italia di fin de siècle* (Rome, 2004), 101. On the theater and social representation see Sorba, *I Teatri: L'Italia del melodrama nell'età del Risorgimento* (Bologna, 2001).
5. Benedetto Croce, *I teatri di Naples dal Rinascimento alla fine del secolo decimottavo* (Bari, 1947), 275; Franco Carmelo Greco "Il teatro del re: dall'istituzione

alla legittimazione," in *Il Teatro del Re: Il San Carlo da Naples all'Europa* (Naples, 1988), 9–37; Gaentana Cantone, "Il teatro del re dalla corte alla città" in *Il Teatro del Re*, 45–77.

6. While some states became satellite principalities (The kingdoms of Italy and Naples) others were directly annexed to France as *départments réunis* (Piedmont, Liguria, Tuscany, Rome, Umbria, and the Marche). See Alexander Grab, "From the French Revolution to Napoleon," in John A. Davis, ed., *Italy in the Nineteenth Century* (Oxford, 2000), 25–50.
7. Federico Doglio, *Teatro e Risorgimento* (Bologna, 1972), 6.
8. "De principes, de bonnes moeux, et de patriotisme," cited in Italo Cubedden, "Stato e spettacolo," in *Enciclopedia dello Spettacolo* (hereafter *EdS*), IX (Rome, 1956), 314–23; Croce, 275.
9. Cubedden, 317; Doglio, 17–19. Joseph Fouché (1759–1820) was Napoleon's police chief; he was dismissed on suspicion of plotting against Napoleon.
10. Beauharnais' French theater company, "La Compagnie des Commédiants Ordinaires de Sa Majesté Imperiale," moved to Naples in 1818 and took the name "Compagnia Reale di Naples" (1818–26); see Cubbeden, 318. On Domenico Barbaja, see Rosselli, *The Italian Opera*.
11. For Restoration Italy, see David Laven, "The Age of the Restoration," in Davis, *Italy*, 51–73.
12. See especially Sorba, *I Teatri*, 17–93; L. Zingarelli, "Teatri nuovi e nuova domanda," in A. Massafra, ed., *Il Mezzogiorno Pre-unitario: Economia, societé, istituzioni* (Bari, 1988), 945–64.
13. Doglio, 22–3. According to Doglio, Pellico's play, first performed in 1816, is considered to be the first Italian example of Romantic drama.
14. On Milan see Rosselli, *The Italian Opera*, 82–3; on Rome, Philippe Boutry, "La Restaurazione, 1814–1848" in Giorgio Ciucci, ed., *Roma Moderna* (Bari, 2000). The Neapolitan official is cited in John A. Davis, "Opera and Absolutism in Restoration Italy, 1815–1860," *Journal of Interdisciplinary History*, 36 (2006), 583.
15. Luciana Di Lernia, "La Visita al San Carlo del Viaggiatore Straniero," in *Il Teatro del Re: Il San Carlo da Naples all'Europa* (Naples, 1988), 159–71.
16. Luciana Di Lernia, "La Visita al San Carlo del Viaggiatore Straniero," in *Il Teatro del Re: Il San Carlo da Naples all'Europa* (Naples, 1988), 159–71.
17. John Roselli, "Opera Production 1780–1880," in Lorenzo Bianconi and Giorgio Pestelli, eds., *Opera Production and its Resources* (Chicago, 1998), 81–164; Philip Gossett, "La fine dell'età borbonica, 1838–1860," in *Il Teatro di San Carlo*, I (Naples, 1987), 167–72; Giuseppe Berti, *Censura e circolazione delle idee nel Veneto della Restaurazione* (Venice, 1988), 9.
18. Carlo Vincent, "Censura" in *EdS*, III, 399–435 (quotation on 403); Di Stefano, 67–72.
19. Di Stefano, 51–83.
20. Vincent, 404.
21. Rosselli, *The Italian Opera*; John Rosselli, "Censorship," in Stanley Sadie, ed., *New Grove Dictionary of Opera* (London, 1992) IV, 57–67; Doglio, 28–30; David Kimbell, "Italian Opera since 1800," in P. Brand & L. Pertile, eds. *The*

*Cambridge History of Italian Literature* (Cambridge, England, 1996), 394; Pietro Calà-Ulloa, *Il Regno di Ferdinando II* (Naples, 1967), 31–34.

22. Roberto Leydi, "The dissemination and popularization of opera," in Lorenzo Bianconi and Giorgio Pestelli, eds., *Opera in Theory and Practice, Image and Myth* (Chicago, 2003), 309–13; Mary Ann Smart, "Liberty on (and off) the Barricades: Verdi"s Risorgimento Fantasies," in Albert Ascoli and Krystyna von Henneberg, eds., *Making and Remaking Italy: The Cultivation of National Identity around the Risorgimento* (Oxford, 2001); Giuseppe Mazzini, *La Filosofia della Musica* (Milan, 1836).
23. Rosselli, *The Italian Opera;* Rosselli, "Censorship."
24. David Kimbell, *Italian Opera* (Cambridge, 1991), 406.
25. See John A. Davis, "Italy," in Robert Justin Goldstein, ed., *The War for the Public Mind: Political Censorship in Nineteenth Century Europe* (Westport, CT, 2000), 81–124.
26. Doglio, 30; Davis, "Italy," 98–99.
27. On Habsburg censorship, see especially David Laven, *Venice and the Venetia under the Habsburgs, 1815–48* (Oxford, 2002). On Verdi, see Jane Phillips-Matz, *Verdi: A Biography* (Oxford, 1993), 131–33; Julian Budden, *The Operas of Verdi* (London, 1984); and Doglio, 30. Among Verdi's operas, *Joan of Arc,* for example, was always performed with different titles, including *Ovietta di Lesbo,* leading Budden to comment, "The implication is clear: better a lesbian than a heretic."
28. See the book by journalist Francesco Predari, *I primi vagiti della libertà in Piemonte* (Milan, 1861).
29. Doglio, 31; Carlotta Sorba, "Il Risorgimento in musica: l'opera lirica nei teatri del 1848," in Alberto Banti and Roberto Bizzochi, eds., *Immagini della Nazione nell'Italia del Risorgimento* (Rome, 2002).
30. Sorba, "Il Risorgimento"; Smart; Doglio, 33; Ottavio Tiby, *Il Reale Teatro San Carolino e l'Ottocento Musicale Palermitano* (Milan, 1958), 69.
31. Gossett. According to Herbert Weinstock, *Rossini: A Biography* (New York, 1968), 47, "During the earlier 1820–21 revolution in Naples, Rossini had waited impatiently in Rome for the revolution to collapse so that he could return to resume the interrupted season at San Carlo," which he did within weeks of the Austrian occupation of Naples in March 1821.
32. Raffaele De Cesare, *La Fine di un Regno,* I (Rome 1909); Calà-Ulloa, *Il Regno di Ferdinando II,* 152–53.
33. Gossett.
34. De Cesare, 152–53; Anthony Cardoza, "Cavour and Piedmont," in Davis, *Italy,* 108–31.
35. Rosario Romeo, *Cavour e il suo tempo, 1854–1861,* III (Bari, 1984), 399; E. Arbib Pensieri, S*entenze e ricordi di uomini parlamentari* (Firenze, 1901), 125; Vincent, 404–6.
36. Di Stefano.
37. For a more general discussion, see John A. Davis, *Conflict and Control: Law and Order in Nineteenth Century Italy* (London, 1988).

38. Vincent, 405; V. E. Imperatori, "Teatri e libertà: La censura in Italia del secolo XIX," *Nuova Antologia,* series V, 157 (1912): 318–28. In addition to Vincent, the fullest and most-recent description of the Italian government's policies toward the theater is Irene Piazzoni, "Il governo e la politica per il teatro: tra promozione e censura (1882–1900)," in Sorba, *Scene di Fine Ottocento,* 61–100; and in Piazzoni's *Spettacolo: Istituzioni e Societé nell'Italia post-Unitaria (1860–1882)* (Rome 2001), on which the following section draws extensively. As in France, the prefect was the senior representative of the state in each of the country's administrative provinces or regions, responsible, among other things, for all matters of policing and with wide-ranging powers to overrule local elected assemblies and officials.
39. Piazzoni, *Spettacolo,* 8–9, 17–18, 137. There was one theater for every 75,000 Italians, compared with one for every 100,000 French, every 184,000 English, every 235,000 Austrians, and every 500,000 Russians. However, most Italian theaters were temporary halls and other venues, making the figures very unreliable.
40. Piazonni, *Spettacolo,* 74, 186.
41. Piazonni, *Spettacolo,* 148, 167.
42. Piazonni, *Spettacolo,* 174; V. Gorresio, *Risorgimento Scommunicato* (Florence, 1958), 171.
43. Gorresio, 174; and the important essay by Axel Körner, "The theater of social change: nobility, opera industry and politics of culture in Bologna between papal privilege and liberal principles," *Journal of Modern Italian Studies* 8 (2003): 341–56.
44. On the "bourgeois theater," see Francesco Socrate, "Commedia borghese e crisi di fine secolo," in Sorba, *Scene di Fine Ottocento,* 21–60; Piazzoni, *Spettacolo,* 207
45. Piazzoni, "Il governo," 82–84; Vincent, 405; Imperatori, 319.
46. See Vincent, 406–7, for discussion of the Fascist law on theater censorship (1931), which banned any play that "defends vice or crime, criticizes established international relations, incites hatred between the social classes, gives offence to the king, the Supreme Pontefix, or foreign rulers, or shows disrespect for the clergy and the public authorities, for the military or the state police." A separate clause banned plays hostile to the regime; in 1938 the ban was extended to include plays by Jewish writers, actors, or producers

# The Habsburg Monarchy

Norbert Bachleitner

## Introduction

The Austrian (Habsburg) monarchy developed from the Habsburg hereditary lands (mostly modern Austria and Slovenia) accumulated by the dynasty since 1278. By the nineteenth century, the monarchy also included the Bohemian crownlands, initially consisting of the provinces of Bohemia, Moravia, and Silesia, and the Kingdom of Hungary. Over the course of history, other lands also came under Habsburg rule. The most important among them in the nineteenth century were Galicia, Bukowina, Venetia, Lombardy, Dalmatia, and Bosnia. The monarchy was therefore a multinational and multilingual state, with about a dozen different languages spoken within its borders, including German, Italian, Hungarian, Czech, Polish, Ruthenian/Ukrainian, Slovenian, and Croatian.

Attempts at centralization began under Empress Maria Theresia and her son Emperor Joseph II in the mid to late eighteenth century, but were abandoned because of large-scale resistance to Joseph's radical reforms. The period of enlightened reform and a certain liberalism was followed by a phase of conservative reaction. In spite of intense repression, both liberalism and nationalism prospered in the underground and culminated in the Revolution of 1848. A constitution was enacted in March 1848, but it had little practical impact. However, one of the concessions to revolutionaries with a lasting impact was the freeing of Austrian peasants from serfdom. This facilitated industrialization, as many peasants moved to the newly industrializing cities of the Austrian domain (the key industrial centers were Bohemia, Lower Austria with Vienna, and Upper Styria). The formation of an industrial working class led to growing social unrest.

In 1848, the long-dominant "prime minister" Klemens von Metternich and the mentally handicapped Emperor Ferdinand I were forced to resign, with the latter replaced by Ferdinand's young nephew Franz Joseph. Separatist tendencies (especially in Lombardy and Hungary) were suppressed by military force and the absolutist regime was prolonged until the 1860s. Following the Habsburg defeats in the wars of 1859 and 1866 with, respectively, Piedmont (the core of modern Italy) and Prussia (the core of modern Germany), the Compromise (*Ausgleich*) of 1867 was reached, by which the so-called Dual Monarchy of Austria-Hungary was set up and Hungarian nationalism appeased. In this system, the Kingdom of Hungary was given sovereignty and a parliament, and in Austria a constitutional system with a parliament, the Reichsrat, was created, and a bill of rights was enacted. Suffrage to the Reichstag's lower house was gradually expanded until 1907, when equal suffrage for all male citizens was introduced. However, the effectiveness of parliamentarianism was hampered by conflicts between parties representing different ethnic groups. Nationalist strife increased during the decades before World War I. The assassination of Archduke Franz Ferdinand, the presumed heir to Franz Joseph as emperor, in Sarajevo in 1914 by a Serb nationalist triggered the war's outbreak, and the defeat of Austria and its allies in 1918 led to the disintegration of the monarchy.

The development of economic and cultural life was extremely varied in the different provinces. In the hereditary lands and in the Italian and Czech territories with old cultural centers like Vienna, Prague, Venetia, and Milan, a bourgeois literary and theatrical life was comparatively well developed, whereas other regions remained overwhelmingly rural until far into the nineteenth century. In the German-speaking areas, theatrical entertainment took place in court theaters or on stages where itinerant troupes performed. Vienna was one of the European centers of court entertainment. As it was a multinational court, its repertory was international, consisting mainly of Italian Baroque operas and, in the eighteenth century,

French drama; besides this there was a tradition of popular theater with a permanent theater house in Vienna from the early eighteenth century onward. In the last third of the eighteenth century, public and commercial theaters were founded elsewhere. The introduction of regular censorship coincided with this development. Theater censorship at first as an instrument of enlightenment above all targeted bad morals, nonsense, and coarseness on the scene, but in the nineteenth century it became more of a political device suppressing enlightenment and progress. The main censorship aim became the suppression of all attempts to criticize or abolish the monarchical system, and thus the monarch and his administration were protected against all manner of attacks. Sensitivity on this point was high to a degree that makes the majority of censorial interventions seem ridiculous today. One major threat to the monarchy was the national movements that strove for independence from the central government, so suppressing perceived nationalist propaganda became an important censorship motivation. In the second half of the century, the social question—the conflict between rich and poor—gained importance and added a further motivation for bans and cuts of plays. In general, the basic structure of society was protected against criticism. Thus, the aristocracy, clergy, officials or even trades, crafts, and manufacturers could not be shown in an unfavorable light on the stage.

The number of theaters in Vienna remained the same from the beginning of the century until 1893, but increased to thirty-eight by 1914. Only at the turn of the century did censorship somewhat relax its grip on the theater. This development, together with the population increase, led to an upswing of theatrical life. Not only the commercial theater flourished in the years before World War I, but the political parties established in the 1880s, especially the Socialists, opened new theaters that appealed to the masses.

## The Introduction of Stage Censorship by Maria Theresia and Joseph II (1770–90)

Until the era of enlightened reform under Maria Theresia and Joseph II, the theater was considered not a medium of education or an instrument for the refinement of manners, but mainly a form of entertainment that provided consolation in hard times and prevented debauchery. Theatrical productions were exclusively offered by wandering companies. There was no permanent theater in Vienna prior to 1708, when Italian comedians occupied a comedy house (Komödienhaus), which was soon to become the Kärntnertortheater. From 1712 onward the local troupes of Joseph Anton Stranitzky and Gottfried Prehauser played their pompous historical scenes (*Haupt- und Staatsaktionen*), Punch (*Hanswurst*) farces, and other popular comedies there. The only other stage in Vienna was the traditional court theater, where Italian operas were performed.

Licensing and observation of plays were the responsibility of the city council. Since no scripts existed and the actors extemporized, censorship in a strict sense was impossible. There were some general rules as to decency and modesty, though, that could not be transgressed if further representations were to be allowed. In 1761 the Kärntnertortheater was bought by the court, a step that facilitated the control of its repertoire. But in 1776 Joseph II broke the monopoly of the two court theaters and paved the way for privately owned commercial theaters in the suburbs. Within a few years, three theaters of long-lasting importance were founded: the Theater in der Leopoldstadt (a suburb) in 1781, the Theater an der Wien (the river Wien) in 1787, and the Theater in der Josefstadt (another suburb) in 1788.

During the reform of the educational system in the second half of the eighteenth century, the Austrian government, following the tenets of enlightenment, started to reform the theater. Above all, the practice of all kinds of rude jokes and jests were repressed and extemporization was eliminated. Moreover, popular plays, most of them with a religious background (Adam and Eve, Christmas, the three Magi), were banned since Empress Maria Theresia considered them improper or supportive of superstition.[1] At the same time the empress watched over the morals of actresses and exiled some of them from Vienna in the 1750s because she considered their behavior too licentious. On the other hand, permanent theaters that performed regular plays, particularly adaptations from the French, Italian, or Spanish, were encouraged by the authorities, until, in the late 1760s, Josef von Sonnenfels began to fight against the hegemony of foreign plays in Austrian theaters. Sonnenfels, a professor of politics (*Polizei- und Kameralwissenschaft*), journalist, and short-time censor, was the central figure of enlightened theater reform. He succeeded—at least temporarily—in repressing extemporization and propagating the creation of a national drama in the German language after the model of the French well-made play (*pièce bien faite*).

As a step toward more "regular" plays, scripts were now printed and sold at the ticket offices. But the theater was considered too important to censor together with books. Its potential to reach and influence a large audience that consisted not only of the educated but of people from all classes, seemed to demand special precautions. Thus, in 1770 censorship of plays was formally established as a branch of control independent from the censorship of books. From 1770 until 1804 Franz Carl Hägelin, nominated as special theater censor, judged the contents of plays as well as their aesthetic qualities. Like Sonnenfels, Hägelin had previously excelled as a reformer of the school system. At the beginning the only rule for his work was to take care "that actors did not improvise and that there were neither fights on the scene nor rude jokes."[2] Extemporization—often of a sexually suggestive nature—was not only a practice that could elude censorship but was considered also characteristic of bad taste and morals.

In the Austrian provinces, the organization of theater censorship was the same as in Vienna. At Prague, for example, Heinrich Carl Seibt, a professor of philosophy, pedagogy and aesthetics, was installed as theater censor in the 1770s. Like Sonnenfels, he was an enlightened reformer who fought against rude jokes and extemporization, performing the role of a "warden of good taste" (*Hüter und Wächter über den guten Geschmack*). The same was true for Lemberg, where in 1776 a censorship commission, led by Wenzel Hann, a liberal and enlightened scholar, was established.[3]

The court theater in Vienna (Burgtheater), opened in 1776, had its own censorship code. Until 1789 a board of actors decided on the admission or rejection of plays, while later an artistic manager was appointed. Thus a kind of self-censorship was installed. Quite obviously the repertory of the court theater was a crucial matter since what was performed on the emperor's own stage was "considered significant for its propriety and political reliability, apart from setting an example for other theaters throughout the nation."[4] Not surprisingly, the representation of monarchs and the discussion of political matters were especially thorny questions for the court stage. Sometimes the monarchs personally decided about a play: for instance, in 1777 Maria Theresia banned *Romeo and Juliet* because she did not like plays that included funerals, cemeteries, tombs, and similarly sad objects. In some adaptations of the play, Romeo and Juliet even survived in order to brighten up the ending.[5]

## The Era of Francis I (1792–1835) and Ferdinand I (1835–48): The Theater in an Authoritarian Police State

### Organization and Principles of Censorship

After the death of Joseph II in 1790 and the traumatic experience of the French Revolution, a reactionary backlash swept the Empire. The suppression of supposed revolutionary movements topped the agenda, notably leading to the Jacobin trials (*Jakobinerprozesse*) of 1794–95 and to dissolution of the Masonic Lodges. After the victory over Napoleon absolutism was reestablished, with the so-called Holy Alliance between Russia, Austria, and Prussia designed to inhibit the progress of liberalism. In 1819, due to the "intrigues" of the German "demagogues" (liberal students and others who opposed absolutism), strict censorship measures (the so called "Karlsbad decrees") were passed, while the European revolutions of 1830 (in Belgium, Poland, and some of the Italian and German states) further intensified watchfulness against progressive forces. Censorship changed from an instrument of enlightenment to an instrument above all of political repression and of maintaining the status quo. Within a few years Emperor Francis, later assisted by Metternich, established one of the most severe systems of censorship in Europe. As Julius Marx has written: "Austrian censorship developed to dimensions one can hardly imagine. Everything was censored, hand-written or printed matters from epitaphs to encyclopedias, pictures from studies to engravings. In the case of rings, needles and pipes, censors tried to ban emblems of secret societies. As concerns music, the lyrics and drawings were checked, revolutionary or political songs were prohibited, as were sometimes even dedications."[6]

It is not surprising that under these circumstances the theater, as a place of public assembly, was closely observed. The opinion that the theater was a political force working against religion, law, and monarchy became general in this era and lasted until 1848 and beyond. The suspicion of the authorities was heightened by the fact that some theaters were now privately owned. If court theaters seemed willing to exercise self-censorship, the private theaters tried to please the audience and were harder to control. There was even a conflict of interest between the court theaters (in Vienna, the Burgtheater and the Theater am Kärntnertor), which tended to favor censorship, and the private theaters (in Vienna the Theater an der Wien, the Theater in der Leopoldstadt, and the Theater in der Josefstadt), which regarded the censors as their enemies.

In 1795 Emperor Francis prohibited extemporization, which had recently been reintroduced on a large scale on the suburban popular stages. Thereafter, actors who extemporized could even be imprisoned: a famous example was the leading actor and playwright Johann Nestroy, who was incarcerated for some days. At the same time, the emperor reminded censors to insure that no play or scene that might be dangerous for the state order was allowed. Reacting to this Imperial decree, the Prague Office of Stage Control (*Bühnenrevisionsamt*) proposed to fine directors of theaters that allowed extemporizing, with the fines to be passed on to poor houses—one of the few reasonable ideas in the course of censorship history. Furthermore, the office indicated that plays like Friedrich Schiller's *Don Karlos, Kabale und Liebe, Die Räuber,* and *Maria Stuart,* or Gotthold Ephraim Lessing's *Emilia Galotti* and most of August Kotzebue's dramas would either not be produced at all or had to be carefully adapted.[7]

The concentration of censorship on political matters is why the police became involved in the censorship and observation of plays. In 1803, the administration of theater censorship was formally taken over by the newly founded police court office (*Polizeihofstelle*). The police now ultimately decided on the admission or rejection of plays, while the censors commissioned to give their opinion on a certain play had only the right to make a recommendation. In the case of the court theaters, the office of the court chamberlain (*Oberstkämmereramt*) was responsible for censorship. But generally this office left the decision about a new play to the police. In sensitive political matters the state chancellery was involved as well. All plays had to be approved in advance, with theaters required to submit two manuscript copies of each proposed play. The censor recommended if the play was acceptable and marked passages to be deleted or reformulated. If the play was approved, the manuscript was returned to the theater. Special police agents, called theater commissioners (*Theaterkommissäre*), who attended rehearsals and first nights, insured that actors did not deviate from the approved text. The theater commissioners even had to approve costumes, decoration, and other details.[8]

Usually plays that were approved in the capital were automatically permitted in the Austrian provinces, with acceptance at the Burgtheater in particular viewed as an official seal of approval. However, a play admitted in the provinces had to be censored again when a Viennese theater wanted to produce it. Censorship in the provinces was in general considered more liberal, as theaters in Graz, Prague, and Hungary staged plays that were prohibited in Vienna. As Viennese theater censor Hägelin stated in 1802: "It is easier by 30 miles for the Prague theater censor to admit a play with a dubious theme than for his colleague in Vienna. If the governor of Prague agrees everything is all right. … There are plays that may be performed almost everywhere but not in Vienna."[9] Such statements must still be verified by comparative studies of bans and adaptations of certain plays. What raises doubt that the treatment of theaters and plays was much more liberal in the provinces is the fact that lists of prohibited plays were sent from Vienna to the provinces in order to provide a certain homogeneity of censorship within the monarchy. Moreover, the works of Friedrich Schiller, considered a revolutionary author in Austria, disappeared from the Buda stages between 1794 and 1808. A theater regulation there decreed that plays were only admitted if they had before been performed at least two times in Vienna. Schiller was also banned from the Krakow stage, but nonetheless two of his plays were performed there. Censorship seems to have been as strict at Lemberg as at Vienna, as the local theater censor cut the word *ojczyzna* (native country) out of Polish plays and in 1813 the announcement of the opera *Kopciuszek* (Cinderella) caused police concern. On some placards the name had been defaced to read "Kosciusko," the name of the patriot who had led the 1794 Polish rebellion.[10]

Besides outright prohibition, the authorities could impose a great variety of restrictive measures. The number of performances could be limited or some specific theaters (e.g., popular stages, theaters in the capital, or theaters in the provinces) could be denied the right to present a particular play. Sometimes the title of a play had to be changed, and sometimes the author's name was suppressed, as in the case of some plays by Schiller, who was considered a particularly "dangerous" author. Furthermore, the abridgement and adaptation of manuscripts was a regular practice. Experienced writers, theater directors like Josef Schreyvogel or Ludwig Deinhardstein, and actors were often employed to adapt plays in accordance with censorship principles. Not only plays were censored but so were reviews of performances: among many other things, allusions to censorship having distorted the texts had to be deleted from the latter.

Sometimes the emperor himself intervened and decided the fate of a play. Theoretically he was the ultimate censorship authority, above the state chancellery and the police censorship. Sometimes he intervened in favor of a play, as in the case of Grillparzer's *König Ottokar* (see below), but more often he acted as a most severe censor. Emperor Francis's opinion of the theater in general is revealed by his ban on amateur performances. In 1800 he decreed that house comedies (*Hauskomödien*) were no longer allowed and argued that "people who perform in comedies are in danger of regarding their playing not as an entertainment in their leisure time, but as their main business and forgetting their proper work. In particular, girls of the lower classes are severed from the sphere they belong to, indulge in romantic ideas and lose the qualities they need for their vocation, i.e. to become good, virtuous and industrious mothers."[11] In 1794 Hägelin, theater censor since 1770, wrote a memorandum, originally intended as instructions for Hungarian censors, in which he summarized his experience. This memorandum served as an unofficial guideline for theater censorship throughout the monarchy during the first half of the nineteenth century. Hägelin argued that censorship of the theater had to be stricter than book censorship because of the "impression which can be made on the minds and emotions of the audience by a work enacted with the illusion of real life," particularly as theatergoers included "people of every class, every walk of life, and every age." He demanded that virtue should be depicted agreeably whereas vice must appear contemptible and be punished. If the plot of a play seemed immoral it must necessarily be altogether prohibited, although in many cases the play might be "repaired" via thorough revision. For the use of censors and adaptors he gave numerous detailed instructions. For example, his memorandum made clear that words like "tyrant" or "despotism" were not to be tolerated on the stage, nor should words like "enlightenment," "liberty," or "equality" be used ("liberty and equality are words which are not to be played with"). Allusions to economic or financial crises, for instance to the enormous inflation in the second decade of the nineteenth century, were to be avoided. Freemasonry was taboo on the stage, with remarks neither for or against the secret order allowed. Battle scenes with firearms were forbidden lest the audience be shocked, and only "single pistol or gun shots may be allowed if they are necessary within a plot and not too loud."[12]

According to Hägelin and all later instructions, censorship had to prohibit three types of transgression: (1) attacks on (Catholic) religion, (2) attacks on the (Austrian) state and the monarchical principle, and (3) representations of immoral acts and crime. Censorship practice reveals a fourth motive for intervention: criticism of or satirical allusion to individuals or groups of citizens, particularly to the aristocracy, but also to trades, crafts, and nations. The following will concentrate on political censorship, but necessarily religious and moral issues will sometimes be implied, as well as the fourth motive for censorship, especially attacks against highborn individuals and nations. Censorship made no distinction between foreign and domestic plays. Clearly, writing under such conditions was extremely difficult, as authors could never be sure if a particular phrase or word would pass censorship. If a text was considered offensive, the consequences were tiresome discussions with officials and, at least, delay of publication and/or production of a play. As Karl Postl, alias Charles Sealsfield, wrote in 1828: "A more fettered being than an Austrian author surely never existed. An Austrian must not offend against any government; nor against any minister; nor against any hierarchy, if its members be influential; nor against the aristocracy. He must not be liberal, nor philosophical, nor humorous—in short, he must be nothing at all."[13] One year later Franz Grillparzer, a lower state official and Austria's best dramatist, wrote in his diary, "An Austrian writer should be held in higher esteem than any other. Anyone who does not completely lose heart under such conditions is truly a kind of hero."[14] In 1845 Grillparzer was among the authors who signed a petition to alleviate and codify censorship, which—rather predictably—failed.

If historical subjects were in general very delicate to handle for Austrian authors, it was almost impossible for historical plays treating the Habsburg Empire in particular to pass the censorship untrimmed. In such cases, historical details like allusions to nationalities or to specific political actions were taboo. Therefore, authors tended to idealize historical events or relegate them to a remote past in order to avoid allusions to contemporary situations. Historical events were to appear as a consequence of the deeds of individual characters, of their virtue or vice. Even the acclaim of emperors or political leaders was considered dangerous, since the audience might protest against such attempts at glorification. As censor Johann Michael Armbruster reported in 1812 about a representation of *Rudolph von Habsburg*, an outright patriotic drama: "No allusion, which should please the heart of each patriot, was acclaimed, and at the end the hissing and trampling of feet were so loud that the last scene, one of the most beautiful scenes containing wishes for the well-being of the Habsburg dynasty and destined to make good effect, could not even be listened to."[15]

The popular stages avoided political matters. During the years of the Restoration, Punch (now called *Kasperl, Thaddädl,* or *Staberl*), banned from the stage since 1770, returned to the scene, together with popular plays with a gothic touch. Until the 1820s, the Theater in der Leopoldstadt, the leading Viennese popular stage, enjoyed a certain license for performing innocent farces, notably comedies featuring knights, ghosts, and fairies. Authorities acted according to the principle of "bread and circuses" and tolerated popular entertainment so long as it avoided political questions. Respectable cheap entertainment was considered necessary for the public of large towns, and especially for the lower classes. From the standpoint of the police, theatergoing "[leads] people away from the more expensive, often unsalubrious pubs, coffee-houses and gambling-houses to better amusements, with some influence on education and morals, and [keeps] the theatergoer under public observation and order for the duration of the performance."[16]

Since authors writing for the popular stages were contracted to provide a certain number of acceptable texts per year, they engaged in a considerable degree of self-censorship. Carl Carl, the dominant director of the popular theater in Vienna, would not sign a contract for a new play without ensuring that it passed censorship. Even a popular playwright like Charlotte Birch-Pfeiffer would not receive a single Kreutzer for a manuscript before Carl had received the censor's approval.[17] Nevertheless, theater directors often submitted doctored manuscripts in order to obtain approval quickly. But in the course of the representations, actors often deviated from the text. Johann Nestroy's improvisations and his aggressive wit when acting were notorious. Even if he recited the approved text, he was always prone to insert sexual innuendos or political allusions by the way the words were spoken or the gestures accompanying them. As theater historian Johann Hüttner observes, "allusions were detected because they were expected" by the public.[18] The police considered such interactions between playwright, actor, and audience as dangerous for public order and Emperor Francis himself complained about Nestroy's subversive influence on the lower classes. In 1825 and again in 1836 Nestroy was jailed for several days. In the first case, after some manifestations of disapproval of his acting, he had openly shown his contempt for the public. In the second case he had extemporaneously attacked a critic.[19]

## Examples of Censored Plays

As noted above, the monarchical principle was protected against theatrical attacks. Therefore, productions depicting revolutions or conspiracies had to be avoided. Plays about Austrian history in which revolutions like the Swiss rebellion (Schiller's *Wilhelm Tell*) or the Netherlands uprising are central were prohibited. The same applied for dramas in which a sovereign, whether Austrian or foreign, was portrayed as despicable. Representation of regicide (i.e., Charles I, Maria Stuart, Louis XVI) was, of course, impossible on an Austrian stage. Nationalities and members of the ruling orders, notably the aristocracy, the clergy, and the military, were also protected against attacks. Even laws, such as those concerning matrimony, duels, or suicide, were not to be criticized on the stage. Nor should plays incite nationalism or insult the character of a people, as this was feared to endanger peace within the monarchy or threaten diplomatic turbulence.

In the years of the wars against France, plays both in praise of and against Napoleon were prohibited. Even a possible parallel between some historical character and Napoleon could lead to a ban, as when Friedrich Wilhelm Ziegler submitted his play *Thekla, die Wienerin* in 1806, a drama about the 1278 siege of Vienna by the Bohemians. The play was prohibited because censors were afraid that the French embassy might identify the

Bohemians with the French and King Ottokar with Napoleon. Another example is Zacharias Werner's *Attila,* which was admitted in 1807 only after all scenes and remarks that suggested parallels with Napoleon were deleted. When Napoleon married the Austrian archduchess Marie Louise, a play about Frederick the Valiant (Friedrich der Streitbare) by Matthäus Collin was banned because Frederick leaves his first wife to marry another. In these years, even a title like *Mord und Totschlag, oder: So kriegt man die Louise* (Blood and Thunder, or: That's the Way to Win Louise), by Karl Koch, was not tolerated. Carl Ludwig Costenoble, an actor at the court theater, reports that titles like *Der alte Junggeselle* (The Confirmed Bachelor) and *Trau, Schau, Wem?* (Who Can You Trust In?) were changed to *Die Hausgenossen* (The Housemates) and *Wie man sich täuscht* (To Be Deceived), respectively, because the former could be construed as alluding to Emperor Francis and the latter as an attack on the empress.[20]

In 1810 the police minister wrote to Emperor Francis that "it is not possible to foresee which allusions a public as dedicated to puns and sophistry as the Viennese may with the help of its lively imagination infer from a passage—to the detriment of a clear and rational point of view."[21] He was right. According to contemporary reports, the public was eager to draw parallels. Thus the following words of Sopir in Voltaire's *Mahomet,* staged in 1812 at the Theater an der Wien, were enthusiastically acclaimed:

> And every hardy traitor may
> Put man into chains? Has
> He the right to cheat, if it is done with
> Grandeur?
>
> (Und jeder muthige Betrüger dürfte
> Den Menschen eine Kette geben? Er
> Hat zu betrügen Recht, wenn er mit Größe
> Betrügt?)

Furthermore, the following words lead to acclaim that was clearly meant as an anti-Napoleonic manifestation.

> On your lips is peace but
> Your heart knows nothing of it.
> You will not deceive me!
>
> (Auf deinen Lippen schallt der Friede, doch
> Dein Herz weiß nichts davon. Mich wirst du nicht
> Betrügen!)[22]

The public was ready to draw parallels and decode allusions even when none were intended, as the paranoid suspicion of politicians and censors apparently engendered a real mania for detecting such perceived references.

An example of the censoring of supposed nationalist propaganda is Zacharias Werner's play *Wanda, Königin der Sarmaten* (Wanda, Queen of the Sarmates), which in 1815 was not allowed in the Polish-speaking provinces because censors were afraid it might remind Poles of their times of national independence. An example of the protection of minority groups was the ban on *The Merchant of Venice*, after members of the Viennese Jewish community had urged suppression as they viewed the main character as a specimen of satanic malice that could provoke hatred of the Jewish religion.[23]

The history of classics on Viennese stages is one of constant embarrassment. Many such plays were prohibited altogether, while others, after long discussions and exchanges of notes between the parties involved, were allowed only in bowdlerized versions. The plays of Schiller, the literary fighter par excellence for political freedom, regularly caused trouble when Austrian theaters wanted to stage them. Thus his *Fiesco's Conspiracy at Genova* was performed in 1800 in a version cleansed from all political matters, with a title lacking the "conspiracy" and a script lacking the word "liberty." In 1803 performances were forbidden until 1807, when a new adapted version was allowed, with references to tyranny and violence deleted along with many other phrases. In 1802 *Die Jungfrau von Orleans* (Joan of Arc) was staged without specifying the two countries opposed in war: the audience learned only that two "empires" were at war, and the English were introduced as a "daring insular people." Charles VII was called "a king," his mistress Agnes Sorel was transformed into his legally married queen (named Mary), the bastard Dunois became Prince Louis, cousin of the king, and the character of the archbishop was deleted. After the French victory over Austria, Schiller was treated less severely, perhaps because he was deemed useful to foster Austrian patriotism. Nevertheless *Don Karlos,* a play first performed during the French occupation of Vienna in 1809, could only be staged in a severely cut version. *Wilhelm Tell,* the story of Swiss insurrection against Habsburg rule, in which a Habsburg is assassinated, was admitted in 1810 at the Theater an der Wien in a bowdlerized version, in which the fault of tyranny is ascribed exclusively to governor Geßler, while the emperor is exculpated and hardly mentioned, and the final act was entirely omitted. In the Austrian version, Geßler's rule appears legitimate and Tell appears as a mere renegade. Still, the play seemed highly suspicious to the censors because it might provoke "painful reminiscences" of the recent insurrection in the Tyrol. When the play reappeared at the Burgtheater in 1827, the censors still hesitated in allowing the staging of an insurrection against Austrian rule, but the emperor had already approved an adapted version. As late as 1904, allusions to the emperor and mentions of Austria were deleted from *Wilhelm Tell* in the Burgtheater.[24]

Schiller's *Maria Stuart,* largely due to the motif of the queen's execution, and the *Wallenstein* trilogy could not be produced until 1848 and then only in modified versions. The trilogy was severely condensed to fit into one evening's performance, with the remaining text expurgated. A version performed in Prague was not admitted in Vienna in 1802. In an 1814 adaptation, phrases like "No Emperor is allowed to dictate what the heart feels" were changed to "There is no rule for the heart." In 1827, court theater secretary Schreyvogel went around the censors by having his somewhat "bold" version approved by Emperor Francis before submitting it to them. Schiller's *Die Räuber* (The Brigands) was banned from Vienna and only allowed in the suburban Theater an der Wien. Strangely enough, Schiller was not utterly averse to censorship. In 1799 he authorized his colleague Kotzebue to adapt his *Wallenstein* for a performance in the Burgtheater and bent to the higher insight of the censors "if a remark that might be misinterpreted by the audience should have slipped his attention."[25] What obviously counted most for him was to have his plays performed. He seems to have clearly believed that staged cut versions were preferable to none at all and that even severe cuts did not prevent a performance from conveying some of his ideas to the public.

Almost all of Shakespeare's plays were cut and altered when prepared for Austrian presentation. In 1822, Schreyvogel sought to preserve the tragic ending in *King Lear,* but his adaptation was banned because a king's downfall was inadmissible and the play was allowed only in a version in which Lear and Cordelia remain alive, with the good king triumphing over his evil children. In *Hamlet* the graveyard scenes were omitted because no bearer of a religious office was allowed to appear on stage. *The Merchant of Venice* was banned in 1822 as Christian-Jewish animosity was considered too delicate a subject; presumably the Jewish community's protest, mentioned above, was taken into account. When *Merchant* was finally allowed in 1827 a great deal was omitted.[26]

As to contemporary foreign dramas, Victor Hugo's romantic plays, among others, were viewed very suspiciously by Austrian censors. His *Hernani* (in German, Die Milde der Majestät) was banned because the king behaved very dishonorably in things amorous and provoked a conspiracy. Hugo's *Angelo, Podesta von Padua* (Angelo, Tyrant of Padova) was banned because it was considered a mere series of atrocities; in addition, the play featured the character of a confidant of the reigning Signoria who abuses his position.

The censorship of an Austrian historical drama may be studied in detail by the example of Grillparzer's *König Ottokars Glück und Ende* (King Ottokar's Fortune and Fall). Another play on the conflict between Ottokar and Rudolph by August Kotzebue had encountered difficulties with the Vienna censors because it included some clerical figures. It was finally performed in 1815, but the title *Rudolph von Habsburg und König Ottokar von Böhmen* had to be changed to *Ottokars Tod* so that the overt allusion to the imperial house was avoided. Grillparzer's play is set in the thirteenth century. The Bohemian king Ottokar's military success fosters his hubris. He divorces his wife, Margaretha of Austria, marries the young daughter of the king of Hungary and claims the crown of the Holy Roman Empire. But the electorate prefers Rudolf of Habsburg, the incarnation of the rightful sovereign. Ottokar wages war against Austria but is defeated, his wife deceives him, and finally he is killed by a member of a family that he has wronged. In 1823 the play's manuscript was submitted by Schreyvogel to the police for production at the Burgtheater. Count Josef Sedlnitzky, the president of the police censorship office, decided that the play was inadmissible and pointed to two major flaws, first that the king's fall appeared as a consequence of his ambition and neglect of the law when divorcing Margaretha, and secondly that the plot might evoke parallels with Napoleon and his recent divorce. In fact, reviewers of the play did draw this parallel. Thus, in 1825 Josef Sigismund Ebersberg wrote in the journal *Der Sammler* that Ottokar's success and fall were depicted in such a way that readers and audience must necessarily be reminded of "a conqueror and usurper of recent times," adding that these reminiscences were "too fresh not to be automatically revived." Ebersberg also wrote that the representation of discord between nations of the monarchy, notably between Bohemians and Austrians, was not suitable for a Viennese stage. The state chancellery, involved in censorship if political issues were at stake, decided that the play was liable to produce a "bad impression" on Austrian stages. In spite of interventions on Grillparzer's behalf by court chamberlain Count Johann Rudolf Czernin and the director of the court theaters Count Moriz Dietrichstein and an appeal by the author, the play remained banned. Only publication in print was granted, after some delay. Emperor Francis took a personal interest in the play and asked his personal physician and state councillor, Friedrich Freiherr von

Stifft, to write a report on the drama. Stifft argued against the censors and concluded that the play was more antidote than poison. In particular, he highlighted the figure of Rudolf, the model of a wise monarch who reigns for the best of his peoples. In Stifft's opinion, only a liberal could find the play offensive. It was the empress who finally convinced her husband that the play should be admitted. In a rather singular procedure, censorship was overruled from "above," and more than a year after it had been submitted, *Ottokar*'s performance was finally allowed. But still passages had to be cut or rewritten, with especially almost all mentions of Austrians and Bohemians fighting each other deleted.

About a month after the February 1825 Burgtheater opening, which proved a big success, another Viennese theater, the Theater an der Wien, followed with its own production of *Ottokar*. The manuscript submitted for this production had to run through the censorship again and has been preserved; thus the alterations can be documented in detail. A total of 125 passages were changed. In accordance with Hägelin's memorandum three categories of censorial interventions can be distinguished, involving religious, moral, and political questions. Since the clergy could not appear or be mentioned on the stage, the chancellor of the archbishop of Mainz appears as a subordinate "delegate" from Mainz, and an allusion to the Pope's power over worldly sovereigns was deleted. As concerns morals, words like *Kuppler* (which can be translated as either matchmaker or procurer), applied to the father of Berta, the bride rejected by Ottokar, were omitted and allusions to Ottokar's moral blemish when dismissing his wife and turning to Berta attenuated. References to the "child-bearing womb" of the queen were expurgated as well as the phrase "no man should ever touch her little finger after the death of her first husband." Furthermore, the king's vassal Zawisch's lascivious thoughts about the future queen, his flirtation with her and references to her infidelity to Ottokar were censored. But most interventions related to political matters. Words like *scoundrel*, applied to noblemen, were deleted, and the well-known name Rosenberg was changed to Rosenburg. As to the characterization of nationalities, the remark that the Hungarians were weak and no longer a threat to peace was deleted. The king was not allowed to attack (on the stage) his own people, the "old Bohemians," whom he thinks too conservative and not interested in innovation, and the Bavarians were not to be called untrustworthy allies. When Ottokar learns that Vienna has surrendered to Rudolf he exclaims, "Damned! O Viennese! You fickle people!" (Verdammt! O Wiener! Leichtbeweglich Volk!). The censor changed this to "O Vienna! This I owe to you!" (O Wien! Das dank ich dir!).

When Ottokar's chancellor warns his master, "The lands are malcontent, Prepared to upsurge and to mutiny" (Die Lande sind nun einmal mißvergnügt, Bereit zu Aufstand und zu Meuterei), the allusion to an imminent insurrection was cut. Emperor Rudolf was not to behave too informally on the stage, for instance by addressing a little girl colloquially as "toad" (Kröte). Rudolf confesses that, prior to his nomination as emperor, he had been as ambitious as Ottokar, fighting every country whatsoever for the sake of conquering: "I was not content with the limits/ Which Empire and Church too timidly set/ To courage and the room it demands" (Doch murrt' ich innerlich ob jener Schranken/ Die Reich und Kirche allzu Ängstlich setzen/ Dem raschen Mut, der größern Spielraums wert). This confession was deleted as well as his too-martial words before the battle against Ottokar, in which he imagines the Austrian flag drawing a line through bloody corpses, and chooses as a battle song "Maria, pure maid." All sorts of invectives against kings were deleted: Berta, the rejected bride, throwing a lump of earth on her abusive father, the "vile and evil man" (den argen, bösen Mann); Ottokar's second wife Kunigunde calling her husband a coward and comparing him to a mule that roars if it sees a wolf approaching but no longer resists when the wolf comes close; the revengeful Rosenbergs who think of "stepping on the king's foot"; or Ottokar cursing the emperor, "Vivat Rudolphus? To hell with him!" (In der Hölle leb er!) Finally, Ottokar is not allowed to inventory his possessions (Bohemia, Moravia, Styria) and his future acquisitions (Carinthia, Silesia, Hungary, Poland), perhaps because parallels with Napoleon's conquests might have arisen. Due to such changes the play was toned down, its realistic portrayals were attenuated, and its passions and vices assuaged to fit into a Biedermeier environment. Conflicts were softened, especially where the public might detect parallels with the contemporary situation. Clearly, in spite of Rudolf prevailing, the central issue of the play, the legitimacy of sovereigns, was a question of utmost delicacy.[27]

Grillparzer attracted the attention of censors with yet another drama, *Ein treuer Diener seines Herrn* (His Master's True Servant), a play about a tyrannical ruler who misuses his power. After the police had approved the play, which was performed with great success at the Burgtheater in 1828, Emperor Francis sought to buy the exclusive rights from Grillparzer so that the Burgtheater became sole proprietor of the drama and further circulation could be avoided. His idea was to treat Grillparzer, a true servant and state official, as considerately as possible and at the same time to withdraw the play from the public. Francis apparently wanted to particularly prevent presentations in Hungary. Grillparzer argued that copies of the play were already circulating and that a complete withdrawal of the play was therefore impossible. He denied the proposal and was assisted by the censorship office, so Francis dropped the plan. Grillparzer was frustrated by censorship to such a degree that he did not even try to publish some of his later dramas. Thus, openly political plays such as *Ein Bruderzwist in Habsburg* (A Fraternal Quarrel in Habsburg) and *Libussa* were not published until his death in 1872.[28]

Although political topics were excluded from the popular stages, extemporization and especially the insertion of additional stanzas in songs provided the opportunity for all sorts of allusions. Sometimes even intonation and accentuation could alter the meaning in an offensive way. In one of Nestroy's comedies, a song about the coming of a comet was left out. The refrain "Da wird einem halt Angst und bang, Die Welt steht auf kein Fall mehr lang" (So fear creeps up on one fast, This world cannot possibly last) was left out in the course of authorial "pre-censorship" since a stress on the first word of the last line ("*This* world") might have been interpreted as an allusion to present Austria under Metternich.[29] Nestroy exercised a sort of double bookkeeping, habitually marking suspicious phrases and providing alternative wordings for them. The revised text was submitted to the censor, but the original versions were copied into the manuscript used in rehearsals. Thus passages omitted in the "official" version could be smuggled into the performance, as there was always the chance that the supervising theater commissioner might not be attentive enough to realize that the spoken text deviated from his script.

The relation between the classes was a standard subject on the popular stage, leading to frequent censorship interventions in passages referring to the conflicts between rich and poor. Thus, in Nestroy's *Zu ebener Erde und im ersten Stock* (Ground Floor and First Floor), a play pitting a poor family on the ground floor with a rich family in the belle étage, the line, "If the rich would not invite other rich, but poor people, all would have enough to eat" (Wenn die reichen Leut' nit wieder reiche einladeten, sondern arme Leut' dann hätten alle g'nug z'fressen) was changed to "They should have invited *us*." (Uns hätt man einladen sollen).[30] In *The Talisman*, another Nestroy comedy, the hero searches for work and is invited by a beautiful girl to go into service with her brother. His answer, "An inner voice from above advises me not to bend to servitude" (Eine innere Stimme über mir rät mir, mich nicht der Knechtschaft zu beugen) was deleted because it might be interpreted as subversive. The reply, "Being a servant is not a bad job, you can advance to upper servant or even chief servant. A servant is well-off" (Ein Knecht ist ja nichts schlechts, mit der Zeit können's Oberknecht werden, oder sogar Hausknecht, oh so ein Knecht ist ein gemachter Herr) was deleted as well, since upstarts of humble origin might have been offended by this remark. Members of the upper classes and especially the aristocracy were not to even carry derogatory names on the stage; thus the censors changed the name of a certain Herr von Platt (plain) to Herr von Plitt.[31]

Opera was treated analogously to the theater by the censorship. Even in the days of the liberal regime of Emperor Joseph II, plays like Beaumarchais' *Les Noces de Figaro* could not be performed in Vienna because of its anti-aristocratic and "revolutionary" contents. The play, translated by Joseph Rautenstrauch in 1785, was approved for print but not for the stage. A play forbidden in German prose might still be, with luck, allowed as Italian opera, however. Lorenzo Daponte proved the right man to adapt the play so that it remained effective and yet avoided everything that "might offend good taste or public decency at a performance over which the Sovereign Majesty might preside."[32] Daponte particularly cut Figaro's highly ideological monologue in scene V of *Les Noces de Figaro* and concentrated on the private aspect highlighted in the aria "Aprite un po' quegl'occhi." Another opera that displeased the censors was Beethoven's *Fidelio*. Although the plot was located in "a Spanish state prison, some miles from Seville, in the eighteenth century," some "gross" passages had to be deleted in the first version of the libretto, so that the opening night in 1805 was delayed for two-and-a-half months.[33]

During the Restoration era, Weber's *Der Freischütz*, first performed in Austria in the Kärntnertortheater in 1821, was severely molested by the censors. Emperor Francis would not allow any shooting of bullets on the stage, so the Wolf Glen's scene was placed in a hollow oak tree, with Max and Kaspar fashioning "magic arrows" to be fired by a crossbow instead of magic bullets. Moreover, since maintaining a dichotomy between stage and reality was very important for the censors, references to contemporary and geographically nearby realities were considered dangerous, so the censors rejected setting *Freischütz* in Bohemia and relegated the plot to the Middle Ages. The changing of titles and settings was a very widespread practice that was viewed as an easy way of preventing parallels with contemporary situations. Thus Giacomo Meyerbeer's *Les Huguenots* was re-baptized *The Ghibellines of Pisa* and, as the new title indicates, set in a completely alien milieu. The religious conflict between Catholics and Protestants was unquestionably political dynamite, but the adaptation led to the singing of Protestant chorals long before the times of Luther. Schubert also had to cope with the censors' resistance to some of his operas.

*Fierabras,* based on a libretto by Joseph Kupelwieser, passed censorship in 1823 only after deletions regarding allusions to particular nations (Spain, France). In the case of *Die Verschworenen* (The Conspirators), to which Ignaz Franz Castelli had provided the text, the title was changed to *Der häusliche Krieg* (The Domestic War) in 1823 in order to avoid political implications. Another Schubert opera, *Der Graf von Gleichen,* based on a libretto by Eduard von Bauernfeld, was banned altogether in 1826 for it referred to the bigamy of a nobleman, although Schubert had already composed much of the music.[34]

## Theater Censorship during Neoabsolutism and the Constitutional Era (1849–1918)

In the two years immediately following the revolution of 1848, which abolished censorship, theater producers had a relatively free hand. Thus in a Burgtheater production of *Julius Caesar,* director Heinrich Laube represented a responsible middle class suggestive of the liberals who had been at the heart of the recent revolution, and in *Coriolanus* conflict between the aristocratic and democratic elements was given due attention. Productions like these would never have passed the previous censorship. But liberty did not last long. A 1850 theater decree (Theaterordnung) reintroduced strict regulations that defined the outlines of censorship until the end of the monarchy. The motives of intervention remained the same as before 1848: Hägelin's 1794 memorandum still seemed to serve as a guide for the censors, who once more had to approve every production in advance. In fact the new code was a synthesis of the various regulations passed during the Vormärz (pre-1848 era). The only major change concerned the authority charged with the supervision of plays: henceforth the governor (Statthalter) of each province was responsible for censorship decisions. Usually he appointed an official as censor, but he could also establish an advisory board of acknowledged experts to help make decisions adequate from an artistic point of view. In Vienna such a board existed between 1854 and 1881, when it was dismissed and censorship reverted to the police. The 1850 theater code was applied in all Austrian provinces: thus, even despite the autonomy granted to the northeastern Polish-dominated province of Galicia in 1867, censorship was enforced in accordance with the rules passed in Vienna. The police censored plays before the governor (in the capital) or the mayor (in smaller towns) decided if a performance would be allowed.[35]

Overall, after 1848 fewer plays were completely prohibited than in the Vormärz, but cuts and changes were still on the daily agenda. During the Neoabsolutist period under Prime Minister Alexander Freiherr von Bach (1849–59) censorship was at least as severe as in the Vormärz, but in the last decades of the nineteenth century and after the turn of the nineteenth century timid steps toward censorship liberalization were evident. A first step in this direction was an 1868 decree, but soon censorship became a focus of disagreement between the newly established political parties. Only Liberals and Social-Democrats favored its total abolition, while conservative politicians and the clergy regarded censorship as a proper means of maintaining public order. The theater became an especially disputed subject during the so-called *Kulturkampf*, the fight for supremacy in religious questions, as conservatives demanded strict censorship to fight anticlerical plays defended by Liberals. Moreover, the social question became increasingly salient as modernization of economic structures, industrialization, pauperization of workers and artisans, and social unrest with strikes and demonstrations seized the country, igniting fears of revolutionary and anarchist actions among the government and general population. Class confrontation among the aristocracy, bourgeoisie, and the rising proletariat was the main political issue of the 1880s and 1890s, while new literary movements such as naturalism introduced political and social questions in a radical manner on the stage, furthering, in the view of conservatives, pessimism and hatred among the classes. After the Liberals came to power, censorship practices were finally relaxed as criticism of the theater censorship increased, leading to public protest meetings and hearings by an extra-parliamentary Theaterzensurkommission (theater censorship commission) in 1897, comprising left and liberal politicians, journalists, artists, and theater directors, who unsuccessfully sought to abolish all special regulations of the theater in favor of reliance upon common law. In 1903 prime minister Ernest von Koerber decreed that henceforth no issue should be banned from the stage on principle, and that in particular the discussion of political and social questions should generally be allowed. Furthermore, a board of competent theater censorship advisors was reinstalled and given an authoritative voice. Nonetheless, in 1914 the Austrian parliament officially called for including among the censors those "of a psychological and literary education" in hopes of avoiding censorship absurdities, as well as a general end to theater censorship except when there were strong grounds to believe that a performance might lead to a breach of the peace or render the author subject to criminal proceedings.[36]

In the immediate aftermath of 1848, as before, Burgtheater productions were commissioned and adapted by the First Court Chamberlain (Obersthofkämmerer) and the artistic director, and the motives for interventions by censors were also as in previous times. In an 1850 performance of Schiller's *Die Räuber,* remarks against Austria were deleted. When Spiegelberg utters "It is a pity that you are not a general, you would have chased the Austrians through a button-hole," the text was changed to "you would have chased the Turks through a button-hole."[37] Topical political questions were avoided, with even allusions to the precarious nature of state finances or the bad quality of cigars forbidden. In 1855 Burgtheater director Laube tried to stage *King John* in order to protest against the recent Konkordat between Austria and the Catholic Church, which secured the latter's control of the educational system, but his plan to depict the conflict between the English monarchy and the Holy See was barred. *Richard III* was not welcome either, because censorship feared that the play might arouse unsympathetic feelings toward high-born persons. In 1863 Laube's production of *Richard II* showed traces of (self-)censorship: "The dethronement of a rightful monarch was a subject of which no imperial censor could approve and the drama was held back until Laube produced a version which invented a party loyal to the King and the King was made to appear a victim of his environment rather than a foolish ruler."[38]

Censorship of Burgtheater productions was transferred to the ministry of foreign affairs in 1867. Higher officials Freiherr Leopold von Hofmann and his successor Freiherr Josef von Bezeczny were charged with the responsibility. In 1898 Hofrat Emil Jettel von Etternach, head of the Literary Bureau in the ministry, was appointed as responsible for the repertory of the Burgtheater. Officially he was considered a counsellor who should help avoid "scandal" and avert drama productions liable to displease the public. As Jettel admitted, his wife was sometimes involved in his decisions, as in the rejection of a French comedy by Decaillavet and Flers. Jettel had a delicate literary taste, abhorring the rude style and "nudities" of naturalism, including the mention of underwear. The Literary Bureau was supervised by the general management of the Burgtheater, so Jettel had to take into account not only the opinions of his wife but also that of Freiherr Plappart von Leenheer. Plappart was much more severe than Jettel, who mostly agreed with director Paul Schlenther, coming from the milieu of German naturalism. And still, quite naturally in the court theater, the opinion of the majesties was ultima ratio, as in the case of Gerhart Hauptmann's *Rose Bernd,* which had to be abandoned since archduchess Marie Valerie disliked the play and ostentatiously left one of its performances.

In 1909 Archduke Francis Ferdinand protested against the production of Richard Strauß's opera *Salome*, assisted by Marie Valerie. It is little wonder that the duchess was nick-named "court croaker" (*Hof-Unke*).[39]

Popular drama was still at least as severely censored as productions of classics. Thus, in Carl Haffner's 1861 comedy *Die Studenten von Rummelstadt* (The Students of Rummelstadt), about the legitimate heir of a castle who acts as a reformer of the local administration, criticism of state officials was deleted. When the students declare the heir to be a "monarch of the new times" (Fürst der neuen Zeit), this "revolutionary" scene was struck. In another play, *Localsängerin und Postillion* (1865), the remark that "Hungarians begin to dance to the Austrian music" (daß die Ungarn anfangen zu tanzen nach österreichischer Weise), an allusion to the Austro-Hungarian conflict leading to the 1867 compromise (*Ausgleich*), was considered disturbing. In the same play a song that accused the press of flattering government and of corruption was deleted. Nestroy, who had become a patriot, remained a rock of offence. In his late play *Häuptling Abendwind*, he attacked Austria's enemies and in reference to the French occupation of parts of Austrian-controlled Italy and the unwillingness of Prussia to aid Austria on acceptable conditions, he extemporized about Prussian officers kissing the hands of French Emperor Napoleon III. One day after being fined by the police for this improvisation, in Offenbach's *Orpheus in der Unterwelt,* Nestroy alluded to the self-coronation of Prussian King Wilhelm I. When Mercury tries to put the crown on Jupiter's head, he remarked: "I will put it on by myself." A new fine for the actor resulted after the police supposedly responded to Prussian protests.[40]

After 1850 censors were obsessed by the fear that the theater tried to incite "the poor against the rich, the servant against his master, the uneducated against the educated, and that contempt, hatred and feelings of revenge towards persons holding a favorable position in society should be implanted into the lower-classes."[41] A play such as *Der Reichtum des Arbeiters* (The Working-Man's Wealth) by Ida Schuselka-Brüning was banned because it hailed honesty, contentedness, and jollity as the specific virtues of a poor working-man's family. In the 1870s productions of *Vater Brahm,* a proletarian play by Hippolyt Schaufert, and of Ernst Wichert's *Die Fabrik zu Niederbronn* (The Mill at Niederbronn) were prohibited because the police interpreted them as glorifying workers as martyrs oppressed by the force of capital, represented by bad masters and their bosses. The fear of revolutionary class-based agitation on the stage intensified around the turn of the century. Gerhart Hauptmann's *Die Weber* (The Weavers), a play earlier banned in Berlin, Paris, Russia, and even New York, was prohibited in Austria between 1894 and 1904. The police considered it void of all higher sentiments, depicting figures directed by animal instincts and degenerated by hardship and toil. In the censors' view, the working-class rebellion depicted in the play developed almost according to natural laws as a consequence of poor living conditions. In short, naturalist drama was too true to reality and nature to be acceptable. Censors were afraid that *Die Weber* might incite working-class anger against manufacturers and lead to protests. In fact, after workers' unions organized demonstrations in Budapest, the play was soon banned there as well. After the 1903 censorship reform, the play was approved in Vienna. The advisory board argued that the play no longer threatened to stimulate agitation, since the socialist party had in the meantime become a force of reform rather than of revolution. But still the text had to be changed: manufacturers were not to be attacked in general, but only as individuals called by their surnames, as "the Dreißigers" or "the Dietrichs."[42]

Nationalist propaganda and supposed attacks on foreign states were another motive for censorship after 1850, with censorship decisions in such areas related to the overall political and diplomatic climate and to local situations. In Galicia, for instance, with a slight Polish majority and large Ukrainian minority, nationality issues were critical and the censors were sensitive to plays dealing with relations between the two ethnic groups. Visions of revenge for injustice done to the Polish nation, for instance the bloody Austrian suppression of the insurrection in Galicia in 1846 (considerably aided by Ukrainian peasant massacres of their Polish landlords), were especially considered offensive. On the whole, however, theater censorship was relatively liberal in Galicia, the Austrian portion of formerly independent Poland, compared with the zones ruled by Russia and Prussia. Thus the Romantic tragedies by Juliusz Słowacki (*Mazepa, Mary Stuart, Beatrix Cenci*) were first staged in Lwow and Krakow in the Austrian partition, some time before their production was permitted in Warsaw. However, in the 1860s, when Russian Poland revolted against the czar, Polish patriotic plays were treated rather severely and dramas like *Die Belagerung von Warschau* (The Siege of Warsaw) by L. A. Smuszewski were prohibited. Around the turn of the century, when relations between Austria and Germany were friendly, plays that could be interpreted as an attack on the Germans like *Gefangen* (Captive) by L. Rydel were prohibited.[43]

The application of censorship varied considerably with the intensity of nationalist feeling in the different provinces. For instance, irredentism loomed large in Trieste, capital of Küstenland province and dominating the one remaining region with an Italian majority. The repertoire of Trieste theaters consisted primarily of Italian plays, leading often to nationalist manifestations, so Austrian censorship was on the alert and representations apt to excite nationalist feelings were prohibited or strictly controlled by the police. Thus, in 1864, when *Il vero blasone* (Real Aristocracy), a comedy by Gherardi del Testa, which ridiculed the conservative pro-Habsburg party in Tuscany and praised partisans of the Italian government, was presented in Trieste, the censors deleted many "patriotic" phrases such as "amar il proprio paese, desiderarlo libero e grande, chiamate idee esaltate" (to love your own country, to want it to be free and great, ideas called eccentric). As often in cases of politically suspect plays, the setting was removed to a fairyland, and the censors inserted "patria" instead of "Italia" and "Kora" instead of "Venezia." They also sought to ensure that no symbols of irredentism like the tricolore, the Italian star, the marguerite or certain names, words and songs were included in theatrical productions. Thus, in 1878, in the comedy *Le due dame* (The Two Ladies) by Ferrari, the line "Margherita is the most beautiful of our flowers" was rejected after it provoked frenetic applause. After the line was cut, the audience still acclaimed the entrance of the character, so the police prohibited the play. In 1878, after a representation of the patriotic ballet *Ettore Fieramosca* by Pogna, the conductor and his musicians were banned from the city because they had performed parts of the nationalist hymn *Marcia reale*. Between 1888 and 1903 Verdi's *Ernani* was prohibited in Trieste after a presentation triggered vehement manifestations (and counter-manifestations by a group of hired supporters of the monarchy), despite the stationing of twenty police officers in the audience. The scene of these events, the Politeama Rossetti, lost its theater license. Another example of a prohibited piece was D'Annunzio's *La nave* (The Ship), forbidden in 1909. Not only Italian nationalism but also supposed abuse of Slavic nationalist pride sparked manifestations, as during a 1907 Trieste performance of Léhar's *Die lustige Witwe* (The Jolly Widow).[44]

The rise of nationalist theater and opera among the Empire's minorities was accompanied by a permanent fight against censorship. The libretto of Verdi's *Rigoletto*, adapted from Victor Hugo's *Le roi s'amuse*, had to be changed before its 1851 premiere in Venice. The setting was changed from the France of François I to the fictive Duchy of Mantua to attenuate the attacks on the morals of a king. Due to censorship pressures, few Czech operas or plays could depict the oppression of the Slav population or appeal to Czech nationalism and even terms referring to "Czech lords" or "Czech kings" were forbidden along with virtually any portrayals of Czech resistance to Habsburg rule or to the Catholic Church. Hussitism, one of the subjects very often used to incite feelings of national unity and tradition, "did not appear on the Czech stage at all for the first two thirds of the nineteenth century, except for a brief period in 1848–50," according to Czech opera historian John Tyrrell. Thus, the play *Jan Hus, Death of Ziska* could only be presented after 1860. Karel Bendl's opera *The Montenegrins* could not be performed in Prague until 1881, since the subject of the Turks' treatment of the Montenegrins was considered too sensitive with regard to nationalist conflicts, no doubt especially since the topic could be interpreted as analogous to Austrian treatment of the Czechs. In Prague, the post-1850 campaign to build a Czech national theater became a major nationalist rallying movement, "a substitute for [forbidden] political activity," in the words of historian Stanley Kimball. The laying of the theater's foundation stone in May 1868 was characterized by one observer as the "greatest national celebration the Czechs, up to that time, had ever experienced" (when the theater burned down in 1881, before it was completely finished, it was regarded as a national tragedy, and a renewed fundraising campaign was massively successful, leading to the complete rebuilding and reopening of the theater by 1883).[45]

In Hungary, as historian Alice Freifeld has written, the theater "as linguistic battlefield was already a fixed motif" in Hungarian nationalism before 1848, as in 1819, when, in response to the line "Long live freedom," declaimed during the play *The Tatars in Hungary* (presented in Pest in Hungarian), the crowd spontaneously roared, "Long live Hungarian freedom!" Especially after the founding of a national Hungarian theater in Pest in 1837, the stage, in Freifeld's words, became a "central venue of patriotic activity," critical to "galvanizing the nation" and igniting "the oppositional cultural politics of the Metternichean period." During the post-1848 Neoabsolutist period, references to religious, national, or political issues were strictly forbidden on the Hungarian stage, for fear of nationalist demonstrations, such as those that erupted in 1850 when the imperial hymn played in honor of the new emperor Francis Joseph's birthday was disrupted by screeching, whistling, and banging in the Pest Hungarian Theater, bringing the orchestra to a halt three times and culminating in the arrest of seventeen Hungarian nationalists and the beating of many others, three of whom were seriously injured. Banned Hungarian playwrights were widely viewed as martyrs, and the funerals of famous actors and dramatists became the focus of mass nationalist demonstrations, as in 1858, when twenty thousand attended the funeral procession of matinee idol Márton Lendvay, a veteran of the 1848 Hungarian uprising against the Habsburgs. Lendvay's statue was soon placed on the square in front of the

National Theater, which, at a time when public assemblies were banned, had become "the new gathering ground" and "a stage for new democratic feelings." Even after the 1867 *Ausgleich* gave Hungary substantial internal autonomy, the Hungarian national music drama, Ferenc Erkel's *Brankovics György*, first performed in 1874 in Budapest, incurred difficulties with the authorities and was withdrawn from the repertoire after two years.[46]

Nationalist spectators had to be cautious, as too frenetic applause easily led to arrests. Thus, in 1867 during a representation of the opera *Tutti in maschera* in Zara/Zadar (Dalmatia), the police noted extraordinary applause after the aria "Viva Italia, terra del canto" and the alleged instigators (a bookseller, a shop assistant, and a journeyman tailor) were arrested, although the motive for the "manifestation" was quite unclear. Some suspected that the applause referred to the recent introduction of Croatian in the schools. Sometimes spectators were "incarcerated" without having given offence at all. Thus, after some fireworks had been detonated in previous representations, Venice police, as a precaution, closed the boxes and released the occupants only after the performance. In an 1862 presentation of the comedy *Sand in die Augen* (Sand in the Eyes) in Pest, the audience applauded when, in the enumeration of prominent persons portrayed in an album, the name Victor Emanuel appeared. Reportedly, the applause for the recently nominated king of Italy lasted only four seconds and was therefore not considered particularly dangerous, but the existing album names were replaced by those of contemporary artists.[47]

Around 1900 and in the tense pre–World War I years Viennese theater censors increasingly reflected the state of diplomatic relations with foreign countries in their decisions. *Helene* (1896), by H. R. Savage, portrays a female anarchist who crosses the Russian border disguised as the wife of an American officer, in order to plot against the government. Undoubtedly the censors were alarmed by the character's anarchist activities, but they banned the drama because they viewed it as insulting Russian society and particularly the Russian state police, who were duped. Another play in a similar vein, P. Angel's *Das heilige Rußland* (Sacred Russia, 1907), depicting revolutionary activities against a stubborn and corrupt upper class, was also prohibited out of respect for a friendly empire. In general the Russian revolution of 1905 provided a strong motive for striking theatrical allusions to national insurgencies. Mentions of Balkan conflicts, as in George Bernard Shaw's *Heroes*, a caricature of military "heroes" in the war between Serbia and Bulgaria of 1885, aroused similar concern, and passages openly alluding to Austria or Serbia and their respective officers and armies were therefore deleted.[48]

Attacks against kings were still prohibited at the turn of the century, even if they appeared as sovereigns of fairy kingdoms. Rudolf Lothar's *König Harlekin* (King Harlequin, 1900) presents a harlequin disguised as the king of a fictive empire, who plays his part so well that his subjects do not realize the fraud. Police considered the play an attack on the system of monarchy and required changes so that no parallel with any recognizable country could possibly be drawn. At the Burgtheater the conventions of a court theater naturally had to be respected, but outstanding conflicts were scarce, mainly because the repertory was thoroughly discussed within the house. Productions of Ibsen's *Ghosts* and *The Wild Duck* were prohibited in 1889, however, and in 1899 Arthur Schnitzler's *Der grüne Kakadu* (The Green Cockatoo) was banned after a few nights because the play, set in revolutionary Paris, alluded too openly to the decadent society of fin de siècle Vienna. The play is set on the day of the occupation of the Bastille in a Parisian gin shop visited by criminals and revolutionaries. The host, a former theater director, and his troupe perform a revolution. The aristocratic public enjoys the decadent milieu and the theatrical performance until the play suddenly becomes real and the murder of a duke signals a revolutionary riot. Some openly anti-Semitic plays were also forbidden around the turn of the century. In 1912 Schnitzler's *Professor Bernhardi* was banned from the Deutsches Volkstheater. The play focuses on the anti-Semitism current in Austrian public life by depicting rivalries in a hospital headed by Professor Bernhardi, a Jewish physician who bars a priest from administering last rites to a dying woman to preserve her illusion that she will live. This decision creates a scandal, outraging the Christian population, and Bernhardi is punished for disturbing the free practice of religion. However, Bernhardi is celebrated as a martyr by the liberal press and public opinion ultimately turns in his favor. The play thus portrays both anti-Semitism and anti-clericalism; the police, fearing it would incite demonstrations, banned it. The minister of interior affairs, in answer to an appeal, added that the play depicted Austrian public institutions in a false and pejorative manner and presented the political parties as involved in permanent quarrel.[49]

After World War I the former Habsburg Empire was reduced to a small state of some six million inhabitants, the "Republik Deutschösterreich" (Republic of German Austria). The new Republican spirit found symbolic expression in the abandonment of censorship in a 1918 legislative decree that was later confirmed by the 1920 constitution. The practice of censorship was, however, far from over, as the long tradition of control of every public utterance could not be swept away with a simple stroke of the pen.

In the early years of the republic, even lawyers were uncertain whether the abandonment of censorship related only to the press or to theater and film also. Thus, the theater advisory board remained in place and the 1850 decree was applied until 1926. After a few years of freedom, censorship was reintroduced by the authoritarian Christian-Social Party government in 1934. After the 1938 *Anschluss* Nazi censorship was applied in Austria, and in the post–World War II decade occupying Allied forces controlled the media, including theater. Austrian theater censorship was finally abolished only in 1955.[50]

## Conclusion

Undoubtedly censorship had a negative influence on the development of Austrian theater. From the days of Emperor Francis, who did not permit a single new theater, the number of stages in Vienna remained the same until the 1860s and even, after some fluctuations, until 1893. During this period there were only five theaters in Vienna, the two court theaters (Burgtheater, Theater am Kärntnertor) within the city walls and three private and popular stages (Theater an der Wien, Theater in der Leopoldstadt, Theater in der Josefstadt) in the suburbs. Whereas Vienna's population increased considerably after the 1820s, mainly due to migration from the country, seating capacity in the theaters did not increase.[51] In spite of programmatic avowals about the necessity of public entertainment ("circuses"), the theater did not flourish because of the restrictive policy of licensing, which may be interpreted as a measure of censorship. The interest of the public in theatergoing seems to have diminished during the Biedermeier and Vormärz eras, and it is very likely that severe censorship was a reason for this, since it made theatergoing less attractive.

The overall effect of Austrian censorship in the first half of the nineteenth century was "a prescribed escapism from problems which the authorities did not want to see solved."[52] Political and social problems and conflicts were denied and delayed. The message to the citizens, deductible from the theater regulations, may be formulated as: stay where you belong, that is, in the social class you were born into, be content with the world you live in, do not criticize or try to change anything; the world is a desexualized, infantile dollhouse; there is nothing to be afraid of as long as the legitimate emperor reigns for your best interest and that of the public. It is hard to tell whether censorship really helped to preserve the monarchy, as censorship seems rather a symptom of the situation than the cause.

The Austrian bourgeoisie, elsewhere the pivot of change and reform, was overwhelmingly ready to compromise with the regime, content with relative freedom for economic enterprise and expectations of ennoblement. Most state officials grew up with the myth of the "good" and liberal monarch that harkened back to the days of Joseph II. Most Austrian bourgeois were afraid of changing the system, as such, in their view, threatened to ignite a reign of the lower classes. Even authors like Grillparzer, who had much trouble with the censors, never supported radical reform.

## Bibliographical Essay

Two good English-language histories of the nineteenth-century Habsburg Empire are C. A. Macartney, *The Habsburg Empire, 1790–1918* (New York, 1969), an extraordinary work of scholarship, although somewhat intimidating at almost nine hundred pages; and the much shorter Alan Sked, *The Decline and Fall of the Habsburg Empire, 1815–1918* (New York, 1989). There are no comprehensive histories of either the theater or censorship in the Empire. The best overview of Viennese theater history is W. E. Yates, *Theater in Vienna: A Critical History, 1776–1996* (Cambridge, 1996), which includes a chapter on censorship. In a recent article ("Two Hundred Years of Political Theater in Vienna," *German Life & Letters* 58 (2005): 129–40) Yates argues that the Viennese theater was never only shallow amusement, but subliminally political, and introduces censorship as an important factor leading to this situation. The best introduction to censorship in the first half of the nineteenth century is Julius Marx, *Die österreichische Zensur im Vormärz* (Vienna, 1959), but the focus is on book censorship. Still invaluable are the works of Carl Glossy, who mainly exploited (or simply copied) police archival material, most of which burnt during the 1927 fire in the Justizpalast. Glossy collected an immense amount of material written by theater censorship officials: "Zur Geschichte der Wiener Theatercensur," *Jahrbuch der Grillparzer-Gesellschaft* 7 (1897): 238–340; "Zur Geschichte der Theater Wiens, I (1801 bis 1820)," *Jahrbuch der Grillparzer-Gesellschaft* 25 (1915): 1–334; "Zur Geschichte der Theater Wiens, II (1821 bis 1830)," *Jahrbuch der Grillparzer-Gesellschaft* 26 (1920): 1–155; "Zur Geschichte der Theater Wiens, III (1831 bis 1840)," *Jahrbuch der Grillparzer-Gesellschaft* 30 (1931): 1–152. He also published several case studies including questions of censorship: "Zur Geschichte des Trauerspieles *König Ottokars Glück und Ende*," *Jahrbuch der Grillparzer-Gesellschaft* 9 (1899): 213–47; *Vierzig Jahre Deutsches Volks-*

*theater: Ein Beitrag zur deutschen Theatergeschichte* (Vienna, 1929); and a short article on the situation after the introduction of the 1850 Theaterordnung, "Theaterzensur," *Österreichische Rundschau* 58 (1919): 228–32.

Other German case studies include Jakob Zeidler, "Ein Censurexemplar von Grillparzer's *König Ottokars Glück und Ende*," *Ein Wiener Stammbuch* 9 (1898): 287–311, which analyzes in detail a censored version of Grillparzer's play; Christian Grawe, "Grillparzers Dramatik als Problem der zeitgenössischen österreichischen Theaterzensur," August Obermayer, ed., *Was nützt der Glaube ohne Werke: Studien zu Franz Grillparzer anläßlich seines 200. Geburtstages* (Dunedin, NZ, 1992), 162–90, who places Grillparzer's troubles with the censors in the context of general Austrian censorship; Franz Hadamowsky, *Schiller auf der Wiener Bühne 1783–1959* (Vienna, 1959), and Theo Modes, *Die Urfassung und einteiligen Bühnenbearbeitungen von Schillers Wallenstein* (Leipzig, 1931), who refers to the cuts in Schiller's play. Three English case studies, often concerning religious and moral, rather than political, censorship are Michael Jones, "Censorship as an Obstacle to the Production of Shakespeare on the Stage of the Burgtheater in the Nineteenth Century," *German Life & Letters* 27 (1973/74): 187–94; Gilbert Carr, "Corridors of Power and Whispered Plots: The Banning of Otto Stoessl's and Robert Scheu's *Waare* in 1897–1898," in W. E. Yates, ed., *From Perinet to Jelinek: Viennese Theater in Political and Intellectual Context* (Oxford, 2007), 127–41; and Colin Walker, "Zacharias Werner's *Die Mutter der Makkabäer* and Biblical Drama in Vienna," *Forum for Modern Language Studies* 18 (1982): 23–38.

Johann Hüttner, "Vor- und Selbstzensur bei Johann Nestroy," *Maske und Kothurn* 26 (1980): 234–48, a leading expert on Nestroy, and Helmut Herles, "Nestroy und die Zensur," Jürgen Hein, ed., *Theater und Gesellschaft: Das Volksstück im 19. und 20. Jahrhundert* (Düsseldorf, 1973), 121–32, dedicate their studies to Nestroy's main reaction to censorship, namely (feigned) self-censorship, which was reversed on the stage via extemporization. Hüttner has published an expanded English version, "Theater Censorship in Metternich's Vienna," *Theater Quarterly* 10 (1980): 61–69. English studies on Nestroy include W. E. Yates, *Nestroy* (Cambridge, 1972), John McKenzie, "Nestroy's Political Plays," in W. E. Yates, ed., *Viennese Popular Theater: A Symposium* (Exeter, 1985); and John McKenzie, "Political Satire in Nestroy's *Freiheit in Krähwinkel*," *Modern Language Review* 75 (1980): 322–32. Yates has also published *Grillparzer: A Critical Introduction* (Cambridge, 1972) on the great Austrian dramatist.

On music, Alice Hanson, *Musical Life in Biedermeier Vienna* (Cambridge, 1985), includes a chapter on "Musicians and the Austrian police," providing an overview of the observation of musicians and the censorship of the various musical genres. Ulrich Weisstein's essay, "Böse Menschen singen keine Arien: Prolegomena zu einer ungeschriebenen Geschichte der Opernzensur," in Peter Brockmeier, ed., *Zensur und Selbstzensur in der Literatur* (Würzburg, 1996), 49–73, raises fundamental questions of opera censorship, analyzes a lot of examples, and concludes that opera censorship acts according to the same principles as theater censorship. Michael Walter, *'Die Oper ist ein Irrenhaus': Sozialgeschichte der Oper im 19. Jahrhundert* (Stuttgart, 1997), has a chapter on "Zensur und Oper" that is internationally oriented (France, Italy, Germany, Austria), but the examples are mainly taken from Italy. Margret Dietrich, *Die Wiener Polizeiakten von 1854–1867 als Quelle für die Theatergeschichte des Österreichischen Kaiserstaates* (Graz, 1967), reproduces documents from the Viennese police archive concerning different matters related to the theater throughout the Hasbsburg monarchy, but censorship plays only a rather marginal role. Marcel Prawy, *The Vienna Opera* (Vienna, 1969), a masterful overview of the history of the Vienna opera, abounds in illustrations and gives some occasional hints on opera censorship. R. B. Moberly, *Three Mozart Operas: Figaro, Don Giovanni, The Magic Flute* (New York, 1967), contains some remarks on the censorship of the operas mentioned in the subtitle. On Schubert's problems with the censors, Elizabeth McKay, *Franz Schubert's Music for the Theater* (Tutzing, 1991), contains the most comprehensive analyses of the librettos he used, whereas Walter Obermaier's article "Schubert und die Zensur," Otto Brusatti, ed., *Schubert-Kongreß Wien 1978* (Graz, 1979), 117–25, is based on archive material.

For the second half of the nineteenth century, an article by Barbara Tumfart must be mentioned: "Vom 'Feldmarschall' zum 'Eroberer': Über den Einfluß der österreichischen Theaterzensur auf den Spieltext in der zweiten Hälfte des 19. Jahrhunderts," *Internationales Archiv für Sozialgeschichte der deutschen Literatur* 30 (2005): 98–117, which analyzes censorship of plays in the 1850s and 1860s based on the archives of the Government of Lower Austria, which supervised Viennese theaters. Concerning the situation around the turn of the century, Djawid Borower, in his unpublished dissertation, *Theater und Politik: Die Wiener Theaterzensur im politischen und sozialen Kontext der Jahre 1893 bis 1914* (Vienna, 1988), has collected information about a great number of censored plays, mainly from the contemporary press, highlighting the ideological conflicts around the theater and censorship. The only case studies on this period are Werner Schnabels "*Professor Bernhardi* und die Wiener Zensur. Zur Rezeptionsgeschichte der Schnitzlerschen Komödie," *Jahrbuch der Deutschen Schillergesellschaft*

28 (1984): 349–83, and Hans Wagner, "Die Zensur am Burgtheater zur Zeit Direktor Schlenthers, 1898–1910," *Mitteilungen des Österreichischen Staatsarchivs* 14 (1961): 394–420, on censorship at the Burgtheater, based on material from the Haus-, Hof- und Staatsarchiv. The situation after 1918, especially the juridical quarrel about the abolition of theater censorship, is documented by Franz Dirnberger, "Theaterzensur im Zwielicht der Gesetze (1918–1926)," *Mitteilungen des Österreichischen Staatsarchivs* 36 (1983): 237–60.

Studies on the theater in the Austrian provinces are rare. The focus is on censorship in Mariola Szydłowska's *Cenzura Teatralna w Galicji: W Dobie autonomicznej, 1860–1918* (Censorship in Galicia at the Time of Autonomy) (Krakow, 1995), whereas Kazimierz Braun, *A Concise History of Polish Theater from the Eleventh to the Twentieth Centuries* (Lewiston, 1999); Oscar Teuber, *Geschichte des Prager Theaters: Von den Anfängen des Schauspielwesens bis auf die neueste Zeit. Zweiter Theil: Von der Brunian-Bergopzoom'schen Bühnen-Reform bis zum Tode Liebich's, des größten Prager Bühnenleiters (1771–1817)* (Prague, 1885); Wolfgang Binal, *Deutschsprachiges Theater in Budapest von den Anfängen bis zum Brand des Theaters in der Wollgasse (1889)* (Vienna, 1972); and the two studies by Jerzy Got, *Das österreichische Theater in Krakau im 18. und 19. Jahrhundert* (Vienna, 1984) and *Das österreichische Theater in Lemberg im 18. und 19. Jahrhundert* (Vienna, 1997) contain only a few remarks on censorship. There are similarly only scattered remarks on theater censorship in two recent outstanding studies focused on nineteenth-century Hungary, Robert Nemes, *The Once and Future Budapest* (Dekalb, IL, 1995), and Alice Freifeld, *Nationalism and the Crowd in Liberal Hungary, 1848–1914* (Baltimore, 2000). While material on censorship is limited, two important studies on the role of theater in the national revivals of Czechs and Hungarians are Stanley Kimball, *Czech Nationalism: A Study of the National Theater Movement, 1845–1883* (Urbana, IL, 1964) and Edith Mályusz, *The Theater and National Awakening* (Atlanta, 1980). Adriano Dugulin, "Der Irredentismus im Triestiner Theaterleben, 1878–1918," in Cornelia Szabó-Knotik, ed., *Wien—Triest um 1900. Zwei Städte—eine Kultur?* (Vienna, 1993), 37–61, is dedicated to the manifestations of Italian nationalism in Trieste theaters and provides some information on the reactions of the Austrian censorship.

Useful information about censorship of the opera in the second half of the nineteenth century can be found in Michael Walter's *'Die Oper ist ein Irrenhaus'* (see above), although it is not always clear *where* a certain opera was censored; the same applies to Philip Gossett, "Zensur und Selbstzensur: Probleme bei der Edition von Giuseppe Verdis Opern," in Stefan G. Harpner, ed., *Über Musiktheater* (Munich, 1992), 103–15. On the rise of national opera among the minorities, Jim Samson, "East Central Europe: the Struggle for National Identity," in Sampson, ed., *The Late Romantic Era: From the mid-nineteenth century to World War I* (London, 1991), 205–39, and John Tyrrell, *Czech Opera* (Cambridge, 1988), are paramount sources; remarks on censorship are quite rare, however, and it is not always clear if certain characteristics of the librettos are due to official censorship or self-censorship. John Neubauer, "Zrinyi, Zrinyy, Zrinski," *Nehelicon* 29 (2002): 219–34, discusses the rise of Croatian national opera.

## Notes

1. Carl Glossy, "Zur Geschichte der Wiener Theatercensur" *Jahrbuch der Grillparzer-Gesellschaft* 7 (1897): 238–340, 250.
2. Glossy, "Zur Geschichte der Wiener Theatercensur," 275.
3. Oscar Teuber, *Geschichte des Prager Theaters: Von den Anfängen des Schauspielwesens bis auf die neueste Zeit*, II: *Von der Brunian-Bergopzoom'schen Bühnen-Reform bis zum Tode Liebich's, des größten Prager Bühnenleiters (1771–1817)* (Prague, 1885), 15; Jerzy Got, *Das österreichische Theater in Lemberg im 18. und 19. Jahrhundert* (Vienna, 1997), 142–43.
4. Johann Hüttner, "Theater Censorship in Metternich's Vienna," *Theater Quarterly* 10 (1980): 61–69, 63.
5. Glossy, "Zur Geschichte der Wiener Theatercensur," 283. From 1798 on, the Prague National theater was owned by the Bohemian estates. A committee of representatives of the estates was responsible for the repertoire and for the censorship of plays produced on the leading Prague stage. The National theater thus became a court theater; its handling of censorship as an internal affair resembled that of the Vienna Burgtheater, Teuber, II, 338–39).
6. Julius Marx, *Die österreichische Zensur im Vormärz* (Vienna, 1959), 55.
7. Teuber, II, 316–17.
8. Glossy, "Zur Geschichte der Wiener Theatercensur," 59–64.
9. Carl Glossy, "Zur Geschichte der Theater Wiens, I (1801 bis 1820)," *Jahrbuch der Grillparzer-Gesellschaft* 25 (1915): 1–334, 17.
10. Wolfgang Binal, *Deutschsprachiges Theater in Budapest von den Anfängen bis zum Brand des Theaters in der Wollgasse (1889)* (Vienna, 1972), 61, 72; Jerzy Got, *Das österreichische Theater in Krakau im 18. und 19. Jahrhundert* (Vienna, 1984); Got *Das österreichische Theater in Lemberg*, 143; Alice Hanson, *Musical Life in Biedermeier Vienna* (Cambridge, 1985), 42.
11. Got *Das österreichische Theater in Lemberg*, 129.

12. W. E. Yates, *Theater in Vienna: A Critical History, 1776–1996* (Cambridge, 1996), 25; Glossy, "Zur Geschichte der Wiener Theatercensur," 328; Glossy, "Zur Geschichte der Theater Wiens," 144.
13. Hüttner, "Theater Censorship," 63.
14. Hüttner, "Theater Censorship," 66.
15. Glossy, "Zur Geschichte der Theater Wiens," 156.
16. Hüttner, "Theater Censorship," 62.
17. W. E. Yates, "Two Hundred Years of Political Theater in Vienna," *German Life & Letters* 58 (2005): 129–40, 131.
18. Hüttner, "Theater Censorship," 67.
19. Helmut Herles, "Nestroy und die Zensur," in Jürgen Hein, ed., *Theater und Gesellschaft: Das Volksstück im 19. und 20. Jahrhundert* (Düsseldorf, 1973), 121–32, 122–23.
20. Christian Grawe, "Grillparzers Dramatik als Problem der zeitgenössischen österreichischen Theaterzensur," in August Obermayer, ed., *"Was nützt der Glaube ohne Werke ..." Studien zu Franz Grillparzer anläßlich seines 200. Geburtstages* (Dunedin, NZ, 1992), 162–90, 171.
21. Karl Glossy, "Zur Geschichte des Trauerspieles *König Ottokars Glück und Ende*," *Jahrbuch der Grillparzer-Gesellschaft* 9 (1899): 225.
22. Glossy, "Zur Geschichte des Trauerspieles," 213–47.
23. Glossy, "Zur Geschichte der Theater Wiens," 5.
24. Franz Hadamowsky, *Schiller auf der Wiener Bühne, 1783–1959* (Vienna, 1959), 70; Glossy, "Zur Geschichte der Theater Wiens," 5; Glossy, "Zur Geschichte der Wiener Theatercensur," 116; Hans Wagner, "Die Zensur am Burgtheater zur Zeit Direktor Schlenthers, 1898–1910," *Mitteilungen des Österreichischen Staatsarchivs* 14 (1961): 394–420, 415.
25. Theo Modes, *Die Urfassung und einteiligen Bühnenbearbeitungen von Schillers Wallenstein* (Leipzig, 1931), 53; Hadamowsky, 16.
26. Yates, *Theater in Vienna*, 31–32; Michael R. Jones, "Censorship as an Obstacle to the Production of Shakespeare on the Stage of the Burgtheater in the Nineteenth Century," *German Life & Letters* 27 (1973/74): 187–94.
27. Yates, "Two Hundred Years," 130; Jakob Zeidler, "Ein Censurexemplar von Grillparzer's *König Ottokars Glück und Ende*," *Ein Wiener Stammbuch* (1898): 287–311, 310.
28. Carl Glossy, "Zur Geschichte der Theater Wiens, II (1821 bis 1830)," *Jahrbuch der Grillparzer-Gesellschaft* 26 (1920): 1–155, 103–7.
29. Yates, *Theater in Vienna*, 40.
30. Johann Hüttner, "Vor- und Selbstzensur bei Johann Nestroy," *Maske und Kothurn* 26 (1980): 234–48, 244.
31. Herles, "Nestroy und die Zensur."
32. R. B. Moberly, *Three Mozart Operas: Figaro, Don Giovanni, The Magic Flute* (New York, 1967), 41.
33. Ulrich Weisstein, "Böse Menschen singen keine Arien: Prolegomena zu einer ungeschriebenen Geschichte der Opernzensur," in Peter Brockmeier, ed., *Zensur und Selbstzensur in der Literatur* (Würzburg, 1996), 49–73.

34. Elizabeth McKay, *Franz Schubert's Music for the Theater* (Tutzing, 1991), 36, 231, 249, 294; Michael Walter, *'Die Oper ist ein Irrenhaus': Sozialgeschichte der Oper im 19. Jahrhundert* (Stuttgart, 1997), 316; Walter Obermaier, "Schubert und die Zensur," in Otto Brusatti, ed., *Schubert-Kongreß Wien 1978* (Graz, 1979), 117–25; Marcel Prawy, *The Vienna Opera* (1969), 17.
35. Jones; Mariola Szydłowska, *Cenzura Teatralna w Galicji: W Dobie autonomicznej, 1860–1918* (Krakow, 1995).
36. Gilbert Carr, "Corridors of Power and Whispered Plots: The Banning of Otto Stoessl's and Robert Scheu's *Waare* in 1897–1898," in W. E. Yates, ed., *From Perinet to Jelinek: Viennese Theater in Political and Intellectual Context* (Oxford, 2007), 129–30; Roy Pascal, *From Naturalism to Expressionism: German Literature and Society, 1880–1918* (London, 1983), 268.
37. Hadamowsky, 40.
38. Jones, 192.
39. Wagner, 401; Djawid Borower, "Theraterzensur im politischen und sozialen Kontext der Jahre 1893 bis 1914," dissertation (Vienna, 1988), 84–85.
40. Barbara Tumfart, "Vom 'Feldmarschall' zum "Eroberer': Über den Einfluß der österreichischen Theaterzensur auf den Spieltext in der zweiten Hälfte des 19. Jahrhunderts," *Internationales Archiv für Sozialgeschichte der deutschen Literatur* 30 (2005): 98–117, 113–15; Herles, 124.
41. Karl Glossy, *Vierzig Jahre Deutsches Volkstheater: Ein Beitrag zur deutschen Theatergeschichte* (Vienna, 1929), 45.
42. Glossy, *Vierzig Jahre Deutsches Volkstheater,* 46, 50; Borower, 273–84.
43. Szydłowska; Kazimierz Braun, *A Concise History of Polish Theater from the Eleventh to the Twentieth Centuries* (Lewiston, 1999), 81–82.
44. Margret Dietrich, *Die Wiener Polizeiakten von 1854–1867 als Quelle für die Theatergeschichte des Österreichischen Kaiserstaates* (Graz, 1967), 58–59; Adriano Dugulin, "Der Irredentismus im Triestiner Theaterleben, 1878–1918," in Cornelia Szabó-Knotik, ed., *Wien—Triest um 1900: Zwei Städte—eine Kultur?* (Vienna, 1993), 37–61.
45. Philip Gossett, "Zensur und Selbstzensur: Probleme bei der Edition von Giuseppe Verdis Opern," in Stefan Harpner, ed., *Über Musiktheater* (Munich, 1992), 103–15; John Tyrrell, *Czech Opera* (Cambridge, 1988), 125, 132; Stanley Kimball, *Czech Nationalism: A Study of the National Theater Movement, 1845–83* (Urbana, IL, 1964), 19, 70, 80.
46. Jim Samson, "East Central Europe: the Struggle for National Identity," in Samson, ed., *The Late Romantic Era: From the mid-nineteenth century to World War I* (London, 1991), 205–39, 226; Robert Nemes, *The Once and Future Budapest* (Dekalb, IL, 1995), 33, 156; Alice Freifeld, *Nationalism and the Crowd in Liberal Hungary, 1848–1914* (Baltimore, 2000), 97, 157–58; Alice Freifeld, "The De-Germanization of the Budapest Stage," *Yearbook of European Studies* 13 (1999): 161.
47. Dietrich, 21, 105–6, 133–34.
48. Borower, 331–34, 337–38, 341–42.
49. Borower, 250–59; Werner Wilhelm Schnabel, "*Professor Bernhardi* und die Wie-

ner Zensur: Zur Rezeptionsgeschichte der Schnitzlerschen Komödie," *Jahrbuch der Deutschen Schillergesellschaft* 28 (1984): 349–83.
50. Franz Dirnberger, "Theaterzensur im Zwielicht der Gesetze (1918–1926)," *Mitteilungen des Österreichischen Staatsarchivs* 36 (1983): 237–60.
51. Hüttner, "Theater Censorship," 62.
52. Hüttner, "Theater Censorship," 68.

# Summary

ROBERT JUSTIN GOLDSTEIN

### Nineteenth-Century European Theater Censorship Mechanics

The eighteenth century and early nineteenth century witnessed in many European countries attempts to tighten and centralize regulation of the theater (reflecting a general trend toward expansion and centralization of state powers), as in the directives of eighteenth-century French king Louis XIV and Hapsburg emperor Joseph II and in the formal imposition of theater censorship in Russia in 1804. In Britain this trend was manifested in the Licensing Act of 1737, largely a response by Prime Minister Robert Walpole to a series of political satires directed against him by Henry Fielding and other dramatists. The Licensing Act contained two major provisions which generally became standard throughout much of Europe by the nineteenth century: (1) only officially licensed theaters could present plays (popularly known as the "theater monopoly"), and (2) no plays could be performed for "gain, hire or reward" without the prior approval of government officials; in Britain, this was the Lord Chamberlain, head of the royal household, who soon delegated most of his theater responsibilities to a member of his staff known as the examiner of plays. These twin requirements of theater licensing and censorship paralleled provisions that had been earlier adopted throughout Europe to control the printed word. By the early eighteenth century, no European printer could function without government license, and no material could be printed without censorship clearance (except in Britain, where such press restrictions were abolished in 1695). The general adoption by about 1800 of parallel provisions for regulation of the stage gave the ruling classes effective tools that, on the whole, succeeded in controlling the theater and eliminating serious social and political criticism from the stage during most of the nineteenth century, particularly during the period before about 1860 when political repression was especially severe in most of Europe. Thus, in 1781 French drama critic Thomas Rousseau bitterly attacked the censorship for destroying all serious theater: "If one surrenders his production to their censure, they cut, prune, trim, mutilate, and dissect it to the extent that there does not even remain for the poor child the shadow of its first form. After this blow, they return it to its father. Reduced to this state of languor, or even more, annihilation, this shapeless skeleton can only revolt; he makes such a heavy fall that it appears he will never be revived; he ... dies, is buried, and everything is finished."[1]

By the early nineteenth century, the mechanics of theater censorship were fundamentally similar in almost all European countries, although many details of the legal basis and administration of theater censorship varied somewhat. Theater managers generally had to submit a copy of all scripts to the censors at least a week or two before opening night, with the censors empowered to approve the text as submitted, ban the play entirely or approve only with deletions. In some countries, including France and Russia, changes could sometimes be negotiated in meetings between the censors (or their superiors) and playwrights and/or theater managers. In Britain after 1737 and in France after 1835 stage censorship was based on statutory law, but in Russia (where there was no elected parliament before 1905) it was based solely on imperial decree. In the German states the censorship was mostly based on royal decree before 1850 and a mixture of decree and law thereafter, while in Denmark censorship was exercised by the government solely on the basis of its traditional role in licensing theaters.[2]

In Britain the examiner of plays functioned as chief censor for the entire country, while in Russia a similar role was played by the notorious Third Section (the secret political police) under Nicholas I (1825–55) and by the Press Affairs Administration thereafter, with a special office established in 1888 to censor popular theaters. In France the Parisian theater was controlled by a board of four or five censors under the jurisdiction of the Bureau of Theaters, which was attached at various times to the Ministries of State, the Interior, Fine Arts, and Education; in the departments censorship decisions were made by the prefects, who could ban locally plays approved for Paris, but who could not allow in their departments dramas forbidden in the capital. Until 1866 the French censors wrote full reports on the reasons behind their decisions, which have largely survived in the French archives and therefore provide a goldmine of information for historians. As in Britain, Russia, and France, Habsburg theater censorship bans reached in the capital applied throughout the realm, although both in Austria and Russia (as in France), local officials could invoke even harsher restrictions. Particularly after 1850, as minority ethnic regions in Russia (such as Ukraine), Austria (such as the Bohemian lands), Germany (the former Polish and French regions), and Spain (especially Catalonia) developed increasingly nationalist aspirations, often including demands for linguistic autonomy and the creation of native language theaters, the central authorities were especially sensitive to the contents of plays and operas in local theaters. For example, puppet theaters in Prague were banned from performances using the Czech language, an 1867 Spanish law banned Catalan in theatrical performances in Barcelona and German censors were especially harsh in treating French language plays in general and appeals to French patriotism, in particular, in theaters in Alsace-Lorraine, which Germany had annexed after the 1870 Franco-Prussian War. In sharp contrast to the centralized theater censorship administrations in France, Austria, Russia, and Britain, after German unification in 1870 each state (and in some cases each city within various states) had its own theater-censorship administration, which was generally in the hands of the Theatersicherheitspolizei (police responsible for theater security), a special branch of the Sittenpolizei (moral police). While the most important German states, such as Prussia, Bavaria, and Saxony, all enforced strict drama censorship, some of the other states, including Württemberg, Baden, Brunswick, and Hamburg, operated without stage censorship. As in Germany, in Italy (after 1864), the Netherlands (after 1851), Sweden (before the 1872 abolition of theater censorship), and Spain (after 1886) stage censorship was controlled by local or provincial officials, with the result, as discussed below, that not only were the same plays treated differently in different countries, but sometimes even within the same country (or political subdivision). In Denmark between 1853 and 1893 a different censor supervised each theater, but after 1893 a single censor appointed by the justice minister supervised all theaters. Following Belgian independence from Holland in 1831, local authorities had the legal right to censor the theater but rarely, if ever, exercised it. Portugal by 1910 had a unique system under which theater managers could either submit scripts in advance to the police, on the understanding that any approved play could be thereafter safely performed without interference, or they could proceed without prior censorship at the risk of having the performance stopped by the police and of facing criminal prosecution. Censorship generally applied to all forms of theatrical presentation, including opera and other forms of musicals, as well as to "spoken" theater. Thus, the 1820 Prussian regulation was typical in requiring submission of texts of "all published and non-published tragedies, drama, comedies, and/or musical plays, which, without expressed permission … [of] those persons assigned authority to grant permission, may not be performed."[3]

Appeals against negative censorship decisions could generally only be taken to higher levels of the bureaucracy. Thus, in Italy after 1889 appeals from adverse decisions by provincial governors could only be addressed to the minister of the interior, and in France and the German state of Bavaria they likewise had to be taken to the supervising minister (although in France and some other countries, including Russia, playwrights with the right "connections" sometimes succeeded in having the censors' rulings reviewed, and sometimes reversed, personally by the ruling monarchs). Apparently uniquely in Europe, in some German states, notably Prussia and Saxony, it was possible to appeal adverse drama censorship decisions to the courts, which exercised considerable independence, overturning administrators on at least six occasions between 1892 and 1896. However, the decentralized nature of the German censorship meant that a court decision overturning a ban in one city did not guarantee that censors would permit a play elsewhere. In the most notorious case Gerhart Hauptmann's *The Weavers* was banned by Berlin officials as an *Umsturzdrama* (subversion drama), then allowed there in 1894 following a court ruling, but subsequently banned by police in seventeen other German cities until it was repeatedly rescued by the courts.

Aside from variations in administrative procedures, European countries (and, in the case of Germany and other decentralized systems, the various states and cities) varied greatly in the intensity with which they administered theater censorship. Thus, French novelist Stendhal wrote in his diary, while visiting Naples in 1817, that a friend had informed him that among the various separate Italian states "only three of [Italian dramatist Vittorio] Alfieri's tragedies are permitted here [in the Kingdom of the Two Sicilies]; four in Rome; five in Bologna [both in the Papal States]; seven in Milan [in Austrian-ruled Lombardy]; none in Turin [in the Kingdom of Piedmont]." Strindberg's *The Father* was censored in Berlin but allowed intact in Copenhagen, while his *Miss Julie* was banned in the Danish capital yet allowed in the German. Within the German state of Bavaria, the theater censorship of Munich was quite strict while that in Nuremberg was relatively lax. Comparative censorship data is scarce, but, what is available, along with strong impressionistic evidence, suggests that the French censorship was considerably harsher than that in England, where only 1 percent of all plays were completely banned between 1852 and 1912, but generally less drastic than that in Austria, most of the Italian and German states before 1860, and especially Russia, where in 1866–67 about 10 percent of all plays were completely rejected and another 13 percent were approved only if modified, and about 15 percent of all plays were banned by the special popular theater censorship between 1888 and 1915. In France about 2.5 percent of plays were entirely forbidden and another 18 percent suffered enforced modifications between 1835 and 1847. During the entire decade of the 1890s, 22 plays were banned in Britain, but 157 were forbidden in Berlin alone; that the Russian censorship was far harsher yet is suggested by the fact that in 1903 alone 249 plays were banned.[4]

Although particular censorship decisions often defy explanation, "censors at all times and places being notoriously unpredictable," in the words of theater historian Tom Driver, the relative harshness of the stage censorship unquestionably generally reflected the overall level of political repression in each country. Thus, the highly repressive regimes in Russia under Tsar Nicholas I (ruled 1825–55) and in Austria and most of the Italian and German states before 1860 tended to have the strictest controls on the stage. In Austria, where the censors decreed that Shakespeare's characters King Lear and Romeo and Juliet could not die on stage, even the notoriously reactionary Emperor Francis I (ruled 1792–1835) termed the censorship "'really stupid," declaring once, "I must go to the theater today. Any time now the censorship might find a hair in the milk and forbid the play and I won't get to see it!" Even in such countries, however, a dedicated and determined director could create a respectable, if not terribly thought-provoking, theater. Such was the case with Josef Schreyvogel, director of the Vienna Burgtheater, who was able to develop a fine ensemble that produced superb productions in the face of one of the harshest censorships in Europe.[5]

The theater-monopoly provisions enforced in most European countries greatly restricted the number of theaters and ensured that only "reliable" theater managers and companies would be licensed. In London after 1737 only two theaters, Drury Lane and Covent Garden, were tolerated, with actors performing illegally at other theaters deemed "rogues and vagabonds" subject to imprisonment. Abolition of the monopoly in 1843 quickly led to the establishment of twenty-five more theaters in the London area. In

France licensing officials were more tolerant, with the number of approved theaters in Paris allowed to increase from eight in 1814 to twenty-three in 1850, but the licensing requirement itself (which in France included strict limits on what "genre" of theater was allowed at each stage) was not ended until 1864, when Napoleon III decreed that henceforth anyone could build or operate a theater and "dramatic works of all types ... can be represented in all the theaters." By 1905 the number of Parisian theaters had increased to forty-three. In Germany and Italy, most of the individual states originally gave exclusive rights to one or two theaters, typically under strong court control, but the monopolies gradually faded away between the 1848 revolutions and the unification of Italy and Germany by 1870. In Germany both the number of theaters and theater employees tripled during the twenty-five years after the theater monopoly was formally abolished in 1870. The Russian theater monopoly in Moscow and St. Petersburg, informally begun in 1827, was maintained until 1882. Until then only two or three imperial theaters under rigid governmental control could legally present legitimate drama in the two capitals, while during the next thirty years hundreds of stage groups blossomed.[6]

## Capriciousness of the Censorship

Nineteenth-century European drama censorship was characterized by capriciousness and inconsistency. Not only were plays banned in some countries but not others, but many plays were first approved and later banned, or first banned and then allowed later, by the same regimes. In one of the most spectacular instances of such capriciousness, the leading Russian dramatist Alexander Ostrovsky's play *Kozma Zakharich Minim, Sukhoruk* (named after its hero) was approved for publication in 1862 and so pleased Tsar Alexander II that he sent the author a ring worth 500 rubles; yet it was banned from the stage the following year, then allowed again in 1866. In France *La Dame aux Camélias,* the play by Alexander Dumas fils based on the life of a courtesan (providing the inspiration for Verdi's opera *La Traviata,* censored before it was allowed in Italy in the 1850s) was forbidden in 1849 by the French censors, but when a personal friend of Dumas, the Duc de Morny, became minister of the interior in 1851, he reversed the ruling. At the same, Morny banned Honoré de Balzac's previously approved play, *Mercadet,* about business corruption. His reasoning, according to theater historian F. W. J. Hemming's sarcastic account, was apparently that financiers, "who render the state no small service, have a right to be shielded from the darts of impertinent satirists; whereas no offence is given to any influential segment of the community by revealing that young men about town habitually frequent the houses of loose women." Such reversals of previous decisions were quite common, although typically they took much longer to occur and reflected a change in the political climate rather than as a result of the mere whim of individual censors or officials (or the use of personal influence, which, in France at least, was quite frequent and often effective among the well-connected, spurring rumors that censors were being offered monetary bribes or even the sexual favors of actresses). For example, in Russia, Pushkin's play *Boris Godunov* (1825) was allowed in 1870 after being banned for forty-five years; Alexander Griboyedov's masterpiece *Woe from Wit* (1825), originally banned and then allowed in 1831 in such mutilated form that, as one observer noted, it had "nothing left but woe," was finally performed uncut in 1869; and Ivan Turgenev's *A Month in the Country*, banned in 1850, was eventually permitted in 1872. Each of these original bans occurred during the reign of Tsar Nicholas I (1825–55), a period of unrelieved reaction. Nicholas insisted on deleting any passage that might "'evoke applause for its independent views by the 'non-privileged' classes." and, panicked by the 1848 revolutions, personally headed a secret censorship committee and stamped "performance forbidden" on rejected scripts. However, conditions eased considerably under his successor, Alexander II (1855–81), who even allowed dramas accurately depicting former tsar Ivan the Terrible as a mass murderer.[7]

Many censorship decisions produced ludicrous results. In Austria the censorship changed a father into an uncle in one of Schiller's plays because his attitude to his son was deemed unworthy of a father; as a result, at one point the son was forced to declaim, "There is a region in my heart whither the word uncle never penetrated." In Britain the phrase "Bring my grey hairs in sorrow to my grave" was struck from a play on the grounds it was profane. The Russian dramatist Mikhail Lermontov was forced to change virtually the entire plot of his play *Masquerade,* because, among other things, the censorship was scandalized by his "indecent criticism of costume balls" among the aristocracy and "impertinences against ladies belonging to the fashionable social sets." Such offences were viewed as "more than horrible: there is no name for it." In France censors in the 1820s refused to approve a play that had the son of a count marrying the daughter of a shopkeeper; the daughter of a great businessman was suggested as an acceptable alternative. The noted Italian actress Adelaide Ristori wrote in her memoirs that in Turin, capital of independent Piedmont before 1860, all religious references, including all mention of angels and devils, were banned, as were the words *Italy* and *fatherland*. Thus, in one play "Beautiful sky of Italy" was changed to "Beautiful sky of the world," and, in another, a stage direction reading, "Here the actor must express the joy which he experiences in beholding his fatherland," had "native land" substituted for the forbidden word to avoid any apparent expression of patriotism in pantomime. After the suppression of the 1848 Roman revolution, the authorities banned the appearance of the Italian national colors (red, white, and green) altogether. One actor recalled that when an actress had white and green in her dress, "another who wore a red ribbon must not come near her," and that he was fined once "for wearing a blue uniform with red facings and white ornaments, for the excellent reason that the blue looked green by artificial light."[8]

European authorities routinely insisted that the settings of operas be changed in both space and time to hopefully avoid any allusion to contemporary events. Thus, according to a standard opera history, in Austrian-ruled Hungary and Czechoslovakia and Russian-ruled Poland, nineteenth-century "historical operas inevitably created problems with the censors unless the subject appeared so remote as to present no threat to the present occupying force." The Italian opera censorship was especially pernicious. Roman authorities would not approve Verdi's opera (performed eventually under the changed title *Un Ballo in Maschera*) based on the 1792 assassination of Swedish King Gustav III until its setting was changed to seventeenth-century North America and the assassination target transformed into the "colonial governor" of Boston; in Naples Verdi canceled a performance of the same opera after the censors insisted on changes in 297 of the 884 lines. The censors in Milan insisted that the heroine of Gaetano Donizetti's 1841 opera *Maria Padilla* die of a "surfeit of joy" rather than commit suicide, while the Roman censors forced the heroine in Gioacchino Rossini's *L'Italiana in Algeri* to substitute the nonsensical phrase "Think of your spouse!" for the original "Think of your country!" In Austria Eugène Scribe's opera *Les Huguenots*, about seventeenth-century French religious strife, could only be performed after it was retitled *The Ghibillenes of Pisa* and provided with a new libretto that featured thirteenth-century Italians singing a hymn composed in the sixteenth century by Martin Luther, while Rossini's *William Tell*, about a medieval Swiss revolt against Habsburg rule, could only be performed if the setting was shifted to a Scotland suffering from English oppression (*Tell* suffered censorship bans or modifications in other countries also, including in some German cities, which insisted that its "revolutionary spirit" be damped down; in Russia, as Anthony Swift notes in his chapter above, *Tell* was approved in the late nineteenth century for only one theater, where the censor reported the audience consisted mostly of the "well off," and where it was "impossible to make out the words" in the cheap seats in the back that ordinary people might be able to afford). In Russia the central plots of Peter Tchaikovsky's 1873 *The Oprichnik* (about the abuses of Ivan the Terrible) and Nicholas Rimsky-Korsakov's *Christmas Eve* (about Catherine the Great) were reduced to nonsense by enforcing an absolute ban on the depiction of tsars in operas (it was explained to Rimsky that "well, it would be unseemly" were a tsar to "suddenly sing a ditty," but as he had been promised by the Tsar Nicholas II that *Christmas Eve* could be presented as written, he wrote bitterly to a friend that the authorities had forgotten "the saying: 'Don't give your word unless you intend to keep it.'"). As was the case with plays, when operas were censored, sometimes the artists were informed why, but often they were given, at best, vague explanations. Thus, when the Naples censors offered Donizetti no explanation at all for the 1834 ban on his opera *Maria Stuarda*, he fumed in a letter, "Stuarda was prohibited. Heaven knows why. It is enough that one must hold one's tongue, for the king commands it."[9]

There were three major reasons for the inconsistency and capriciousness of the censorship: (1) the general vagueness of the censorship laws and decrees (which was probably inevitable given the nature of the censor's task); (2) the personalities of individual censors; and (3) perhaps most important of all, the censorship generally reflected the political situation in particular countries at any given time and thus varied with the changing political temperature. Although some censorship rules, such as the British ban on all representations of living individuals and all dramas based on the Bible, and a French decree of 1840 banning all references to Napoleon, were clear, many theater censorship laws and decrees did not even try to lay down any clear guidelines. Among the 1822 Tuscan drama-censorship rules was a ban on "performances of any kind which could in any way offend the conscience and the principles of modern times," while the 1843 British Theater Regulation Act simply authorized the Lord Chamberlain to suppress plays where he felt it "fitting for the Preservation of good Manners, Decorum, or of the Public Peace." The 1871 Bavarian police code directed stage censors to protect "morality, propriety or public peace." As Anthony Swift notes in his chapter above, the 1804 Russian censorship regulations instructed censors to ban any publications or performances that attacked "God's law, the government, morality or the personal honor of any citizen," and the 1828 Russian statute was similar and equally vague, calling for a ban on works "harmful with respect to faith, the throne, morality and the personal honor of citizens." Tsar Alexander II's 1865 decree regulating theaters added to such bans interdictions on any historical or political topics with material "offensive to the Russian government or to those governments friendly to Russia."[10]

When questioned, theater censors could generally shed little light on their operating principles. One British examiner of plays said he tried to strike anything that "may make a bad impression on the people at large" and another told a 1909 parliamentary inquiry, "There are no principles that can be defined. I follow precedent." When Austrian dramatist Franz Grillparzer met the censor who was responsible for banning his 1823 play *King Ottokar*, the censor responded when asked what was objectionable, "Nothing at all, but I thought to myself, 'One can never tell!'" When Berlin theater manager Oscar Blumenthal asked the Berlin police president to explain the ban on play around 1900, he was told that the police had acted because "it just suits us," rather than due to any particular scenes or language. A French theater censor testified at an 1849 hearing on stage censorship that in making decisions, "We have no other guide than our conscience," and "in seeing a scabrous passage, we would ask ourselves: 'Would we take our wife and daughters to a theater to hear such things?' That was for us a criterion."[11]

Particularly, given such vague guidance, the personalities of individual censors inevitably played a major role in determining policies. Although a number of theater censors, such as Francesco Ruffa (1792–1851) in Naples, Jean-Louis Laya (1761–1833) in France, and John Kemble (1807–57) in Britain, were well-known authors and scholars, many censors once in office seem to have let their power and idiosyncrasies get the better of them. Thus, Giuseppe Belli, a well-regarded poet who wrote over two thousand witty and realistic sonnets about plebeian Roman society, was known for unparalleled pedantry as a censor, leading one observer to comment that, if his principles were strictly observed, "all that could be recited in the theater would be the rosary." George Colman, who served as British examiner of plays between 1824 and 1836, was also notorious for his odd decisions, which extended to striking the word "thighs" as indecent, and banning a reference to members of the royal family as "all stout gentlemen." One critic declared of Colman, "An inordinate fear of the devil, working on a mind reduced to the last gasp of imbecility, could alone originate such a ludicrous, yet injurious, abuse of paltry power." Another examiner, E. F. Smyth Pigott, who banned Ibsen's *Ghosts*, declared, "I have studied Ibsen's plays pretty carefully and all the characters in Ibsen's plays appear to me morally deranged." When Smyth Piggott died in 1895, George Bernard Shaw wrote a savage obituary, terming his censorial reign "one long folly and panic, in which the only thing definitely discernible in a welter of intellectual confusion was his conception of the English people rushing towards an abyss of national degradation in morals and manners, and only held back on the edge of the precipice by the grasp of his strong hand."[12]

## The Goals of the Censorship

Nineteenth-century European theater censorship (as well as censorship of other media) aimed above all to uphold the general political and social order, and especially to protect the existing political regime. Thus, French theater censorship historian Odile Krakovitch notes that "whether the censors based their actions on political, religious or moral grounds, they always acted on one and the same principle: the defense of the social class in power" and "respect for the established order." Even without specific guidance, the censors understood what was expected of them: in 1849 the French censor who testified, as noted above, that while ultimately "we have no other guide than our conscience," added, "In seeing passages with a political or social significance we asked ourselves, 'Does that aim at causing the different classes to rise up against each other, to excite the poor against the rich, to excite to disorder?' We asked ourselves in principle if it was possible to allow ridicule on the stage of the institutions of the country, and especially those who maintain order most effectively; if it was right to disarm the latter [e.g., the police and militia] in advance and expose them to the laughter and mockery of the crowd. We had no trouble in answering no." Sometimes there was clear guidance from above along the same lines: an 1850 directive ordered the French censors to clamp down on plays that presented "socialist ideas" or "inspired class antagonism" and directed provincial prefects to ensure that no play "made with an injurious or exaggerated political sentiment or attacking morals or religion is presented in the theaters of your department." Similar criteria applied to other media: with regard to caricatures and drawings, French censors were informed in 1829 that "that which belongs to the royal majesty and the august dynasty of the [ruling] Bourbons" must be spared "guilty attacks or allusions of whatever kind," and were directed in 1879 to "refuse absolutely" drawings "directed against the head of state" and to approve only with "the greatest circumspection" those targeting other state officials, religion, or the clergy.[13]

An 1875 Swedish cabinet protocol declared that the drama censors should ensure that "nothing is introduced which is contrary to religion, the mode of government, the King's highness, respect for the notability, the respect due to the other estates and offices" or other material that "might diminish these among an easily misled public," while, as John A. Davis points out in his chapter above, the interior minister of the short-lived French-dominated Republic of Naples declared in 1799 that as "theaters constitute a form of public education of the greatest importance," they should be subjected to "rigorous scrutiny by the public authorities who must ensure that the people are not moved by sentiments other than patriotism, virtue and sound morality." An 1819 Wallachian decree proclaimed that all dramas "libelous to religion, the state and public morality" should be banned. The 1865 Russian censorship statute, which governed both press and theater, directed the censors to ban "offence to the respect due to the teachings and rituals of Christian faiths, protect the inviolability of the Supreme Authority [i.e. the tsar] and its attributes, [maintain] respect for members of the reigning house," and "the steadfastness of the basic laws," while forbidding "the harmful teachings of socialism and communism, which lead to the undermining or overthrow of the existing order" as well as other material that aroused "the enmity of hatred of one class towards another" or "offensively ridicule entire classes or officials in the state or public service."[14]

Under these circumstances the hero of Beaumarchais's *Marriage of Figaro,* banned in France for six years in the late eighteenth century, no doubt spoke for many dramatists in declaring, "They all tell me that if in my writing I mention neither the government, nor public worship, nor politics, nor morals, nor people in office, nor influential corporations, nor the opera, nor the other theaters, nor any one who has aught to do with anything, I may print everything freely, subject to the approval of two or three censors." In any case, criticism of the established order was generally blue-penciled (when playwrights and theater managers were courageous enough to submit such dramas to the censors), with even historical plays that seemed to imply criticism of the status quo frequently banned. In Britain not only were all stage representations of living persons forbidden, but so were even historical dramas viewed as containing implicit criticisms of the monarchy or the reigning monarch. For example, virtually all presentations dealing with the deposed and executed king Charles I (ruled 1625–49) were banned from the British stage between 1825 and 1852 as "insulting to monarchy." Similarly, the Prussian theater regulations banned all stage depictions of any member of the ruling Hohenzollern dynasty, living or dead, in a manner that might "undermine popular loyalty toward the royal family." In France Victor Hugo's 1829 play *Marion de Lorme* was banned because it unfavorably depicted Charles X's long-dead ancestor Louis XIII, and Alfred de Musset's 1861 *Lorenzaccio,* a play about Renaissance Italy, was banned since, as the censor put it, "The discussion of the right to assassinate a sovereign whose crimes and iniquities, even including the murder of the prince by his parents, cry out for vengeance," was "a dangerous spectacle to present to the public." In Austria Schiller's play *William Tell,* like Rossini's opera based on the same subject, could only be presented after, as a report to the theater director noted, the play had been "adapted" so that "Austria and her former relations to Switzerland are not mentioned, and the democratic tendency, which one might ascribe to the original, disappears in favor of a merely domestic and generally human interest."

Even trivially critical comments about ruling elites were often barred. Thus, the French dramatist Emile Augier had to strike from his 1853 play *La Pierre de touche* the comments of one character that "society was ill ordered," while the British censor struck from an 1829 play the remark that "honest men at court don't take up much room." In the 1850s the French censors rejected a play that showed a postman who neglected his official duties and insisted that a customs official who was mocked be changed into a wine taster, in both cases, apparently to avoid lowering public esteem for government officials. They also struck out of George Sand's play *Moliere* (1851) a passage in which the hero toasted "the poor people of France, who pay the fiddlers for all the festivals and the trumpets for all the wars," refused to allow, in an 1853 play, the comment that "the rich, in the design of God, are only the treasurers of the poor," and banned from Victor Sejour's 1860 play *Les Aventuriers* the phrase "if a rich man wants to go hunting or dancing, they roll out a carpet for him on the way lest he weary his feet." Austrian playwright Johann Nestroy had to delete from his play *Der Talisman* the comment "so many true good fellows walk around in torn jackets," which was viewed as too sympathetic to proletarians, while late nineteenth-century Bavarian censors cut even the feeblest jokes about the state legislature.[15]

Serious treatments of social problems, especially those depicting lower-class protests, generally ran into a censorship wall. Thus, among the plays banned near the end of the century (when political censorship had generally eased somewhat) were four dramas sympathetically depicting strikes: Hauptmann's portrayal of the 1844 Silesian weavers' revolt in *The Weavers,* forbidden in the 1890s in Austria, Russia, France, and in many German cities (until allowed by the German courts); Emile Zola's *Germinal,* temporarily banned in France in 1885 for, as the official censors' report put it, the play's "socialist tendency" and especially for depicting "troops firing at striking miners in revolt"; Maxim Gorky's 1907 *The Enemies,* interdicted in Russia for its portrayal of a clash between textile workers and their employers; and the 1874 British play *Lords and Labourers,* banned because relations between employees and their supervisors was held a subject "not fit for representation on the stage at any time." As is demonstrated in the chapters of this volume, most European regimes occasionally banned plays with anti-Semitic themes, also in the interests of damping down internal conflict, and to preserve their foreign policy interests, periodically banned plays perceived as offending allied nations.[16]

Such censorship had similar results throughout Europe, as all too often, in the words of theater historians Vera Roberts and Robert Boyer, the nineteenth-century stage presented only "glitter and tinsel, with impossibly noble heroes, ideally sweet heroines, romantic love stories, happy endings and lavish productions" with "only the remotest connection with real life" and "not a modicum of thought," while providing the theater patron with a "mindless, amnesiac experience" that invited him to "check his intelligence, along with his coat, at the playhouse door." In short, the censorship generally achieved its objective of creating a socially politically safe and sterile stage, one that rarely presented material dealing realistically with the problems of modern life. The Italian playwright and critic Giovanni Pindemonte lamented in 1827 that, "among the other miseries of our Italy is that it has no theater worthy of the name," while in her memoirs Italian actress Ristori attributed the "decadence of our drama" mainly to the censorship in Austria and the Papal States before 1860, declaring that "the plays were mutilated to a mass of contradictions" and were "at times rendered completely silly and bereft of any interest." In 1879 British writer Matthew Arnold blamed the censorship for insuring that "in England we have no modern drama at all." Historians have concluded that, due to the censorship, the Russian stage was dominated by "cheap melodrama, farce and trivia," that Austrian controls forced theater there to be "dominated by total political apathy and absolute indifference to public life," and that the German stage was "rarely inspired" as the censorship "contributed to mediocrity by discouraging anything potentially offensive" and that immediately after the failed 1848 revolutions plays "had to be so inoffensive as to become almost mindless."[17]

The impact of censorship on the opera was similar to that on the spoken theater. Although, as pointed out below, politically attuned audiences in Italy and elsewhere were able to find contemporary political allusions even in operas (and dramas) set in the distant past and far-away or imaginary settings (as was routinely required by the censorship), composers and librettists were not free to write directly about subjects of interest and had to work with the censorship constantly in mind. As European music historian Henry Raynor writes, under these conditions, most operas were "romanticized out of reality" and focused on events that "if they had ever happened" did so "a long time ago and preferably a long way away," and composers and librettists had to "either risk a series of headlong collisions with the authorities" or produce material that "could never be more than a pleasant decoration of the surfaces of life," existing in a "vacuum where political and social realities no longer applied" with characters "falsified by their removal from social reality." Similarly, Russian opera historian Robert Oldani finds that "any composer or dramatist had to be careful to exclude politically unacceptable material"; German opera historian John Warrack concludes that, at least before 1848, the impact of Austrian chancellor Clemens von Metternich's censorship was to limit the opera hall to "almost entirely a place of recreation, with cosy pieces drawing reassuringly on local color, stock figures and popular tunes"; and Italian opera historian William Ashbrook notes that since the "ultimate authority" over plot and libretto resided with the censors," their influence, at least until a marked easing of the opera censorship after about 1860, "can scarcely be exaggerated" and that the "intimidation of librettists," who avoided "potentially censurable situations" was "the most insidious aspect of the whole ugly situation, as well as the most far-reaching in view of its ultimate effect upon the composer seeking his inspiration in such a compromised text."[18]

## Opposition to the Censorship

While censorship's impact on the content of plays and operas is reasonably clear, it also had a far subtler and more difficult to measure, but extremely serious, impact on the ability of dramatists, composers, and librettists to freely write or even think. Thus, in France, Alexander Dumas likened theater censors to "customs officers of thought," while Victor Hugo compared censorship to the Inquisition, terming it "detestable" and a "prison" for writers that "like the other holy office" had its "secret judges, its masked executioners, its tortures and mutilations and its death penalty." Following the reintroduction of stage censorship in 1850 after two years of theatrical freedom, Hugo declared, "It brought sobs to the depths of my heart."

His compatriot Henry Becque complained in 1888 that the censorship reduced dramatists to sticking to "banal passions, to comic foibles of a trivial kind" or to "matters of only passing interest, which appear daring but do not seriously alarm anyone." Emile Zola, who compared the drama censors to a "torturer," declared, "Books have been freed, periodicals have been freed. Why is the theater condemned to eternal servitude?" Russian author Anton Chekhov, as Anthony Swift mentions above, compared the censorship to "writing with a bone in your throat."[19]

Similar reactions to the drama censorship were common throughout Europe. Thus, British playwright Elizabeth Inchbold lamented that the novelist "lives in a land of liberty, whilst the dramatic writer exists but under a despotic government," while Spanish socialist Fernando Garrido similarly declared, "Dramatic literature, like all manifestations of intelligence, needs to breathe in the gentle breeze of freedom." German dramatists and brothers Heinrich and Julius Hart complained to Chancellor Otto von Bismarck in 1882 along the same lines that "there is no reason for separating the censorship of books from that of theater by removing the one and keeping the other." Seventy British playwrights complained in a 1907 letter to *The Times* of London that their "art [should] be placed on the same footing as every other one," and bitterly protested against a system "opposed to the spirit of the Constitution, contrary to common justice and to common sense," in which a "single official, who judges without a public hearing, and against whose dictum there is no appeal" could "cast a slur on the good name and destroy the means of livelihood of any member of an honorable calling." They added that the censorship created a "menace hanging over every dramatist," of having their work "destroyed at a pen's stroke by the arbitrary action of a single official, neither responsible to Parliament nor amenable to law," a concern clearly reflected in the 1909 parliamentary testimony of H. G. Wells that censorship had "always been one of the reasons I have not ventured into play writing." In Russia famed writer Lev (Leo) Tolstoy (whose *Power of Darkness,* a depiction of brutal poverty and its consequences in Russia was banned from the stage in Russia, England, and Germany) declared, "What matters is not what the censor does to what I have written, but to what I might have written," while his compatriot Alexander Gribodoyev censored much of his masterpiece *Woe from Wit* even before submitting it to the censors (who further mutilated it), explaining that "the childish ambition to hear my verses in the theater, the ambition that it meet with success there, prompted me to spoil my creation as much as possible." Russian writer and playwright Nikolai Gogol wrote to a friend that he never completed one play after noticing "that my pen kept knocking against such passages as would never be permitted by the censorship," and despaired, "There remains nothing else for me than to invent an innocent plot to which even a police precinct officer will take no offense. Yet what is a comedy without truth and indignation?" The great Austrian dramatist Franz Grillzparzer declared in his autobiography and private writings that in his homeland "invisible chains rattle on hand and foot" and that any writer "who does not completely lose heart" was "truly a kind of hero," as the "system" did not "pin crosses on genius, but nails genius to the cross." Austrian actor and playwright Johann Nestroy compared the censorship to a "mind with the root pulled out" and to a "crocodile" that bit "off the heads" of writers, and termed it the "living admission of our rulers that they can only kick stupefied slaves, not govern free people." German playwright Gerhard Hauptmann remained embittered by the harassment endured by *The Weavers* for the rest of his life, recalling fifty years later in 1942, "I was treated like a criminal, like a common rogue!" In his chapter above, Gary D. Stark quotes two other German censorship opponents as comparing the censors' evaluations of plays to how "a blind man evaluates colors" or an elephant making judgments about playing the flute. Russian director Konstanin Stanislavsky demanded in 1905 that something be done to save the theater from being "strangled by the arbitrary action of the authorities," while his compatriot director Vsevolod Meyerhold bitterly complained that "in Russia, they always begin by saying it's forbidden."[20]

Opera composers and librettists reacted similarly to the censorship. Thus, Verdi, probably Europe's most famous nineteenth-century opera composer, termed the pre-1860 Neapolitan censorship "too strict to permit interesting subjects," although he exulted that with its (brief) collapse during the 1848 revolution he could finally "compose absolutely on any subject." When informed in 1850 that *Rigoletto* (based on Hugo's play *Le roi s'amuse*, banned in France for fifty years) had been forbidden in Venice (it was later allowed with modifications), Verdi wrote to a friend that he had "almost lost my head" and was reduced to "desperation," feeling "hurt and displeasure ... so great that I do not have words to describe them." He wrote to a sculptor friend in 1851 that *Rigoletto* and *Stiffelio* had been "ruined" by the Roman censorship and asked, "What would you say if a black mask were stuck on the nose of one of your fine statues?" Verdi once suggested that the credits for *Rigoletto* should read "poetry and music by Don _____," with the censor's name inserted. He termed the changes required in Naples for the 1858 performance of *Un Ballo in Maschera* "artistic murder," which placed him "in a real hell," and reported feeling "nauseated" by the Roman butchery of that opera. In response to Roman censorship demands that Violetta, the heroine-courtesan of *La Traviata* (based on the play *La Dame aux Camélias* by Alexander Dumas fils, originally banned in France) be "purified," Verdi stormed that censorship had "ruined the sense of the drama," along with "all the situations, all the characters" by making Violetta "pure and innocent. Thanks a lot! ... A whore must remain a whore. If the sun were to shine at night, it wouldn't be night any more. In short, they don't understand anything."[21]

Other composers expressed similar revulsion at the opera censorship. Thus, Donizetti, after seeing a censored performance in 1841 of his *Maria Padilla* in Naples, complained that it had been "massacred unrecognizably" and in a "horrible fashion," and after hearing reports about the presentation of his *Caterina Cornaro* in the same city two years later, lamented, "God knows what a slaughterhouse the censorship has created." The Russian composer Nicholas Rimsky-Korsakov, responding to the censorship of his opera *Christmas Eve,* based on a story by Gogol, declared bitterly in private, "it would be better if all of Gogol's works were banned along with my opera. Then, at least, no one would be tempted to write on his subjects."[22]

Toward the end of the nineteenth century most European countries witnessed at least some alleviation of the theater censorship, partly because those opposed to it became increasingly organized and vocal and obtained increasing public support. In France heated parliamentary debates on the subject occurred almost annually after 1885, leading to a major 1891 legislative inquiry, inspiring a 1901 petition against the censorship from most of France's leading literary figures and, ultimately, through a gradual legislative de-funding of the censors beginning in 1903, forcing (uniquely in major European countries before World War I) termination of the censorship in 1906. In Britain opposition to the censorship from such leading authors as J. M. Barrie, H. G. Wells, John Galsworthy, George Bernard Shaw, and Oscar Wilde forced a 1909 parliamentary inquiry (which led to no changes). (In England, as in France, where an earlier major investigation of the theater censorship was convoked in 1849, drama censorship attracted continuing contention throughout the nineteenth century: British parliamentary inquiries were also held in 1832, 1866, and 1892, all leading to recommendations to maintain it.) In Germany towering artistic and literary figures such as Thomas Mann and Richard Strauss spoke out against the censorship and growing opposition to it, especially in Munich, including mass demonstrations, led to the creation of a censorship advisory council there in 1908 (upon which Mann briefly served), a concession that was also accepted in Austria in 1903. In Russia leading directors spoke out against the censorship during the 1905 revolution, with Stanislavsky comparing its procedures to Dante's circles of hell in the *Divine Comedy*. Spanish playwrights expressed their opposition to the censorship at a major meeting in 1897, while the Austrian parliament in 1914 called for a major retrenchment of the censorship as well as the appointment of censors who had a "psychological and literary education," in the hopes of avoiding the worst absurdities. While the French censorship was abolished in 1906, following years of recurrent and intense debates, parallel action was not taken by any other major European country before World War I (although Sweden permanently terminated drama censorship in 1872, after an earlier period of theatrical freedom beginning in 1809 was ended in 1835).[23]

Dramatists, composers, actors, and, especially, theater directors were by no means unanimously opposed to prior theater censorship, and at least some of them felt it could even be beneficial for several reasons. First, it provided an excuse for failed works or an inability to produce, since, as the great Austrian actor and playwright Nestroy noted during the breakdown of Austrian censorship amid the 1848 revolution, "Writers have lost their favorite excuse. It wasn't a bad thing after all, when you'd run out of ideas, to be able to say to people, 'God, it's awful. They won't let you do a thing.'" Secondly, especially in those countries where censored or banned plays could be printed and sold, producing a forbidden drama could be the road to fame and fortune. Texts of censored plays sold so well in England that one paper reported that a recently produced uncensored play "only requires an edict [banning it] from the Lord Chamberlain to render it the success of the season." Victor Hugo gained much of his early fame via his battles with the drama censorship during the 1829–32 period (involving his banned plays *Marion Delorme* and *Le roi s'amuse*), while Emile Zola clearly deliberately sought, and obtained, a confrontation with the censors with his 1885 play *Germinal*. After German dramatist Hermann Sudermann's play *Sodoms Ende* was banned in Berlin in 1890, he wrote to his mother that "if anything was still lacking regarding my popularity, it is [remedied by] this brutal police decree." He reported receiving dozens of requests from German theaters to produce it and added, "You can hardly imagine the excitement this ban has created in the theatrical world. In Vienna, Rome and London they are writing newspaper editorials about it, American journalists come to interview me, and artists come to sketch my portrait." The ban also increased interest in one of Sudermann's earlier plays, and, when it was lifted after several months, large crowds came to see *Sodoms Ende,* as was almost invariably the case in Germany when forbidden dramas were later allowed. Some dramatists and many directors and actors were not riled up about the censorship because it theoretically (if not always in practice) assured them that once a play had been approved the authorities would not suppress it, as this would lead to a total loss of production costs and unemployment for the cast and crew. Thus, in the 1909 British parliamentary committee hearings, the Actors Association supported continued censorship, as did the French Society of Dramatic Authors during the 1891 legislative inquiry. Directors, who had the most to lose if a production was halted midstream, were especially likely to support continued prior drama censorship.[24]

## Resistance to the Censorship

Opponents of nineteenth-century European drama censorship in France went far beyond words in fighting it: they also repeatedly defied or evaded it at the risk, not only of the suppression of their material, but of prosecutions, fines, and jail terms. As Victor Hugo told a 1849 French legislative inquiry, theater censorship could be resisted in virtually innumerable ways, including by a dramatist writing material that s/he knew would be unacceptable, the use of gestures or inflections by actors to provide meanings or innuendos not evident in a written text, using stage decoration and costumes, such as employing "seditious emblems," and the "offences of the public, an applause which accentuates a verse, a whistle which goes beyond what the actor or author intended." Similarly, the Russian official charged with monitoring Moscow theatrical performances reported in 1901 that "in the continual struggle with the demands of the censorship, the theater disposed of a quite wide arsenal of weapons, which are perfected from year to year," including how actors "realize their roles, diction, mimicry, makeup, gesture and costume."[25]

Such means of censorship resistance or evasion, if ultimately infinite, can be broadly classified into two broad categories: (1) defiance of censorship regulations, such as presenting an unauthorized play or including censored dialogue in a performance; and (2) technical censorship evasions, complying with the letter of the law while subverting its spirit, such as publishing the written text of plays banned from the stage and highlighting censored material, or presenting plays to a supposedly "private" audience technically not subject to censorship regulations. Although it is usually difficult to prove definitively, there is considerable evidence that, at least in some instances, plays were performed without being submitted to the censorship, as required, or were performed even though banned by it. Thus, the British dramatist J. R. Planche publicly stated in 1872 that censorship instructions were "never paid the slightest attention to" and that forbidden material "continued to be uttered and to excite the roars and plaudits of the galleries to the last night of representation." The Russian censorship administration found in 1901 that 75 out of 190 plays recently presented at "popular" theaters in St. Petersburg were unapproved for such venues, while a 1906 Russian censorship directive lamented that frequently, "by the deletion of separate expressions and whole phrases, a play is intentionally given a tendentious character which it does not actually have." The author of a French play dealing with prostitution banned in 1897 claimed several years later to have presented it over three hundred times.[26]

In general, as these reports suggest, the inability of the censors to attend every play to ensure that their orders were being enforced opened up plenty of opportunities for evasion by actors and directors willing to risk the consequences of improvising or restoring censored lines. Thus, French theater historian F. W. J. Hemmings writes that under Napoleon III, "at the dress rehearsal and for the first few performances, the passages that had been blue-penciled would be obediently omitted; but as performance succeeded performance, the cuts would be imperceptibly restored by the players, or the author would even add new matter that the censor had never seen." The great Austrian dramatist/actor Johann Nestroy was notorious (and was jailed twice) for improvising uncensored material on stage, as well as for frustrating the censors through gestures and inflections. In countries where prior press censorship was enforced, banned plays generally could not be legally published either, but they were sometimes clandestinely printed or circulated in manuscript. Thus, Italian dramatist Giovanni Niccolini's *Arnalda da Brescia* could neither be performed nor printed due to its nationalistic appeal, but it was published in France in 1843 and subsequently circulated throughout Italy, with its fiery patriotic passages memorized by those favoring Italian freedom and unity. Similarly, Russian dramatist Griboyedov's banned *Woe from Wit* (1825) became widely known as the result of clandestine circulation of handwritten copies.[27]

Far more common than such outright defiance of the censorship were a variety of techniques that clearly violated the spirit of the laws while technically remaining within their boundaries. For example, Polish audiences could, at least after approximately 1860, legally evade the worst excesses of the censorship in Russian-occupied Poland by crossing the frontier into Galicia (Austrian Poland), since stage censorship was by then considerably less harsh there. During an 1860 performance in Warsaw (Russian Poland), the great polish actor Jan Królikowsi simply raised his manacled hands in silence during a performance of Hugo's *Les Burgraves,* leaving as the only sound the clanking of his chains at the point where the censors had deleted a patriotic speech; a deathly hush accompanied the scene, and the performance ended in a national patriotic demonstration. In a particularly notorious example of technical evasion of the censorship, Balzac's play *Vautrin,* which had been cleared by the French censors on its fourth revised submission, was banned in 1840 after one performance because the famous actor Frédérick Lemaître appeared in makeup and costume that made him resemble King Louis-Philippe. In a similar 1873 British incident the censors cracked down after three characters in *The Happy Land,* co-authored by W. S. Gilbert (of Gilbert and Sullivan fame) were made up to resemble three cabinet members. French café-concert performers often imaginatively alluded to forbidden material by what one scholar has termed "a game of evocative words, repetitive or frankly absurd, by a comic 'visual code,' a gesture, a cry, a whistle, a game of body language, a mask, a costume or make-up." Even more frequent than such technically legal "alterations" to the approved texts were audience interventions by applause or hooting that effectively underlined particular passages and attributed to them unintended political connotations; in 1827 the Paris prefect of police directed his subordinates to report on "any political or other allusion upon which the subversive might seize," and "all those elements that tend to elicit a response from the audience," including a detailed account "of the effect it has produced," with "the nature of the applause or expressions of disapproval it has provoked," as it was "particularly in places of assembly which are as heavily frequented as theaters are nowadays that subversion endeavors to influence public opinion" and it was "vital" for the "authorities not to be unaware of anything that you may have occasion to observe."[28]

Since prior press censorship was abolished in most countries while theater censorship remained in force, authors and publishers sometimes "helped" audiences along in such interventions by publishing the uncensored texts and drawing especial attention to the suppressed passages by underlining them, printing them in capital letters, printing them next to the censored version, and so on, often accompanied by bitter written denunciations of the censors. Thus, the French censors complained in 1836 that text of the opera *Esméralda,* based upon Victor Hugo's famous novel *Notre-Dame de Paris* (which was completely banned as a play until 1879) was being sold in the very lobby of the Paris Opéra where it was being performed, "containing almost all of the passages whose suppression had been demanded by the censors," and that some of them "have even been recited by the actors." The enraged director of the censored English play *Happy Land*, discussed above, published an unexpurgated text, with all excisions printed in capital letters, accompanied by a preface that informed readers that if they took "the trouble to compare the original text with the expurgated version" they would be able to "appreciate the value of the Lord Chamberlain's alterations." When Nepomucene Lemercier's *La Démence de Charles VI* (The Madness of Charles VI), an unflattering portrayal of an insane fourteenth-century French king, was banned from the Odeon theater in Paris in 1820 on the personal orders of King Louis XVIII, even the royalist newspaper *Le Drapeu blanc* wrote a sympathetic account, adding that "curious readers" can "buy the play; it is published and sold at the Barba bookstore, Palais-Royal, stone gallery, behind the Theater Français, number 51."[29]

Audience interventions to underline particular dramatic passages or to otherwise use the theater as a platform for political protests was extremely common throughout Europe, particularly during periods of political tension and tumult, such as during the 1905 Russian Revolution and amid the Italian Risorgimento (between the suppression of the 1830–31 revolutions and the 1860 unification of Italy). Thus, as Norbert Bachleitner notes in his chapter, an 1810 memo (during the Napoleonic wars) from the Vienna police president to Emperor Francis I lamented that it was "not possible to foresee which allusions a public as dedicated to puns and sophistry as the Viennese may with the help of its lively imagination infer from a passage—to the detriment of a clear and rational point of view." The French author Stendhal's similar comment, about Italians, that, "If you are dealing with a race which is at once dissatisfied and witty, everything soon becomes an allusion," was repeatedly borne out by the tendency of Italian audiences during this period to, for example, interpret any literary reference to past French and Spanish domination of their land as a metaphor for current Austrian domination. Thus, a French minister in Milan reportedly became indignant when the audience cheered anti-French references in Niccolini's *Giovanni da Procida* (1830), about a thirteenth-century Sicilian revolt against French rule. Reassuring him, the Austrian minister present observed, "Don't take it badly; the envelope is addressed to you but the contents are for me." The play was soon suppressed as a result of French and Austrian pressure, but was clandestinely circulated.

In at least one instance Italians used the theater, without the aid of any stage action at all, to express their opposition to the post-1848 Austrian occupation of their land: Italian patriots in Pavia boycotted the theater to protest against Austrian rule, so angering the Austrian commander that he declared, "If anybody by criminal political obstinacy should persist in not frequenting the theater, such conduct should be regarded as the silent demonstration of a criminal disposition which merited to be sought out and punished."[30]

In France politicized responses to theatrical presentations were so common that they were dubbed "making applications," characterized by historian Nicholas Harrison as "a creative act on the part of the audience, pressing words into a political service for which they had not been intended by the playwright." For example, the play *Edward in Scotland*, which dealt with an exiled ruler, was approved by both the Napoleonic and Restoration censors as inoffensive, but in performance was applauded under Bonaparte as a pro-Bourbon royalist piece and then subsequently hailed as a pro-Bonapartist piece during the Bourbon Restoration. When a censored version of Hugo's *Hernani* was allowed in 1867 (after being banned, along with all of Hugo's other works, for fifteen years under Emperor Napoleon III), crowds greeted it with a delirious acclaim that turned the performances into an anti-regime demonstration, and responded to the omissions by shouting out the correct words. In a variant of "making applications," during the late 1820s, when the French Restoration regime of King Charles X was intent upon reinforcing the power of the Catholic Church, theater audiences in numerous cities responded to bans on performances of Moliere's bitterly satirical anti-clerical comedy *Tartuffe* by demanding that it be performed, a phenomenon labeled "Tartufferie."[31]

Another legal means of evading theater censorship was the presentation of plays at so-called "private clubs," theoretically open only to members who paid an annual subscription fee, thereby avoiding any charge at the door and thus technically avoiding the censorship laws, which typically applied only to dramas that charged required admission fees and/or were open to the general public. (Sometimes even more brazen techniques were used to evade the censorship, as in Britain, where sometimes before the ending of the theater monopoly in 1843 unlicensed stages put on supposedly "free" performances under the guise of asking patrons to "tea at 6:30" or to share a "dish of chocolate," on the understanding that interested persons would purchase tickets by paying an exorbitant price at a nearby shop for tea or peppermints or supposedly pay an admission fee only for a concert or an "auction of pictures" with a play thrown in supposedly at no cost.)

The most famous of the so-called "private clubs" was the Théâtre Libre of Paris, which flourished under the direction of André Antoine, a former clerk at the Paris Gas Company, between 1887 and 1894. It closed for financial reasons in 1896 after presenting a total of sixty-two programs with 184 plays (including a number of dramas that had suffered widely publicized official censorship bans) that attracted over fifty thousand subscribers.[32]

Similar "free" theaters, generally clearly modeled on or highly influenced by the Théâtre Libre, sprang up throughout Europe after 1885. Among the most prominent were the Freie Bühne of Berlin, the Independent theater of London, the Abbey theater of Dublin, the Modern Life Society of Munich, and the Ibsen theater of Leipzig; similar groups appeared in Vienna, Hamburg, Hanover, Dresden, and many other cities. The founding statement of the Freie Bühne called for a theater "free from conventions, censorship and commercial aims," while one of its founders declared that the theater was "'above all" created to rap "the nose of the police censor." The first presentation of both the Freie Bühne and the London Independent Theater was Norwegian playwright Henrik Ibsen's *Ghosts,* which had been banned in at least Russia, Britain, France, Norway, and much of Germany for its treatment of syphilis and marital infidelity. In general the authorities turned a blind eye to the activities of the "free theaters," perhaps because their high annual subscription fees kept out the lower classes. However, there was a limit to tolerance: Bavarian authorities imposed censorship on the Munich cabaret Elf Scharfrichter (Eleven Executioners) in 1901 in response to the increasingly political character of its satires, and a socialist offshoot of the Freie Bühne, the Freie Volksbühne, founded in 1890, was subjected to censorship in Berlin after 1910.[33]

With the major exception of the Freie Volksbühne and its rival Neue Freie Volksbühne (established after an 1892 split), with a combined membership of almost seventy thousand by 1913 (whose successors still play a significant role in German theater), most of the "free" theaters had brief lives. This was sometimes due to their very success, as when Antoine and Freie Bühne director Otto Brahm were hired by regular theaters or the plays they pioneered became so well regarded that barriers to their performance in mainstream playhouses broke down. However, in other cases their short durations resulted from audience limitations due to high subscription fees. But if few of the "free theatres" were long-lived, they played a significant role in bringing to the stage forerunners of the modern, socially concerned drama, as well as helping to break down censorship barriers. As historian Roy Pascal has noted, they demonstrated to their audiences "the dramatic quality of works known only in print and often decried on theatrical grounds" and gave authors "whose works were banned from the stage the chance of seeing them played," thereby helping them to "develop their own style" and enhancing the "self-awareness and solidarity of the new generation of writing." The great British playwright George Bernard Shaw declared, "Among all German theatres, there is none by which I would rather be produced than by the Freie Volksbiihne."[34]

Aside from the British technique described above of evading the "theater monopoly," other methods were also used. Thus, although the Russian theater monopoly theoretically kept the number of stages in Moscow and St. Petersburg to two or three until 1882, the monopolies were quite regularly violated by private entertainments that were facilitated by large bribes or that were disguised under such code names as "family reunions" or "dramatic evenings." Such gatherings were commonly sponsored in Moscow by the Circle of Lovers of Dramatic Art, established in 1861, and in St. Petersburg by the Nobility Assembly and such groups as the Painters' Club and Merchant Club. By 1875 about twenty-five such groups were regularly putting on performances in the two cities. In a society as highly regulated as tsarist Russia, these goings-on could not remain unknown to the authorities and their toleration no doubt reflected the fact that the sponsoring groups were regarded as politically reliable. But their very widespread existence, combined with the fact that private theaters were allowed in the provinces, undermined the legitimacy of the monopolies well before their official abolition in 1882.

In Britain while the monopoly established in 1737 restricted the "legitimate theater" in London to two playhouses, the vague distinction between "legitimate" and "non-legitimate" theater provided another means of evasion. A number of London venues were licensed for "music, dancing and public entertainments," as distinct from stage plays under the Disorderly Houses Act of 1751, with such forms of entertainment often categorized as "burlettas," a term encompassing all performances with at least five pieces of music in each act. By technically putting on a "burletta," through some subterfuge such as rewriting *Macbeth* in doggerel verse and having a piano constantly tinkling in the background, or adding a chorus of singing witches, theaters that were not licensed for "legitimate" drama could evade the monopoly, finally abolished in 1843 after having been, as theater historian Vera Roberts has noted, often "respected more in the breach than in the observance." The same was true in France where, under legislation dating back to Napoleonic decrees, only eight Parisian theaters were licensed for the "legitimate" stage, and no other theaters were theoretically allowed to present the various "genres" reserved for them. However, since other theaters were licensed to present additional "genres" such as pantomime or acrobatics, or even plays under various severe restrictions, and especially as the definitions of the various genres were often vague, it was possible to evade the monopolistic restrictions with a touch of imagination: one Parisian venue, which was licensed to present drama so long as no more than two actors were simultaneously on stage, evaded this restriction by using quick-change artists and marionettes who "mouthed" their lines via off stage actors.[35]

## Conclusion: Theater Censorship as a Reflection of General Political Trends

As indicated above, the overall success of censorship and licensing controls in "taming" the theater is fairly clear (even if, as documented above, such regulations were often subverted). Moreover, it is obvious from the amount of energy and time that nineteenth-century European authorities devoted to regulating the theater that they viewed a free stage as posing a serious threat to the existing power structure. However, because theatrical regulations were only a small part of the much broader network of social and political controls in nineteenth-century Europe summarized in this book's introduction, it is virtually impossible to isolate the effect of theatrical restrictions upon the broader European social and political scene. However, if it would place too heavy a burden on theatrical controls to seek to attribute to them a significant causative role in shaping broader European trends and developments, studying this subject remains worthwhile, not only for its intrinsic interest, but also because such restrictions provide an extremely accurate and useful index of such broader trends and clearly illuminate, in an unusually nuanced manner, the thoughts, hopes, and fears of ruling nineteenth-century European elites. In short, although it would be difficult or impossible to prove that theatrical regulations by themselves *caused* significant broader developments, they very clearly *reflected* them, and in doing so frequently provide highly detailed and interesting insights into the mentalities of ruling authorities.

Almost everywhere in Europe, changes in the theater censorship regulations tracked broader social and political trends. Thus, the collapse of authoritarian regimes in Austria, France, Germany, and Italy during the 1848 revolutions was accompanied by a lapse in the theater censorship, but when the "law and order" was restored generally in each of these countries, so was the censorship. A general move in the direction of liberalism and constitutionalism in each of these countries after 1860 was, sooner or later, accompanied by a relaxation of censorship enforcement and termination of licensing requirements. Thus, as David Gies demonstrates in his chapter above, the political turbulence in Spain was fully reflected in changing theater regulations: liberal revolutions in 1820, 1834, and 1868 each led to abolition of the censorship, but when the political pendulum swung back, censorship was restored. Perhaps the record for such parallel general political and theater censorship changes was held by France (as is discussed at length in the chapter on France above), where drama censorship was abolished five times between 1790 and 1914, the first four times in connections with revolutions (1789, 1830, 1848, 1870) that eventually turned in a conservative direction accompanied by a restored theater censorship, and a final, permanent end to the censorship in 1906, reflecting a more gradual democratic consolidation and stabilization. Not only did the repeated abolition and restoration of nineteenth-century French theater censorship reflect broader political developments, but its specific characteristics when in place intricately and minutely mirrored the twists and turns of French politics. Thus, as documented in more detail in the chapter on France, during the latter part of the Restoration (1815–30), which featured an attempt to revive the role of the Catholic Church, the censorship was especially sensitive to any signs of theatrical anti-clericalism; during the post-1835–48 period the censors were particularly attuned to attacks on a highly unstable political regime (about as many dramas were censored for overtly political as for all other reasons, such as attacks on religion or alleged immorality, during this period); between 1850 and 1870 the censors were especially sensitive to appeals to class conflict amid the emergence of a significant urban industrial labor force; and for over thirty years subsequent to the 1871 Commune—a radical Parisian lower-class rebellion—that entire subject was essentially verboten on the stage. During the 1835–47 era under July Monarchy king Louis-Philippe, of 8,330 plays submitted to the censorship, 219 (2.6 percent) were completely banned and another 488 (5.6 percent) underwent enforced modifications. The general impression that the Second Empire of Napoleon III (1851-70) was the most repressive French regime of the 1815–1914 period—at least in the immediate aftermath of the 1851 coup which brought him to power—is supported by an 1853 report that found that, of 682 submitted plays, only 246 were approved intact, while 59 (8.4 percent) were completely rejected and changes were demanded in another 323 (47.4 percent) (decisions were pending in the remaining cases). The general political relaxation during the last years of Napoleon III's rule (the so-called "liberal empire") was clearly reflected by a lifting of the previous ban on all of Hugo's plays after 1867. During the intense period of immediate post-Commune repression, about 40 plays were forbidden between 1870 and 1874, but as the Third Republic (1870–1940) gradually stabilized thereafter, theater interdictions became quite rare, with only 8 plays forbidden between 1874 and 1891 and perhaps another dozen banned thereafter before the 1906 abolition of theater censorship.[36]

Not surprisingly, French caricature censorship followed much the same irregular, politically determined path as theater censorship (it was abolished also in 1830, 1848, and 1870, but restored during post-revolutionary conservative political swings). However, perhaps because drawings were not typically "consumed" in a crowd setting, caricatures were viewed as less threatening than theater, and its censorship was permanently abolished in 1881, twenty-five years before theater censorship ended (similarly, caricature censorship terminated years *after* the abolition of press censorship but *before* the abolition of theater censorship in other countries, including Germany and Russia). The same conclusion observers of French politics reached in the late nineteenth century concerning how closely the caricature censorship followed and reflected France's political tides applies equally well to the theater censorship: according to an 1874 caricature journal, "One day one could write an exact history of the liberty which we enjoy during the era that we live through by writing a history of our caricatures."[37]

## Notes

1. Robert Isherwood, *Popular Farce and Fantasy: Popular Entertainment in Eighteenth-Century Paris* (New York, 1986), 254.
2. For surveys of nineteenth-century European theater censorship, including its mechanics, which are covered in this and the next several paragraphs, see Robert Justin Goldstein, *Political Censorship of the Arts and the Press in Nineteenth-Century Europe* (London, 1989), 113–54; Goldstein, "Political Censorship of the Theater in Nineteenth-Century Europe," *Theater Research International* 10 (Fall, 1987): 220–41; and Goldstein, ed., *The War for the Public Mind: Political Censorship in Nineteenth-Century Europe* (Westport, CT, 2001), 7–15. There are short, but very useful sections on theater censorship in different European countries in Alberic Cahuet, *La Liberté du Théâtre en France et a l'Etranger* (Paris, 1902), 310–26; Frank Fowell and Frank Palmer, *Censorship in England*, (London, 1913), 318–23; and scattered in Neville Hunnings, *Film Censors and the Law* (London, 1967). Dawn Sova, *Banned Plays* (New York, 2004), primarily focuses on the American stage, but includes some material relevant to nine-

teenth-century Europe. Essays on "censorship," "theater," and/or "censure" with limited, although nonetheless useful, information about the nineteenth-century European stage censorship can be found in Martin Banham, ed., *The Cambridge Guide to World Theater* (Cambridge, 1988); Dennis Kennedy, *The Oxford Encyclopedia of Theater and Performance* (Oxford, 2003); Derek Jones, ed., *Censorship: A World Encyclopedia* (London, 2001); Michel Corvin, ed., *Dictionnaire encyclopédique du Théâtre* (Paris, 1998). Cambridge University Press has published a series of books with collections of documents on theater history, a few of which focus on censorship: see Donald Roy, ed., *Romantic and Revolutionary Theater, 1789–1860* (2003); Charles Schumacher, ed., *Naturalism and Symbolism in European Theater, 1850–1918* (1996); George Brandt, ed., *German and Dutch theater, 1600–1848* (1993); and Laurence Senelick, ed., *National Theater in Northern and Eastern Europe* (1991). For detailed information on individual countries see the chapters in this book and their bibliographies. For the Habsburg Empire and Germany, especially helpful are W. E. Yates, *Theater in Vienna: A Critical History, 1776-1990* (Cambridge, 1996), 25–48; Roy Pascal, *From Naturalism to Expressionism: German Literature and Society, 1880–1918* (New York, 1973), 261–76; and Lothar Hobelt, "The Austrian Empire," and Robin Lenman, "Germany," both in Goldstein, *War*, 86–93, 228–33; for the Netherlands, the English summary in Tjeerd Schipfof, *De Vrijheid van het Toneel* (Amsterdam, 1994), 229–33, and Gabrielle Cothereau and Suan van Dijk, "George Sand and Dutch theatre censorship," in van Dijk, ed., *I have Heard about You: Foreign Women's Writing Crossing the Dutch Border* (Hilversum, 2004), 275–80, and Cothereau, "Un cas de censure en 1851 aux Pays-Bas," in Gislinde Seybert, ed., *George Sand* (Bielefeld, 2000), 417–28; on Italy, Belgium, and Portugal, see Cahuet, 318–21, 322–25 (also, for Italy, John Davis, "Italy," in Goldstein, *War*, 114–15); for Sweden, see Senelick, 92–93; for Spain, see David Gies, *The Theater in Nineteenth-Century Spain* (Cambridge, 1994), and Adrian Shubert, "Spain," in Goldstein, *War*, 189–96, 200–203; for Russia, see Murray Frame, *School for Citizens: Theater and Society in Imperial Russia* (New Haven, CT, 2006); Frame, *The St. Petersburg Imperial Theaters: Stage and State in Revolutionary Russia, 1900–1920* (London, 2000); Anthony Swift, *Popular Theater and Society in Tsarist Russia* (Berkeley, CA, 2002); Gary Thurston, *The Popular Theater Movement in Russia, 1862–1919* (Evanston, IL, 1998); and Charles Ruud, "Russia," in Goldstein, *War*, 241–42, 259–62. The most comprehensive English-language studies of Italian and Scandinavian theater, Joseph Farrell and Paolo Puppa, ed., *A History of Italian Theater* (Cambridge, 2006), and Frederick and Lise-Lone Marker, *A History of Scandinavian Theater* (Cambridge, 1996), have little or nothing on nineteenth-century theater censorship, which in the latter (but definitely not the former) case may reflect the rarity of its use.

3. On discrimination against ethnic theater, see the chapters in this book and also John McCormick, *Popular Puppet Theater in Europe, 1800–1914* (Cambridge, 1989), 29; and Stefan Hoffman, "Scenes du conflit franco-allemand au Théâtre muncipal de Strasbourg: La Censure et le Public," in Jean-Marc Leveratto, ed., *Culture et Histoire des Spectacles en Alsace et en Lorraine* (Bern, 2005), 243–56.

See also, generally, Edith Málusz, *The Theater and National Awakening* (Atlanta, 1980), which unfortunately has little about censorship. For the text of the 1820 Prussian law, see William Grange, "Censorship," in *Historical Dictionary of German Theater* (Lanham, MD, 2006), 62. While theater censorship encompassed light opera and opera everywhere, such restrictions were especially significant in Italy due to the tremendous popularity of opera there. Good summaries of European opera censorship can be found in John Rosselli, "Censorship," in Stanley Sadie, ed., *New Grove Dictionary of Opera* (New York, 1992), 801–3 (with an excellent bibliography), and Henry Raynor, *Music and Society Since 1815* (New York, 1976), 1–14. For Italy and, especially, Guiseppe Verdi there is an immense literature on opera censorship, among which the most useful sources in English are Walter Rubsamen, "Music and Politics in the 'Risorgimento'" *Italian Quarterly* 5 (1961): 100–120; John Davis, "Opera and Absolutism in Restoration Italy," *Journal of Interdisciplinary History* 36 (2006): 569–94; John Rosselli, *Italian Opera* (Cambridge, 1991), 404–7; Rosselli, *The Opera Industry in Italy from Cimarosa to Verdi* (Cambridge, 1984), 81–99; David Kimbell, *Verdi in the Age of Italian Romanticism* (Cambridge, 1981), 23–32, 256–79; Andreas Giger, "Social Control and the Censorship of Giuseppe Verdi's operas in Rome (1844–1859)," *Cambridge Opera Journal* 11 (1999): 233–65; and Roberta Marvin, "The Censorship of Verdi's Operas in Victorian England," *Music and Letters* 82 (2001): 582–610. For Russia, see Walter Zidaric, "Traduction/adaptation des livrets d'opéras: le rôle de la censure en Russie au XIXe et XXe siècles," in Gottfried Marschall, *La traduction des livrets* (Paris, 2004), 495–504. For France, see the chapters dealing with opera in Janice Best, *La subversion silencieuse: Censure, auto censure et lutte pour la liberté d'expression* (Montreal, 2001); Odile Krakovitch, "L'Opéra Comique et La Censure," in Herbert Schneider, ed., *Die Opéra Comique und ihr Einfluß auf das europäische Musiktheater im 19. Jahrhundert* (Hildesheim, 1997), 211–34; and Frank Hochleitner, "La censure à l'Opéra de Paris aux débuts de la Troisième République," in Pascal Orly, ed., *La Censure en France* (Paris, 1997), 233–49.

4. Gary Stark, "Trial and Tribulations: Authors' Responses to Censorship in Imperial Germany," *German Studies* 12 (1989): 449; Richard Findlater, *Banned! A Review of Theater Censorship in Britain* (London, 1967), 73; Daniel Balmuth, *Censorship in Russia, 1865–1905* (Washington, 1979), 42, 55; Thurston, *Popular*, 175; E. Anthony Swift, "Fighting the Germs of Disorder," *Russian History* 18 (1991): 43; Odile Krakovitch, *Hugo Censuré* (Paris, 1985), 224, 248–49, 286–87.

5. Tom Driver, *A History of Modern Theater* (New York, 1970), 201; Marianna Cholden, *A Fence Around the Empire: Russian Censorship of Ideas under the Tsars* (Durham, NC, 1985), 16; Johann Hüttner, "Theater Censorship in Metternich's Vienna," *Theater Quarterly* 37 (1980): 65.

6. On the Russian theater monopoly and its termination, see Frame, "Freedom of the Theaters," *Slavic and E. European Studies* 83 (2005).

7. Marjorie Hoover, *Alexander Ostrovsky* (New York, 1981), 327; F. W. J. Hemmings, *Culture and Society in France, 1848–1898* (London, 1971), 48–49; Ronald Hingley, *Russian Writers and Society, 1825–1904* (New York, 1967), 229;

Sidney Monas, *The Third Section: Police and Society in Russia under Nicholas I* (Cambridge, MA, 1961), 184; B. Varneke, *History of the Russian Theater* (New York, 1951), 203–7, 220–22; Marc Slonim, *Russian Theatre from the Empire to the Soviet* (Cleveland, OH, 1961), 45; George Freedly and John Reeves, *A History of the Theater* (New York, 1941), 396; Jack Weiner, *Mantillas in Moscow: The Spanish Golden Age Theater in Tsarist Russia, 1672–1917* (Lawrence, KS, 1970), 58; Christine Edwards, *The Stanislavsky Heritage* (New York, 1965), 13.

8. Margot Berthold, *A History of World Theater* (New York, 1972), 537; Findlater, 53; Varnecke, 237; Marvin Carlson, *The Italian Stage from Goldoni to D'Annunzio* (London, 1981), 101, 119; Kimbell, 25.
9. Roger Parker, *The Oxford Illustrated History of Opera* (Oxford, 1994), 247; William Ashbrook, *Donizetti and His Opera* (Cambridge, 1982), 47, 103, 495; Mary Matz, "The Road to Boston," *Opera News* 44 (1980): 14; Edward Dent, *The Rise of Romantic Opera* (Cambridge, 1976), 173; Marcel Prawy, *The Vienna Opera* (New York, 1970), 17–18; Francis Toye, *Rossini* (London, 1954), 148–49; Rosa Newmarch, *Russian Opera* (New York, n.d.), 338; Gerald Abraham, *Rimsky-Korsakov*, (London, 1945), 98–102; Jeremy Commons, "Maria Stuarda and the Neapolitan Censorship," *Donizetti Society Journal* 3 (1977): 162.
10. Kimbell, 25; John Stephens, *The Censorship of English Drama, 1824–1901* (Cambridge, 1980), 10; Cahuet, 217; Peter Jelavich, *Munich and Theatrical Modernism: Politics, Playwriting and Performance, 1890–1914* (Cambridge, MA, 1985) 121; Charles Ruud, *Fighting Words: Imperial Censorship and the Russian Press, 1804–1906* (Toronto, 1982), 251–52; Balmuth, 140.
11. Findlater, 54; Stephens, 168–69; W. E. Yates, *Grillparzer* (Cambridge, 1972), 12; Horst Claus, *The Theater Director Otto Brahm* (Ann Arbor, MI, 1981) 47; Cahuet, 206.
12. Stephens, 27, 80; Commons, 164; Findlater, 55, 58, 74–75.
13. Krakovitch, *Hugo,* 150, 224–25, 227, 286; Cahuet, 206, 217; James Allen, *In the Public Eye: A History of Reading in Modern France* (Princeton, NJ, 1991), 94; Archives Nationales, F18 2342, 2363.
14. Senelick, 70, 303; John Davies, *Naples and Napoleon* (Oxford, 2006), 100; Claus, 47; Swift, "Germs," 7.
15. Findlater, 54; Stephens, 10, 42–43; John and Muriel Lough, *An Introduction to Nineteenth-Century France* (London, 1978), 273; W. D. Howarth, *Sublime and Grotesque: A Study of French Romantic Drama* (London, 1975), 306; Hüttner, 66–67; Hemmings, *Culture,* 51; W. E. Yates, *Grillparzer,* 12; Hohenberg, 72; Claus, 47.
16. Marin Kanes, "Zola, 'Germinal' et la Censure dramatique," *Les Cahiers Naturalistes* 29 (1965): 35–42; Clélia Anfra, "*Germinal* en rouge," *Théâtre/Public* 181 (2006): 18–22; Lawson Carter, *Zola and the Theater* (New Haven, CT, 1963), 136–42; Marc Slonim, *Russian Theatre from the Empire to the Soviets* (Cleveland, 1961), 145; Stephens, 127; Gary Stark, "Hauptman: *Die Weber,*" in Jones, 1036–37. Laurence Senelick's article, "Anti-Semitism and Russian Theatre: The *Smugglers* Riots," *Theatre Survey* 44 (2003), is a case study of an anti-Semitic play that touched off widespread riots in Russia in 1900–1901. On theater censor-

ship and foreign policy concerns, see Gary Stark, "Diplomacy by Other Means: Entertainment, Censorship and German Foreign Policy, 1871–1918," in John McCarthy and Werner von de Ohe, eds., *Zensur under Kultur zwischen Weimar Klassik und Weimarer Republic* (Tübingen, 1995), 123–33.

17. Vera Roberts, *On Stage: A History of Theater* (New York, 1962), 411; Robert Boyer, *Realism in European Theater and Drama, 1870–1920* (Westport, CT, 1979), xvii; Barry Daniels, *Revolution in the theater: French Romantic Theories of Drama* (Westport, CT, 1983), 193; Krakovitch, *Hugo*, 43, 69; Nikolai Gorchakov, *The Theater in Soviet Russia* (New York, 1957), 50; Robert Waissenberger, ed., *Vienna in the Biedermeier Era, 1815–1848* (New York, 1986), 162–63; Marianna Tax Choldin, *A Fence Around the Empire: Russian Censorship of Western Ideas under the Tsars* (Durham, NC, 1985), 16; Adelaide Ristori, *Memoirs and Artistic Studies* (New York, 1907), 16–17; Oscar Brockett, *History of the Theater* (Boston, 1977), 369; MacGowan, 178; Marvin Carlson, *The German Stage in the Nineteenth Century* (Metuchen, NJ, 1972), 121.

18. Raynor, 11, 14; Robert Oldani, "Boris Gudonov and the Censor," *Nineteenth-Century Music* 2 (1978): 246; John Warrack, *German Opera* (Cambridge, 2001), 297; William Ashbrook, *Donizetti* (London, 1965), 47–48.

19. Daniels, 193; Krakovitch, *Hugo*, 43, 69, 219, 245; Schumacher; Roger Berthet, *Anastasie, Anastasie: Groupement de textes sur la censure* (Reims, 1992), 18; Carter, 141.

20. L. W. Conolly, *The Censorship of English Drama, 1737–1824* (San Marino, CA), 111; Lemar Beman, *Selected Articles on Censorship of the Theater and of Moving Pictures* (New York, 1931), 254; Varneke, 203–4, 302; W. E. Yates, *Nestroy* (Cambridge, 1972), 149–50; Yates, *Grillparzer*, 221; Waissenberger, 84, 243; Hüttner, 63, 65–66; John Osborne, *The Naturalist Drama in Germany* (Manchester, 1971), 119; David Magarshack, *Stanislavksy* (New York, 1951), 276.

21. Spike Hughes, "Verdi and the Censors," *Musical Times* 95 (1954): 651; Francis Toye, *Giuseppe Verdi* (New York, 1972), 69; Paul Hume, *Verdi* (New York, 1977), 87; Joseph Wechsberg, *Verdi* (New York, 1976), 99; Kimbell, 269, 279; D. Rosen, "Virtue Restored," *Opera News* 42 (1977): 39; George Martin, *Verdi* (New York, 1963), 350; Francis Abbiati, "Years of *Un Ballot in Maschera*," *Verdi* 1 (1960): 818–22.

22. Herbert Weinstock, *Donizetti and the World of Opera* (New York, 1963), 202, 213; Ashbrook, 662; V. V. Yastrebtsev, *Reminisences of Rimsky-Korsakov* (New York, 1985), 129, 391.

23. On the various parliamentary inquiries and growing opposition to the censorship, see Marvin Carlson, "The French Censorship Inquiries of 1849 and 1891," *Essays in Theater* 5 (186): 5–13; Odile Krakovitch, "De Thermidor aux Paravents: La Liberté théâtrale, objet de débat politique à l'Assemblée," *Théâtre/Public* 181 (2006): 6–18; Pascal, 268; Gilbert Carr, "Corridors of Power and Whispered Plots: The Banning of Otto Stoessl's and Robert Scheu's *Waare* in 1897/1898," in W. E. Yates, ed., *From Perinet to Jelinek: Viennese Theater in its Political and Intellectual Context* (Oxford, 2001), 129; Thurston, 207; and Findlater, 100–110. On Sweden, see Senelick, 92–93.

24. W. E. Yates, "Cultural Life in Early Nineteenth-Century Vienna," *Forum for Modern Language Studies* 13 (1977): 110; Alice Hanson, *Musical Life in Biedermeier Vienna* (Cambridge, 1985), 43–44; Magarshack, 276; Waissenberger, 230; Stephens, 123; Gary Stark, "The Censorship of Literary Naturalism, 1890–95: Prussia and Saxony," *Central European History* 18 (1985): 341–43.
25. Krakovitch, *Hugo*, 84; Swift, "Germs," 46. In general, on resisting nineteenth-century French censorship, including but not limited to the theater censorship, see Robert Justin Goldstein, "Fighting French Censorship, 1815–1881," *The French Review* 71 (1998): 785–96.
26. Findlater, 65; Swift, "Germs," 45; Hochleitner, 246.
27. Hemmings, *Culture and Society in France, 1789–1848* (Leicester, 1987), 50; Yates, *Nestroy*, 150; Carlson, *Italian*, 73; Simon Karlinsky, *Russian Drama from its Beginnings to the Age of Pushkin* (Berkeley, CA, 1985), 305.
28. George Freedley, *A History of the Theatre* (New York, 1941), 425; Zygmunt Hubner, *Theater & Politics* (Evanston, IL, 1988), 64; Krakovitch, *Hugo*, 84–85, 87; Concetta Condemi, *Les Café-Concerts* (Paris, 1992), 57.
29. Stephens, 122; Barbara Cooper, "Censorship and the Double Portrait of Disorder in Lemercier's *La Demence de Charles VI*," *Orbis Litteratum* 40 (1985): 300, 306.
30. Murray Frame, "Censorship and Control in the Russian Imperial Theatres during the 1905 Revolution and Its Aftermath," *Revolutionary Russia* 7 (1994): 164–91; Frame, *St. Petersburg*, 121–33; H. Hearder, *A Short History of Italy* (Cambridge, 1963), 131; George Martin, *The Red Shirt and the Cross of Savoy: The Story of Italy's Risorgimento* (New York, 1969), 394.
31. Nicholas Harrison, "Colluding with the Censor: Theater Censorship in France After the Revolution," *Romance Studies* 25 (1995): 16; Krakovitch, *Hugo*, 55; Sheryl Kroen, *Politics and Theater: The Crisis of Legitimacy in Restoration France, 1815–1830* (Berkeley, CA, 2000), 229–84. See also, on theatrical demonstrations, Jean-Claude Yon, "Du droit de sifflet au théâtre au XIXe siècle," in Philippe Bourdin, ed., *La Voix & Le Geste: Une Approche Culturelle de la Violence Socio-Politique* (Paris, 2005), 321–37; and Alain Corbain, *Time Desire and Horror: Towards a History of the Senses* (New York, 1995), 39–52.
32. On Antoine, see Jean Hothia, *André Antoine* (Cambridge, 1991); Samuel Waxman, *Antoine and the Théâtre Libre* (Cambridge, MA, 1926); Sally Charnow, "Commercial Culture and Modernist theater in Fin-de-Siècle Paris: André Antoine and the Théâtre Libre," *Radical Historical Review* 77 (Spring 2000): 60–89, Charnow, *Theater, Politics and Markets in Fin-de-Siècle Paris* (New York, 2005), 13–53.
33. On the "free theaters" generally, see Anna Miller, *The Independent Theater in Europe* (New York, 1931); Oscar Brockett and Robert Findlay, *Century of Innovation: A History of European and American Theater* (Englewood Cliffs, NJ, 1973), 89–111; MacGowan, 185–95; Jelavich, 167–85; Cecil Davies, *Volksbühne Movement: A History* (Amsterdam, 2000); Andrew Bonnell, *The People's Stage in Imperial Germany* (London, 2005).
34. Pascal, 276; Davies, 58.

35. Slonim, 84; Findlater, 47; Roberts, 355.
36. Krakovitch, *Hugo,* 224, 248–49, 286–87; Findlater, 73; Balmuth, 42, 55; Stephens, 119–21; Thurston, *Popular,* 175, Swift, "Germs," 43.
37. *L'Eclipse,* 20 September 1874.

# List of Contributors

**Norbert Bachleitner** is associate professor of comparative literature at the University of Vienna, Austria. His specialties include censorship, the history of the book, and the reception of English and French literature in the German-speaking world. His publications include "The Politics of the Book Trade in Austria," *Austria History Yearbook* 28 (1997), and two books entitled (in English translation) *History of the German Serial Novel* (2000) and *History of the Book Trade in Austria* (2000).

**John A. Davis** (PhD, Oxford) holds the Emiliana Pasca Noether Chair in Modern Italian History at the University of Connecticut. Author most recently of *Naples and Napoleon: Southern Italy and the European Revolutions* (2007), he is general editor of the multi-volume *Oxford Short History of Italy* and editor of the *Journal of Modern Italian Studies*. Other publications include *Conflict and Control: Law and Order in 19th-Century Italy* (1988) and "Cultures of Interdiction: The Politics of Censorship in Italy from Napoleon to the Restoration," in David Laven and Lucy Riall, eds., *Napoleon's Legacy* (2000).

**David T. Gies** (PhD, University of Pittsburgh) is commonwealth professor of Spanish at the University of Virginia and editor of *Dieciocho*, a journal focused on the Spanish Enlightenment. His specialties include Spanish romantic and enlightenment literature and theater, as reflected in his publications: (ed.) *The Cambridge History of Spanish Literature* (2004), *Theater and Politics in Nineteenth-Century Spain* (1994), and *The Theater in Nineteenth-Century Spain* (1994).

**Robert Justin Goldstein** (PhD, University of Chicago) is research associate at the Center for Russian and East European Studies at the University of Michigan, Ann Arbor, and emeritus professor of political science at Oakland University. A specialist in nineteenth-century European political censorship, his publications include *Censorship of Political Caricature in Nineteenth-Century France* (1989), *Political Censorship of the Arts and the Press in Nineteenth-Century Europe* (1989), and (ed.) *The War for the Public Mind: Political Censorship in Nineteenth-Century Europe* (2000).

**Gary D. Stark** (PhD, Johns Hopkins University), professor of history at Grand Valley State University, Allendale, Michigan is the author of *Banned in Berlin: Literary Censorship in Imperial Germany, 1871–1918* (2009). His other publications include "Cinema, Society and the State: Policing the Film Industry in Imperial Germany," in Gary Stark and Bede Lackner, eds., *Essays on Culture and Society in Modern Germany* (1982) and "Trials and Tribulations: Authors' Responses to Censorship in Imperial Germany, 1885–1914," in *German Studies Review* 12 (1989).

**Anthony Swift** is lecturer in history at the University of Essex, England. He specializes in the history of late tsarist and early Soviet Russia. His publications include *Popular Theater and Society in Tsarist Russia* (2002), "Fighting the Germs of Disorder: The Censorship of Russian Popular Theater, 1888–1917," *Russian History/Histoire Russe* 18 (1991), and "Workers Theater and 'Proletarian Culture' in Pre-Revolutionary Russia, 1905–1917," *Russian History/Histoire Russe* 23 (1996).

# Index

Note: Places and individuals referred to only once or twice in passing are generally not indexed and, with the exception of a few plays of exceptional interest for nineteenth-century theater censorship history which are referred to in multiple chapters (i.e. *The Weavers* and *William Tell*), individual plays and opera are not indexed by name, but can be located by looking up their authors/composers/librettists. For additional information concerning index entries preceded by an asterisk (*), please also consult the appropriate specific country, regional and/or city listings (i.e. for "Theater censorship in nineteenth-century Europe" also consult individual countries, and for "Germany," also consult individuals regions and cities).

Alexander I, 132, 134, 135
Alexander II, 139–42, 144, 148, 270, 271, 274
Alexander III, 10, 16, 144, 153
Alfieri, Vittorio, 193, 197, 268
Antoine, André, 116, 289
Asquerino, Eusebio, 173, 174, 180
Auber, Daniel, 138, 190
Augier, Emile, 102, 277

Baden, 34, 35, 52, 267
Balzac, Honoré de, 84, 93, 114, 270, 286
Barbaja, Domenico, 192, 197, 225
Barcelona, 178, 267
*Bavaria, 5, 18, 27, 30, 34, 35, 39, 47, 49, 52, 243, 267, 268–69, 273, 288, 289
Beaumarchais, Pierre, 78, 86, 143, 145, 154, 171, 246, 276
*Belgium, 2, 3, 7, 14, 29, 76, 90, 217, 253, 267
Bellini, Vincenzo, 193, 199, 203, 204, 205, 210, 222, 269, 274, 283, 289

Berlin, 15, 24, 26–27, 31–34, 38–39, 40, 41, 43, 44, 45, 46, 47, 48, 51–58, 250, 262, 275, 289
Bismarck, Otto von, 41, 56–57, 280
Bohemia: see Czech lands
Bonaparte, Joseph, 162, 197
Bonaparte, Louis Napoleon (Napoleon III), 79, 80, 81, 82, 83, 86, 92, 97, 98,103, 213, 217, 250, 270, 285, 288, 292–93
Bonaparte, Napoleon (Napoleon I), 12, 23, 27, 39, 40, 53, 56, 71, 75, 77, 80, 81, 82, 87, 89, 92, 94–95, 97, 100–01, 113, 115, 163, 190, 192, 193, 195–98, 199, 201, 202, 233, 238–39, 242, 244, 273, 274, 290
Bremen, 25, 34, 51
Breslau, 25, 55, 43, 44
Bretón de los Herreros, Manuel, 167, 169, 170, 171
Brussels, 7, 90
Budapest, 235, 251, 253, 254
Burguera y Serrano, Father Amado de Cristo, 180, 183

# INDEX

Café-concerts, 15, 86, 102, 103, 104, 109, 113
Cánovas del Castillo, 163, 177
Caricature and drawings, regulation of, 14, 70, 73, 77, 91, 103–04, 106, 293
Carl, Carl, 237, 238
Carrillo, Father Fernando, 167, 171
Catherine the Great, 10, 132–33, 138, 148
Cavour, Count Camillo Benso, 210–12, 213, 224, 226
Charles I, 94, 236, 276
Charles X, 78, 81, 88, 89, 90, 115, 277, 288
Chekhov, Anton, 130, 144, 146, 154, 155, 280
Congress of Vienna, 27, 52, 191, 192, 198
*Czech lands, 57, 199, 228, 229, 238, 239, 242, 243, 244, 252, 253, 267, 272

Decembrist Uprising, 135, 137
Denmark, 6, 266, 267, 268
Díaz, José María, 173, 174, 179
Dicenta, Joaquín, 181, 182
Dobroliubov, Nikolai, 143–44
Donizetti, Gaetano, 79, 80, 193, 199, 204, 205, 210, 222, 272, 273, 282
Dostoevsky, Fedor, 144–45
Dresden, 23, 34, 46, 48, 289
Dumas, Alexander (fils), 84, 270, 282
Dumas, Alexander (père), 84, 89, 101, 111, 177, 178, 192, 279
Düsseldorf, 25, 33, 46

Education and literacy in nineteenth-century Europe, 2–3, 9–10, 73, 75
Eguílaz, Luis, 176, 180
*England, 2, 4, 6, 9, 17, 54, 58, 101, 210, 218, 265–66, 269, 271, 273, 274–75, 276, 278, 280, 283, 286, 287, 288, 290
  Theater censorship in nineteenth century:
    as reflecting fear and importance of theater, 7, 9
    character of censors, 274–75
    defense of, 283, 289
    earlier history of, 17, 18
    goals and mechanics of, 6, 9, 165, 166, 267, 269, 276, 277, 278, 290
    impact of, 178
    legislative inquiries on, 282, 284
    licensing requirements related to, 265–66, 169, 290
    opposition and resistance to, 280, 282, 235, 286, 287, 288, 290
Evreinov, Nicholas, 147, 155

Fernández de Moratín, Leandro, see Moratín
Fernando VII, 164, 165, 167, 168, 170, 171, 175
Florence, 194, 199, 208, 216, 224, 227
Foscolo, Ugo, 193, 196, 197, 202
*France, 2, 3, 11, 23, 54, 56, 58, 112, 113, 116, 117, 133, 140, 195, 197, 205, 238, 247, 252, 285, 289
  press and press regulation in nineteenth-century, 72, 73, 74, 76, 81, 87, 89, 91, 92, 93, 96, 98, 103–04, 106, 107, 111, 113, 116
  theater censorship in nineteenth century:
    and opera, 76, 78, 79, 80–81, 83, 85, 90–91, 95, 100, 101, 103, 104, 107, 286
    as reflection of fears about and importance of the theater, 5, 6–7, 8, 9, 70–78
    as reflection of political events and local issues, 71–72, 73–74, 78, 79, 80, 83, 87, 88–89, 91–93, 97–98, 291, 292
    before 1815, 86–88
    capriciousness of, 270–71, 273, 274
    character of censors in, 82–83, 274
    class biased administration of, 14, 15, 77–78, 80–81, 94–95, 98, 103, 104–05
    defense of, 283, 284
    during July Monarchy (1830–48), 91–96
    during Restoration (1814–1830), 88–91

during Second Empire (1851–
1970), 98–103
during Second Republic (1848–
1851), 96–98
during Third Republic (1870–
1914), 103–110
earlier history of, 17
"free theaters" (private clubs),
289
foreign policy considerations of,
101, 107–08
goals of, 78–82, 191, 275, 276,
277, 278
impact of, 111–12
legislative and other inquiries
concerning, 96–97, 108, 282,
284
mechanics of, 6, 9, 82–86, 265,
266–67, 268, 269, 273, 275
opposition and resistance to,
102, 111–16, 279–80, 282,
284, 285, 286–87, 288, 289,
290–91
statistics concerning, 93–94, 98,
101, 102, 103, 105, 292–93
theater licensing, 85–86, 87, 91,
102, 270, 290–91
Francis I (France), 80, 92
Francis I (Habsburg), 232, 233, 235, 238,
239, 241, 242, 244–46, 256, 269
Francis Joseph, 229–31, 253
Frankfurt, 25, 33, 46, 236
Freie Volksbühne, 11, 41–43, 46, 289–90
French Revolution (1789), 1, 3, 18, 27, 44,
39–40, 44, 71, 89, 92, 94, 95, 96, 101,
108, 133, 164, 191, 192, 194, 195, 225,
232
French Revolution (1830), 71, 73, 91, 101,
204
Friedrich Wilhelm III, 30, 47, 53
Friedrich Wilhelm IV, 30, 47–48

*Galicia (Austrian Poland), 237, 247, 251,
286
García Gutiérrez, Antonio, 171, 174, 176
Garibaldi, Giuseppe, 208, 212, 213, 215,
216

Garrido, Fernando, 175, 181, 182, 280
*Germany, 2, 9, 20, 22, 14, 15, 80, 117,
140, 229, 251, 267, 270, 282, 284, 289,
291, 293
press and press regulation in
nineteenth-century, 5, 24, 30, 32,
38, 40–41, 44, 50, 55
theater censorship in nineteenth-
century:
and class conflict, 37–46
and depictions of military, 50–52
and depiction of monarchs,
46–50
and foreign policy and
diplomatic issues, 54–58
and French Revolution, 39–40,
44
and municipal theaters, 25–26,
31–32, 34, 47
and opera, 15, 31, 39, 272–73,
279
and Polish nationalism, 52–54
and private commercial theaters,
25–27, 32–34, 43–44, 56, 58
and royal court theaters, 22–23,
25, 27, 30–31, 34, 38–39,
47–48, 55–56
and theater licensing, 25–27, 31,
33–34, 37, 42, 58, 270
as reflection of fear and
importance of theaters, 5, 8,
22–30
as reflection of general political
trends, 291
before 1848, 27–32, 38–39,
47–48, 53, 55–56
between 1848 and 1870, 32–33,
39
between 1870 and 1914, 33–35,
36–37, 39–46, 48–54
capriciousness of, 272–73
class biased administration of,
15–16
defense of, 283–84
"free theaters" (private clubs), 289
goals of, 37–38, 58–59, 277–78
impact of, 278, 279

mechanics of, 6, 9, 27–32,
    58–59, 266, 267, 269
  opposition and resistance to,
    35–37, 280, 281, 282, 289
  statistics concerning, 48, 56–58
*Germinal* (play), 15, 43–44, 250, 268, 278
Gil y Zárate, Antonio, 171, 175, 178
Goethe, Johann Wolfgang von, 23, 27, 38, 135, 154.
Gogol, Nikolai, 10, 136–37, 148, 278, 280–81, 282, 284
Goncourt, Edmond de, 108, 111
Gorky, Maxim, 146, 147–148, 154, 155, 278
Greece, 16, 39, 79
Griboedov, Alexander, 137, 271, 280, 285
Grillparzer, Franz, 24, 235–37, 242–45, 257, 274
Grimaldi, Juan de (Jean-Marie), 167, 168, 169, 171
Gutzkow, Karl, 28, 35–36, 40, 47, 56

*Habsburg Empire: 2, 4, 6, 8, 12, 13, 14, 17, 27, 27, 38, 39, 55–58, 81, 138, 150, 157, 185, 191, 198, 200, 267, 268, 269, 271, 272, 274, 277, 278, 279, 281, 282, 283, 285, 286, 287, 288, 291
  and pre-1860 Italy, 191, 194, 195, 198, 199, 200, 202, 203, 205, 206, 208, 209, 211, 212, 213, 222
  theater censorship in nineteenth-century:
    and opera, 229, 231, 235, 246, 247, 250, 252, 253, 254, 277
    and popular theatre, 230, 245, 250
    as reflection of fears about and importance of theater, 5, 7–9, 235–46
    as reflection of general political trends, 291
    between 1815 and 1848, 237, 241–47
    between 1849 and 1918, 247–56
    capriciousness of, 271, 272, 274
    defense of, 283
    earlier history of, 17, 230–41

extemporization as device to avoid, 231, 233, 238, 245
extra-parliament inquiry on, 248
impact of, 256–57, 278, 279
motivations and mechanics of, 6, 230–36, 245–46, 251–55, 265, 267, 269, 277
of historical plays, 237, 252, 253
of nationalism, 229, 230, 240, 248, 249, 251–54
of opera, 246, 247, 252, 253, 272, 279
opposition and resistance to, 236–37, 238, 245, 281, 282, 283, 285, 287, 289
Hägelin, Carl Franz, 232, 234–36, 243, 247
Hallays-Dabot, Victor, 7, 70, 74, 76, 84, 95, 100
Hamburg, 23, 25, 44, 45, 46, 47, 50, 52, 267, 289
Hanover, 25, 33, 43, 44, 46, 289
Hartzenbusch, Juan Eugenio, 179, 180
Hauptmann, Gerhardt, 15, 42–45, 146, 249–51, 268, 277, 281
Heine, Heinrich, 28, 45–46
Hemmings, F. W. J., 5, 72, 113, 285
Hesse, 27, 34, 55
Hugo, Victor, 11–12, 78, 80, 89, 91, 92, 95, 96, 97, 99, 101, 102, 104, 105, 111, 112, 113, 114, 115, 116, 117, 138, 169, 217, 241, 242, 252, 277, 279, 281, 283, 284, 286, 289, 293
*Hungary, 2, 228, 229, 234, 242, 244, 253, 254, 272

Ibsen, Henrik, 31, 153, 154, 255, 274, 289
*Italy, 2, 3, 5, 13, 39, 79, 82, 229, 259, 254, 267, 268, 270, 271, 272, 277, 278, 279, 285, 289, 291
  press and press regulation in nineteenth century, 192, 193, 201, 203, 206, 211, 212, 214, 215, 218, 219, 220, 221
  theater censorship in nineteenth century:
    and Catholic Church, 201–02 203, 205, 216–18

and opera, 5, 13, 192, 197, 203, 204, 205, 207, 215, 217, 219, 272, 273, 279, 280, 286, 287
as reflections of fears and importance of theater, 8, 192–93, 194, 196, 199, 200, 201, 102–03
as reflection of general political trends, 190–93, 196–97, 206–08, 209–10, 214–17, 220–26, 291
capriciousness of, 205, 209, 215–16, 218, 271–72, 273
during post-unification era (1860–1900), 213–219
during Restoration (1814–30), 198–203
during revolutionary and Napoleonic period (1796–1815), 195–7,
during Risorgimento (1830–1860), 203–13
earlier history of, 190, 193–4, 195, 198
goals and mechanics of, 194–95, 196–97, 201–02, 203, 205, 209–10, 212–13, 214–16, 218–19, 221, 267, 268, 269, 273, 276,
impact of, 278, 279
licensing requirements of, 270
nature of censors, 194, 201, 202, 203, 205, 207, 209–20, 211, 212, 215, 216, 217, 220, 274
opposition and resistance to, 203–04, 206–08, 281, 282, 285, 287–88
statistics on, 266
theaters in, 190, 192–93, 194, 199–200
Carignano Theater (Turin), 194, 199, 206
La Fenice (Venice), 194, 199
La Scala (Milan), 192, 194, 197, 199, 203, 206, 208, 224,
San Carlo (Naples), 192, 194, 197, 199, 200, 201, 209, 210, 224, 225, 226
See also: Habsburg Empire, and pre-1860 Italy

Joseph II, 17, 228, 230, 232, 246, 257, 265

Karlsbad Decrees, 27, 38, 205, 233
Kotzebue, August, 234, 241, 242
Krakovitch, Odile, 15, 70–71, 77, 78, 87, 88, 91, 110, 117, 275
Krakow, 235, 251

Larra, Luis Mariano de, 180, 181
Larra, Mariano José de, 163, 168, 169, 170, 171, 172, 180
Laube, Heinrich, 28, 49, 56
Leipzig, 11, 25, 34, 44, 159, 289
Lemaitre, Frederick, 94, 114, 206
Lermontov, Nikolai, 137, 271
Lessing, Gotthold Ephraim, 22, 234
*Lombardy-Venetia, Kingdom of (Habsburg Italy, 1814–60), 191, 199, 200, 208, 209, 213, 224
London, 267, 280, 283, 289, 290
Louis XIII, 17, 80, 86, 277
Louis XIV, 17, 86, 265
Louis XVI, 83, 86, 100, 238
Louis XVIII, 89, 116, 156, 158, 287
Louis-Philippe, 9, 71, 75, 78, 82, 84, 90, 91, 92, 93, 94, 96, 99, 105, 114, 115, 286, 292

Madrid, 10, 167, 168, 170, 171, 172, 173, 178, 179, 180, 181, 182
Mann, Thomas, 35–36, 282
Manzoni, Alessandro, 193, 215
Maria Theresia, 228, 230, 231, 232
*Marriage of Figaro* (play and opera), 86–87, 143, 145, 171, 246, 276
Mazzini, Giuseppe, 204, 205, 213, 220, 224, 226
Mesonero Romanos, Ramón de, 167, 171
Metternich, Klemens von, 27, 229, 233, 245, 253, 279
Meyerbeer, Giacomo, 83, 210, 246
Meyerhold, Vsevolod, 130, 147, 155, 281

Milan, 13, 17, 192, 194, 195, 196, 197, 199, 200, 201, 205, 207, 208, 218, 221, 224, 225, 229, 268, 272, 287
Modena, Gustavo, 208, 215, 217
Modernization, European in nineteenth-century, 3–4
Molière, 115, 138, 147, 288
Moratín, Leandro Fernández de, 166, 167, 170
Moscow Art Theater (MAT), 10, 130, 146–47
Moscow, 7, 11, 132, 133, 134, 136, 139, 140, 144, 146, 151, 152, 270, 284, 290
*Muette de Portici* (opera), 7, 76, 90, 138
Munich, 25–27, 31, 34–36, 39–40, 43, 58, 261, 268, 282, 289
Musset, Alfred de, 78, 100, 277

Nantes, 76, 77, 115
Naples, 3, 90, 192, 194, 195, 196, 197, 198, 199, 200, 201, 205, 206, 209, 210, 216, 222, 224, 225, 268, 272, 273, 274, 276, 281, 282
Napoleon I: see Bonaparte, Napoleon
Napoleon III: see Bonaparte, Louis Napoleon
Narváez, Ramón de, 162, 172
Nestroy, Johann, 35, 233, 238, 245, 250, 277, 281, 283, 285
Netherlands, 2, 6, 7, 38, 90, 135, 238, 267
Niccolini, Giambattista, 193, 202, 208, 212, 285, 287
Nicholas I, 135–39, 140, 141, 266, 269 271
Nicholas II, 144, 146, 147, 148, 153
Nocedal, Cándido, 163, 175
Nuremberg, 25, 269

Offenbach, Jacques, 80, 81, 199, 162, 250
Ostrovsky, Alexander, 16, 140, 141, 143–44, 155, 270

*Papacy and Papal States, 13, 194, 195, 198, 202, 203, 204, 205, 213, 216, 268, 278
Paris, 5, 9, 11, 12, 17, 29, 72, 73, 78, 81, 83, 85, 86, 87, 90–91, 93, 94, 95, 96, 98, 102, 104, 105, 114, 116, 182, 196, 201, 205, 206, 250, 255, 266, 267, 270, 286, 287, 289, 290, 291 See also Paris Commune.
Paris Commune, 40, 72, 103, 107, 292, 293
Pellico, Silvio, 193, 199, 208
Pérez Galdós, Benito, 181, 182
Persil, Jean-Charles, 71, 73–74
Peter the Great, 131, 132, 138
*Piedmont (Kingdom of Sardinia), 16, 194, 198, 199, 203, 205, 206, 208, 209, 210–12, 213, 214, 224, 225, 226, 229, 268, 271
*Poland, 52, 54, 56, 151, 154, 233, 244, 251, 267, 272, 285,
Pope Pius IX, 204, 206, 207, 208, 209, 213, 214, 217
Portugal, 2, 3, 267
Poverty, European in nineteenth-century, 3–4
Prague, 229, 232–34, 241, 253
*Press and press regulation in nineteenth-century Europe, 2, 5–6, 8, 9, 14, 266, 276, 285, 286, 293
*Prussia, 24–27, 30, 32–33, 35, 38, 43–44, 46–48, 50, 52–59, 101, 267, 268, 274, 276–77
Pushkin, Alexander, 135, 137, 143, 148, 149, 271
Pyat, Felix, 92, 95, 104

Quintana, Manuel José, 169, 170

Revolution of 1848, 28, 32, 39, 71, 96
Riego, Rafael de, 162, 166
Rimsky-Korsakov, Nikola, 138, 148–49, 273, 282
Rodríguez Rubí, Tomás, 173, 174, 176
Rome, 16, 194, 196, 199, 200, 203, 205, 207, 208, 209, 211, 212, 213, 217, 223, 224, 268, 272, 274, 276, 282
Rossini, Gioacchino, 38, 39, 79, 81, 138, 146, 150, 167, 168, 193, 199, 204, 205, 222, 226, 272, 277
Rousseau, 77, 89
Rumania, 10, 21, 149 See also Wallachia

*Russia, 2, 3, 4, 5, 6, 7, 9, 10, 11, 13, 14, 16, 46, 54, 55, 56, 57, 101, 244, 285, 267, 268, 269, 270, 271, 272, 273, 274, 276, 278, 279, 280, 281, 282, 283
   press and press regulation in nineteenth century, 131, 136, 139, 140, 141, 142, 147, 154, 155
   theater censorship in nineteenth century:
      and church, 132, 142, 143, 146–47, 148 154
      and minority ethnic/religious groups, 149–51
      and opera, 132, 136, 138, 141, 142, 146, 147, 148–49, 150, 273, 279
      and "popular" theater, 16, 131, 145–46, 148, 150, 151, 154
      as reflection of fears and importance of theater, 5, 7, 9, 131, 140, 145
      capriciousness of, 148–49, 270, 271, 273–74
      earlier history of, 132–33
      evasion of, 150, 151–54
      impact of, 139, 151, 155, 278, 279
      licensing and imperial theaters' monopoly on public performances, 134, 140, 144, 270, 290
      limitations of, 151–54, 155
      mechanics and motivations of, 9, 131, 132, 134–36, 137–38, 140–43, 145–46, 147, 148–52, 153, 154, 266, 267, 268, 269, 273–74, 276, 277, 278
      opposition and resistance to, 130–31, 143–45, 151–54, 280–81, 282, 284, 285, 287, 290
      statistics concerning, 137, 144, 151, 285
      under Alexander I (1801–25), 134–35
      under Alexander II (1855–81), 139–44
      under Alexander III (1881–94), 144–45
      under Catherine the Great (1762–96), 132–33
      under Nicholas I (1825–55), 135–39
      under Nicholas II, 146–54
   Revolution of 1905, 130, 148, 149, 150, 153–54, 155

St. Petersburg, 132, 133, 134, 135, 136, 139, 143, 144, 148, 149, 151, 152, 153, 154, 270, 285, 290
Sancha, Tomás, 170, 171
Sardinia: see Piedmont
Sardou, Victorien, 99, 100, 108
*Saxony, 27, 37, 34–35, 39, 41, 47, 56, 267, 268
*Scandinavia, 2, 133
Schiller, Friedrich, 10, 22–24, 29, 32, 38–39, 56, 59, 138, 139, 143, 151, 154, 234, 235, 238, 240, 241, 249, 272, 277
Schnitzler, Arthur, 40, 255, 271
Schreyvogel, Josef, 235, 241, 242, 269
Scribe, Eugene, 90, 95, 97, 100, 272
Sejour, Victor, 79, 277, 279
Serra, Narciso, 176, 177
Seville, 166, 182, 246
Shakespeare, William, 138, 141, 154, 232, 240, 241, 247, 249, 269
Shaw, George Bernard, 254, 275, 282, 290
Sicily, 195, 198, 204, 208, 209, 212, 213, 215, 216, 287
Sonnenfels, Josef von 231, 232
*Spain, 2, 3, 8, 17,114, 115, 208, 211, 247, 267, 292
   press and press regulation in nineteenth century, 164, 165, 168, 170, 171, 173, 174
   theater censorship in nineteenth century:
      and Catholic Church, 163, 169, 182
      and individual censors, 164, 170, 173, 175

and opera and *zarzuela*, 167,
168, 178
as reflection of fears and
importance of theater, 8, 163,
171, 178, 179, 180, 183
as reflection of general political
trends, 162–3, 164–66, 176
before 1868, 164–71, 178–81
between 1868 and 1914, 177–
78, 181–82
capriciousness, 75–81
earlier history of, 17, 163
goals and mechanics of, 164–70,
173–75, 176, 177, 178, 180,
181, 267
opposition to, 164, 175, 178,
182, 280, 282–83
political motivations of, 177,
178, 181
Stanislavsky, Konstantin, 10, 130, 144–45,
146, 147, 153, 155, 281, 282
Stendhal, 200, 268, 287
Strauss, Richard, 147, 282
Sudermann, Hermann, 283–84
Sue, Eugene, 95, 99, 111
Suffrage, European in nineteenth-century,
2
Sweden, 6, 16, 263, 272, 276, 276, 283
Switzerland, 2, 3, 41, 38, 81, 138, 150,
239, 240, 272, 277

Tchaikovsky, Peter, 148, 273
*Theater censorship in nineteenth-century
Europe:
and opera, 267, 268, 269, 272–73,
278–79
as reflection of fears about and
importance of the theater, 4–10
as reflection of general political trends,
291–93
capriciousness of, 270–75
character of censors, 274–75
class bias in administration of, 14–16
dates of imposition and ending, 6,
283, 293
defense of, 283–84

earlier (pre-nineteenth-century)
history of, 16–18
"Free Theaters," (private clubs) as
device to evade, 288–90
goals of, 275–79
impact of, 266, 278–79
licensing requirements associated with,
9, 15, 18, 263, 265–66, 269–70,
288, 290, 291, 292
mechanics of, 265–70
opposition to, 279–84
resistance to censorship, 284–91
social and political context of, 1–4
statistics concerning, 269
Tolstoy, Aleksei, 143, 145, 146.
Tolstoy, Lev, 144, 145, 151, 152, 155,
280
Trieste, 251, 252
Turgenev, Ivan, 137–38, 271
Turin, 168, 194, 199, 206, 208, 211, 212,
215, 223, 268, 271
*Tuscany, 8, 194, 195, 202, 205, 206, 208,
209, 213, 225, 273
*Two Sicilies, Bourbon Kingdom of, 194,
198, 203, 209, 213

Ukraine, 149, 150, 151, 251, 254, 267

Vega, Lope de, 144, 167
Venice, 194, 195, 198, 199, 207–08, 211,
213, 222, 226, 229, 252, 254, 281
Verdi, Giuseppe, 80, 193, 201, 203, 206–7,
208, 210, 215, 216, 222–5, 226, 252,
270, 272, 281–82
Victor Emanuel I, 199
Victor Emanuel II, 199, 213, 214, 215,
216
Vienna, 30, 32, 35, 49, 205, 229, 231,
234, 235, 238, 240, 241, 242, 243, 246,
247, 252, 255, 256, 289
theaters in:
Burgtheater, 232–34, 241–44,
247, 249, 256
Deutsches Volkstheater, 255
Kärntnertortheater, 231, 233,
246, 256

Theater an der Wien, 231, 233, 239–41
Theater in der Josefstadt, 231, 233, 256
Theater in der Leopoldstadt, 231, 233, 237, 256

Voltaire, 10, 89, 133, 239

Wagner, Richard, 39, 80
Wallachia, 9–10, 276
Warsaw, 149, 251, 286
*Weavers, The* (play), 15, 43–44, 250, 268, 272, 277
Wedekind, Frank, 15–16, 36, 148
Wells, H. G., 280, 282
Wilde, Oscar, 147, 282
Wilhelm II, 24, 42, 48–49, 57
*William Tell* (opera and play), 39, 81, 138, 146, 150
Wurttemberg, 34, 47, 267

Zola, Emile, 45, 46, 107, 108, 111, 112, 115, 278, 280, 283
Zorrilla, José, 180, 181

www.ingramcontent.com/pod-product-compliance
Lightning Source LLC
Chambersburg PA
CBHW051419290426
44109CB00016B/1360